The Language Wars

For Geordie,
with seasonal best wishes

The
Language Wars

A History of Proper English

Henry Hitchings

HENRY HITCHINGS

December 2010.

JOHN MURRAY

First published in Great Britain in 2011 by John Murray (Publishers)
An Hachette UK Company

I

© Henry Hitchings 2011

The right of Henry Hitchings to be identified as the Author of the Work has been
asserted by him in accordance with the Copyright, Designs and Patents Act 1988.

A CIP catalogue record for this title is
available from the British Library

ISBN 978-1-84854-208-2

Typeset in Bembo by Palimpsest Book Production Ltd, Falkirk, Stirlingshire

Printed and bound by Clays Ltd, St Ives plc

John Murray policy is to use papers that are natural, renewable and recyclable
products and made from wood grown in sustainable forests. The logging and
manufacturing processes are expected to conform to the environmental regulations
of the country of origin.

John Murray (Publishers)
338 Euston Road
London NW1 3BH

www.johnmurray.co.uk

Contents

1 'To boldly go'

Truths and myths about English

It seems as if no day passes without an argument over the English language and its 'proper' use. We debate the true meanings of words, the nuances of grammar, the acceptability of slang, attitudes to regional accents, resistance to new-fangled terms, confusion about apostrophes, the demise of the semi-colon.

Why do questions of grammar, spelling and punctuation trouble us? Why are we intrigued or unsettled by other people's pronunciation and vocabulary? Why does the magazine *The Awl* report 'the awful rise of "snuck"', and is the word *ilk* really, as *The Economist* counsels, 'best avoided'?[1] Do we laugh or grimace when we see outside the entrance to a friend's apartment block a sign reading: 'Please Ring the Buzzard'? What about if the sign says 'Please, Ring the Buzzard!'? Why do we object to someone sighing 'I could care less' rather than asserting 'I could not care less'? What is it that irks people about *alleged* being vocalized as three syllables rather than two?

The ways in which we and others use language have implications for our relationships, our work and our freedoms. Much of the time we select our words deliberately, and we choose to whom we speak and where we write. We may therefore feel uncomfortable about others' less careful use of language.

Perhaps you are feeling uncomfortable right now. You are likely to have spotted those queasy inverted commas around 'proper' in my opening paragraph. Maybe you disapproved of them. I might have deployed them in several other places, save for the suspicion that you would have found them irritating. But immediately we are in the thick of it, in the mêlée of the language wars. For notions such as 'proper', 'true meaning' and 'regional' are all contentious.

To sharpen our sense of this contest, I'll introduce a quotation from a novel. One character says, 'I cannot speak well enough to be unintelligible.' 'Bravo!' comes the response. 'An excellent satire on modern language.' When was this novel written? Recently? Twenty years ago, or sixty? Actually, it is *Northanger Abbey*, written by Jane Austen in the late 1790s.

I cannot speak well enough to be unintelligible. The words, said by Austen's teenage heroine Catherine Morland, are not meant to be satirical. They give pleasure now because they present, in miniature, some of the more vexed issues of English usage. Catherine is struck by the indirectness of polite conversation, and sees her own clarity as a mark of being unsophisticated. That strikes a chord: we all have experience of speech and text in which unintelligibility is displayed as though a badge of educational or social refinement. The American academic Alan Sokal has parodied this deliciously, publishing in a scholarly journal a spoof article entitled 'Transgressing the Boundaries: Towards a Transformative Hermeneutics of Quantum Gravity', which uses smart words to dress up claims about the non-existence of laws of physics and the need for a 'multiculturalist' understanding of mathematics.[2]

There are other concerns humming in the background of the extract from Jane Austen. Who decides whether someone speaks well? As for 'well enough' – is the insufficiency of Catherine's speech something perceived by her or by others, and, if the latter, how have they let her know about it? Are there, in fact, any virtues in unintelligibility, or in not being immediately intelligible? To put it another way, are there times when we benefit from expressing ourselves in a warped or aberrant fashion, our individualism saturating our idiom? And what does Henry Tilney, the rather flirtatious clergyman who is the object of Catherine's affections, mean by 'modern language'? Austen's writing invites this kind of close attention. Ironies are everywhere, and her characters are forever picking their way through the linguistic hazards of polite society.

Next, here is the title of an essay: 'The Growing Illiteracy of American Boys'. When do you suppose it was published? 2010? 1980? In fact this piece was the work of E. L. Godkin, founder of the magazine *The Nation*, and was published in 1896. Godkin lamented the absence of practical language skills among college students. He based his arguments not on research in some unlettered backwoods, but on an extended study of written work done at Harvard. In America in the late nineteenth century, universities were criticized for failing to prepare students for professional life. In 1891, the future President Herbert Hoover was required to take a remedial English course before being admitted to Stanford, and that same year James Morgan Hart, a professor at Cornell, could write that 'the cry all over the country is: Give us more English! Do not let our young men and women grow up in ignorance of their mother tongue!'[3]

Now, moving back in time to 1712, this is Sir Richard Steele, a usually convivial observer of London life, writing in *The Spectator* – a periodical which influenced eighteenth-century ideas of polite usage, though in its original form it ran for only twenty-one months and sold about 3,000 copies per issue: 'The scandalous abuse of Language and hardening of Conscience, which may be observed every Day in going from one Place to another, is what makes a whole City to an unprejudiced Eye a Den of Thieves.' Here is the same author, the previous year: 'The Dialect of Conversation is now-a-days so swelled with Vanity and Compliment . . . that if a Man that lived an Age or two ago should return into the World again he would really want a Dictionary to help him to understand his own Language.' Finally, here he is in 1713 in a newspaper called *The Guardian* (no relation of the more famous paper founded by Manchester businessmen in 1821): 'As the World now goes, we have no adequate Idea of what is meant by *Gentlemanly* . . . Here is a very pleasant Fellow, a Correspondent of mine, that puts in for that Appellation even to High-way Men.'

Reflecting on Steele's complaints, we may well say to ourselves that little has changed in the last three hundred years. But the history of talking about language's imperfections goes back even further than this. It is not exclusive to English. In the first century BC the critic Dionysius of Halicarnassus celebrated recent improvements in oratory by rubbishing the rhetoric of the previous generation; this, he said, was 'intolerable in its melodramatic shamelessness' and possessed of a crudeness that made Greece 'like the household of some desperate roué, where the decent, respectable wife sits powerless in her own home, while some nitwit of a girl . . . treats her like dirt.'[4] This is the way critics of language use are apt to express themselves; we can quickly lose sight of the fact that they are discussing language, because they deploy such extravagant images.

In the late nineteenth century the American linguist William Dwight Whitney argued that language is an institution. It is 'the work of those whose wants it subserves; it is in their sole keeping and control; it has been by them adapted to their circumstances and wants, and is still everywhere undergoing at their hands such adaptation'. Its elements are 'the product of a series of changes, effected by the will and consent of men, working themselves out under historical conditions, and conditions of man's nature, and by the impulse of motives, which are, in the main, distinctly traceable'.[5] Whitney's model has flaws, but he alights on an important idea: 'Every existing form of human speech is a body of arbitrary and conventional signs . . . handed down by tradition.' Crucially, therefore, change is 'the fundamental fact upon which rests the whole method of linguistic study'.[6] Common assent and custom are, he argues, fundamental to meaning, and at any moment we may experience a kind of amnesia about what the words we employ used to mean and where they came from.

Although many will agree with Whitney's view of language as a set of habits, other conceptions of language persist. English-speakers are touchy about questions of usage. This sort of touchiness is not uncommon among speakers of other languages, but English is the most contested major language. By this I mean that its small details and large presence are fought over more vociferously than those of any other language.

The fight is most often about 'the fundamental fact' of language identified by Whitney. Change happens. All living human languages alter: meanings shift, and so do pronunciations and grammatical structures. We may feel that the language we use is stable, but this is an illusion. For all that it may unnerve us, there is nothing weird or wrong about change; it would be much weirder if change did not happen. Language is form, not substance; not communication, but a system of communication – a point on which I shall expand.

We are the agents of change. The 'facts' of language are social: changes occur in a language because there are changes in the condi-

4

tions under which the language is used. Needs alter, values shift, and opportunities vary. For many, the experience of being caught up in language change is maddening. It requires a large effort of detachment to think that the rise of Textspeak may be one of the glories of minimalism. But feeling outrage is not the same as being right.

The idea that we are doomed to disagree about language is, of course, the subject of one of the most memorable stories – and one of the most enduring images – in the Old Testament. This is in chapter 11 of the Book of Genesis. In the King James Version, the text reads as follows:

> And the whole earth was of one language, and of one speech. And it came to pass, as they [the families of the sons of Noah] journeyed from the east, that they found a plain in the land of Shinar; and they dwelt there . . . And they said, Go to, let us build us a city and a tower, whose top may reach unto heaven; and let us make us a name, lest we be scattered abroad upon the face of the whole earth. And the Lord came down to see the city and the tower, which the children of men builded. And the Lord said, Behold, the people is one, and they have all one language; and this they begin to do: and now nothing will be restrained from them, which they have imagined to do. Go to, let us go down, and there confound their language, that they may not understand one another's speech. So the Lord scattered them abroad from thence upon the face of all the earth: and they left off to build the city. Therefore is the name of it called Babel; because the Lord did there confound the language of all the earth: and from thence did the Lord scatter them abroad upon the face of all the earth.

This has become a defining myth in Western culture. Notionally we are the descendants of the families of the sons of Noah, and we suffer the effects of our forefathers' arrogance. Our punishment is incomprehension of other people; their minds are shuttered from our gaze. The myth of Babel fosters the idea that we are doomed to be separated by language not only from other societies, but also from people within our own society.

Samuel Johnson, the eighteenth-century polymath who was the author of the first really good English dictionary, claimed that 'Tongues, like governments, have a natural tendency to degeneration.' It is true that languages in the past have tended to divide and proliferate. Yet rather than thinking of this as degeneration, we can see the diversity of languages in a different way: as permitting through its richness greater possibilities for creativity and adaptability, and as generating opportunities for collaboration and reciprocity that are powerful precisely because they are difficult. The world is a boisterous parliament of tongues. And not only between different languages, but also within each language, there is this disparity, this scattering, this dissociation – which can be seen as a problem, as a mere fact, or as the very wellspring of the efforts we pour into communicating.

A language is a transcript of history, not an immutable edifice. Whoever makes this point, though, is at risk of being labelled permissive. In fact, a derogatory adverb usually accompanies 'permissive': 'hopelessly' or 'dangerously' or 'recklessly' – as if one has been encouraging anonymous sex or the sharing of hypodermic needles. There is a gulf of difference between, on the one hand, questioning bogus rules and, on the other, urging people to use language insensibly and promiscuously. But to many self-appointed guardians of good usage (and almost all such guardians *are* self-appointed) the gulf is invisible. These guardians come in many guises. They may be teachers, retired civil servants, senior broadcasters, seasoned editors, people who like writing letters to newspapers, word-fanciers, or the semi-educated. Some make sensible observations, but many are hypocrites. Their rage can be tempestuous. Just ask the language professors who have received hate mail for refusing to take a stand against split infinitives.

In the chapters that follow, I shall explore the history of arguments about English. The movement of the book will be, in broad terms, chronological. Yet digging into the past will often prompt thoughts about the language as it is today. Rather than unfurling a narrative of what-happened-next, I shall move between the past and the present. The connections between them are essential to my story.

The geographical focus will at first be Britain; then I shall range more widely, reflecting the emergence of English as an international language. Some chapters will dwell on a concept, for certain subjects require a single sustained treatment. I shall also zero in on people who have exerted an especially strong influence on ideas about English; one of my themes is the role of individuals in shaping the language and our beliefs about it. Ralph Waldo Emerson has a lovely line that 'Language is a city to the building of which every human has brought a stone'. This captures the sense – vital here – of language as a consensual, communal but also ongoing construction. My account of the building of this city will be investigative. But, as I proceed, a polemical strand will become apparent.

I sometimes give talks about English, and I am always keen to take questions afterwards. My first book was about Samuel Johnson's dictionary. My second was a history of words absorbed into English from other languages. Whenever I speak about these books and the time for questions comes, the past has to make way for concerns about the present: my feelings about apostrophes or the perceived evils of instant messaging. We are dogged by the notion that the English language is in a state of terrible decline. Here, writing in the 1980s, is the distinguished American educator Jacques Barzun: 'Two of the causes in the decline of *all* modern European languages have been: the doctrines of linguistic science and the example of "experimental" art,' and 'The language we have now has suffered damage wholesale, the faults encountered come not as single spies but in battalions.'[7] I hear this kind of thing a lot: individual words are being cheapened, diction is on the slide, grammar is getting bastardized, and 'In fifty years English literature will mean nothing to us.' Once, after an event in Edinburgh, an audience member bearded me to ask, 'Don't you think this is a very uniquely sad moment in the history of our language?'

In truth, I don't. I could pedantically reply that there are no degrees of uniqueness. More to the point, though, the present moment does not strike me as sad. It is normal to imagine one is living in an age of exceptional violence and anarchy, yet this is to be blind to the problems of every other age. Our sense of the particular ser-iousness of the difficulties we face is sharpened by narcissism, and more than that by the belief that we can improve matters. We take a morbid pleasure in believing that the special randomness of our world requires of us a special heroism. Yet novelty is not the same thing as decline. English is no more going to the dogs than it was in the middle of the nineteenth century when pessimists predicted that within a hundred years the speech of Britons and of Americans would be mutually unintelligible, or in the 1550s when the humanist scholar Thomas Wilson complained in *The Arte of Rhetorique*, a book 'for the use of all suche as are studious of eloquence sette forth in Englische', that well-travelled gentlemen had lately started to 'powder' their conversation with confusing 'oversea language'.

To say this, I recognize, is to provoke. Experience suggests that you can always start a row by staking a claim about English usage. Get mixed up in the question of plurals, for instance. Insist that, since the word *data* is plural in Latin, if we have been given only one piece of information it is a 'datum'. Allege that when confronted with more than one hippopotamus, one should speak not of hippopotamuses, but of 'hippoipotamou'. Say that a Birmingham accent – be it Birmingham, England, or Birmingham, Alabama, or one of the two Birminghams in Ohio – is inferior to a middle-class London one. Claim for that matter that some languages are spoken much faster than others or that Americans are ruining English. Protest, as someone did to me at a festival, that 'However stupid English grammar is, at least English has got grammar – unlike Chinese.' Assert that 'The crowd is on its feet' is better than the 'The crowd are on their feet', or insist that you cannot say 'The class of '89 is having a reunion, and there's a big surprise in store for them'.

When we argue about language, we are often concerned with the ways in which it impairs thought. Words seem to lack the precision of numbers or symbols, and the elasticity of language propels misunderstandings. This argument is not new. Those who have studied language most deeply have done so in the hope that it will enable them to understand thought and indeed life itself. Meanwhile, philosophy is forever encroaching on linguistic concerns.

These are sensitive areas, and there is a distinguished tradition of thinkers who have created philosophical mayhem by kicking against conventional and unreflective images of what language is and how it works. We can trace this tradition back as far as Plato's *Cratylus* in the fourth century BC, which examines some of the basic problems in the study of language (such as the conventions of how we name things), and the more sustained efforts of Plato's pupil Aristotle, who was especially concerned with establishing the vocabulary we use to describe and categorize reality. Their successors have included St Augustine of Hippo in the fifth century, who speculated about the process by which language skills are acquired; John Locke in the seventeenth, who argued that words are arbitrary signs denoting our ideas; Wilhelm von Humboldt, a Prussian diplomat and educational theorist, who insisted on treating language as a phenomenon situated in reality rather than as something abstract (a 'dead contraption'), and thought of it as a creative activity, making infinite uses of a finite number of elements; Jacob Grimm, famous with his brother Wilhelm for collecting folk tales, and responsible also for making historical research the cornerstone of linguistics; and Ferdinand de Saussure, who changed this, emphasizing the idea of language as a system of relationships, and positing the need to study a language system not through its historical development (a *diachronic* approach), but at a particular moment in time (a *synchronic* one).

Modern linguistics owes something to all these figures, but is especially indebted to Saussure. Its message is that the present is the key to the past. By this I mean that the forces that created languages are at work right now. Looking at languages as they exist today enables us to understand their history. What this also suggests is that things we may consider problems in the present are in fact evidence of the powerful creative forces of language.

Many of the large challenges that face us may be new, but the issues at stake are familiar, and the little details that niggle us have niggled previous generations just as much, if not more. We hear worriers disparaging imported words (does *nouvelle vague* accomplish more than *new wave*?), slang (today's term of approval, let's say *hot*, may tomorrow seem stale), abbreviations (sometimes with justice – it amazes me that 'Accid anal prev' is used instead of 'Accident analysis and prevention'), rickety grammar ('Once she'd been neutered, the princess went to collect her cat') and the lapses of public figures who 'ought to know better' (George W. Bush saying 'Rarely is the question asked: "Is our children learning?"'). As a result we may imagine that we are living in an age of egregious stupidity and crassness – and of remarkable linguistic precariousness. But this suspicion was just as common in the England of Chaucer, Shakespeare or Milton, in the Britain of Dickens, and in the America of the Pilgrim Fathers, George Washington or Martin Luther King.

Furthermore, some things we now consider to be mistakes or solecisms were once quite acceptable. Do we pretend not to understand Edgar in *King Lear* when he vows 'to take the basest and most poorest shape'? Are we racked with indignation when we hear Bassanio in *The Merchant of Venice* read a letter from Antonio containing the words 'All debts are cleared between you and I'? The stout defenders of the Queen's English – a construct first mentioned in 1592 by the Elizabethan pamphleteer Thomas Nashe – or indeed of the King's English – mentioned in 1553 by Thomas Wilson – pretend that they exert themselves in order to ensure that the language remains a channel for clear communication. But the sorts of usage that offend them hardly prevent communication. When Mick Jagger sings 'I can't get no satisfaction', none of us can in good faith claim that his double negative has led us to believe he feels blissfully satisfied. When Chaucer writes of the Knight in *The Canterbury Tales* 'He nevere yet no vileynye ne sayde', we may be thrown by 'vileynye' (it means the Knight never said anything defamatory or discreditable), but the accumulation of negatives does not prevent us from sniffing the courtly aroma of the Knight's politeness.

One obvious difference here is that Mick Jagger is speaking (after a fashion), whereas Chaucer is writing. Different standards should be applied to the spoken and written forms of the language. Yet often people discussing the use of English fail to recognize the distinction. I shall be saying plenty more about this. Or rather, *writing* plenty more.

With reference to both speech and writing, most of us practise linguistic hygiene, brushing or swabbing away what we see as pollutants – jargon, vulgarisms, profanity, bad grammar and mispronunciations – and sometimes in the process replacing one kind of evil with another. Alarmists are apt to vilify the types of people they think most culpable: they have in the past condemned travellers, shopkeepers, journalists, university students, nurses, hairdressers, people who live in cities, homosexuals, the authors of translations, and women.[8] All of us, besides using language, comment on it, and we complain about others' usage far more often than we applaud it. Where language is concerned, some are engineers, but more of us are doctors.

This kind of appraisal can be entertaining, but its main appeal is that it allows us to tidy up reality. At the same time it reveals our aversion to disorder. We fear not being able to make ourselves understood, and fear also that the essentials of our world-view are not shared by others. When we practise what the linguist Deborah Cameron has designated 'verbal hygiene', we expose our anxieties about otherness and difference.[9] It can seem as though we positively want to feel that our language is coming unstuck. Even if other aspects of our existence appear beyond our control, language feels as if it can be rescued from the chaos of modernity. If we can arrest language change, the thinking goes, we can hold off other kinds of change.[10] All the while, people who stress that change is inevitable are dismissed as wimpish egalitarians, pluralists, relativists – as 'Shit happens' defeatists. Yet if the 'Anything goes' approach seems an abdication of responsibility, its opposite, pernickety micro-management, recalls in its desperateness King Canute's mythic efforts to turn back the waves.

It is time to look at a rule, to see pernicketiness in action. I want to consider something seemingly humdrum, which is nonetheless one of the most enduringly contentious subjects in English grammar. My chosen issue is the split infinitive, perennial bugbear of neo-Victorians and TV's (fictional) Dr Frasier Crane. The opening credits of *Star Trek* contain the best-known of all split infinitives. The mission of the *Starship Enterprise* is, we are informed, 'to explore strange new worlds, to seek out new life and new civilizations, to boldly go where no man has gone before.' It's a line much satirized, as by Douglas Adams in *The Hitchhiker's Guide to the Galaxy*, where the heroes of the wild and long-lost Galactic Empire are said to have dared 'to boldly split infinitives that no man had split before'. But is this phrasing so dreadful? Leaving aside for a moment the question of what rule there is about the treatment of infinitives (and also the decision to say 'no man' rather than 'no one'), we might usefully focus on the rhetorical force of the statement as it is at present couched. The rhythm here is important. The three-part structure 'to explore . . . to seek . . . to go' is disrupted by the abrupt introduction of 'boldly'. Rather than being a bad thing, this accentuates our impression of the narrator's excitement about the sheer boldness of the quest. The assonance of 'to boldly go' is more striking – not only because of its rhythm, but also because less compressed – than that of 'to go boldly'. 'Boldly to go' would just seem precious.

The split infinitive is found at least as early as the thirteenth century. It occurs a couple of times in Chaucer, rather more often in the writings of John Wyclif, and a huge amount in the fifteenth-century works of Reginald Pecock, a Welsh bishop who delighted in the form. It seems to have been considered inelegant for most of the two centuries that followed – Shakespeare has only one, in a sonnet ('Thy pity may deserve to pitied be') – and was uncommon until the later stages of the eighteenth century, when it began to appear in the writings of even the most punctilious authors, such as Samuel Johnson. Hostility to the practice of splitting infinitives developed in the nineteenth century. A magazine article dating from 1834 may well be the first published condemnation of it. A large number of similar prohibitions followed. The first to call it a 'split infinitive' was a contributor to the magazine *Academy* in 1897.[11]

The prohibition originates in a regard for Latin, and for some people today is reinforced by the split infinitive's impossibility in German. The experimental psychologist Steven Pinker has suggested that 'forcing modern speakers of English . . . not to split an infinitive because it isn't done in Latin makes about as much sense as forcing modern residents of England to wear laurels and togas'.[12] But let's just probe the rule for a moment. In Latin, the infinitive is expressed by a single word: *amare* means 'to love', *venire* means 'to come'. It is, in short, unsplittable. Now consider Latin's treatment of nouns: in Latin there is no definite or indefinite article – 'a girl' is *puella*, 'the threads' is *fimbriae*. No one would suggest that we cannot say 'a clever girl' or 'the broken threads'. Yet isn't this a split nominative? Is it not as much of a crime as a split infinitive?

'I am going to really do it' means something different from 'I am really going to do it' and 'Really I am going to do it' and 'I am going to do it really'. The location in this sentence of the adverb *really* is not – should not – be a matter merely of propriety or euphony. It should be determined by which version best conveys one's intended meaning.

This principle can be illustrated by the case of another common adverb, *only*. It pays to keep *only* as close as possible to the word it modifies. Consider, for instance, the disparity between 'I only take off my socks when she asks' and 'I take off my socks only when she asks'. For good measure, let's add 'I take off only my socks when she asks'. Three rather different pictures of domestic life emerge here. A fourth develops if I change the sentence again: 'Only I take off my socks when she asks.' Obviously there is no infinitive to split in these examples, but they suggest the importance of where we place an adverb. Sometimes we have to split infinitives, not only because anything else sounds weird, but because the prissy avoidance of a split infinitive results in a distortion of our meaning. It's hard to see how I could neatly and economically reformulate the sentence 'I expect our output to more than double next year'. The proper thing to do is whatever seems most natural, least fidgety. But what kind of a guideline is that?

Most people cleave to certain rules about English. They behave as though these are eternal, immutable edicts – the violation of which is a symptom of low intelligence and poor breeding. I can remember being chastised at school by a teacher who insisted that a civilized person could never put a comma before *and* or use the words *lot* and *got*. Most of us have been encouraged to believe that rules of this kind are important. And there are a large number of them – perhaps as many as 3,500. This is the number of distinct points of grammar identified in the index to *A Comprehensive Grammar of the English Language* (1985), a 1,779-page tome by the eminent scholars Randolph Quirk, Sidney Greenbaum, Geoffrey Leech and Jan Svartvik.

I am not going to claim to be immune from these 'rules'. I find myself wincing when someone says 'between you and I'. I'll admit, too, that when I hear this I suspect that the person who has said it is trying to sound smart and educated. But, even as I wince, my inner linguist recognizes that the response is aesthetic and is one

13

which I have been conditioned to express. For these rules – note my earlier inverted commas – are not really rules, but conventions. At different times, and in different places, different conventions are the norm. Of course, some of these conventions become so deeply ingrained in us that we find it hard to grant they are merely that; we think of them as timeless, profound and inherently sensible. Conventions can put down deep roots; they can be hard to eradicate. Yet they have changed before and will change again.

Conventions are contingent. Communication may depend on our observing them, but, examined dispassionately, many seem odd. (To get away from language for a moment, consider the conventions of chess, video games, formal dress or opera.) If I stop to think about why it's correct to say X but not to say Y, I may not be able to come up with much of an explanation. We generally adhere to the conventions because it is practical to do so. A convention is a solution to a recurrent problem of coordination; by sticking to it, one not only overcomes the problem, but makes it invisible. If you are playing football and you decide to pick the ball up and run with it, you are likely to be sent from the pitch; few people are going to think you have done something clever, witty or original, and most will find your behaviour difficult to understand, because you have violated the rules of the game. Where language is concerned, we play by what we understand to be the rules because we sense – on the whole unconsciously – a responsibility to the people with whom we are communicating.

This book is written in what I hope is a crisp kind of standard English (of which more anon), because that is what I have been taught, that is what I have tended to absorb as a reader, and that is what I imagine the audience for this book is likely to favour. Writing more colloquially would feel wrong. Yet as soon as one begins to analyse the idea of what is correct and what incorrect, one sees how entangled it is with notions of what's appropriate, felicitous, effective, useful and socially acceptable.

2 The survival machine

The power of language and
the fight for English

You and I know what language is, and we know that we have a command of it. We would, I imagine, be relaxed about saying this. But what exactly is it that we know?

The linguist Leonard Bloomfield provides an answer: 'Language has been developed in the interchange of messages, and every individual who has learned to use language has learned it through such interchange.' Accordingly, the language an individual uses is not his or her creation, but consists of adopted habits. From childhood, we practise language until the details of it are 'mechanized and unconscious'. As a result we rarely consider exactly what our use of language involves.[1] Think for a moment about the movements you have to make with your tongue and lower lip merely in order to articulate a single word: on reflection, the precise mechanics of the process seem – unless you are an actor or a singer perhaps – quite strange, and this is before you take into account the operations of the larynx, the glottis, the soft palate and so on. We rarely consider the physical basis of language. The complex set of processes which enables us to achieve anything from a little interjection to a sophisticated speech is something we tend not to examine. And this lack of examination is a theme of our entire relationship to language – for language is a central plank of our existence about which we nevertheless have beliefs and opinions that, while passionate, are primitive and unscientific.

The capacity for language is biological. Language is one of what Richard Dawkins has called the 'survival-machine actions' that impel our existence. However, the form that language takes – the signs and sounds we learn, and many of the ways we combine them – is determined by the community in which we grow up. In Tahitian the verb

15

comes at the start of a sentence. Speakers of Dyirbal in Queensland have traditionally had for all things an everyday word and an alternative one for use in the presence of their mothers-in-law. The Burushaski language spoken in some northern parts of Pakistan distinguishes four genders. Kalam, spoken in Papua New Guinea, has a mere ninety-six verbs. Language is natural; languages are culturally created.

It is worth being clear, though, that there seem to be rules of language shared by all humans. The brain is a set of computational systems, a shrink-wrapped lump of molecular hardware. We are familiar with its inputs and outputs, but rather less familiar with the circuitry inside the black box, which performs its functions in ways that seem magical. The brain processes information, and within our neural networks there are systems that manage language according to a computational logic that is genetically specified. There is a level of grammar that is, to a significant degree, biologically determined.

This 'universal grammar' is capable of generating the very different syntaxes of all human languages – that is, the different ways in which we organize words into sentences. It is one of our basic endowments, rather than something we learn. Modern views of the subject draw heavily on the work of Noam Chomsky, an academic maverick who by his own account experienced linguistic enlightenment while suffering from seasickness during an Atlantic crossing. Chomsky's model of grammar, presented in the late 1950s, built on von Humboldt's idea that an infinite number of utterances can be achieved while following a finite number of rules. Chomsky presented the human capacity for language as a computational system. His account of this, though today professedly 'minimalist', is forbiddingly technical. Its exact nature is not important here; what matters for present purposes is that the complicated and apparently innate rules of universal grammar, within which it is possible to exhibit immense creativity, are different from the elements of language that we learn – among them phoney rules of English usage.

As I have suggested, the conventions of usage result from a sense of responsibility towards other users of our language. There are cogent reasons for trying to use language lucidly. In many everyday settings we are irritated by language that misleads us, unbalances us or needlessly and fruitlessly diverts our concentration. It is no fun to have to read twice a sentence which, on that second reading, we find we didn't even want to read once. Skilful handling of language will tend to reduce the amount of cognitive effort one's audience has to expend in getting at one's meaning. If my expression is confused and ambiguous, I risk losing your attention.

Chomsky has highlighted language's main purposes: to transmit information, establish relationships, express our thoughts or clarify them, pursue knowledge and understanding, exercise our minds creatively, and play. In all but the last two of these, lucidity is vital. Precise and conventional use of language averts painful misunderstandings; for instance, if I am an air traffic controller talking a pilot through an emergency landing I should be scrupulously careful about the words I use when referring to positions and directions.[2] Consider, also, the importance attached to language in the law. Many legal cases turn on issues of interpretation – assessing the intent of legislators, and locating the meanings of statements or assigning meanings to them. Precedent is important here. Habits, associations, taught beliefs, traditions and the generally accepted norms of social groups all inform the metaphysics of legal meaning. Because the occasions when legal writing is scrutinized are usually adversarial, writing of this kind needs to blend an impression of objectivity with a subtle advocacy of its positions.

The justification for linguistic conventions is a pragmatic one. When they appear to be under threat, it does not mean that civilization is falling apart. Rather, the existing conventions are being superseded by new ones. Researchers such as the 'language evolution' specialist Simon Kirby draw a comparison between the behaviour of a language and that of a virus. The properties of a language are shaped by its need to survive in its physical environment. Robustness – structure, infectiousness and ease of assembly – is vital to its survival. This robustness is not the same thing as perfection: languages are full of clutter that's not there for any reason which we can immediately identify, and where the reasons can be seen, their machinery may still be ugly.

Languages are not wholly consistent. They are not perfectly logical. In fact, they are loaded with redundant information. Typically this performs a social function; it may make meaning easier to decode, or it may support the connection between people who might otherwise struggle to communicate. Redundancy can be something as simple as the *u* that tends to follow a *q* in English (inherited from Latin), my saying 'PIN number', or my reciting my phone number twice when leaving you voicemail; or it may be something more complex, such as the harmonious recurrences sewn into a poem. Generally, you need to pick up about three words in ten to get an inkling of what a conversation is about; it is the lack of redundancy in mathematics and its teaching that explains why so much maths bewilders so many people. Redundancy can be rhetorical, but it can also be a practical way of shielding meaning from confusion – a safeguard, a reassuring and stabilizing kind of predictability.

To expect a natural language to behave like mathematics is akin to expecting a child to behave like an iPod. Nevertheless, English is often cited as an example of a language peculiarly ungoverned by logic. This view is especially likely to be advanced by French scholars, who have been arguing for well over three hundred years that theirs is a language of great clarity, possessed of incorruptible syntax and precise terminology. The founding father of this school of chauvinism was Claude Favre de Vaugelas, whose *Remarques sur la langue française* (1647) celebrated the lucid expression of the French royal court. Previously the poet François de Malherbe had, with amusing specificity, canonized the exemplary usage of the longshoremen who worked at the '*port au foin*' (hay port) in Paris. Others, such as Joachim du Bellay and Antoine de Rivarol, believed that French was the closest language to the single tongue that was supposed to have existed before Babel. But French is not the language of reason, and English is not loose and unscientific.

To be clear: this is a book about English, but sometimes I shall drop in on the phenomena and problems of other languages, because doing so promises to afford some extra insight into English's conditions. And sometimes, too, I shall refer to English as 'our' language, although I recognize it may not be your language and in any case the possessive is misleading – for no one owns English.

Besides, English is not monolithic. There are numerous different Englishes, many of which may in some respects strike me as alien. A number of these have a lot of speakers: Australian English, for instance, and the Englishes used in Jamaica and the Philippines. Others, such as the forms used in the Nicaraguan Corn Islands, in Namibia or on Pitcairn Island in the south Pacific, are little documented.

A great many people use English as a second language. They, too, have a stake in its future. A distinction is sometimes drawn between the inner and outer circles of English, its traditional bases such as Britain or the US and those countries where it is not the native tongue but has been important historically – India and Singapore, for instance. The image was developed by Braj Kachru, an American academic born in Kashmir. Kachru also describes a third, 'expanding' circle that encompasses countries where English is used as a lingua franca, typically for business. This circle includes China and Japan.

The English of the inner circle is infused with certain values that are not immediately apparent. Examples of this cultural baggage include an overt concern with accuracy, a liking for hard facts, a careful distinction between facts and opinions, an aversion to emotional display, an emphasis on the autonomy of the individual, a preoccupation with fairness and reasonableness, a hostility to exaggeration which often results in understatement, and explicit recognition of the limits of one's knowledge.[3] Clearly these tendencies pull us in different directions; we cannot manifest all of them at once. It is easy, moreover, to find innumerable examples of times when people from within the inner circle – those who use what the Polish-Australian scholar Anna Wierzbicka calls 'Anglo cultural scripts' – deviate from these norms. But there are concepts central to the ways in which inner-circle English-speakers express themselves that are deeply ingrained, little remarked upon, and different from the concepts embedded in the expressions of people who use other languages.

When I write of 'our' language, the possessive pronoun makes light of a great deal of cultural baggage. At the same time, my wording reflects a simple truth: people are proprietorial about the language they speak and write. Arguments about English have always been coloured by feelings about tradition, the distribution of power, freedom, the law and identity. Many of the debates and disputes surrounding English relate to education: any statement about methods of teaching and learning is grounded in politics, and when someone advances a so-called educational philosophy it is really an ideological programme.

As Chomsky has said, 'Questions of language are basically questions of *power*.'[4] Language is a potent instrument for promoting notions of togetherness and of discord. There's an old joke that a language is 'a dialect with an army and a navy', which spread and defend it. (The line is often attributed to the linguist Max Weinreich, although it was certainly not Weinreich who coined it.) It makes more sense to say that a language is a system of signs, where there is a standard way of writing those signs, and that it is promoted through formal education and government endorsement. Any definition of language will meet with objections in some quarters, but it would be hard to come up with a useful definition that did not convey – even if only implicitly – the idea summed up in the now rather hackneyed maxim 'Language is power'. Power involves relationships, and those relationships tend to be unequal; they subsume loyalties, responsibilities, traditions and systems of control.

Questions of English reverberate through our daily lives. When we use language, we may be making a social connection, answering a question, enjoying ourselves, passing time, or showing off, but fundamentally we imagine that the interest of the person or people to whom we are speaking is engaged.[5] The desire to shape and emphasize this engagement is crucial. How do I get you to listen to me? Can I persuade you to like me, hire me, trust me, come and see my etchings? Manipulations of our language – by the state, advertisers, salespeople, factions, preachers, prophets, poets, cheats – are legion. Then there are other questions. How do we refer to social groups other than our own – people of a different ethnic background, say, or people with disabilities? How do we address strangers, which words are hurtful, and when is it okay to swear? Is the language of an email different from the language of conversation? What songs can we sing, and how should we pray?

The limits of English have long caused concern. In moments of creative despair, Joseph Conrad thought English incapable of conveying feelings. It was a language only for dogs and horses. Charles V, the Holy Roman Emperor, had a precise idea of the scope of different languages, and reputedly chose to speak English only to geese. Voltaire complained to James Boswell that it was not possible for him to speak English because to do so one had to place the tongue between the teeth – and he had lost his teeth. In Harriet Beecher Stowe's novel *Pink and White Tyranny* (1871) the narrator comments, 'Just as there is no word in the Hottentot vocabulary for "holiness," or "purity," so there are no words in our savage English to describe a lady's dress': to do the matter justice it was necessary 'to write half, or one third, in French'. Then there is Nicole Diver in F. Scott Fitzgerald's *Tender is the Night* (1934), who comments with what may seem some justice that 'in French you can be heroic and gallant with dignity . . . But in English you can't be heroic and gallant without being a little absurd.' Bob Dylan offers this: 'You know, the English can say "marvellous" pretty good. They can't say "raunchy" so good, though. Well, we each have our thing.'[6]

It's true: we do each have our 'thing', and English's 'thing' is complaint. When we discuss the English language, we illuminate our foibles, prejudices and ambitions. Language creates communities, and some of these are solidarities of complainers and pedants. A statement about proper English is a statement not only about the language, but also about people – about who the proper English are, or just about who the proper users of English are. Typically, the celebrants and defenders of proper English are celebrating or defending something other than language.

In 1989, Professor Brian Cox presented a report proposing large reforms in the national curriculum. This had been commissioned by the Conservative government, and the Secretary of State for Education, Kenneth Baker, chose to announce its recommendations before the main body of the report was published. A few days later Prince Charles, the heir to the British throne, made a statement that 'We've got to produce people who can write proper English . . . English is taught so bloody badly. If we want people who write good English . . . it cannot be done with the present system and all the nonsense academics come up with. It is a fundamental problem. We must educate for character.'[7] The switch here from 'proper' to 'good' is brisk, as though they are the same. But propriety and goodness are defined in different ways.

If I refer to proper behaviour, something's proper place, a proper course of action, a proper attitude, a person having a proper job, proper care or consideration, proper use or treatment, providing proper training or doing things properly, I am unlikely as I do so to be explicit about what I mean by 'proper'. Instead I assume that you know – that we share a cultural norm or standard. More than that, I am indicating that you should know. Challenge me to explain what I mean by this word, and I am likely to flounder. The 'proper' is negatively defined: it is the absence of proper behaviour, things not being in their proper places, someone not having a proper job, or the neglect of proper training that prompt our aggrieved use of this adjective.

Where does our sense of the 'proper' come from?[8] In arguing about what is right and what wrong in any language, we appeal to authority. This authority is embodied in academies, the Ministry of Education (or its equivalent) and universities, as well as in the pronouncements of people who have appointed themselves authorities and have become known as such. We commonly accept these judges' pronouncements. There are also geographical criteria. These are evident in statements such as 'Natives of Perugia speak the best Italian' or 'People in Alsace have funny accents'. Typically, we feel that there are certain environments in which our language is decently used, and we favour the usage that obtains there. Sometimes, too, we defer to the example of a significant literary figure, saying that so-and-so is a model of correctness. A broader view is that 'correct English is that which is used by the best writers', but who are they, and what are the criteria for their being so esteemed? The definition tends to be circular: the best writers are the ones who best use the resources of English.

When we appeal to aesthetics, our arguments become nebulous. The aesthetically sensitive arbiter will argue that whatever is beautiful in language is good. The problem here would seem to be that the desire for beautiful language concentrates on language as an object – on the sensory pleasure it affords rather than on what it signifies. Besides, as we know from our observation of others, the constant pursuit of beauty can be embarrassing.

Alternatively, we may claim that the most elegant usage is that of the social elite. Perhaps this now seems an absurd position, but not long ago it would have been perfectly normal. The democratic option is to say that all doubtful matters should be decided by referendum, or just to say that the majority is right. This idea was touched upon by Horace in his treatise *Ars Poetica,* published around 18 BC. He wrote of the power of *'ius et norma loquendi'* – i.e. the law and standard of speaking. 'Norma loquendi' is a phrase that has acquired some currency, as in the playful title of the popular journalist William Safire's book *In Love with Norma Loquendi.* We also appeal to logic. Although there are discrepancies between logic and the ways we use language, we frequently use arguments from logic (or from what we imagine to be logic) in order to justify our choice of words or find fault with others' choices. In practice we tend to find our usual practices logical and anything else illogical. 'Logic' is often a mask for smugness and jingoism.

All attitudes to usage can be classified as either prescriptive or descriptive, and current arguments about the subject often involve the words *prescriptivist* and *descriptivist* both as adjectives and as nouns. A prescriptivist dictates how people should speak and write, whereas a descriptivist avoids passing judgements and provides explanation and analysis. So, one says what ought to happen, and the other says what does happen. This antagonism, constructed mainly by modern academic discussions of language and linguists, is now commonly used when discussing writers on language before the twentieth century. Pigeonholing of this kind results in some ludicrous misrepresentations of what these writers thought.

The history of prescriptions about English – of grammar texts, manuals of style and '*O tempora o mores*'-type laments – is in part a history of bogus rules, superstitions, half-baked logic, groaningly unhelpful lists, baffling abstract statements, false classifications, contemptuous insiderism and educational malfeasance. But it is also a history of attempts to make sense of the world and its bazaar of competing ideas and interests. Instinctively, we find the arbitrariness of existence hard to accept. Our desire to impose order on the world, which means inventing the forms of language rather than discovering them, is a creative act. Furthermore, the quarrel between descriptivists and prescriptivists (terms I shall use for want of good alternatives) is a sort of mad confederacy: each party thrives on lambasting the other.

Strong feelings do not beget strong arguments. The default setting for prescriptivists is to say what we should not do, rather than be precise and consistent about what we should. Sanctifying good English is achieved mainly by marking off a category called 'Bad English'. They are thus really *proscriptivists*, and their attitude is captured in the title of the 1883 manual *Don't*, published by the playwright Oliver Bell Bunce under the pseudonym 'Censor'. Bunce's little book, subtitled *A Manual of Mistakes and Improprieties more or less prevalent in Conduct and Speech*, is full of instructions such as 'Don't say *lady* when you mean *wife*' (which may suggest he imagines a male audience), 'Don't fail to exercise tact' (surely the first three words there are redundant?) and – a majestic catch-all – 'Don't speak ungrammatically'.[9] This negativity is something we can all recognize as a recurrent feature of the way we are taught language. It also highlights the contingency of conventions, to which I referred at the end of the previous chapter: many of Bunce's modern counterparts would be critical of his use of what are in effect double negatives. Writing of this kind is symptomatic of one of the most pernicious features of the English-speaker's world: the belief that the avoidance of mistakes is more important than the achievement of excellence. This belief is allied to a tendency to think that one misstep undoes the effect of a hundred perfect strides.

The grumblers, fault-finders, quibblers and mud-slingers frequently profess their passion for English. 'I care about English deeply, and I won't tolerate your use of this vile word,' says one. Another claims, 'I love the language too much to let this solecism pass unremarked.' They have a funny idea of love. Yet the descriptive approach does not provide a perfect alternative. Descriptive grammars are large, complex and in many cases astonishingly expensive. More to the point, they do not supply decisive, straightforward answers to the problems of everyday usage. These perceived problems may be rejected by the descriptivist as chimeras. But they feel uncomfortably real.

It is often claimed that the study of English began in the nineteenth century. There are good grounds for this: there is scant evidence that English literature or the history of the language were taught to young people before about 1820. However, close attention was paid to the mechanisms of the language long before that. Ian Michael, a historian of education, states that 'Formal teaching of the English language intended, in part at least, for schools, is apparent from 1586'.[10] Self-consciousness about English usage dates back further than this.

Tellingly, many early books dealing with grammar were packaged as self-help manuals. A volume dealing with writing skills might also instruct its readers about the best way to keep business records, cure a nosebleed or prune a fruit tree. So, for instance, William Mather's *Young Man's Companion* of 1685 explained how to cure madness (by holding the mad person underwater 'a little and often' and then administering sneezing powder), soften stiff eyelids with deer suet, and cure a sore throat with a plant unhappily known as Dogs-Turd.[11] Mather's book began with guidance on pronunciation, homophones, and how to use punctuation.

We are all familiar with the experience of judging people by the ways they speak: we understand that these convey information to us. Schemes of self-help have frequently involved the development of grammatical confidence. William Pearson's *The Self-Help Grammar of the English Language* (1865) is singular only in being quite so explicit about its conflation of the two concerns.

As far back as we can see, grammatical failings have been associated with moral ones, and those whose grammar has publicly been found faulty – typically in a classroom – have associated grammar with humiliation. To abuse language has been to risk excommunication. St Augustine of Hippo wrote in his *Confessions*, 'O Lord my God, be patient . . . with the men of this world as you watch them and see how strictly they obey the rules of grammar which have been handed down to them, and yet ignore the eternal rules of everlasting salvation.' More than 1,500 years after Augustine's death, this still feels apt. People bicker over the rules of English, complaining that Elvis Presley should say 'I'm all shaken up' rather than 'I'm all shook up', or arguing, less facetiously, that 'From where do you come?' is superior to 'Where do you come from?' They do this instead of struggling to observe what Augustine calls the eternal rules, because, in prospect at least, the fight for English looks easier to win.

3 The emergence of English

Chaucer, Caxton, Cranmer

Between the Norman Conquest and the reign of Queen Elizabeth I, the status and character of English were passionately disputed. Arguments about the language mainly concerned its worth, not the little details of ways in which it was used. It was common to ask which purposes English suited. Today we might answer that it is suitable for all purposes, but until the Renaissance there was a narrow sense of the language's potential.

We like to think of English as an old language, but it is not. The origins of a spoken language cannot be pinpointed, so in making claims about the relative ages of languages we are in fact comparing the ages only of the literatures associated with them. Nevertheless, we can say that even within the British Isles there are living languages older than English – the most robust of these being Welsh – while the oldest European language is probably Basque.

A very brisk summary of English's early history may be helpful here. English originated in dialects brought to Britain by Germanic settlers in the fifth century. We know little of how these dialects established themselves. However, it is clear that they all but eliminated the Celtic languages previously spoken in Britain. The arrival of Christian missionaries at the end of the sixth century led to the development of a form of writing based on the Roman alphabet, and in due course Catholic monasteries were the main centres of (Latin) scholarship and education. From the end of the eighth century, several waves of Viking settlers introduced new elements to English. Under King Alfred, at the end of the ninth century, there was sturdy resistance to the Vikings. By then one Germanic dialect, West Saxon, was dominant, and Alfred vigorously promoted it. The Scandinavian connection remained, though, and became especially important between 1016 and 1042 when England had, in succession, three Danish kings. Soon after this, in 1066, came the Norman Conquest. This forced English into a position of subservience, from which it did not ascend till the fourteenth century.

Our concern is the manner in which English reasserted itself after this period of repression. The development of a standard form of written English spanned the period from 1300 to 1800, mostly happening between 1400 and 1660. This summary is of course crude, not least in implying that by 1800 everything was in immaculate order. The story of standardization is matched – almost – by a countervailing story of dissolution, dissent and dissonance. Convergence, once achieved, creates opportunities for divergence. David Crystal's excellent book *The Stories of English* provides an account of the language that, starting with its very title, makes clear that the orthodox history and the history of orthodoxy are parts of a larger, kaleidoscopic variety of stories (which are stories of variety). Nevertheless, we can say that during this central period from 1400 to 1660 the image of English altered dramatically; the language went from seeming quite precarious to being approved and applauded. In this phase, we can see two important features of English being established: use of the language is intimately linked to a sense of nationality and national purpose, and people's experience of using it is fraught with insecurities.

In 1300, French was the language of administration in England. But the linguistic climate was changing. This hastened with the outbreak in 1337 of what came to be known as the Hundred Years War. Already English poets and chroniclers, celebrating the stable and united kingdom of Edward I and condemning the disastrous reign of his successor Edward II, had endeavoured to project an idea of England and Englishness that was grounded in the English language. This they represented as something robust and clear-cut, bearing witness to the Anglo-Saxon ancestry of the people, and anchoring their patriotism and ethnic solidarity.[1] Now French was the language of the enemy, and, while it remained useful in many careers, antagonism towards France was a fillip to English.

Beginning in 1348, the Black Death killed about a third of Britain's population. The peasants who survived found that labour was scarce;

workers could command higher wages and, if unhappy with the way their masters treated them, knew they could quit their district and find employment elsewhere. As many peasants rebelled against the established labour laws, they craved a voice in government. English was their language of protest. From around 1350, the language was used in schools. In 1362 the Statute of Pleading was enacted, and English became the language of legal proceedings – although records still had to be kept in Latin, and French was not completely eradicated from the legal profession until 1733. These dates mark key moments in the emergence of English, and by the end of the century the Cornishman John Trevisa could claim that children at grammar school knew no more French than their left heel did.

While the language of texts dating from the Middle English period (roughly 1100 to 1500) looks alien to us now, the attitudes to how authors should use the language are familiar. There were areas of broad agreement. Writing should be carefully structured, making dignified use of balance, and slang and archaisms ought largely to be avoided. The adoption of strange foreign words should be limited. It was normal, also, to say that writing should please the ear. We still hear this today, though of course what pleases my ear may distress yours.

People who wrote in English were apt to beg pardon for doing so. A note of apology can be heard in the works of even the most confident contemporary authors. Chaucer acknowledged the problems arising from English's poor scope for rhyme and its lack of sophistication. He presented himself as the man to save the language and shape it. As authors such as Chaucer and William Langland developed a vernacular literature, and as the daily use of French and Latin diminished, English was employed for tasks it had not previously performed. The efforts of Chaucer and his fellow experimenters were part of a turbulent repositioning of the language.

The central role of Chaucer in this period has led some to speak of him as the father of English. This is an overstatement, but it is easy enough to see how it has come about. He might easily have chosen to write in French, and may indeed have done so in the early part of his career. His friend and fellow poet John Gower wrote in both French and Latin, before turning to English for his masterpiece, *Confessio Amantis*. Chaucer's decision to use not the languages of the cultural elite, but instead English, was bold. After all, he was writing works to be performed before a coterie of courtly associates, rather than targeting a large public. After his death, as his poetry circulated widely in manuscript, he was anointed as the inventor of English as a literary language.

Chaucer expressed concern about the diversity of English – regionally and socially – and worried that scribes would mar his texts. But he also revelled in the potential for variety, which was fertile ground for a poet. In Middle English the range of regional variations is obvious. It existed because the language the Germanic settlers brought to Britain had itself exhibited some variation. The parties of settlers, who migrated in several waves, took different forms of the language to the different places where they established new bases. Subsequent influences on English, by Vikings and Normans, varied from place to place rather than having uniform effects. In the Old English period there were four major dialects: Kentish, Mercian (spoken from the Thames to the Humber), Northumbrian and West Saxon. By the Middle English period the picture had not changed greatly, and the standard division – which does not of course allow for subtleties of shading – marks five dialects: South-Eastern, South-Western, East Midland, West Midland and Northern. These large divisions make sense to us still. But in the Middle English period they were evident in writing as well as in speech. There is a clear gap between the Northern dialect of the *Cursor Mundi*, a religious text produced at Durham, and the East Midland dialect of the Lincolnshire monk Orm. Writers used their dialects without self-consciousness. Local ties were strong, and there was little sense of a need to conform to a nationwide standard; the very idea of something 'nationwide' would have seemed outlandish.

The dialect used in Chaucer's works was London English. Because of the large-scale fourteenth-century immigration into London of literate men from the East Midlands, London English had a distinctly East Midland character. By contrast, the unknown author of *Sir Gawain and the Green Knight*, writing at about the same time as Chaucer, used the West Midland dialect, which Londoners found difficult. To a modern audience, the language of *Gawain* poses greater challenges than that of *The Canterbury Tales*. The popularity of Chaucer's writings helped formalize London English. It also consolidated national identity. Another factor in raising consciousness of English was the spread of the scriptures in English, beginning with the translation inspired by John Wyclif in the 1380s. Wyclif's acolytes produced a version of the Bible that circulated widely in manuscript. It was viciously decried and suppressed, with opponents protesting that 'The jewel of the clergy has become the toy of the laity'.

Meanwhile the political status of English was changing. Henry IV, who seized the throne in 1399, was the first English king since the eleventh century to have English as his mother tongue, and he used it when claiming the Crown. At this time, official writing was done in either Latin or French. Under his son, that changed. When in 1415 Henry V inspired a significantly outnumbered English army to victory at Agincourt, the success legitimized his kingship in the eyes of his subjects. Agincourt provided an opportunity for favourable publicity, and two years later Henry found another way to achieve this: having previously conducted his correspondence in French, he chose for the first time to write his letters home in English. This was a premeditated move. It was undoubtedly calculated to stimulate national feeling, and it affected the practices of London's guildsmen, who began to use English for their own documents. English was used alongside French by the London pepperers as early as 1345, and London's brewers resolved in 1422 to note down all their affairs in their mother tongue, a language which they felt 'hath in modern days begun to be honorably enlarged and adorned'.[2]

As a greater number of important documents were written in English, the inconsistencies of English spelling became a source of anxiety. Did one write of a *knight*, a *knyght*, a *knyht*, a *knict*, a *knith* or a *cniht*? There had in fact been a pretty rigid system of spelling in the early eleventh century, thanks to the successful efforts of West Saxon scribes, but, although demand for books was high, the number produced at that time was not great. The West Saxon standard held on for nearly a century after the upheaval of the Norman Conquest, but eventually collapsed. The monk Orm, writing in the twelfth century, was an exceptional and particularly dogged exponent of spelling systematically. When a syllable ended with a consonant and contained a short vowel, he doubled the consonant that followed the vowel: he wrote *and* as *annd* and *under* as *unnderr*. It looks odd, but he was scrupulously consistent. Others were not. The stabilization of spelling was actively pursued again only in the fourteenth century, at a time when writing materials suddenly became much cheaper.[3]

According to the established histories of English, in the early part of the fifteenth century there were institutional efforts to promote a standard, consistently spelled form of English. It is orthodox to say that, beginning around 1420, government cultivated an artificial standard form of written English. Supposedly it had attained maturity by 1430, and was used, for reasons of functional efficiency rather than prestige, in the records kept by scribes in the offices of the Court of Chancery. Some accounts enlarge on this, noting that this standard emerged from four sources: not just Chancery, but also the offices of Parliament, the Signet and the Privy Seal. The problem here is that, having become a familiar part of the story of English, this version of events is rarely examined. Its reception is symptomatic of the way myths about language get recycled. An article published in 1963 by M. L. Samuels is commonly treated as the definitive account of Chancery Standard. Its arguments have repeatedly been amplified.

While the orthodox story is not a grotesque misrepresentation, it is not true that the Court of Chancery was the centre of a rigorously planned attempt at standardizing written English. It comprised about 120 clerks responsible for producing legal documents, and there is some evidence of what one might call a house style. Among other things the clerks mostly spelled *should* without a *c* (previously it had been *schould*), *any* with *a* rather than *o* as its first letter, and adverbs with *-ly* at the end rather than a variety of endings such as *-li* and *-lich*. They also favoured the spellings *such*, *not* and *but*, where earlier writers had used *swich*, *nat* and *bot*. But their style was a matter of fashion rather than policy. It seems likely that the Chancery clerks, rather than being trailblazers, were copying and approving forms that were already in use. In any case most of Chancery's writs were in Latin, not English.[4]

Nevertheless, by the time William Caxton set up his famous printing press at Westminster in 1476, a move towards uniformity was under way. Caxton was a transmitter rather than an innovator, an entrepreneur rather than a scholar. His most astute move was to publish only in English. After all, printed books in other languages could already be imported from the Continent. Books in English were also being printed abroad, but as an Englishman Caxton had an advantage over the printers of Bruges, Cologne and Paris when it came to selling English-language books in the English market-place. Caxton's main concern was to run a profitable business, and it was important to produce books that would sell well over a long period. He recognized that unless the English language were better governed it would not be adequate for good translations of works in French and Latin, and that stabilizing English would help extend his books' commercial life.

Having spent, so he said, thirty years abroad, Caxton was struck on his return to England by what he saw as a north–south divide. He worried also about his contemporaries' affection for 'curyous termes', and was conscious that his roots in Kent had accustomed him to what he called 'brode and rude' English – rude at that time meant 'inexpert' or 'uneducated' as well as 'impolite'. While he was not the first to perceive the differences, he used them to justify making an effort towards standardization. Noting that London English was the most popular written form, he made the decision to print his texts accordingly; the books he published perpetuated the forms of English used by government administrators. So, for instance, when he released Sir Thomas Malory's *Le Morte D'Arthur* in 1485 he tweaked Malory's Midland forms to make them conform to southern usage. In *The Description of Britayne* (1480) and in his prologue to *Enyedos* (1490) he discussed the difficulties of this practice.

Ironically, Caxton's press introduced confusions rather than quelling them. His own habits as a writer were erratic, and he seems not to have had a precise policy in mind. He was lax in his super-vision of the compositors who worked for him; mostly they were foreigners, and they were unlikely, as they set up texts in type, to be confident about regularizing the spelling of English words. The type they used was cast in Germany, and did not include certain letters that appeared in some manuscripts: the *thorn* (þ), the *eth* (ð), and the *yogh* (ʒ). The first two were generally replaced with *th*, and *yogh* with *g* or *gh*, though as late as the 1570s the musician Thomas Whythorne used the old letters in his autobiography, hoping to revive them. The archaic *Ye* we sometimes see today where we would expect *The* – as in 'Ye Olde Tea Shoppe' – was originally the result of printers' misreading of *thorn*, and later came to seem a pleasantly medieval quirk.

Caxton's efforts and those of the next few generations of printers were complicated by the fact that English pronunciation had been changing significantly since around 1400. Whereas consonants have been articulated in the same way since the Old English period – the one exception being *r* which used to have a trilled sound – this is not true of vowels. The Great Vowel Shift, as it is usually known, occurred in England over the course of about three hundred years. As David Crystal points out, Caxton was working at a time when, as well as there being several spellings in London for a single word, some words were being pronounced by Londoners in several different ways. 'These were not the best circumstances for fostering a standard written language. Nor was it a conducive climate for people to develop an intuition about norms of usage.'[5]

To call the change that occurred between the age of Chaucer and the end of the seventeenth century the Great Vowel Shift makes it sound like something that happened suddenly, or indeed steadily, whereas the movements were fitful and had different effects in different regions. It is not clear why the change happened, but during this period there was a general 'raising' of long vowels. If we go back to Middle English, an *a* was usually sounded the way it is today in *father*, an *e* like the first vowel sound in *bacon*, an *i* like the *ee* in *deem*, *o* as in *go* rather than as in *hot*, and *u* as in *blue* rather than as in *bun*. Crystal explains that 'We do say it's time to go now' would have sounded, in the age of Chaucer, roughly like 'Way doe sah it's teem to gaw noo'.[6]

Less important here than a definitive account of the shift is an awareness that attempts to sort out English spelling in the fifteenth, sixteenth and seventeenth centuries were made against a background of changing vowel sounds. In *The English Grammar*, which he wrote around 1620, Ben Jonson stated that 'All our *Vowels* are sounded doubtfully.'[7] This was certainly the case, and printers were attempting to freeze spelling at a time of phonological uncertainty. The correspondence between grapheme and phoneme – that is, between letters or combinations of letters and the smallest units of sound – was thus lost, and the language's spoken and written forms moved further apart.

Caxton's legacy was in other respects profound. Printing created a keener sense of a national literary culture. True, it enabled the spread of junk, but it also made it possible to imagine a virtual library of great English books, and led to a new emphasis on individual authors and their literary property. By enabling the preservation of precious documents, printing changed ideas about the perishability of texts and the language with which they were fashioned. A language with a printed literature can be transported and preserved. Printed books did not just help standardize the written language, but also made a standard form look and feel achievable, and – less obviously – as writers' practices became more alike, so they collected examples of diversity. The historian of print Elizabeth Eisenstein makes the point that 'Concepts pertaining to uniformity and to diversity – to the typical and to the unique – are interdependent'. As a result, 'one might consider the emergence of a new sense of individualism as a by-product of the new forms of standardization. The more standardized the type, indeed, the more compelling the sense of an idiosyncratic personal self.'[8]

It seems likely that print culture changed the ways people used their brains. As consumers of printed reading matter grew more numerous, memory must have played a smaller role in the transmission of texts, and the process of comprehending ideas, which had previously had a strong auditory element, presumably became more visual. The notion of privacy – specifically, of a secular readership engaged in private study – became potent. Readers were able to compare texts, and it was easier to analyse writers' methods of argument. They believed that the printed copy of a text they were reading was the same as the copy another person was reading –

which was certainly not the case when people read manuscript copies of a text. Printing changed the experience of authorship, with authors able to take pleasure at seeing not only their words' crisp existence in print, but also the apparently limitless reproducibility of those words.

The reproductive power of print could be dangerous. Certain types of material, printed in the vernacular, seemed to threaten the status and security of the elite. For two hundred years or so after the arrival of printing, some writers shunned print because they wished to be read only among their own coterie. The clergy were especially worried; their vital social role could be undermined if religious texts were widely available.

In the fifteenth century Europe was Catholic; by the end of the sixteenth it was divided, broadly speaking, into a Protestant North and a Catholic South. Beginning in the 1520s, the English people responded to the new Protestant message that the Roman Catholic Church was neglectful of their needs. Catholic theology was condemned as obscure. The monarch, Henry VIII, had his own reasons for wanting to break with the authority of Rome. Anne Boleyn, who captured Henry's interest in 1526 and eventually married him seven years later, was the patron of many reforming churchmen. She pushed for an English vernacular Bible that would enable ordinary citizens to hear the gospels. One of her prized possessions was an illuminated copy of William Tyndale's recently produced English rendering of the New Testament – at that time illegal. She offered protection to those who imported the scriptures in English from foreign presses.

Tyndale was a heroic figure, repeatedly condemned as a heretic. He exiled himself in Germany in order to produce his translation of the New Testament, and then smuggled copies to England, concealed in bales of cloth. Later he moved to the Netherlands. For the last decade of his life he was constantly in danger. His work was wildly popular. Sir Thomas More censured his use of 'evil' words (*love* instead of *charity*, *elder* instead of *priest*), but people flocked to listen to readings from the new translation. In the end, Tyndale was for his pains strangled to death and then burnt. Yet the reception of his accurate, clear and sometimes beautiful rendering of the sacred

Christian texts offered handsome proof of the power of the vernacular. By the reign of Queen Elizabeth, the right to read the Bible in English was entrenched, and the monumental King James Version of 1611 drew repeatedly on the phrasing of Tyndale.

The language of prayer was changing, too. Dissenters spoke of the Latin Mass as an obstacle to communication between churchgoers and their God. Thomas Cranmer, who took office as Archbishop of Canterbury in 1533, promoted the idea of an English liturgy. This resulted in *The Book of Common Prayer*, published in 1549 and succeeded by a significant revision three years later. Cranmer's prayer book met with hostility, especially in Ireland, the Isle of Man and Cornwall. In England its use would be outlawed in 1645, and when it was reintroduced following the Restoration of Charles II in 1660 some of its terminology was altered in the interests of clarity. Yet Cranmer's text, with its regular and melodious prose, was widely adopted. It survived, with few changes, for four centuries. Cranmer's most arresting achievement was creating a style of formal written English that did justice to the mysteries of faith yet was suitable for being read aloud. His sonorous phrases – 'ashes to ashes, dust to dust', 'till death us do part', 'speak now or forever hold your peace' – have imprinted themselves on the imagination of countless English-speakers.

When Mary Tudor, a Catholic, came to the throne, the power of Cranmer to bring about reform abruptly ended, and in 1556 he was burnt at the stake for treason. But he had created a vehicle for worship that barely changed in the next four centuries. English was now a medium for all kinds of religious expression. It was the language with which to address God, and it was the language of God's word. A language that two centuries before had seemed insecure was now an instrument of astonishing social and spiritual reform. In the reign of Elizabeth I, the feeling would intensify that English had special powers of alchemy.

4 From Queen Elizabeth to John Locke

Ripeness, rightness and the doubtful signification of words

Thomas Cranmer was Queen Elizabeth's godfather, and we may romantically imagine him blessing her with a passion for the vernacular. Shakespeare and John Fletcher, in their play *Henry VIII*, dramatize the connection between them, and have Cranmer salute Elizabeth's birth with the lines: 'This royal infant . . . / Though in her cradle, yet now promises / Upon this land a thousand thousand blessings, / Which time shall bring to ripeness.'

The reign of Elizabeth was in fact scarred by religious conflict, and her citizens were anxious about the stability of the monarchy, but one of the period's chief bequests to posterity was a luxuriant myth of Elizabeth as a heroine and of her era as a golden age. The flowering of English literature during her forty-five years on the throne was used as evidence of the nation's distinctiveness. For a generation of writers born in the 1550s and 1560s, England and its people, together with its history and institutions, seemed the most important subjects to address.[1] Literature became an instrument of political authority. The monarch was glorified, and so was the language used for the purpose. Images of Elizabeth pictured her as richly attired, an object of worship and a symbol of sovereignty in all its glory. The ornaments with which she was bedecked were also a kind of armour. Commentators on the culture of Elizabethan England, both then and now, recognize the same quality in its language: a copiousness that clothes ideas and arguments richly, its sartorial display a sign of military intent.

When John of Gaunt in Shakespeare's *Richard II* hymns 'this sceptred isle', he is articulating an Elizabethan view, not that of a fourteenth-century English prince. Elizabeth and her successor, James I, were not the first monarchs to play a palpable role as patrons of English. I have mentioned Henry V already, and long before him, in the ninth century, King Alfred championed translation and education in English. Before him, Æthelberht I of Kent had codified laws in English. But now there was a more dramatic posture of militant literacy: England's intellectual and cultural climate was unique, and its people were ready to overtake any and every rival. The language was a symbol of unity, and a vehicle for it too.

Today when English-speakers declare that their language is the best, they are renewing this Elizabethan spirit. We have all heard claims of this sort: it's asserted that English has the biggest vocabulary of any living tongue, is particularly well adapted to an ever-changing world, has the most skilful teachers, is inherently civil, is a force for democracy, and is the language that the rest of the world most wants to learn or should most want to learn. Often such claims are supported by the statement that English is the language of Shakespeare. In our unconscious or semi-conscious myths of English identity – tinged with eroticism, and somewhat confused both historically and biologically – Elizabeth the virgin mother of the nation is also the begetter of Shakespeare, and we imagine a relationship between them, a golden meeting of politics and poetry, a perfect image of the majesty of the English language and its speakers.[2] People who would not countenance sitting through a production of *Hamlet* still speak of Shakespeare not only as the greatest of English authors, but also as proof of English's surpassing excellence. Shakespeare the national poet is used to embody ideas about the greatness of English.

It was in the eighteenth century that it became usual to refer to Shakespeare as divine – a habit that frequently struck foreign visitors to Britain.[3] But he was not the only Renaissance English poet to be mythologized, and he was not the first. Sir Philip Sidney, after his death at the Battle of Zutphen in 1586, was celebrated as a model of piety, valour, courtesy and creative brilliance. In *The Defence of Poesy*, which he wrote in the late 1570s, Sidney had suggested that poetry could stimulate men to perform virtuous and even heroic deeds. Posthumously he was acclaimed as a hero, a scholar who was also a soldier. Reflecting on Sidney's achievement, poets of this period were apt to think of themselves as protean creatures, capable of large contributions in other arenas: the court, warfare, history, and the promotion of patriotic feeling.

Samuel Daniel was one of many who used the heroic image of Sidney to justify their own activities as poets. In 1599 he acclaimed 'the treasure of our tongue', and wondered which other nations it might soon 'enrich'. He spoke with confidence of 'the greatnes of our stile' and of English as 'our best glorie'. The language was a prized asset and, potentially, an instrument of conquest. By 1628, when the nineteen-year-old John Milton wrote his poem 'At a Vacation Exercise', which begins with the words 'Hail native language', this attitude had hardened.

This was a significant change, for throughout the sixteenth century anxieties about English beset writers and commentators. Disputes over the language's use were incessant, as were concerns about its inferiority. Now, though, it was its inferiority to Latin and Greek, rather than to French, that occupied the disputants. A recurrent concern was English's lack of expressive resources. The writers of the period were often brilliantly loquacious, but their notions of what one could and could not do with English were made up as they went along. The most contentious issue in the late sixteenth and early seventeenth centuries was the expansion of the English word-stock. Its substance was changing. Around 1570, writers started to worry that their works might not last because of the impermanence of vocabulary. Edward Brerewood, who wrote a study of the diversity of languages and religions, was unusual in finding little cause for alarm in the language's changes. 'There is no language,' he declared, 'which . . . is not subiect to change.' One of the reasons for this, he saw, was that people grow 'weary of old words (as of old things)'.[4]

Yet at the same time, beginning in about 1580, another theme developed – the eloquence of English. Important and original works were beginning to be written in the language, by writers such as Edmund Spenser and Sir Philip Sidney. Devices of Classical rhetoric were being zealously cultivated by English authors. English vocabulary had lately been augmented by significant adoptions from Latin and Greek. Additionally, there was a growing sense that the language was not just in need of regulation, but worthy of it.[5] The resourceful authors of the Elizabethan period used language as though it were something new and ecstatic. Here, and in the Jacobean period that followed, there were outstanding talents writing for the theatre (Shakespeare, Ben Jonson, Christopher Marlowe), along with poets such as John Donne, ambitious experimenters in prose (Francis Bacon, for instance), and theorists of both literature and language.

Gone was the sense of English being fit for few purposes. In 1582 Richard Mulcaster, the highly regarded headmaster of Merchant Taylors' School in London, wrote that English had 'so manie uses, bycause it is conversant with so manie people, and so well acquainted with so manie matters'. Even in classrooms where the speaking of English was forbidden, many teachers were at pains to ensure that their pupils, translating Latin into English, crafted English prose of high quality.[6] The functions of English were becoming more varied, and so, as Mulcaster recognized, was its audience. Hitherto there had not been a great deal of learned writing in English, but that, he saw, could be changed.

It is worth pausing to remember that at this time English was spoken only in England and parts of southern Scotland, as well as by small numbers in Ireland and Wales. It was little valued elsewhere. Its present diffusion was not even the stuff of fantasy. Yet Mulcaster saw that 'all kindes of trade' and 'all sortes of traffik' were beginning to make English 'a tung of account'. 'I love *Rome*, but *London* better,' he wrote. 'I favor *Italie*, but England more, I honor the Latin, but I worship the *English*.'[7] In the seventeenth century, this sense of English's 'account' would dramatically increase: English began to be exported, and the language that was planted abroad developed in different ways there.

To many of its users, Renaissance English seemed alarmingly plastic. 'Thou hast frighted the word out of his right sense, so forcible is thy wit,' says Benedick to his sparring partner Beatrice in *Much Ado About Nothing*. Beatrice's wit is not the only thing springing words from their medieval cages in this late-1590s play. *Thou*, incidentally, had in Old English been used when addressing only one person, and *you* when addressing more. By the sixteenth century, this had changed; the difference was social, with *thou* expressing intimacy or possibly condescension, while *you* was chillier or more respectful. The distinction disappeared in the seventeenth century from written English, and from most spoken English also, though one may still hear it in Yorkshire – it is memorably frequent in Barry Hines's novel *A Kestrel for a Knave*, set in 1960s Barnsley. By contrast, other languages in Western Europe continue to draw such a distinction: in some, notably French, it is important, while in others, such as Spanish and Swedish, the formal address is now not much used. Today's *yous*, widely heard in Ireland, and *youse*, heard on Merseyside and in Australia, revive and make explicit the difference between the plural *you* and the singular. So, too, does the American *y'all*.

More to the point, though, Shakespeare was a coiner of new words and, more interestingly, a great manipulator of the language's existing resources, exhilarated by its semantic possibilities. The notion of 'coining' a new word arose in the 1580s, and before it became usual to talk of 'borrowing' words from other languages one instead spoke of 'usurping' them. Shakespeare was a particularly influential usurper. More than three hundred years later, Virginia Woolf provides an incandescent image of this: while working on her novel *The Waves* in 1930, she writes in her diary of reading Shakespeare straight after every burst of writing 'when my mind is agape & red & hot', and of the thrill of Shakespeare's 'stretch & speed & word coining power': 'the words drop so fast one can't pick them up'.[8]

Some of the changes in vocabulary were achieved by means of prefixes and suffixes (hence the new terms *uncomfortable* and *overindulgence*, *straightish* and *relentless*), and some by compounding existing words (novelties including, for instance, *laughing-stock* and *pincushion*), but borrowing was the chief cause of concern for conservatives. I deal with this in detail in my book *The Secret Life of Words*. Not just Latin and Greek, but also French, furnished many new words at this time, and there were other, less numerous imports, from Spanish, Portuguese, Italian, Dutch and Hebrew. In *Love's Labour's Lost* we hear Holofernes, a character possibly modelled on Richard Mulcaster, speak in a way that should be reserved for writing – if indeed used at all. With lines such as 'Most barbarous intimation! Yet a kind of insinuation, as it were, *in via*, in way, of explication', he embodies the vanity of the Renaissance man addicted to fancy flourishes of erudition. Thomas Wilson's *The Arte of Rhetorique* (1553) disapprovingly mentions 'straunge ynkehorne termes', and for roughly half a century a writer who spattered his text with novelties was likely to be told his work reeked of the inkhorn – a vessel used for carrying ink, a little horn of plenty that became a symbol of authorial self-indulgence.

For many, big words were needed to do justice to big ambitions. A various and copious vocabulary was evidence of literary sophistication. In 1593 the noted gossip and critic Thomas Nashe – a figure at the heart of the period's literary culture, a witty scribbler with a talent for making enemies – published a work entitled *Christs Teares Over Ierusalem*. It warned Londoners of their corrupt city's potential for collapse, and began with an apology to his fellow man of letters Gabriel Harvey, with whom he had previously clashed in print. The following year Nashe presented a new edition; the main body of the text was unchanged, but, after Harvey had rejected the offer of a truce, he took another swing at him. Nashe was offended by the reception his book had received, and specifically by comments about its style. In characteristically noisy but nimble fashion he dashed off his complaints.

Nashe remarked that the 'ploddinger' London critics had accused him of 'a puft-up stile . . . full of prophane eloquence', while others had objected to 'the multitude of my boystrous compound wordes, and the often coyning of Italionate verbes, which end all in Ize, as mummianize, tympanize, tirannize'. He wasn't having any of this: 'To the first array of my clumperton Antigonists this I answer, that my stile is no otherwise puft up, then any mans should be which writes with any Spirite.' Moreover, 'For the compounding of my wordes, therein I imitate rich men, who, having gathered store of white single money together, convert a number of those small little scutes into great peeces of gold, such as double Pistols and Portugues.' His intention was to make up for the limits of his country's language: 'Our English tongue, of all languages, most swarmeth with the single money of monasillables, which are the onely scandall of it. Bookes written in them, and no other, seeme like Shop-keepers boxes, that containe nothing else save halfe-pence, three-farthings and twopences.' Reflecting on his decision to use a particularly obscure word (*mummianize*, meaning not 'to mummify' but to 'to turn something into mummy', *mummy* being a liquid extracted from embalmed carcases), Nashe called on his critics to find one more succinctly conveying his meaning: 'Expresse who can the same substance so briefly in any other word but that. A man may murder any thing if hee list in the mouthing, and grinde it to powder . . . betwixt a huge paire of iawes: but let a quest of calme censors goe upon it twixt the houres of sixe and seaven in the morning, and they will in their grave wisdomes subscribe to it as tollerable and significant.' Finally, he wondered 'wherefore should they hate us for our sting that bring forth Honny as well as they?'[9]

Such showmanship was typical of Nashe the pamphleteer. His prose is spangled with oddities. He is a risk-taker, socially and sexually mobile – his best-known poem circulated in manuscript under the name 'Nashe's Dildo' – and his racy writing delights in all things new and exotic. Nashe at one point in his short career got into trouble for having reviled the entire Danish nation; at another for having upset all his own country's bishops. His style was vital to his invective: sparkling, quarrelsome, brattish. He personifies the fashions of an age in which the possibilities of the printed word were dizzying. It was Nashe, as I mentioned earlier, who first wrote of the Queen's English, and from the many words that appear to be Nashe's coinages or imports – *balderdash, braggadocio, to emblazon, grandiloquent, helter-skelter, hufty-tufty, multifarious, obscenity, silver-tongued, star-gazing, swaggering* – we may construct an image of that English as a many-coloured land.

The opposite position was that of the Saxonists, who, measured against Nashe's exuberance, really do seem 'ploddinger'. They wanted not this flashiness and florid devilry, but instead the gravity of Anglo-Saxon. Among those who promoted a return to that ancient gravity were William Camden and Richard Rowlands Verstegan. In a collection of what he called 'rude rubble and out-cast rubbish', published in 1605 as *Remaines of a Greater Worke, Concerning Britain*, Camden applauded the usefulness of Germanic monosyllables for 'expressing briefly the first conceipts of the minde . . . so that we can set downe more matter in fewer lines, than any other language'.[10] That same year Verstegan, a printer and sometime Catholic spy, brought out *A Restitution of Decayed Intelligence*, in which he went a good deal further.

The English-born grandson of Dutch immigrants, Verstegan was peculiarly attuned to the importance of Englishness. In *A Restitution* he set out to remind his countrymen of their true origins – in Germany – and the dignity of these. Applauding the ethnic integrity of the Germans and the integrity of their language, he complained that English had become 'the scum of many languages'. Borrowing words from other tongues was embarrassing, but, if the words were returned, people would be 'left . . . dumb'.[11] The only solution was for old words to be reclaimed. In making this case, he was extending a political argument that he had previously pursued more directly. During the reign of Elizabeth, he had written pamphlets attacking the government and celebrating Catholic martyrs. Now, two years after the accession of James I, he was hopeful that Catholics would be better treated, especially given the possibility that the new monarch would create at Westminster a monument to the memory of his own martyred Catholic mother, Mary. In order to buoy his hopes, Verstegan chose to think of James as an Englishman, not a Scot, and dedicated *A Restitution* to him. Yet even as he saw the potential for a regime much less hostile to Catholicism than Elizabeth's had been, he anticipated the possibility of England being overrun by Scottish influence. The solution, he believed, was to cement the Catholic identity of England by restoring the German character of its language.

Camden and Verstegan present English as a language of impressive antiquity. We know that this is not really the case, but imagining the deep past of English was a seductive enterprise for them, faced as they were with so much evidence of its strangeness and malleability. It was within their camp that the enduring basic principles of linguistic rightness were established: clarity, decorum, an avoidance of the vulgar and the awkward, a rejection of all things voguish, a nebulous admiration for the past. But nothing like a modern style guide came out of their work; contemporary authors had to rely on their own judgement.

Anxieties about the roots of English and the language's new

directions led scholars to puzzle over the relationships between languages. The word *philology* was not in use in its modern sense; it meant little more than 'love of literature', and would not be used much more specifically till the early eighteenth century. The study of language was in its infancy – in 1598 the lexicographer John Florio called it *toong-work* – and tended to go hand in hand with an interest in old artefacts and family pedigrees. Yet the word *grammarian* was current. A petty or inept grammarian was a *grammaticaster* – the word is used by Ben Jonson – while discussions of grammar were known as *grammatication*.

Jonson is a pivotal figure. Born eight years after Shakespeare, in 1572, he lived until 1637, twenty-one years after Shakespeare's death. Poet, playwright, translator, critic, historian and political shapeshifter, he produced a body of work full of contradiction and experiment. His varied career connects the vertiginous excitement of Elizabethan literature to the religious conflicts of the 1630s. His writings seem to delight in the range of language, mixing the learned and the colloquial, but they also suggest unease about ambiguities, rustic speech and the rise of the letter *q*. Jonson was the author of the first treatment of English grammar that called itself precisely that.

When first used in English, in the fourteenth century, the word *grammar* was synonymous with Latin, for Latin was the only language taught grammatically. Not till the seventeenth century did it become a generic term, such that it was necessary specifically to refer to a 'Latin grammar' or an 'English grammar'. As we shall keep seeing, the association between grammar and Latin has proved hard to escape. During this period the standard work on grammar was what came to be known as 'Lily's Grammar'. Ostensibly this was by William Lily, a distinguished London schoolmaster. Lily was steeped in Classical learning; he had a talent for Latin verse, which he used to bestow moral advice on his pupils at St Paul's School, and he had enriched his understanding of Ancient Greek by spending time with people who spoke the modern version of the language – refugees from Constantinople whom he met at Rhodes on his way back from a pilgrimage to Jerusalem. The grammar book that bore his name was a composite work; drawing extensively on earlier surveys of grammar, it included contributions by Erasmus and by John Colet, the founder of St Paul's.

Lily's Grammar focused on Latin, but provided a template for thinking about English grammar. The examples he included were larded with proverbial wisdom and moral guidance. Published around 1513, and twice substantially revised, it received the approval of Henry VIII. This was renewed by Edward VI, who decreed that no other grammar book be used in schools, and then by Elizabeth I. Its authority endured for two hundred years, and it was reprinted around 350 times. Shakespeare craftily alludes to it in *Titus Andronicus*,[12] and countless later authors refer to it; as late as the midnineteenth century the novelist George Borrow recalls having been forced as a child to memorize Lily's Grammar.

Although Jonson followed convention in insisting on Latin grammatical categories, he broke with it in calling his book *The English Grammar*, declaring the existence of something that had previously been not much more than a mirage. The title page made it clear that his method was descriptive; he based his work on 'observation of the English Language now spoken, and in use'. Jonson's scheme was poorly organized, but was accepted because it was the work of a respected creative writer. Throughout the history of English, statements about grammar by popular writers have been taken seriously, regardless of their depth of expertise, and it is striking how many of those who have launched themselves successfully into the language wars – Jonathan Swift, Samuel Johnson, William Cobbett, George Bernard Shaw and Kingsley Amis, to name a few – have been nonspecialists, admired because of this rather than in spite of it. Jonson's account of English grammar was striking, too, because it was presented as an attempt to 'ripen the wits of our owne Children'. At the same time he sought to 'free our Language from the opinion of Rudenesse . . . wherewith it is mistaken to be diseas'd' and show its 'Matchablenesse, with other tongues'.[13] Even though the finished product was imperfect, Jonson put on an impressive show of combining practical intentions with a proud assertion of English's ability to do what any other language could do.

Until the middle of the eighteenth century, there was an enthusiasm for 'double grammars', in which the grammar of English and that of another language were presented side by side – one way of exhibiting 'Matchablenesse'. But as scholarly interest in English increased, the need for stand-alone grammars of English felt more urgent. One of the most successful responses to this need was John Wallis's *Grammatica Linguae Anglicanae* (1653), which, despite being written in Latin, argues that English should not strictly follow the model of that ancient tongue. Wallis, a mathematician whose most lasting achievement was inventing the sign ∞ for infinity, writes in his preface of how a slavish devotion to Latin had produced unhelpful rules for English usage, creating confusion and obscurity.[14] Among Wallis's more influential propositions was the distinction between the use of *shall* in the first person, to make a prediction, and in the second and third persons, when threatening someone or making a promise.

Wallis suggested that there were links between sounds and meanings: words that began *st* suggested strength, and those that began *sp* often conveyed the idea of expansion. Many of Wallis's contemporaries felt the same way; the mouths of men could make certain simple sounds, and these had a natural, fixed power. This sense that sounds and meaning existed in parallel prompted plans to simplify the way sounds were represented on the page.[15] Some writers on the subject spoke of approaching English as if for the first time: of making it new. There were attempts to develop a scientific or 'philosophic' language – one that was built from the ground up. Samuel Botley boasted of the excellence of a system of tiny symbols which he marketed under the name *Maximo in Minimo*. Francis Lodwick developed 'a common writing', in which, for instance, a 'drinker' was represented by a swollen, drunken sort of *d* with a hook on its shoulder, 'drinking' by the same hieroglyphic with an extra hook, a 'drunkard' by what looks rather like the rounding off of that second hook, and 'drunkenness' by yet another hook.[16] In 1657 Cave Beck set out a system in which all words were replaced by minutely organized combinations of letters and numerals – a fly was r1941, a firefly r1944, a butterfly r1945, and the verb 'to fly' was 1940.

The best-known work in this field was by John Wilkins, who hoped to create a universal language that would eliminate the ambiguous and the inexact from all written communication. Wilkins, a churchman and administrator, in 1668 delivered *An Essay Towards a Real Character and a Philosophical Language*, in which he proposed repairing the ruin of Babel by means of a newly created language. This would be able to catalogue everything in the universe; it would consist not of words, but of basic generic symbols – which could be elaborated to account for all the departments of existence. The elements of this 'real character' must be 'comely and graceful', 'methodical', 'sufficiently distinguishable from one another to prevent mistake', and capable of being 'described by one *Ductus* of the pen, or at the most by two'.[17] The result looks a little like Arabic.

In all these efforts, the emphasis was on words and how best to symbolize them. But in the final quarter of the seventeenth century, largely in response to the pioneering work of the philosophers at the Port-Royal monastery near Paris, the focus widened. The Port-Royal philosophy had two main prongs: a concern with the principles of logic, and a determination to explain the grammatical features shared by all languages. Its exponents set out a grammar that was also a theory of mind: more important than the presentation of individual words were sentences, the ways in which these represented the workings of the mind, and the relationship between language and knowledge. In other words, the grammarian was depicting an activity rather than creating a system of rules. The Port-Royal philosophers suggested a distinction between the surface structures of languages and deeper mental structures – an inspiration, much later, for Noam Chomsky. They argued, moreover, that it was hard to communicate the truth because the apparently close relationship between words and things meant that one often reflected on words more than on what they were intended to denote.

In seventeenth-century England, such problems of meaning occupied the most original thinkers. Francis Bacon distrusted language, arguing that it led reason astray or ensnared it. 'A poor and unskilful code of words incredibly obstructs the understanding,' he wrote in 1620, and 'words do violence to the understanding, and confuse everything; and betray men into countless empty disputes and fictions'.[18] Later Thomas Hobbes presented language in a similar way. He saw it as deeply problematic – full of words that do not really mean anything and of 'inconstant' terms that inconveniently mean different things to different people. The inconstant words are awkward; they are significant, but they tell us as much about the person who uses them as they do about the things of which they are being used. For instance, I may say, 'John is evil.' This is not an insignificant statement, but does it shed more light on John or on me? Hobbes argued that meanings are to be established almost as if by contract; the true senses of words derive from custom and common usage, and we must by political means manage the inconstancy of significant words.

In *Leviathan* (1651), arguably the most important work of political thought ever written in English, Hobbes proposes that the role of the sovereign – the absolute and indivisible ruler who compels people to work for the common good – is to stop arguments about the meanings of words becoming interminably pedantic. Otherwise, a man that seeks the truth 'will find himselfe entangled in words, as a bird in lime-twiggs; the more he struggles, the more belimed'. The sovereign should lead his subjects to agree definitions of good and bad. The alternative is violence, and 'seeing nature hath armed living creatures, some with teeth, some with horns, and some with hands, to grieve an enemy, it is but an abuse of Speech, to grieve him with the tongue.'[19] For Hobbes, as for many of his contemporaries, the disorderliness of language was associated with the story of the Tower of Babel – and thus with sin. Reforming language was a moral necessity. His thoughts owed much to his experience of the English Civil Wars of 1642 to 1651; he had witnessed the disintegration of language and the social bonds it embodied.

Bacon and Hobbes predated Port-Royal, but John Locke's *An Essay Concerning Human Understanding* (1690) was responsive to what was widely known as 'the new logic'. Like the Port-Royal philosophers, Locke wanted to enquire into the origins and extent of knowledge, and he saw the study of language as crucial to a rigorous understanding of how people think. The Port-Royal logicians had argued that a sign, i.e. a word, embraced two ideas: the thing that is represented, and the thing that does the representing, with the first of these being 'excited' by the second. Locke's best-known insight about language is, in its most simple form, that words are the signs of ideas. Although we use words publicly, their significance is private in the sense that the ideas we associate with them are to some degree idiosyncratic. To quote him: 'Words . . . stand for nothing, but the Ideas in the Mind of him that uses them.'[20]

Locke was kicking against the old idea that words are a nomenclature of things – a ready-made list of names for them, like labels. This had been asserted in Lily's Grammar. 'A Noune is the name of a thing,' Lily had written. It follows that the number of nouns should be the same as the number of things. Locke challenged this, and identified other deep problems to do with language and communication. He recognized that many arguments, perhaps even most, have their origins in differences over the significance of words, rather than in a real difference in the understanding of things. He also recognized that readers may well extract from books meanings different from those intended by their authors. Locke suggests our insularity. Our simple ideas – of whether something is round or hot, for instance – have a good chance of being in step, but our complex ideas – which we arrive at voluntarily, and which may include for instance our view of whether something is just or beautiful – are less likely to be. Locke sees language as inherently imperfect, and he is therefore not hopeful about our ability to communicate successfully. The signification of words is mired in 'doubtfulness'.

The new focus on the connection between language and thought gradually encouraged writers to move away from radical schemes and look instead into the rational grounds of grammar. One consequence was an overt concern with 'method', 'order' and 'sequence', which found its most banal expression in grammarians' extensive use of tables to set out the different classes of words – types of verb, for instance, and their conjugations. The layout of the page became a priority; grammarians had to work closely with printers to ensure that the systematic representation of the different parts of language was lucid and as elegant as constraints of space would allow. One rather ironic effect of this was that the philosophy of language – the inspiration for this more rigorous approach to classification, but inherently discursive – was relegated to footnotes. Eventually the footnotes would disappear, and the idea of linguistic discipline would push aside knottier questions of theory.

5 Hitting le jackpot

Arguing about academies

The English love of liberty is fabled. It's one of those 'myths about the English' that is fundamentally true. But really the love of liberty is a characteristic of English-speakers. They have resisted and always will resist any attempt to reorganize their language and regulate it from the top down. Yet they will complain endlessly about problems that could finally be resolved only through such regulation.

The idea that the English language should be sent to school flourishes today. Witness the recent announcement by the Queen's English Society, a British charity, of its plan for an Academy that will act as a 'moderating body' to protect and discipline the language.[1] Schemes of this kind blossomed in the second half of the seventeenth and first half of the eighteenth centuries. There was a determination to achieve greater clarity of syntax. This involved, among other things, doing away with double comparatives (*more wiser*) and double superlatives (*most wisest*), paying attention to concord (mainly the agreement between verbs and their subjects), using tenses more rigorously, and differentiating between *which* and *who*. To many of those who pressed for change, it seemed that an institution was needed to hand down rulings on such matters.

In 1660, the year Antoine Arnauld and Claude Lancelot published the *Port-Royal Grammar*, the Royal Society was founded. Its stated purpose was 'the improvement of natural knowledge'. This 'natural knowledge' was what we now call 'science' – a word that did not attain its current meaning until the early eighteenth century – and in 1664 the Society, hoping to establish a new model of method-ical expression, organized a twenty-two-strong 'committee for improving the English language'. However, the committee met only a handful of times. The real influence of the Royal Society was on the style of scientific writing.

In 1667 the Society's historian Thomas Sprat argued in favour of a 'natural' and 'naked' mode of speech. He thought English was on the slide; there was too much noise in men's prose. Sprat excoriated fineness and abundance of phrasing, which were vain and deceptive – possibly even demonic. Fancy diction was a form of sorcery; in Sprat's view, writing that contained a great deal of ornament was an instrument of wickedness. The sometimes bewilderingly long sentences of sixteenth-century writers, who followed the stylistic example of Cicero, were to give way to a new curtness of expression. Short words and 'primitive purity' were in; digressions and 'specious tropes' were out. It is easy to say that this was inevitable, since the advance of science called for a more clinical style of writing. But the Society's stylistic agenda was shaped by politics: its members advocated plainness (which they didn't always practise) to emphasize their distance from the verbosity and fanciful metaphors of the period's jingling assortment of religious fanatics, alchemists and millenarian bullshitters.

Joseph Glanvill's *The Vanity of Dogmatizing*, an essay on the importance of scepticism and testing ideas by experiment, is an interesting example of the influence of the Society's thinking. Its first version, published in 1661, is flowery. In 1664 Glanvill was elected Fellow of the Royal Society; a second, retouched version of the book appeared the following year. By the time he brought out a third version in 1676, he had absorbed the ideas of Sprat, and he radically stripped back the style. So, for instance, where the 1661 text has 'those that have never travail'd without the *Horizon*, that first terminated their Infant aspects, will not be perswaded that the world hath any Countrey better than their own',[2] fifteen years later we read 'those that have always liv'd at home, and have never seen any *other* Country, are confidently perswaded that their *own* is the *best*'.[3]

However, the Royal Society did not achieve reforms beyond the realm of science. As the Restoration ushered in a self-consciousness about manners, not least about how best to handle one's words and expressions, calls persisted for there to be a national Academy, as there had been in France since 1635. One of the loudest came in

1697 from Daniel Defoe, known then not as a writer but as a risk-taking businessman involved in importing tobacco, making bricks, and farming civet cats in Stoke Newington. Defoe, perpetually interested in money-making schemes and political advantage, declared the need 'to encourage Polite Learning, to polish and refine the *English* Tongue, and advance the so much neglected Faculty of Correct Language, to establish Purity and Propriety of Stile, and to purge it from all the Irregular Additions that Ignorance and Affectation have introduc'd'. He proposed that a society be set up by the king, William III, to achieve this. Its members would be 'Persons Eminent for Learning'; lawyers, clergymen and physicians would be debarred, and instead the panel should consist of twelve noblemen, twelve 'Private Gentlemen' and a final twelve selected 'for meer Merit'. This panel of thirty-six would 'have liberty to Correct and Censure the Exorbitance of Writers'. Moreover, 'no Author wou'd have the Impudence to Coin without their Authority'. In Defoe's eyes, under such a regime it would be 'as Criminal then to *Coin Words, as Money*'. And there would be less swearing, 'that Scum and Excrement of the Mouth' – a mixture of 'Bruitish, Sordid, Senseless Expressions' – that 'makes Conversation unpleasant'.[4] Defoe's proposal did not win strong backing, and a similarly minded individual, a London schoolmaster called Lewis Maidwell, who four times petitioned the government for state subsidy to found an Academy in Westminster, also met with no success.

Fifteen years later Jonathan Swift launched a fresh campaign for such an institution. Swift was at that time an enthusiastic participant in the coffee-house culture of London, and worked as a propagandist for Sir Robert Harley, a Tory who became Lord Treasurer in 1711. Harley was one of the first politicians to grasp the usefulness of the then quite new phenomenon of journalism, and Swift was his pet writer, attending Harley's intimate Saturday Club dinners where the most powerful Tory figures devised their policy. Much of Swift's writing for Harley was trifling, but in 1712 he published a substantial tract in which he sought to reframe his political image: *A Proposal for Correcting, Improving and Ascertaining the English Tongue.*

This pamphlet, which took the form of a letter to Harley, has been seen as beginning the tradition of complaint about English.

There were complainers before Swift, but his proposal initiated a new heightened rhetoric of linguistic disgust. He pronounced the language 'extremely imperfect', noting that 'the Pretenders to polish and refine it, have chiefly multiplied Abuses and Absurdities'. 'In many Instances,' he wrote, 'it offends against every Part of Grammar.' Swift commented that the 'Licentiousness' caused by the Restoration had infected first religion and morality, then language. This was evident in 'affected Phrases' and 'new, conceited Words'. Universities were culpable, and in the speech of the educated men who flocked to the coffee-houses he heard 'monstrous Productions' and 'conceited Appellations'. Swift argued that there should be an Academy to enlarge, polish and fix English. Its members, he foresaw, 'will find many Words that deserve to be utterly thrown out of our Language . . . and perhaps not a few, long since antiquated, which ought to be restored, on account of their Energy and Sound.'⁵ For Swift, an Anglo-Irish Protestant who between 1689 and 1714 spent much of his time in England, stabilizing English would be a patriotic act – a credit to the nation and to its ruler, Queen Anne. It would ensure that future generations were able to understand the texts that recorded history. A fixed language could guarantee the continuity of tradition and a national memory; the alternative, a mutable English, threatened to compromise the future of the social values he and his political paymasters held dear.

Swift savoured his dislikes. He abhorred vagueness; in Dublin he had proposed that beggars be given badges so that people could know their individual circumstances. He worried about cultural amnesia – manifest in a casualness about language, in which the histories of words were ignored. He was anxious about the poverty of conversation; good talk was one of the binding energies of society, and bad talk was a recipe for social meltdown. All these concerns fuelled his satire. One of his more unusual notions was that uneducated rustic folk naturally speak well, having avoided corruption by the spurious sophistication of the urban elite.

He was strikingly hostile to contracted and abbreviated forms of expression. In this he was following Joseph Addison, who had written in *The Spectator* of the Englishman's 'natural aversion to loquacity' and tendency as a result to scrunch up words into 'clusters of consonants'. Swift and Addison were responding to the seventeenth-century flourishing of contractions. Poets were to blame; they had introduced silly abbreviations that helped them fit their thinking to their verse schemes. Only Northerners, Swift claimed, could bear the harsh sounds of these condensed, unnatural words. The objection to *could've* is that it easily becomes 'could of', and the awkwardness on the page of *when'll* or *how're*, which seem perfectly natural in speech, is conspicuous. But Swift could not stomach even *disturb'd* – let alone *mob*, which was short for *mobile vulgus*.

Within a week of the *Proposal* the pamphleteer John Oldmixon published a response, in which he laughed off Swift's distaste for these contractions. Oldmixon also objected to Swift's plea for fixity, commenting that 'every Age, as well as every Nation, has its different manner of Thinking, . . . according as the Times take their Turn'.[6] Yet it's a bit too easy to laugh at Swift's dismissal of *mob* and imagine he achieved nothing, for some of the other modish contractions he disparaged did fall out of use, and his hostility may have helped this.

Affectation nauseated Swift. In *A Letter to a Young Gentleman, Lately Enter'd into Holy Orders* (1721) – the contraction in the title presumably not to his taste – he stressed the need for 'the Study of the *English* Language, . . . the neglect whereof is one of the most general Defects among the Scholars of this Kingdom'. As far as he was concerned, 'Proper Words in proper Places, makes the true Definition of a Style.' The faults in people's use of English were 'nine in ten owing to Affectation, and to the Want of Understanding'.[7] He revisited the matter in a parodic anthology of 'genteel and ingenious conversation' published in 1738. Begun around 1704, it was packed not with wit, elegance and examples of restrained intelligence, but instead with clichés, mangled pronunciations, malicious gossip, innuendoes, mechanical inanities and modish catchphrases. Swift's 'polite' conversationalists were in fact astonishingly rude.

Swift's capacity for outrage may be timeless, but legislating usage was now a matter of fashion. As the rise of a prosperous and socially self-conscious middle class caused the urban gentry to seek ways of marking their own superiority, correct usage and moral excellence were packaged together as tokens of just this. Everyday usage – the language of the social upstarts – was depraved, and for those who wished to keep them at bay it was essential to maintain a standard of elegance. 'Propriety', a keyword for both Swift and Defoe, would become ubiquitous in eighteenth-century discussions of language.

The opening sentence of John Knowles's *The Principles of English Grammar* (1796) is 'Grammar teaches us to speak and to write with Propriety'.[8] Knowles is unusual only in so quickly getting to the point. 'Politeness' was also an important concept, at once moral and aesthetic. Precise definition was difficult, but one was expected to know polite conduct when one found it. There existed a model of correct social behaviour in which conversation and letter-writing were the keys to good relationships and were practised with a chaste delicacy.

Among those who established the relevant principles of polite and proper sociability was the writer and printer Samuel Richardson. When he entertained his many female fans at his home in Fulham – described by his friend John Duncombe as 'that mansion of cheerfulness and grotto of instruction' – he discussed his novels. These had grown out of his correspondence, in which he had attempted to combine moral prescription with a style that was at once rigorous, innocent and agreeably conversational.[9] Both in person and on the page, Richardson was sensitive to the intricacy of relationships. A critic of the theatre, which seemed to him to be too often a force for social disorder, he nonetheless expounded a highly theatrical view of society. To be polite was a posture. Dr Johnson called it 'fictitious benevolence', a highly conventional performance of friendship. Yet, as Swift had earlier recognized, a product of the cult of politeness was a remarkable and, one would probably have to say, distinctively English talent for being impolite.

It is easy to understand why Swift wanted to regulate English. The society in which he lived was expanding. This made the successful traffic of ideas more important and more difficult. In an age when print culture was growing, institutionalized norms seemed desirable. But no one thought seriously about acting on Swift's proposal. Nor have similar proposals since been embraced. The British generally do not trust centralized regulation, so the idea of a government-sponsored system of linguistic regulation is anathema. Moreover, the performance of academies abroad does not encourage a positive view of their effectiveness.

Turning for a moment to the present, we can see that the Académie Française has not succeeded in preventing French from absorbing English words. Nor have other mechanisms for defending French from English. The *Loi Toubon*, passed in 1994, asserts that French is *'un élément fondamental de la personnalité et du patrimonie de la France'* and provides protection for the language in public life, education, the workplace and the media.[10] Successful prosecutions have been brought against, for instance, the company General Electric Medical Systems for the failure of its subsidiary GE Healthcare to issue French workers with security instructions written in French. But despite the large bureaucratic efforts and enthusiastic individual ones to maintain linguistic patriotism, French continues to assimilate words from English. The ninth edition of the Académie's *Dictionnaire* incorporates words such as 'le chewing-gum', 'la cover-girl' and 'le jackpot'.

Wits like to say that the main purpose of the Académie Française is not to affect the behaviour of French-speakers, but to provide amusement for foreign journalists. To observers contemporary with Defoe and Swift, though, this learned body – with its founding motto, '*À l'immortalité*' – seemed regally impressive. One of the leading proponents of an English Academy was the poet and playwright John Dryden, who was England's pre-eminent literary figure in the final decades of the seventeenth century. Dedicating his play *The Rival Ladies* (1663) to his fellow dramatist the Earl of Orrery, he expressed disappointment that there was no English equivalent to the French institution, and he repeated this line in the dedication of his reworking of Shakespeare's *Troilus and Cressida* (1679) to the influential Earl of Sunderland. Dryden was intent on leading an English cultural renaissance, and recognized the importance both of courting political support for this and of collaborating with like-minded men. I have kept Dryden in reserve till now, partly because his main intervention in matters of English usage requires – or at any rate permits – a digression.

There is a well-established American campus joke which goes something like this. On the first day of a new academic year, a freshman approaches a senior and asks, 'Hey, excuse me, do you know where the freshman dorms are at?' To which the senior responds, 'At Princeton, we don't end a sentence with a preposition.' The freshman tries again: 'Excuse me, do you know where the freshman dorms are at, motherfucker?'

Why shouldn't a sentence end with a preposition? One answer often put forward has to do with the etymology of *preposition*, which comes from the Latin for 'place' and 'before': the preposition should be located before the word it governs, as in the sentence 'She sketched his likeness with crayons'. It is also argued that a preposition at the end of a sentence gives the appearance of being stranded, and that in terms of both logic and aesthetics it is therefore undesirable.

The hostility to the stranded preposition begins, however, with a single opponent: Dryden. It was Dryden's habit to assay the purity of his English by examining how smoothly it could be translated into Latin; he then translated the Latin back into English, to see if anything got lost along the way. This was not just a piece of whimsy; he was concerned to establish that English was suited to heroic subject matter, and in promoting its potential he emphasized where he could its connections with Latin. Understandably, given his prominence even in the 1660s, he had been a member of the Royal Society's 'committee for improving the English language', and the idea of improvement had lodged in his mind. Becoming Poet Laureate in 1668, he returned to this theme. Influenced by the way prepositions were treated in Latin, where they always preceded their objects, and mindful of etymology, he became hypersensitive to their use in English. Having pronounced that stranded prepositions were 'a common fault' in the works of Ben Jonson, and knowing that he was himself guilty on this count, Dryden made a point of eradicating them from reissues of his published writings. Thus 'such Arguments . . . as the fourth Act of *Pompey* will furnish me with' becomes 'such Arguments . . . as those with which the fourth act of *Pompey* will furnish me'.

The exact nature of Dryden's alterations was spotted only at the end of the following century when Edmond Malone was preparing an edition of Dryden's prose. Malone compared the 1668 and 1684 editions of Dryden's *Of Dramatick Poesie*, and noted the differences between the two. The most striking was the removal of prepositions from the ends of sentences. In pruning his own prose, Dryden had invented a rule. The circumstances of its invention had eluded everyone up till Malone, but the fact of its existence had not. People simply followed Dryden's example. It impressed eighteenth-century grammarians, and by the end of that century the stranded preposition was conventionally viewed as a grave solecism. Yet there are times when its strenuous avoidance proves ugly. Winston Churchill is often alleged to have responded to a civil servant's objection to his ending a sentence with a preposition, 'This is the kind of pedantic nonsense up with which I will not put.' Though the story is probably apocryphal, this constipated statement usefully illustrates the point that the avoidance of a supposed offence can lead to something far worse.

The aversion to 'sentence final' prepositions has led to condemnation of phrasal verbs. A phrasal verb is one in which a particle (usually a preposition) alters and narrows the meaning of the verb. These verbs tend to be informal. They are also very common, and they can cause confusion. In some cases the distinction between related phrasal verbs may be both large and unobvious. Take, for instance, 'compare with' and 'compare to'. Undoubtedly these get used interchangeably. Yet by convention, if I compare myself *to* Christ, I am suggesting a similarity, whereas in comparing myself *with* Christ I am mainly concerned with the differences between us. There is a tradition of arguing that phrasal verbs are crude; according to this view, 'carry on' is inferior to *continue*, 'open up' to *enlarge* or *expand*, and 'put up with' to *tolerate*. Foreign learners of English find phrasal verbs puzzling – 'He put me down' can mean several different things, and questions such as 'What are you up to?' and 'Are you having me on?' can seem bafflingly indirect. The use of *up* in phrasal verbs can feel especially odd, since it often has to do with completeness rather than upwardness – 'I'm closing up', 'Eat up your sprouts', 'He finished up the season as the club's top scorer' – and often also seems redundant. Today, courses aimed at foreign learners pay special attention to the phrasal verb; its combination of prevalence and potential for confusion makes it an important subject. Phrasal verbs create opportunities for dangling prepositions, and this has been used as an argument for avoiding them. But here, as so often, the fear of a solecism can lead to stilted expression.

To go back to Dryden, though: his concern with the best place for prepositions was part of a larger interest in reforming literary style. He even went so far as to translate passages of Shakespeare (specifically, *The Tempest*) into a plainer, more modern idiom, streamlining his language and in particular its syntax. Dryden shunned the esoteric. He described Shakespeare's style as 'pestered' with figurative phrases, and worried about its obscurity.[11] He spoke for an age that associated stylistic flourishes not just with vanity, but with witchcraft.

Dryden is a creature now thoroughly alien to us: the poet-as-legislator. A sort of one-man equivalent of the Académie Française, he is the leading representative of an age in which poetry, rather than being something that happened at the margin of society, was a central feature of civilization and education. The poet was seen as a practical, useful figure, often involved in politics and acts of patriotism, and capable of prophecy, revolutionary thought and steering or defining popular taste. Some people still cherish the therapeutic powers of poetry, but in the English-speaking world the poet rarely now administers his or her therapies to a wide public – or even often *in* public.

As poet, dramatist and critic, Dryden was involved in a project to cement the status of English as a language that could proudly compete with others – French being the most obvious. In the late seventeenth century it became conventional to characterize English as manly, whereas French was weakly feminine. Dryden played his part in this. But he had what could be called a 'heterosexual' ideal of English.[12] For Dryden, masculinity works best when it coexists with femininity: what seem to be the softness and harmony of feminine expression are an essential means of balancing what he sees as the boldly masculine properties of noble, rational writing. He favours a style in which there is a careful and faithful collusion between male and female qualities. It is, in short, chaste. This may help explain why the dangling preposition had to eliminated. For it is anything but chaste – a slovenly provocation, leaving a sentence gaping open rather than decently closed.

6 The rough magic of English spelling

A 'scarce creddibel' story

If we look at the original published versions of works by Dryden, Defoe and Swift, one of the things that strikes us is their use of capital letters, which appear in places we would no longer expect them. Peep inside a book from the seventeenth or early eighteenth century and it is apparent that, as in German today, nouns were printed with their first letter in upper case. The convention seems to have been introduced by printers who came over from the Continent; its supporters included one A. Lane, a schoolmaster in Mile End, whose *A Key to the Art of Letters* (1700) contained the assertion that capitals should be used to mark 'all proper Names, and Adjectives derived of proper Names' as well as 'all Emphatical or Remarkable Words'.[1] The practice of capitalizing nouns seems to have peaked around 1720 or 1730, having climbed for the previous 150 years or so. But many writers during this period were erratic in their use of capitals. For everyone who was as careful with them as the poet James Thomson there were several who erred in the direction of the notably sloppy Defoe.

Authors of works about spelling tended, from the middle of the seventeenth century, to offer guidance on capitalization. Their instructions varied, and there is evidence that writers who saw the use of capitals as a rhetorical resource had to tussle with printers who were keen to achieve a uniform system.[2] In the 1790s the grammarian Lindley Murray would make the valid point that the practice of capitalizing nouns 'gave the writing or printing a crowded and confused appearance'.[3] As far as he was concerned, it was a thing of the past. There is evidence that this kind of capitalization, along with the frequent accentuation of words by means of italics, fell out of use in mid-century. The influential *Gentleman's Magazine* stopped capitalizing nouns in 1744.[4] In 1756 we find Daniel Fenning, in *The Universal Spelling Book*, stating that 'Substantives should be wrote with a Capital Letter',[5] but later editions of Fenning's popular work dropped this prescription.

An area of significantly greater conflict between printers and writers was spelling. I touched on this three chapters ago, when discussing Caxton. Now, before we turn to the more general stand-ardizing efforts of the eighteenth century, it is appropriate to look at English spelling in some detail, surveying its whole history. The difficulties of spelling and the potential for improving our spelling system are perennial concerns. Scholars of writing systems are known as orthographers: there have been English orthographers since the Middle Ages, and their main concern has been the way we spell. As printed books grew more common after about 1500, printers came to accept and practise a fixed spelling. But progress was slow. If we look at Wyclif's Bible, we find inconsistencies of spelling. *Shall* appears as *shal* and also as *schal*. *Stood* is sometimes *stod*. Similar inconsistencies are rife in the books Caxton printed. Should one write *boke* or *booke*? *Hous* or *hows*? While such uncertainties can now seem quite amusing, anxiety about spelling remains – spelling shows up, after all, in every sentence that we write – and we are guilty of mistakes and irregularities in our correspondence, the notes we make at work, emails, diaries, and domestic jottings such as shop-ping lists.

In the face of ridicule, some people wear their inept spelling with pride. Winnie the Pooh is a classic example of the poor speller who detects some virtue in his mistakes: he concedes that his spelling is 'wobbly' but immediately insists that all the same 'It's good spelling'. Pooh is, famously, 'a bear of little brain', and his attachment to his wobbliness, endearing though it may be, reinforces most people's sense of this. Idiosyncratic spelling is often interpreted as an index of idiosyncratic and indeed defective mental powers, and most readers will have some familiarity with the social penalties of poor spelling, perhaps through having observed the way that dyslexia was (and frequently still is) misunderstood as evidence of stupidity. In *The Three Clerks* (1858) Anthony Trollope portrays a young man who 'persisted in spelling blue without the final *e*' and 'was therefore, declared unworthy of any further public confidence'. The novelist Willam Golding anticipated the day when 'some bugger' would edit his manuscripts and correct his spelling, interrupting the text with ugly parentheses – 'But my bad grammar and bad spelling was me.'[6] Sometimes a person's wayward spelling can become a focus for larger suspicions about his or her worthiness. When in 1992 the gaffe-prone Dan Quayle, the American Vice-President, urged a child to amend his spelling of *potato* to *potatoe* on a blackboard while being filmed, he amplified the ridicule he had already attracted for an official Christmas card that declared his nation 'the beakon of hope for the world'.

But then, we have all at some point observed the inconsistencies of English spelling. Many of us have had occasion to curse them. Compare English with a language such as German, in which the pronunciations of words can be derived from their spelling, and we grasp the problem. In English, what you see is often not what you get. Numerous words are spelled in ways that seem both familiar and – if we trouble to think about them – odd. For instance: *night, knife, psalm, diarrhoea, colonel, aisle, biscuit, rhythm, daughter.* As I have suggested, a key factor in shaping English spelling was the Norman Conquest. In the period that followed, many of the scribes in important centres of learning (monasteries) were men who had been trained in France, and they introduced French spelling habits into the English texts they copied. A few Old English letters were abandoned – for instance, *æ* – and new letters were introduced: *k, q, x, z.* The scribes' work often involved making personal choices, and these were inconsistent. As the Old English model of spelling came under pressure from French methods, irregularities proliferated.

In addition, etymology accounts for some peculiarities. Since the Renaissance, there has been enthusiasm for preserving evidence of etymology in the spellings of borrowed words, and in the sixteenth century many words that had been borrowed from French were treated as though they had in fact been imported from Latin. In his classic study of English spelling and etymology, Walter Skeat explains that 'the old spelling was, in the main, very strictly etymological, because it was so *unconsciously*,' but this changed in the sixteenth century when 'the revival of learning . . . brought classical words, and with them a classical mode of spelling, to the front'. This 'involved the attempt to be *consciously* etymological, i.e. to reduce the spelling of English words, as far as possible, to an exact conformity *in outward appearance* with the Latin and Greek words from which they were borrowed'. Words of Anglo-Saxon or Scandinavian origin were generally let alone, but borrowings from French 'suffered considerably at the hands of the pedants'.[7]

In Chaucer one reads of a 'parfit' knight; the word had been introduced from French some time before 1300. But in the age of Shakespeare and Ben Jonson an awareness of the earlier Latin word *perfectus* – and the use of words such as *perfection* and *perfective* that wore their Latin colours openly – meant that *perfect* became the usual spelling. Today's word *victuals* was originally a borrowing of the French *vitaille*, but the spelling was influenced some time after 1500 by an awareness of the Latin *victualia*. This explains why *victuals* is pronounced to rhyme with *whittles* rather than with an audible *c* and *u*. In some cases the Latinized spelling affected the pronunciation: the noun *aventure*, borrowed from French, had been in use for more than three hundred years before, around 1570, it became *adventure*, on the model of the Latin *adventura*, with the *d* sounded. In other cases, such as *doubt* and *salmon*, the consonants introduced by etymological regard for Latin were audible only in the speech of eccentric, exaggeratedly learned figures, such as Shakespeare's Holofernes, who insisted on sounding the *l* in *calf* and the *b* in *debt*.

A few peculiarities have etymological explanations of a different kind. The Italian word *colonello* entered English via French, and was borrowed twice by French, once as *colonel* and once as *coronel*. In English the two forms were used indiscriminately until the middle of the seventeenth century, when the former spelling became more common. However, the *r* sound held on, partly because it was easier and also, it seems, because of a tacit and incorrect habit of associating the word with the Latin *corona* meaning 'crown'.

There are some words and expressions that seem – and I must stress 'seem' – to be mangled more often than they are presented correctly. You have very likely come across several of the following: 'soaping wet', 'chaise lounge', 'preying mantis', 'tarter sauce', 'baited breath', 'straight-laced', 'just desserts', 'duck tape' and 'dough-eyed'. These substitutions – creative, idiosyncratic and confusing – are known as 'eggcorns'; the term was suggested by the linguist Geoffrey Pullum in ironic homage to a woman who habitually referred to acorns by this name.

Occasionally it is asserted that English spelling is 50 per cent regular. This belief dates back to a research project carried out at Stanford University in the 1960s, with funding from the US Office of Education. The project involved using a computer to analyse the 'phoneme–grapheme correspondences' of 19,000 words – that is, to look at how often a computer program provided with the details of these words' pronunciation would derive their correct spelling. The figure of 50 per cent, though much quoted, improved when the algorithm was refined. But, conversely, the data fed into the algorithm apparently presented some phonemes in a way that made correct spelling more likely. The figure of 50 per cent must therefore be treated with caution.[8]

It is certainly true that spellings are much more predictable in many other languages – in Italian and Spanish, for instance, and in German, where they were fixed mainly by Jacob Grimm. In English, uncomfortably, there are many examples of words that sound the same but are written differently and have different meanings: a few examples are *freeze* and *frieze*, *key* and *quay*, *stationery* and *stationary*, *semen* and *seamen*. These are a rich source of punning humour, but a cause of confusion to learners. Commonly misspelled English words comprise unpredictable elements: for instance, there are silent letters, as in *rhythm* or *parliament*; they contain an *ee* sound, for which there is no obvious pattern (*litre*, *protein*, *people*, *beneath*, *achieve*); and they include double consonants where, according to commonly taught rules, we would not expect them (*dissolve*, *palette*), and lack them where we would (*linen*, *melody*, *element*).

We would be naïve to expect a writing system to reproduce exactly the sounds of talking. It is a set of visual patterns that can be related to speech, rather than a faithful transcription. The shapes of sounds vary from one speaker to the next. Speech is continuous:

when I am talking there is a constant flow of sound, without the breaks that occur between words on the page. A system of visible marks cannot exactly represent sounds. A writing system is conventional – an invented device, not a duplication of speech, and something into which one needs to be initiated by an instructor. Moreover, writing has functions other than representing sounds, and the production of speech and writing are handled differently by the brain; the two activities realize the abstract system of language in distinct ways. In some languages, such as Finnish, the relationship between graphemes and phonemes is almost perfect. In others, such as Japanese, a mixture of systems is used in any written text, and people who learn Japanese have to memorize the written forms of words rather than being able to deduce these forms from the words' component sounds.[9]

In practice, four-fifths of English spellings conform to patterns we can readily see – Steven Pinker gives a figure of 84 per cent[10] – and only about 3 per cent of English words are spelled in ways that are genuinely anomalous. Of more immediate help is the realization that spoken English contains more than forty distinct sounds – forty-four is the number usually stated – but is not written with forty or more letters. Our 26-letter alphabet, an augmented version of the 23-letter alphabet of Latin, contains three arguably redundant letters (*c*, *q* and *x*), but others have to do more than one job. The sounds of English are in fact represented by roughly 1,100 different arrangements of letters. The most common vowel sound in English is not the sound of any of those with which we are familiar; it's the quick 'uh' sound known as a *schwa* – a term borrowed from Hebrew – which we hear in *bottom*, *supply*, *cadet* and *eloquent*.

It has long been customary to suggest that the ability to spell is a social and professional skill, one of those small but telling accomplishments that earn credit at school and in the workplace – and an essential marker of good social standing. In 1750 Lord Chesterfield, who presented himself as a great arbiter of manners, wrote to his son that one false spelling could condemn a man to ridicule for the rest of his life. Noting his son's misspelling of *induce* and *grandeur* as 'enduce' and 'grandure', Chesterfield alleged that few of his housemaids would have been guilty of such slips. I suspect he may have been wrong about this, but in any case there has long been a contrary view – persistent, even if not widespread – that correct spelling is a marker of pedantry rather than authenticity. Fussiness about spelling is, accordingly, associated with dullness. One of the best literary examples is in Alexander Pope's poem *The Dunciad*, published in 1728. Pope suggests in a note that the title should really be *The Dunceiad*, so as not to offend the punctilious Shakespeare scholar Lewis Theobald, who had insisted on restoring to the playwright's name the final *e* that Pope had previously chosen to omit. The 'hero' of Pope's poem is the King of Dunces, Tibbald. Pope implies that, if Theobald's editorial schemes were followed through to their natural conclusion, this would be the true spelling of his name.

For those anxious about English spelling's obstructions and perplexities, systematic reform has seemed the obvious solution. It has been explicitly advocated at least since the 1530s. The reformists can be divided into two camps: those who propose enlarging the alphabet to take account of the sounds it does not deal with adequately, and those who more modestly propose sticking to the existing alphabet but sorting out some of the more troublesome inconsistencies.

In the 1530s the main promoter of reform was Sir John Cheke, a Cambridge scholar of Greek. Cheke was supported by his Cambridge colleague Sir Thomas Smith. The two men followed Erasmus in their approach to the sounds of Greek; rather than pronouncing the Classical form of the language the way contemporary Greek sounded, in which there was often little correspondence between grapheme and phoneme, they recovered what they believed to be the authentic ancient pronunciation, in which this correspondence was exact and sounds were not confused. Having reconstructed the sounds of Greek, they set about doing the same for English. Cheke died in 1557, aged forty-three; Smith lived twenty years longer and had time to develop their work. He wrote an English usage guide (in Latin), in which he put the case for a 34-letter alphabet that used accents on vowels to indicate their length and quality.

Between 1551 and 1570 John Hart mounted a more sustained campaign, producing three works on English spelling and pronunciation. The first of these was graced with the unflinching title

The Opening of the Unreasonable Writing of our Inglish Toung. Struck by the difficulties that the unruliness of English writing posed for foreigners and 'the rude countrie Englishman', he described the existing ways of spelling as 'a darke kind of writing'. Hart argued the need for a new alphabet and phonetic spelling, which he believed would 'save the one third, or at least the one quarter, of the paper, ynke, and time which we now spend superfluously in writing and printing'.[11] Like Smith, he used accents. He also suggested replacing 'ch' with a twirly symbol a bit like a drunken *g*. He was the first person to write about intonation in English speech, and made other original observations, but his work did not find a significant audience.

The ideas of Smith and Hart were built upon in the 1580s by William Bullokar, whose jaundiced view of English spelling was informed by his experiences as a schoolmaster. He proposed spelling reform as part of a three-pronged attack on the peculiarities of English; it would also include an authoritative grammar and a dictionary. He too employed accents and a few new squiggles to represent the forty-four distinct English sounds he identified. His system managed to be complicated without being comprehensive. We can gauge its texture from his translation of *Aesop's Fables.* When he writes of 'A frog being desirous to match to an ox', the word *desirous* is spelled thus: a regular *d* and *e* are followed by what looks like a snoozing *3*, then by a *y* with an acute accent, an *r*, an *o* with a sort of cedilla joined to another *o* with a dot below it, and an ordinary *s*. A couple of sentences on, *though* is presented as 'thowh', and among the few words to appear in completely familiar form are *when, the* and *ox*.[12]

The typical pattern in the sixteenth century was for reform to be mooted, but for schemes of reform to be sketchy or peculiar. It was easy to fulminate about the deficiencies of English spelling, but difficult to conceptualize a plan for sorting them out – let alone enact such a plan. The most widely acknowledged programme was devised by Richard Mulcaster. His *The First Part of the Elementarie* (1582) was intended, as its title suggests, to be the opening section of a substantial work of educational reform. Instead of furnishing a new spelling system, Mulcaster favoured stabilizing the existing one.

A dictionary, he saw, would be invaluable as a means of bringing this about. One of Mulcaster's more successful ideas was that a monosyllabic word with a short vowel sound should not have a doubled final consonant – so, one should write not *bedd* or *bedde*, as was then common, but *bed*. For evidence of this advance, we can look to the (posthumous) First Folio of Shakespeare's plays in 1623: *hadde* appeared there just once, whereas there were 1,398 examples of *had*.

Mulcaster also makes an interesting connection between spelling and handwriting, noticing for instance that a word would often be written with a double *l* at the end where a single one would do because of the unthinking swiftness of cursive handwriting: 'It is the swiftnesse of the pen sure, which can hardlie staie upon the single endling *l*, that causeth this dubling.'[13] The hand of the poet Sir Philip Sidney exemplifies the sixteenth-century tendency for an author's handwriting to accelerate as he approaches a conclusion. From around 1560 the fashion in handwriting was for a compact, rapid and obliquely angled hand, which often descended into an illegible scrawl. It was normal at this time to employ an italic style of handwriting for Latin and a 'secretary' hand – more calligraphic, but also quirkier and more facile – for English.[14] By the end of the seventeenth century, writers such as John Dryden were practising a rounder hand.

Looking at books produced in this period, one sees what these reformers were up against. In a single page one might read of *coronation* and *crownacion*, of a *rogue* and a *roage*, and of something that has *been*, *bin* or *beene*. This was probably down to the compositors who prepared pages for the press, rather than to their authors. Even people's names were spelled inconsistently, the most celebrated example being Shakespeare, who was also Shakspere, Shaxper, Shackspeare, Shexpere and plenty more besides. One sees how important the idea of alphabetical order was, yet it was only during the Renaissance that this became the main principle used to organize and sequence words. The word *alphabet* is not recorded before 1580; in Old English it had been the *abecede* or the *stæfræw*. *Alphabetical*, *alphabetary* and *alphabetic* are first attested by the *Oxford English Dictionary* in 1567, 1569 and 1642, respectively. The noun *alphabetarian*, signifying someone learning or studying the alphabet, appears in 1614.

Up until the eighteenth century there was some uncertainty about which letters were to be considered the true components of our alphabet – for instance, were *i* and *j* to be treated as separate or essentially the same? Plenty of those who produced spelling books believed that the letter *q* served no useful purpose, and some felt the same way about *c* and *x*. In *The English Primrose* (1644), a book aimed at helping young learners to spell, Richard Hodges proposed that the letter *w* be known as *wee*; more than a hundred years later its name was still debated, with John Yeomans, a Chelsea schoolmaster, one of several proposing it be called *oo*.

These attempts at tidying up the language may have contained some odd ideas, but the impulse behind them was practical. Teachers lamented the obstinacy of printers, and the desire for progress was evident in spelling books, which were plentiful. These slim volumes comprised lessons that guided learners from a grasp of the alphabet to a full command of reading. A feature of spelling books is that they allow only one spelling per word. The first truly successful one was *The English Schoole-Maister*, published by Edmund Coote in 1596. Coote wrote the book shortly after being appointed master of a school in Bury St Edmunds. Ironically, not long after its appearance he was obliged – for reasons now unknown – to give up this post. But his practical approach was much copied. It was soon conventional for spelling books to be marketed as 'easy', 'brief', 'delightful', 'true' or 'pleasant'. In the seventeenth century they often have long-winded but congenial titles; examples include Thomas Crosse's 1686 *The experienc'd instructer, or a legacy to supply poor parents and their children to read distinctly, by the rule of spelling exactly* and George Fisher's 1693 *Plurimum in minimo, or a new spelling book; being the most easy, speedy, and pleasant, way to learn to read and write true English*. Their eighteenth-century inheritors tend to sound more severe, and the emphasis then is on completeness, extensiveness and comprehensiveness.

Useful progress was made. The real achievements of the seventeenth century were standardization and rationalization. Towards the end of the eighteenth century, with the standard entrenched, criticism of wayward spelling became commonplace. By 1750 there was not much doubt about how words should be spelled, and the result was increased disparagement of those who appeared uncertain. That said, the gap between what we do in public and what we may do in private has never been completely closed. Even Dr Johnson could be inconsistent; in the *Dictionary* he listed as the correct forms *chapel*, *duchess* and *pamphlet*, but elsewhere he wrote *chappel*, *dutchess* and *pamflet*. Dickens in his letters wrote *trowsers* rather than *trousers*, George Eliot *surprize*, Darwin *cruize*, and Queen Victoria *cozy*.[15] In Edward Bulwer-Lytton's novel *The Caxtons* (1849) there is a whimsical figure by the name of Dr Herman who is known to have written 'a great many learned works against every pre-existing method of instruction', and 'that which had made the greatest noise was upon the infamous fiction of Spelling-Books'. In Dr Herman's opinion, 'A more lying, roundabout, puzzle-headed delusion than that by which we Confuse the clear instincts of truth in our accursed systems of spelling, was never concocted by the father of falsehood.' 'How,' he wonders, 'can a system of education flourish that begins by so monstrous a falsehood, which the sense of hearing suffices to contradict?' Herman, who is one of 'those new-fashioned authorities in education', teaches 'a great many things too much neglected at schools', his particular speciality being 'that vague infinite nowadays called "useful knowledge"'.

The desire to improve the English spelling system did not abate. A Scottish schoolmaster, James Elphinston, occupied himself with the matter for the last four decades of the eighteenth century. The character of his efforts can be gauged from a single sentence of his writing: 'Scarce creddibel doz it seem, to' dhe anallogists ov oddher diccions, dhat hiddherto', in Inglish exhibiscion, evvery vowel and evvery consonant ar almoast az often falsifiers az immages ov dhe truith.' A better scheme was that of Isaac Pitman, who first publicized his Stenographic Soundhand in 1837 when he was just twenty-four. Eventually Pitman proposed that the familiar letters of the alphabet be replaced with a new set of thirty-eight characters. His grandson James joined with Mont Follick, the Labour Member of Parliament for Loughborough, in order to try and establish the Initial Teaching Alphabet for use in children's education. Follick in fact wanted to rebuild the language from the ground up, and his proposals included doing away with plurals as well as both *a* and *the*.

In the 1890s H. G. Wells published an essay entitled 'For Freedom of Spelling. The Discovery of an Art', which began with the observation: 'It is curious that people do not grumble more at having to spell correctly.' Wells continued, 'It is strange that we should cling so steadfastly to correct spelling. Yet again, one can partly understand the business, if one thinks of the little ways of your schoolmaster and schoolmistress. This sanctity of spelling is stamped upon us in our earliest years. The writer recalls a period of youth wherein six hours a week were given to the study of spelling, and four hours to all other religious instruction.' Reflecting on the numbing effects of this, he wondered, 'Why, after all, should correct spelling be the one absolutely essential literary merit? For it is less fatal for an ambitious scribe to be as dull as Hoxton than to spell in diverse ways.' We may be thrown by the idea of Hoxton being dull – either it means nothing to us, or the characterization of this now vibrant London neighbourhood seems off-beam – but Wells builds to an important point: that 'spelling has become mixed up with moral feeling'.[16]

The Simplified Spelling Society was founded in 1908, to raise awareness of the problems caused by irregularities in English spelling and promote remedies for them. It still exists, and its website likens the modernization of spelling to the decimalization of currency – a specious parallel. In America a similar organization, the Simplified Spelling Board, was established in 1906. It was a pet interest of the hugely rich steel magnate and philanthropist Andrew Carnegie, who subsidized it to the tune of $25,000 per annum. President Theodore Roosevelt took it seriously enough to decree that the federal printing office adopt three hundred of its new spellings: among them *instil*, *good-by* and *thorofare*. He attracted ridicule, with the *Baltimore Sun* going so far as to wonder whether he would be amenable to spelling his name *Rusevelt* – or 'get down to the fact and spell it "butt-in-sky"'.[17] Roosevelt's enthusiasm waned, and within a few years so did that of Carnegie. Unimpressed by the Board, he told the publisher Henry Holt that 'A more useless body of men never came into association.'[18] The Board relocated from Manhattan's

Madison Avenue to the Lake Placid club in upstate New York – there to fade into oblivion. In 1922 members taking breakfast at the Club would have perused menus offering 'sausaj', 'cofi' and 'huni gridl cakes'.[19] But golf and tennis were higher priorities for them than orthographic reform.

Altogether more extreme was the Shaw alphabet. This was a system of forty new letter shapes devised by George Bernard Shaw and generously sponsored in his will. Shaw, who described himself as a 'social downstart', became interested in spelling reform as a young man in the 1870s, and he pursued the matter right up till his death in 1950. There is a popular story that he highlighted the inconsistencies of English spelling by pointing out that, bearing in mind relationships between letters and sounds that could be found elsewhere in English, the word *fish* could be spelled *ghoti*. After all, *gh* sounded like *f* in *enough*, *o* sounded like an *i* in *women*, and *ti* was pronounced *sh* in *nation*. In fact, it was probably not Shaw who first came up with the example of *ghoti*, and in any case there are reasons why the suggestion is flawed – the *i* sound in *women* is unique, and *gh* is only pronounced *f* when it appears at the end of a morpheme, while for *ti* to be pronounced *sh* it needs to be followed by a vowel. But Shaw was passionately concerned with amending the inconsistencies of spelling, which he connected with injustice, noting that a child who was asked to spell the word *debt* and offered as his answer *d-e-t* would be punished for not spelling it with a *b* because Julius Caesar had spelled its Latin original with a *b*. Ever a speculative dealer in bright new ideas, H. G. Wells acknowledged the value of such amendments in principle, but confessed that Shaw's revised spellings 'catch at my attention as it travels along the lane of meaning, like trailing briars'.[20]

Radical reform, with its large proposals, has been characterized by hyperbole. The more credible evangelists have made more modest claims. A nice parody of reformed English, often attributed to Mark Twain, appears to have been the work of the comparatively obscure M. J. Shields:

> In Year 1 that useless letter 'c' would be dropped to be replased either by 'k' or 's', and likewise 'x' would no longer be part of the alphabet. The only kase in which 'c' would be retained

would be the 'ch' formation, which will be dealt with later. Year 2 might reform 'w' spelling, so that 'which' and 'one' would take the same konsonant, wile Year 3 might well abolish 'y' replasing it with 'i' and Iear 4 might fiks the 'g/j' anomali wonse and for all. Jenerally, then, the improvement would kontinue iear bai iear with Iear 5 doing awai with useless double konsonants, and Iears 6–12 or so modifaiing vowlz and the rimeining voist and unvoist konsonants. Bai Iear 15 or sou, it wud fainali bi posibl tu meik ius ov thi ridandant letez 'c', 'y' and 'x' – bai now jast a memori in the maindz ov ould doderez – tu riplais 'ch', 'sh', and 'th' rispektivli. Fainali, xen, aafte sam 20 iers ov orxogrefkl riform, wi wud hev a lojikl, kohirnt speling in ius xrewawt xe Ingliy-spiking werld.

By the end of the proposal M. J. Shields has become M. J. Yilz.

Even when the revamped orthography promises to be a little more pliable than this, there are economic reasons for resisting spelling reform. For instance, every publisher would have to adopt the revised spelling, at great cost, and a huge amount of written material would in one stroke become obsolete. There would also be difficulties in enforcing the changes. Historical information about where words come from would be lost – perhaps not a cause for universal lamentation, but a dismaying depletion of our heritage. Yet fundamentally the objection is this: spelling reform will work only if it is universal. Reforms that seem appropriate in, say, Oxford will seem strange and unacceptable in Winnipeg or Wellington, because they will be based on the phonetics of the English mostly spoken in Oxford rather than that spoken hundreds or thousands of miles away.

Imagine an international referendum to achieve English spelling reform. Who would be consulted? And who would win? Not the British, that's for sure. English's spellings, as they stand, accommo-date a variety of pronunciations. You only have to think about some of the disparities in pronunciation within your own social circle to see the wider difficulties. How would you feel if the pronunci-ations underlying the new system of spelling were not your own? Some readers will recall the hostility felt in many quarters towards metrication. Compared to the introduction of a new system of spelling, that ill feeling would seem minuscule. Unlike adopting the metric system, this change would not be a one-off. It would be huge, but would nevertheless have to be repeated; pronunciations would continue slowly to shift, and spellings would have to be updated from time to time in order to fit the new pronunciations. Ask the proverbial man in the street whether simplified spelling might be a good thing, and he will probably say it would. Explain what would be involved, and he will very likely change his mind. In any case, the appetite for reform is not widespread. The proponents of reform are capable of making a lot of noise, but most people care a good deal less about the issue than the agitators like to make out.

In any case, you cannot suddenly decouple a language from its historical freight. In the sixteenth century, when English was spoken only by a few million people, the case against reform was not watertight. Now, the educational arguments notwithstanding, it is impregnable. In its present form, English spelling makes it possible for texts to be shared by people who speak in very different ways. It would be tragic to lose that.

7 The many advantages of a good language

Reforming grammar, and the eighteenth-century doctrine of correctness

Reforming grammar can seem less difficult than reforming spelling – because, although the territory is larger, the reforms can be accomplished piece by piece. But what is grammar? The word is used frequently, and it is used with an air of authority, yet ask its advocates and apologists to say what it is and you will hear some strangulated responses.

The word *grammar* has a number of meanings. People speak of 'bad grammar' or 'correcting' someone's grammar as though there is agreement about what grammar itself is, but the word is elastic. One of the definitions provided in the single-volume *Oxford Dictionary of English* is 'a set of actual or presumed prescriptive notions about correct use of language', and it is this aspect of grammar that excites most discussion and anxiety. 'Actual or presumed' gets to the heart of the matter: there are notions, and then there are the mere notions of notions. However theoretically pleasing they may be, the categories into which language is organized by grammarians are porous. Edward Sapir, a hugely influential twentieth-century thinker whose work straddled anthropology and linguistics, put the matter succinctly when he said that 'All grammars leak'.[1]

There is an important distinction to be drawn between 'grammar' and 'a grammar'. Fundamentally, 'grammar' is a system of rules expressing the regular forms of a language; 'a grammar' is a book providing a particular model of that system. Today a grammar is likely to map what we know about how a language is used. In its ideal form, it is a complete description of the language, but, as we know, grammar books have not always been descriptive.

The distinction I have drawn matters because grammar exists whether or not it is recorded in books. One can know grammar without being conscious of it. In fact, most of the time we are unaware of its workings. Learning a language involves mastering its grammatical rules, but once we have mastered them we may struggle to give an account of them.

When we refer to 'good English' we mean English that is grammatically secure. But 'good writing' or 'a good speech' are different matters: we are thinking here of the effects achieved more than of grammatical integrity, and, while these performances are likely to be grammatically sound, they need not be so.

I can speak or write grammatically without communicating in a pleasing or especially effective way. The flipside of this is my being able to convey my thoughts to you without abiding by grammatical rules: you will know what I mean if I say, 'I would of loved one of them chicken pies what you done cook.' Less obviously, perhaps, I can write grammatically without making sense. Noam Chomsky illustrated this principle with the sentence 'Colourless green ideas sleep furiously'. Grammatically, this is fine; it is well-formed, unlike the same group of words in reverse – 'Furiously sleep ideas green colourless'. But it means nothing. We intuitively judge the first version to be better than the second, which suggests that our determination of whether a sentence is well-formed is to some degree independent of our grasp of its meaning.

Yet this is not what is taught in schools. Teachers focus on the procedures that allow us to form sentences well, rather than on the underlying philosophy. You may have read the last two sentences with raised eyebrows, for, if English grammar is taught at all in English schools today, it is taught vaguely. Exposure to the idea that there is this frumpy thing called grammar may happen only when other languages are taught. This is where students come across concepts such as 'genitive', 'pluperfect' and 'preposition'. And the information that there is in French such a thing as the pluperfect subjunctive (*'O toi que j'eusse embrassée!'*) may not carry over into students' perception of English.

Grumblers say teachers' neglect of grammar is a recent development. Yet in 1921, a government-sponsored report into the teaching of English in England declared that 'Grammar is certainly badly taught as a rule' and went on to wonder, 'Is it . . . impossible at the present juncture to teach English grammar in the schools for the simple reason that no one knows exactly what it is?' The report is written in a relaxed style unlikely to be used in its modern equivalent. 'We are happily free,' say its authors, 'from most of the cumbersome inflections which hampered the utterances of our ancestors and which still hamper that [sic] of our old-fashioned cousins, the Germans.' We can see influential patterns in its arguments. Teaching of 'correct speech in schools' should be based 'first of all, on correction of mistakes when they arise; secondly, on the great power of imitation; and thirdly, at a later stage, . . . on the teaching of the general rules to which our standard speech conforms.' These priorities are familiar. More of a surprise is the authors' decision to cite with approval an earlier report on teaching in secondary schools, which claimed that 'There is no such thing as English Grammar in the sense which used to be attached to the term.'[2]

Those 'cumbersome inflections' are worth a moment of our time. One of the things that strike students of highly inflected languages such as Russian or Arabic is that they pack a lot of information into words. English does not. However, Old English was a largely synthetic language, which is to that say that it had many inflections: for instance, nouns had four cases (nominative, accusative, genitive, dative) and there were three genders, all clearly marked. This system decayed, and Middle English was largely analytic; it had fewer inflections, especially in its nouns and adjectives, and typically it signalled the grammatical role of a word, X, by using an extra word, Y, rather than binding the information into X. The reasons for this change are not our concern here. But the uninflected nature of English means that sentences have to be structured by other means. Word order is crucial. Something that appeals to novice learners of Latin is the way it is possible to scramble the word order and still make perfect sense; the way the words are tagged ensures that *Caesarem occidit Brutus* and *Brutus Caesarem occidit* both convey the information that Brutus killed Caesar. This seems neat. English, as we are perhaps uncomfortably aware, does not work like that. While it is nonsense to say that English has no inflections – I have just made *inflection* plural by adding an *s*, and *adding* is an inflected form of *add* – it is true that English does not have great inflectional complexity. Its lack of inflections when compared with Latin or Russian explains the common perception that it has little grammar. But it is precisely the absence of inflections that makes the grammatical arrangement of words – i.e. syntax – important in English.

While grammar used to be taught more vigorously than it is today, the philosophy behind such teaching has always been hazy. The principles of English grammar, as presented to schoolchildren, are a patchwork. Students typically understand the subject as a network of traps for the unwary. The machinery of communication is ignored. Instead, teaching has traditionally focused on eliminating common mistakes, and the approach has been punitive, not positive. It would be unusual (and illegal) for a schoolchild today to be beaten for making a grammatical mistake in class, but older readers of this book may remember being given the cane or the strap for doing so. Perhaps the most lasting memory of grammar instruction, though, is the impression it creates that within something that is presented to us as a science there can be great inconsistencies. This is unnerving: how can I do the right thing if the principles of doing right are so full of exceptions? The experience is one we are likely to have again – for instance, in our encounters with the law.

The eighteenth century is often portrayed as an age of grammarians. There had been accounts of grammar before, as we have seen, and there would be many afterwards, but commonly it is to this period that a lot of our grammatical notions are traced. It is usually characterized as an age of regulation, discipline, logic and prescription – summed up in the title of a 1929 study by Sterling Leonard called *The Doctrine of Correctness*.

At this time, complaining about English became a force for unity. During the two previous centuries, writers had looked forward optimistically to a time when the state of English would be much improved. But in the eighteenth century, commentators switched to lamenting the passing of a golden age of English. Dr Johnson described the writers 'which rose in the time of *Elizabeth*' as 'the wells of English undefiled' (words originally used by Spenser of Chaucer, with wistful inaccuracy). The Elizabethans, he believed, were 'the pure sources of genuine diction'. The genuine diction remained until the Restoration of the monarchy in 1660. In this view Johnson was close to Swift, who felt that the period of excellence had occurred between the beginning of Queen Elizabeth's reign in 1558 and the start of the First English Civil War in 1642. Nostalgia for that period was common, though not universal.

The sense of slippage was widespread. It helps explain why the eighteenth century was the period when ideas of correctness became an obsession. In an attempt to prevent any further deterioration, writers began to make specific pronouncements about what was good usage and what was its scandalous opposite. They did so against a background of linguistic affectation, bombast and snobbery, in which commercialese was ever more rampant.

Writing in 1724, the author of *The Many Advantages of a Good Language to Any Nation* (generally believed to be Thomas Wilson, Bishop of Sodor and Man) examined the state of English and complained of the lack of a decent dictionary, the raw ignorance of students arriving at university, the 'silliness' of women's choice of words, and the shortcomings of the alphabet. 'We have no Grammar of it that is taught in any School that we ever heard of,' he wrote.[3] Wilson died in 1755, the year Johnson brought out his famous *Dictionary*; he did not live to see what would turn out to be a glut of grammars in the decades following the publication of Johnson's magnum opus.

The title of Wilson's book is significant. It avoids specificity – a knowing sort of indirectness – yet really the book ought to have been called *The Many Advantanges of Good English to Britain*. Getting English in order was increasingly seen as a way of solidifying national identity. For some, this was an egalitarian mission; for others, a means of papering over the cracks in relations between the different parts of Britain. Grammatical security was regarded as a way of cementing the Constitution by other means. But let us be clear: there is no single document that sets out a British constitution. Rather, we have a collection of laws. There are key statutes of a constitutional nature – ranging from Magna Carta, issued in 1215, to, for instance, the Freedom of Information Act in 2000 – but there are also elements of the *de facto* constitution that are unwritten. Its sources are scattered, and it has evolved for practical purposes. It is amorphous and in many places indistinct, and as a result it is much contested.

The most arresting thing about the systems of grammar promulgated in the seventeenth and eighteenth centuries is their profusion. The standard modern overview of the subject, by Ian Michael, examines more than 270 grammars produced between 1586 and 1800, and identifies in these no fewer than fifty-six different systems, while even among those that stuck closely to Latin patterns there were twenty different systems.[4] The authors of these books frequently lifted material from those of their predecessors, and few of them could make much claim to originality. But it is striking that so many people thought they could profitably contribute to this field – that there was money to be made, and that they had something valuable to say.

Reviewing the efforts of English grammarians for the ninth edition of the *Encyclopaedia Britannica* (1875–89), Archibald Sayce wrote that 'The endeavour to find the distinctions of Latin grammar in that of English has only resulted in grotesque errors and a total misapprehension of the usage of the English language'. That view was far from orthodox at the time. In 1914 H. G. Wells could still wonder, 'Is it not time at least that this last, this favourite but threadbare article of the schoolmaster's creed was put away for good? Everyone who has given any attention to this question must be aware that the intellectual gesture is entirely different in highly inflected languages such as Greek and Latin and in so uninflected a language as English, that learning Greek to improve one's English style is like learning to swim in order to fence better, and that familiarity with Greek seems only too often to render a man incapable of clear, strong expression in English at all.'[5] He had previously had this to say:

At present our method in English is a foolish caricature of the Latin method; we spend a certain amount of time teaching children classificatory bosh about the eight sorts of Nominative Case, a certain amount of time teaching them the 'derivation' of words they do not understand, glance shyly at Anglo-Saxon and at Grimm's Law, indulge in a specific reminiscence of the Latin method called parsing, supplement with a more modern development called the analysis of sentences, give a course of exercises in paraphrasing (for the most part the conversion of good English into bad), and wind up with lessons in 'Composition' that must be seen to be believed.[6]

Wells's image of 'classificatory bosh' would have affronted most teachers in the eighteenth century. Until recently English had been taught only in so-called dissenting academies, but now the increased emphasis on English in schools created a market for doctrine about language and for schemes that helped impart it. As Sterling Leonard points out, 'the claims for the study of language made at this period were entangled with the idea of formal discipline', and there was 'obvious educational value' in 'pursuing rather subtle analogies' and in 'mastering abstract differentiae in the resolution of false syntax'. The result was 'the multiplication of formal niceties'.[7] 'Educational value' is conceived here from the point of view of the educators rather than those they educate: the job of teaching is made more straightforward when lessons are broken down into exercises and tests.

The established methods of teaching Latin offered a model for this. English did not develop from Latin, so it seems crankish to expect it to conform to the patterns of Latin. It would be more reasonable to expect it to behave like German, since the two languages have shared ancestry, although in moving away from that ancestry they have of course both altered. But, whereas many seventeenth-century grammarians such as John Wilkins had wanted to erect a completely new system, in the eighteenth century it was common to accept uncritically that Latin provided a set of grammatical concepts that could be mapped on to English. One of the founding works in this tradition was George Snell's 1649 *The Right Teaching of Useful Knowledg (sic)*, which argued that 'the present, exquisite, and elaborate times . . . seem to bee the most advantagious for settling . . . our English tongue' and glorified Latin as 'a Grammatical language, elegant, certain, and perfect' and 'a book language, which no force of arms can alter'.[8] Later contributions of note included Elisha Coles's *Nolens Volens* (1675), a primer promising 'You shall make Latin whether you will or no' and promoting Latin as a model for good English, and Richard Johnson's *Grammatical Commentaries* (1706), which laboriously identified the shortcomings of Lily's nearly two-hundred-year-old Grammar yet deified Latin as a universal language, suitable moreover for everyday speech.

Writing in *The Spectator* in 1711, Sir Richard Steele complained about the poor delivery of those leading church services, suggesting that it stemmed from 'the little Care that is taken of their Reading, while Boys and at School, where when they are got into *Latin*, they are looked upon as above *English*'. Over the rest of the eighteenth century, as Latin, which had already ceased to be the shared language of European scholarship, ceased also to be the language of classroom instruction, it increasingly became a symbol of an intellectual rigour of which the modern world seemed incapable. Known only in its written form, it seemed impeccably formal and secure. It connoted discipline, justice and equilibrium. Conservative writers on English wanted their language to resemble Latin in its precision and stability.

'When in Rome, do as the Romans do' – or rather, if you dream of recreating the spirit of the Roman Empire, start by exalting the spirit of its language. In the latter part of the eighteenth century and for most of the nineteenth, the idea that Britain was a new Rome seduced grammarians, and their enthusiasm for the Latin way of doing things was not so much nostalgic as self-legitimizing. The story of Latin should really have been a cautionary one, though that is more apparent now than it would have been then. Here was a language which spread through the political aggression of its original speakers, became the lingua franca of urban trade all around the western Mediterranean, and was disseminated further through the medium of its literature and by Christianity, but which later became a sort of arcane scholastic code, trampled into the minds of hapless schoolchildren, and later still became merely obscure.[9] A further cautionary point: the decline of Latin was brought about by its supporters more than by its opponents.

There is a delightful table in John Stirling's *A Short View of English Grammar* (1735), which shows – in the style of a Latin declension – the various forms of the adjective *wise*: the masculine, feminine and neuter, both singular and plural, of its nominative, vocative, accusative, genitive, dative and ablative. Delightful, that is, because all thirty-six entries in the table are the same: 'wise'. In his preface, Stirling assures readers that his little volume will 'particularly be of singular Service to young Ladies'.[10]

Stirling, who also translated Virgil and Ovid, has not been canonized as one of the eighteenth century's most valuable thinkers about grammar, but he is representative of the period's polite amateurism in matters to do with language. While we may doubt whether Stirling's declension of *wise* was of singular service to any of his readers, his mention of young ladies is significant, reflecting the emergence of a new audience for ideas of correctness. In Britain in the second half of the eighteenth century, grammatical instruction was a commodity. Advertisements from the period make this clear. When schools, and especially new academies for young women, sought teachers, the ability to provide 'proper' and 'grammatical' instruction in English was to the fore. The largely middle-class parents of prospective pupils saw a command of grammar as a guarantee of social opportunity: their children, properly instructed, could enter the upper ranks of society.

English was being gentrified and commercialized. The first half of the century had witnessed a massive surge in printing and the appetite for print. Books circulated freely thanks in part to the new commercial lending libraries, and second-hand copies could be picked up cheaply from dealers who traded from stalls or barrows. Even those on modest incomes could afford chapbooks, the contents of which might include recipes, jests and reports of sensational events. The most notable new form of literature was the novel; Daniel Defoe was a trailblazer, creating his plot lines in accordance not with history, myth or legend, but with his own sense of what his invented characters might plausibly do. Original fiction had a sizeable female readership, and creating it became a way for women to earn a living, although anonymous or pseudonymous publication was in many cases deemed necessary in order to get the books a fair critical hearing. By mid-century it was normal to think of women as the likely readers of these works, and this prompted comment – applause, certainly, but also sneers – about the democratization of literature.

At the same time there was a wealth of other printed material: newspapers, magazines and pamphlets, in addition to calendars, posters, price tags, labels, tickets and maps. Readers became consumers of words – often silently and in private – and society was seized by a mania for ink and paper. As this happened, printed matter began to seem less precious. Books became commodities. The increased public visibility of books, and the busy trade in them, created opportunities for writers to set themselves up as instructors of popular taste. The entire system of literature seemed new. The society in which Dr Johnson lived experienced a 'literacy crisis' that was the opposite of the one we worry about today.[11] There was immense anxiety that the increasing literacy of people outside the social elite would upset the established cultural and political order.

From the 1750s on, there was a flood of not just grammars, but also dictionaries, spelling books and theories of language, as well as guides to penmanship, letter-writing and other 'small literary performances'. Books that showed how to write a letter tended to include some rudimentary advice about grammar: one of the best examples is Charles Johnson's *The Complete Art of Writing Letters* (1770), which presented twenty pages of 'useful' grammar before its instructions about how to write letters appropriate to courtship, friendship, business, education and compliment. Equally, grammars gave guidance on letter-writing. The literary historian Jack Lynch explains, 'These were not books by aristocrats for aristocrats; they were written by aspiring middle-class writers who hoped to pull other middle-class would-be writers up with them,' and 'the middle classes were imitating their social betters, hoping to pass among them unnoticed.'[12] While not exactly subversive, these books were far from being prim endorsements of the status quo.

There was, fundamentally, more sharing of the written word. In the nineteenth century this would escalate – for instance, the Penny Post was introduced in 1840, and within thirty years almost a billion letters were being sent annually in Britain[13] – but it was in the eighteenth century that attitudes to this word-traffic crystallized. Although language was not in great flux, discussions of language and the formation of opinions about it were fervent. Assessing Charles Wiseman's *A Complete English Grammar on a New Plan* in the *Monthly*

Review in 1765, the satirically minded critic William Kenrick wondered, 'How many *complete* English Grammars on *new plans*, have we not already had, or been threatened with?'[14] It is easy to lose sight of the fact that the authors of these proposals all believed they had something genuinely original to offer.

There were, essentially, two schools of thought about such plans. On the one hand, there were those who believed that language could be remodelled, or at least regularized; they claimed that reason and logic would enable them to achieve this. On the other hand were those who saw language as a complicated jungle of habits that it would be impossible to trim into shape. The former were more numerous. Beginning around 1700, and especially after 1750, the orthodox approach to English was prescriptive. Much of the time the intent was not to establish new rules, but to be explicit about existing ones, and to insist on them. Unfortunately, these existing rules were often misapprehended. Moreover, the grammarians neglected the possibility that several kinds of English can exist at once; they made little allowance for the different contexts in which the language is used and the ways in which context affects people's practices.

It was common to suppose that language was a gift from God. Common, too, to think of language as an entity; to believe that it possessed something often dubbed a 'genius', an ideal form ordained by its original theorist, the Creator; and to conceive of it as a mirror, reflecting the qualities of its users. The wonders and copiousness of English were a consequence of the excellence of English-speaking society – its refinement, the magnitude and multitude of its achievements. The ideas of Locke were available to inform a different view – namely that language was a type of behaviour, lacking any inherent correspondence with reality – but the linguistic amateurs of the eighteenth century tended not to have much time for him. One of the more complex engagements with Locke came in a novel: Laurence Sterne's *Tristram Shandy* (1759–67), in which the patterns of thought are realized with great imagination. Many of today's wonky ideas of language in general – and of our language in particular – can be traced back to the eighteenth-century neglect of Locke's philosophy.

This may seem an odd thing to say, given that Locke was, with Isaac Newton, the greatest influence on eighteenth-century thought in Britain. These two, moreover, can in retrospect be seen as responsible for ending the role of Latin as the language of higher thought and learning; Newton wrote *Principia Mathematica* (1687) in Latin, but switched to English for *Opticks* (1704). But Locke was mainly valued as a political thinker, and Newton's thought was popularized by means of simplified versions and public lectures. For most people, the prevailing voices were the authoritarian ones of the period's grammarians. These were often retired gentlemen of a pious disposition; commonly they had been clerics or schoolmasters. They revered the elegance of Latin and, to an even greater extent, Greek. English constructions were measured against their Latin and Greek prototypes; differences were seen as unfortunate departures from these models. The grammarians had little concern with the actual problems of daily usage, preferring instead to take language out of context. They viewed it under the microscope, but theirs was a limited notion of language – brief and easy summary was their goal, though brevity and easiness were not always manifest in the results.

As I have suggested, the market for grammatical law-making was a result of increased social mobility. But it was not just the socially aspiring who wanted rules and guides; an upper-class revulsion at the thought of being contaminated with middle-class vulgarity was a strong motive for the eighteenth-century codification of grammar. There was an intricate relationship between linguistic intolerance and the twin energies of aspiration and insecurity. This remains.

However, close attention to the books that advanced the doctrine of correctness shows that they were not so very doctrinaire. It has become orthodox to lay into 'eighteenth-century prescriptivists' and accuse them of establishing silly rules. Yet while there really were some hardcore prescriptivists in this period, it is an oversimplification to say that eighteenth-century thinking about English was militarily rigid. In truth, it is the uncertainties and ambivalences we can find in eighteenth-century books about the language that are their most lasting legacy.

8 'Bishop Lowth was a fool'

Getting under the skin of prescriptivism

Samuel Johnson's *Dictionary* of 1755 stands as the great monument of eighteenth-century philology. Like most great monuments, it has its dusty corners, and while the structure is impressive, what strike us most are its little ornaments of idiosyncrasy. Before Johnson, there was no authoritative dictionary of English. It is a mistake to say that there had been no work whatsoever in this vein; in fact, there had been dictionaries of English for the previous 150 years. But these had at first been glossaries of difficult words, and even when their scope became more ambitious their content remained patchy. Johnson's is the first really good English dictionary. By the time he began work on it, in the late 1740s, the lack of such a reference book was a national embarrassment. The French and the Florentines had impressive dictionaries. Where was their British counterpart? 'We have long preserved our constitution,' Johnson wrote in the preface to the *Dictionary*. 'Let us make some struggles for our language.'[1]

A consortium of London booksellers, led by Robert Dodsley, realized that the publication of a good English dictionary might be an opportunity to make a handsome amount of money. Dodsley, who had been in domestic service before embarking on a career in publishing, had a gift for spotting gaps in the market. In Johnson, whom he had previously published, he identified an author fit for this particular task.

Johnson was not an obvious choice. He was a self-tormenting, sickly man whose domestic arrangements were irregular, and he was given to bouts of debilitating melancholy. He did not have a degree, and he had failed in his attempts to run a school, mainly because he suffered from tics and convulsions that disconcerted the parents of prospective pupils. However, Dodsley knew his appetite for hard work and his formidable erudition. While Johnson's main motive for compiling a dictionary was financial – the booksellers were prepared to pay him the apparently grand sum of £1,575 – there can be little doubt that the project appealed to his unfulfilled ambitions as an educator.

Setting out his plans, Johnson declared that he would record only those words he could find in books, and consequently the *Dictionary* does not include a good deal of slang that was in use at that time. In principle, it was not enough for him to hear something as he passed along Fleet Street or through the gin-soaked slums of the parish of St Giles; if he could not find a word or expression in a printed source, it would not be included. In practice, he did pick up some words 'as industry should find, or chance should offer'. Yet the emphasis on printed texts was crucial to his achievement. Thanks to his insistence on having documentary evidence and on supporting his definitions with quotations that illustrated words in use, he achieved a much fuller portrait of the language than his predecessors had.

Instead of beginning with a word list, Johnson began with books, reading widely in the literature of the previous two hundred years. In drawing his evidence about the language from books, he was implicitly accepting that words mean what people use them to mean. In the Plan of the *Dictionary* he published in 1747, he claimed that etymology would be the mechanism for producing his definitions, yet in the finished work he does not pay much attention to it. Precedent was his guide; most of the time he did not issue proclamations about what words 'should' mean. Whereas initially he presents a strict and limited system for distinguishing the meanings of each word, in the end he demarcates a vast number of senses for some common words. His illustrations of the word *etymology* suggest a complete loss of faith in the power of that discipline, as in his citation of the historian of theatre Jeremy Collier: 'When words are restrained, by common usage, to a particular sense, to run up to etymology . . . is wretchedly ridiculous.'

Nevertheless, for all his skill in discerning the different senses of a word and for all his aplomb in writing definitions, Johnson displayed some prejudices, stigmatizing particular words and types of word. He identified some words as 'low', 'cant' or 'barbarous'. Other labels included 'ludicrous', 'improper', 'redundant', 'bad' and even 'vicious'. He was not the first English lexicographer to do this, and in fact more of his usage labels are descriptive than evaluative. The vast majority of words are not labelled in this way at all, and, had he really been the hard-line prescriptivist of myth, he would surely just have excluded words that he disliked. Still, the evaluations stand out.

Johnson was suspicious of words imported from French. In the preface he ominously declared that if the 'idleness and ignorance' of translators be 'suffered to proceed', it will 'reduce us to babble a dialect of *France*'.[2] He omitted from the *Dictionary* words such as *bouquet*, *liqueur* and *vignette*. Perhaps he did not find them in the texts he consulted, but his attitude is apparent in his condemnation of borrowings such as *ruse* ('a French word neither elegant nor necessary') and *trait* (which is 'scarce English'). He defines *to Frenchify* as 'to infect with the manner of France; to make a coxcomb' and provides a pungent illustrative quotation from William Camden about the unpopularity of the 'Frenchified' Edward the Confessor.

Although Johnson's hostility to French was not unusual, many of his contemporaries admired the language. The position was well stated by Hugh Blair in *Lectures on Rhetoric* (1783), in which he collected material he had been using for more than twenty years in his university teaching at Edinburgh. Blair claimed that 'It is chiefly, indeed, on grave subjects, and with respect to the stronger emotions of the mind, that our Language displays its power of expression. We are said to have thirty words, at least, for denoting all the varieties of the passion of anger.' However, 'the French Language surpasses ours, by far, in expressing the nicer shades of character; especially those varieties of manner, temper, and behaviour, which are displayed in our social intercourse with one another,' and 'no Language is so copious as the French for whatever is delicate, gay, and amusing. It is, perhaps, the happiest Language for conversation in the known world.' 'National character', Blair concluded, will 'always have some perceptible influence on the turn of Language'.[3]

Johnson's view of national character is apparent in the *Dictionary*. For instance, he explains that bulldogs are 'so peculiar to Britain, that they are said to degenerate when they are carried to other countries'. Some of his assertions feel implausible. He claims that 'The English language has properly no dialects', which implies a unity that a time-traveller touring the country in 1755 would struggle to recognize.[4] There are other statements that suggest linguistic partiality.

'I could not visit caverns to learn the miner's language, nor take a voyage to perfect my skill in the dialect of navigation,' he says. Nor did he visit merchants and shops – but then, 'of the laborious and mercantile part of the people, the diction is in a great measure casual and mutable'. This has been interpreted by many modern critics as an arrogant dismissal of the language of the working man and the poor. But the 'laborious and mercantile part' includes many middle-class people, and in any case Johnson is saying these things to manage readers' expectations. In truth, one of the strengths of the *Dictionary* is its coverage of these very areas. He argues that the 'fugitive cant' of such people 'is always in a state of increase or decay' and 'cannot be regarded as any part of the durable materials of a language'. Accordingly, it must be allowed to 'perish with other things unworthy of preservation'.[5] This, too, has been seen as evidence of Johnson's middle-class dismissal of demotic speech. But examination of the cant that does find its way into the *Dictionary* shows that what he had in mind was not the language of the disenfranchised. Rather, it was often the smart talk of the upwardly mobile – the sort of modish hypocrisy that had troubled Swift.

In many respects Johnson is a surprising thinker. After completing his work, he reflected that at the outset 'I found our speech copious without order, and energetick without rules: wherever I turned my view, there was perplexity to be disentangled'. But he half admires the tangle even as he labours to sort it out, and when he writes of 'the boundless chaos of living speech' and 'the exuberance of signi-fication' it is possible, I think, to hear a note of awe. He regards the efforts of academies, set up 'to guard the avenues of their languages, to retain fugitives, and repulse intruders', as empty, for language is volatile, and it is as foolish to think one can 'enchain syllables' as to believe one can 'lash' – that is, bind – 'the wind'.[6] This is the language of a poet – which Johnson was.

Johnson's efforts were painted as heroic by his friends and admirers. Claiming that the *Dictionary* was better than the Académie Française's *Dictionnaire*, David Garrick wrote that 'Johnson, well arm'd like a hero of yore, / Has beat forty French, and will beat forty more'. Johnson characterized lexicography as 'dull work', but it was a Herculean sort of dullness, which established a potent image of

Britain's linguistic and cultural heritage. His selection of authors, for the more than 100,000 quotations he provided to show words in use, established an English literary canon.

The guide to grammar that Johnson included in the *Dictionary* was limited. It was not methodically produced. Much of it was borrowed: Johnson relied on John Wallis, Ben Jonson and Lily's Grammar. Within the main body of the *Dictionary*, he copiously illustrated what he considered correct usage, but made few comments about the practices of the authors he cited. The *Dictionary*'s chief contribution to grammar was that it goaded others into examining English more minutely.

The development of the *Dictionary* reflected Johnson's own changing attitude to English. When he began work on the project, he believed he could embalm the language, yet by the time he completed it he was conscious of the necessary mutability of English; he had also come to recognize the need for lexicography to say how things are rather than to specify how they ought to be. Even in the Plan of 1747, he oscillates between active and passive imagery; he writes of fixing and guarding, but also of observing and recording, and he pictures himself as both a conqueror and a collector. Eight years later, in the preface to the finished work, he sounds less like a legislator than a sort of cleaner. He opens by characterizing 'the writer of dictionaries' as one of those 'who toil at the lower employments of life . . . rather driven by the fear of evil, than attracted by the prospect of good', and as 'doomed only to remove rubbish and clear obstructions from the paths through which Learning and Genius press forward to conquest and glory, without bestowing a smile on the humble drudge that facilitates their progress'. When he began, he says, he fantasized about the 'obscure recesses' of learning he would 'enter and ransack' and about being able to 'pierce deep into every science' and 'limit every idea by a definition strictly logical' – 'But these were the dreams of a poet doomed to wake a lexicographer.'[7] Some of the grandeur of his original design persists, but reality has infringed upon it. We sense this in all that Johnson wrote about creating the *Dictionary*. The battle that occurred within his intellectual conscience was a reflection of the quarrel between prescriptivists and descriptivists, which would become a large and public matter in the twentieth century.

Johnson is an important figure in the history of arguments about English not only because of his creation of the *Dictionary*, but also because his sheer presence as a cultural panjandrum made him *the* point of reference for several generations of writers on usage. Over the next century it was a feature of works dealing with English that they engaged with Johnson's legacy, often explicitly and disparagingly. They seemed to be animated either by the desire to augment his achievements or by a manic conviction that those achievements needed extirpating.

When we hear today about the prescriptive tradition, Johnson is often wrongly identified as its founding father. It is usually claimed that its other begetter was Robert Lowth, who in 1762 published a book entitled *A Short Introduction to English Grammar*. Despite its success this volume has repeatedly been castigated in recent times. Its reputation now is undeservedly low; anyone looking on the internet for information about Lowth will soon come across a website proclaiming that 'Bishop Lowth was a Fool'(he was Bishop of London from 1777 to 1787), and there is plenty more in this vein.

Yet rather than being a narrow-minded nit, Lowth was a man of formidable learning, a scholar of Hebrew who was Professor of Poetry at Oxford and later a Fellow of the Royal Society. His lectures on sacred Hebrew poetry were subtly attentive to different traditions in the reading of the scriptures, and his biblical scholarship was celebrated for its detail. Yet when he wrote *A Short Introduction to English Grammar*, he was responding to an immediate need: the education of his young son Thomas. He intended the book as a broad and gentle overview of the language, and he published it in 1762 only at the suggestion of his friend Robert Dodsley, whom we previously saw urging Johnson to embark on his *Dictionary*. Even then, he did not put his name to it. It is tempting to imagine an encounter between Lowth and Johnson, given that Dodsley was their mutual friend, but there is no evidence that they met. Still, it is remarkable that Dodsley was responsible for bringing both works to the market, and it may be that his awareness of the limitations of Johnson's remarks on grammar in the *Dictionary* lay behind his encouragement of Lowth. His close familiarity with the popular periodicals of the day, in which critics often condemned writers' grammar, must also have helped him see that there was an audience for a clear-sighted overview of the subject.[8]

The first edition of the *Short Introduction* was a sort of trial run, used to gauge public interest in a book of its kind. Lowth invited feedback, and the second edition incorporated some of this. A third edition continued the process. Issued in small and large formats, and repeatedly tweaked by Lowth over the next two decades, the *Short Introduction* was popular not only in Britain but also in America and Germany, and was still being actively used by students in leading American universities such as Harvard almost a hundred years after its publication.

It is often suggested that at the heart of Lowth's *Short Introduction* is the notion that antiquity offers solutions to the linguistic problems of the modern world. According to this view, Lowth's idea of grammar was grounded in his knowledge of Latin – indeed, it is claimed that the essence of his grammar *was* Latin. Lowth is regarded as the culmination of a tradition which emphasized the usefulness of Latin as a means of categorizing and stabilizing English – of imposing consistency on its wildness.

The truth is not so simple. Lowth seems to have worked with a selection of the writings of what he calls 'our best Authors', and to have spotted in them moments when even these leading writers used English poorly. He provides examples of what he considers their mistaken usage. He thus shows the language in use, and then comments on it, rather than simply chiselling out a set of eternal commandments.

Lowth's readers loved his exposé of famous authors' grammatical misadventures. Shakespeare is a favourite target, and when Lowth adds thirty-eight new snippets of Shakespeare to the second edition, twenty-three of them are disparaged.[9] Yet while Lowth considers his own judgement superior, and seems to enjoy finding the blips and slips, the most dogmatic moments are kept to the footnotes, rather than appearing in the main text. Moreover, he is proscriptive more than he is prescriptive. And his admiration for Latin was less deep than his admiration for Hebrew.

Notions of logic and propriety are plainly important to Lowth: he has a brisk and serious way of laying down the law. He tells his readers that a full stop signals a pause twice as long as a colon, a colon 'or Member' one twice as long as a semi-colon, and a semi-colon 'or Half-member' one twice as long as a comma.[10] He complains about the use of *worser*, noting its occurrence in a line by Dryden, considers the pronoun *thou* all but obsolete – though William Cobbett was still concerned with its correct use more than half a century later – and thinks the word *because*, 'used to express the motive or end', is 'either improper or obsolete'.[11] Other matters that trouble him are what he sees as the erroneous use of adjectives instead of adverbs, as when something is said to be 'marvellous graceful' rather than 'marvellously graceful'; 'you was' ('an enormous Solecism'); the use of *who* rather than *whom* in what he calls the 'Objective Case'; and the confusion of *lay* and *lie*.[12]

'You was' is of particular interest. Judging from collections of private correspondence, it seems that the form began to spread towards the end of the seventeenth century, peaking twenty or thirty years before Lowth was writing. Many well-educated writers were inconsistent, making no clear distinction between 'you was' and singular 'you were'. Apparently, men started to write 'you was' earlier than women did, and women maintained the form longer.[13] Lowth was not the first to condemn 'you was', but his explicit disparagement – when he writes 'an enormous Solecism' we may imagine him holding his nose – was a seminal moment, establishing a principle that the next generation of grammarians would reassert.

Perhaps most influentially, Lowth popularizes the distinction between *would* and *should*, and in the second edition emphasizes it by adding that the former 'primarily denotes inclination of will', the latter 'obligation'.[14] He also inserts in the second edition the rule that double negatives are to be avoided; they equal an affirmation, since they 'destroy' each other.[15] Occasionally this destruction can serve a rhetorical purpose. The statement 'He's not unamusing' subtly differs from 'He's amusing'. Some would say the difference is not even subtle. But Lowth's real target was utterances such as the protest 'I didn't steal nothing'. We may well find this statement clumsy and may complain that it is open to misinterpretation, but in practice few of us would hear someone say this and believe it equalled an affirmation – an admission of guilt. In English, as the Danish linguist

Otto Jespersen observed, negation is logically important but often formally unimportant; we mark it modestly, as by adding *-n't* to *does*, and consequently the urge to reinforce the negation is strong.[16]

Still, Lowth's line on double negatives has proved lastingly popular. At the time he was writing, double negation was not common in written English, and it seems likely that Lowth was motivated to condemn it because it was regarded as a mark of poor education or breeding, and was thus the sort of thing his son (and other learners) must avoid. Since he did not mention it in the first edition of the *Short Introduction*, it seems plausible that double negation was not something he had come across in practice, and that it was brought to his attention by one of his early readers. Alternatively, he may have seen it condemned in another grammar – the most likely being James Greenwood's *An Essay Towards a Practical English Grammar* (1711).[17] The examples Lowth gives of double negatives are from books more than a hundred years old, though his contemporary Robert Baker writes in *Reflections on the English Language* (1770) that in 'very animated Speeches, where a Man were delivering himself with Vehemence and Heat' two negatives 'might perhaps be used not with an ill Grace'.[18]

Although Lowth is clear about double negatives and 'you was', he is sometimes tentative. The very first thing he says in the *Short Introduction* is that 'Grammar is the Art of rightly expressing our thoughts by Words'. When he calls it an art, he is implying that it is an acquired ability and also that it is governed by aesthetics. He then states, 'The Grammar of any particular Language . . . applies . . . common principles . . . according to the established usage and custom of it.' 'Established usage' and 'custom' are not rock-solid. A little later he writes, 'Words are articulate sounds, used by common consent as signs of ideas.'[19] Again, his model of usage suggests room for manoeuvre. He admits that some of his rules are flimsy. Of *would* and *should* he concedes in the second edition, though not in the first, that 'they both vary their import'.[20] Of the marks of punctuation, he admits, 'The precise quantity or duration of each Pause or Note cannot be defined,' and 'Much must be left to the judgement and taste of the writer.'[21] Additionally, he is unclear about the use of apostrophes, and spells the possessive pronouns *hers, ours, yours* and *theirs* with an apostrophe before the *s*. *His*, he explains, is really *hee's*.[22] The use of apostrophes was very uncertain during the eighteenth century, and Lowth does not clear matters up. He says that the possessive form of *it* is *its*, but is not emphatic about the need to write *its* rather than *it's*.

The eighteenth-century uncertainty about *its* and *it's* may surprise us now; getting them muddled is widely considered a sloppy, immature error. Yet the possessive *its* was a sixteenth-century novelty, and even in the early nineteenth century many educated people wrote *it's* when signifying possession. The *OED* shows the scholarly Irish clergyman Thomas Sheridan – father of the more noted Thomas Sheridan, an actor and elocutionist – using possessive *it's* in 1728, and the novelist and educational writer Maria Edgeworth using it in 1802. In a work entitled *Aristarchus, or The Principles of Composition* (1788), Philip Withers writes, 'I hope that the English Language will come in for it's Share of Improvement'.[23] Until the sixteenth century, *his* was the possessive form of *it* in written English, and this use of *his* continued into the seventeenth century. But in the sixteenth, writers started to avoid using *his* of subjects that were not male, and would find roundabout ways of expressing themselves, writing 'of it' or using the Old English *thereof*. In the King James Bible, *its* appears only once: in a verse in Leviticus which begins 'That which groweth of its own accord of thy harvest thou shalt not reap'. *Its* occurs in none of the works of Shakespeare published in his lifetime, and in the First Folio of 1623 possessive *it's* occurs nine times and *its* once.

Lowth draws a distinction between what one may say and the forms of expression one should use when writing. He states that in formal written English it is unacceptable to end a sentence with a preposition, but accepts the practice in 'familiar' use. To make the point he even writes that 'This is an Idiom which our language is strongly inclined to'; he then uses a semi-colon and continues his sentence, but the phrasing seems like a small joke on his part, since a moment before he was remarking on the unloveliness of writing 'Horace is an author, whom I am much delighted with.'[24] There is other evidence that Lowth has a sense of humour. He describes the power of speech as 'bestowed' by the Creator – 'but alas! how often do we pervert it to the worst of purposes?' Shortly after this he writes, 'The interjection *alas!* expresses the concern and regret of the speaker; and though thrown in with propriety, yet might have been omitted without injuring the construction of the sentence.'[25] The self-referential gesture is almost cute.

Most tellingly, in his correspondence Lowth again and again breaks his own rules, and he is inconsistent in his habits. He writes 'you was', ends sentences with prepositions, uses contractions such as *'twill*, doubles final consonants unexpectedly ('admitt', 'success-full'), and forms the past tense with 'to be' rather than 'to have', saying that a letter 'is just come'.[26] In this he is behaving normally: there is one standard for casual communications, another for formal ones. Nevertheless, Lowth's inconsistency is a key part of his legacy. His successors in prescriptivism (and in his real speciality, proscriptivism) hand down their judgements in the name of science, but their message is unscientific and their efforts originate not in the rigour of research and philosophy but in a sense of life's encroaching chaos and myriad uncertainties.

Lowth is concerned with usage, not with the structure of language. He sustains the convention in books about English of making simple statements about the language and then in footnotes (which most people will not read) addressing more complex theoretical matters. As John Barrell observes, in the second half of the eighteenth century 'the rational grounds of grammar almost disappear and they come to be regarded as the subject of a different sort of book'. Sceptical about the search for a universal grammar, which seemed too dependent on psychological intuitions rather than the facts of a particular language, Lowth pointed interested parties in the direction of James Harris's *Hermes* (1751), a difficult work which investigated grammar from a philosophical perspective. Whereas French grammarians were interested in the relationship between grammatical structures and the structure of reality, British grammarians were suspicious of the abstract. 'With the disappearance of theory from the grammars,' notes Barrell, 'they become simply manuals of rules, teaching how to conform.' Theory was kept out of grammar books because they were intended for learners and had to be of an affordable length, but also to repress public awareness of how controversial language could be. It made custom seem comfortable, rather than a matter for debate.[27] The *Short Introduction* represents the general condition of English grammars up until the twentieth century: there is a reluctance to wrestle with difficult questions, an emphasis on using literature to illustrate aspects of language, an affection for examples and learnable points rather than larger rational procedures, an inherited set of labels that are variably used, and a rarely explored awareness that there is something wrong with all of this.

Why was Lowth so successful? Partly, it seems, because Robert Dodsley was his publisher. Dodsley was among the period's most powerful publishers and was one of the main shareholders in the influential *London Magazine* and *London Evening Post.* The commercial success of books had a lot to do with who published them, how they were published, and how effectively they were promoted – something that still holds true. Dodsley was perhaps the leading light of a newly proactive book trade, in which publishers went looking for talent, rather than waiting for the talent to come to them.

Lowth had other useful friends, having dabbled in diplomatic work. He had also enjoyed a good deal of attention as a result of a public spat with the religious controversialist William Warburton about the Book of Job – from which he emerged the victor. One early reflection of his book's popularity was the decision in 1763 to reissue John Ash's *Grammatical Institutes*, originally published in 1760, with the new subtitle 'An easy introduction to Dr Lowth's English Grammar'. When Johnson revised his *Dictionary* for its fourth edition (1773) he respectfully mentioned Lowth's work twice, and, asked by an ambitious student for a reading list, he recommended Lowth's Grammar rather than his own.

Lowth's liking for displaying other writers' mistakes has impressed his prescriptive and proscriptive heirs. Today a writer making a case for correctness will exhibit examples of others' stylistic and syntactic cock-ups, enjoining the reader to share a delight in their absurdity. It is no surprise that Lowth's approach was popular with pedantic Victorian commentators. William Hodgson, Professor of Political Economy at Edinburgh University, published in 1881 a book called *Errors in the Use of English*, and his opening words were: 'Acting on the principle that example is better than precept, the Spartans impressed upon their children the wisdom of sobriety by showing them the folly of intemperance ... Similarly this work is meant to set forth the merits of correctness in English composition by furnishing examples of the demerits of incorrectness.'[28] But is example better than precept? Examples are most useful when they are marshalled in support of an argument, not when they stand alone. Hodgson's book leads students to be more familiar with mistakes than their opposites. There is a risk that instead of avoiding errors readers will replicate them, having absorbed them by osmosis.

Students were certainly made to learn Lowth's Grammar. They were expected to memorize the rules and then recite them. Ditto the examples. William Cobbett, whom I have a couple of times mentioned in passing, chose to do this while a soldier garrisoned at Chatham. Awaiting posting to Canada, he copied Lowth out, learnt the text by heart, and then recited it while on sentry duty. The experience informed Cobbett's *A Grammar of the English Language*, which he published in New York in 1818 and in London the following year. This volume consisted of letters written to his teenage son James Paul, and its declared audience was 'Schools and . . . Young Persons in general; but, more especially . . . Soldiers, Sailors, Apprentices, and Plough-boys'. Cobbett mentions Lowth several times; he appears keen to shrug off his influence.

Johnson and Lowth mark the beginning of a period in which the style of written English becomes noticeably more formal. Characterizing this formality, H. G. Wells wrote that at that time 'one's natural hair with its vagaries of rat's tails, duck's tails, errant curls, and baldness, gave place to an orderly wig, or was at least decently powdered. The hoop remedied the deficiencies of the feminine form, and the gardener clipped his yews into respectability. All poetry was written to one measure in those days, and a Royal Academy with a lady member was inaugurated that art might become at least decent. Dictionaries began. The crowning glory of Hanoverian literature was a Great Lexicographer.'[29] Wells's picture is intended to be mischievous, and not all his facts are straight, but his assessment has a provocative appeal.

Certainly there was a heightened attention to the craft involved in using English effectively, and self-consciousness about the writer's art gave rise to a style that was often pompous, elaborate and abstract. Whereas Swift tends to seem cleverly conversational, serious writers in the second half of the eighteenth century appear intent on sounding more decorous. Their prose is fussy. For Hugh Blair, any writer who used a large number of everyday words degraded his arguments; verbal ornaments created an air of dignity. Vocabulary became more courtly and genteel. Johnson in his periodical essays, especially for *The Rambler*, used 'philosophic words' which he thought had not been tarnished by daily use. The *OED* suggests that *colloquial* became a term of disapproval in the 1750s; its first authority for this sense is Johnson in *The Rambler*. In his pieces for periodicals and his longer prose works, Johnson constructed his arguments with the balanced precision of an architect. His style embodied the grammarians' preference in written English for parallelism, explicitness and an avoidance of the casual and the chatty.[30]

For many, though, there were more immediate concerns than how best to write: none more so than the snob value of having a good speaking voice and – among the merchant class – expressing oneself in a manner appropriate to commerce. One's pronunciation was evidence of the company one kept. Thomas Sheridan the younger, of whom we shall later see a good deal more, insisted that his daughters read him long passages from the works of Dr Johnson. He would then correct their faults. Sensitivity to such matters was more acute in the middle portion of society than at either of its extremes. The actor John Philip Kemble, asked by George III if he would 'obleedge' him with a pinch of his snuff, is alleged to have replied, 'With pleasure, your Majesty; but it would become your royal lips much better to say "oblige".'[31]

The period's one descriptive voice belonged to Joseph Priestley – or such, at least, is the conventional wisdom. A theologian, educationalist, political reformer, historian of science and prolific pamphleteer, he is today known mainly as an experimental chemist; among other things he discovered oxygen, which he none too catchily called 'dephlogisticated air'. Priestley's unorthodoxy in political and religious matters, which had prevented him from attending a leading university, later imperilled his career in the Church. In 1766, aged thirty-three, he was elected a Fellow of the Royal Society, but his polemical works on political and theological questions made him a controversial figure, and his support for the Revolution in France caused riots in Birmingham, where he presided over a dissenting congregation. His reaction was to accept French citizen-ship, which hardly improved his public image. Shunned and fearful for the welfare of his children, he emigrated to America in 1794, settling in Northumberland, Pennsylvania.

In his views on language Priestley was at odds with most of his contemporaries. His thinking was inconsistent, but he was committed to examining usage, and drew his findings from the data that appeared to him, rather than starting with a thesis and then looking for the data to support it. His short book *The Rudiments of English Grammar* (1761) was the result of his experiences teaching grammar at a school he ran at Nantwich in Cheshire. Priestley insisted that there could be no institution to lay down a standard for correct English. 'As to a publick *Academy*,' he wrote in his preface, 'I think it not only unsuitable to the genius of a *free nation*, but in itself ill calcu-lated to reform and fix a language. We need make no doubt but that the best forms of speech will, in time, establish themselves by their own superior excellence: and, in all controversies, it is better to wait the decisions of *Time*, which are slow and sure, than to take those of *Synods*, which are often hasty and injudicious.'[32]

As Priestley saw it, custom was 'all-governing'. Where there were two different ways of approaching a linguistic problem, the democ-racy of common usage would eventually decide in favour of one. Moreover, in matters of style there was room for 'infinite diversity': 'every man hath some peculiarity in his manner ... [and] likewise, hath every man a peculiar manner of conceiving things, and expressing his thoughts, which, were he so fortunate as to hit upon subjects adapted to his genius, would not want propriety or beauty.'[33] Priestley also had a dig at the efforts of his predecessors and rivals, remarking that some were 'clogged with superfluous words'; their materials had not been 'regularly and thoroughly digested', and their rules often did 'not correspond with the present state of the language, as it is actu-ally spoken and written'. As for exemplifying the grungy realities of current usage, it struck Priestley that an appendix showing samples of *'bad English'* would be 'really useful', but for the fact that these sloppy sentences would 'make so uncouth an appearance in print'.[34]

However, when Priestley produced a second edition of *The Rudi-ments of English Grammar* in 1768, it was noticeably different. Whereas in 1761 his introduction strikes a positive note, seven years later he is downbeat and sees that making sense of English grammar is a bigger task than he originally believed. He is uncomfortably aware of the success of Lowth, whose *Short Introduction* was published soon after the first edition of *The Rudiments of English Grammar*. Reading Lowth made Priestley question his own thinking.[35] In the 1768 edition Priestley writes, 'I must . . . acknowledge my obligation to *Dr Lowth* . . . It is from an amicable union of labours . . . that we may most reasonably expect the extension of all kinds of knowledge.'[36] Lowth in the many editions of the *Short Introduction* never says anything about Priestley, and this 'amicable union of labours' was a fantasy.

It would be wrong to think of Priestley as a purely descriptive observer of English. He frequently says what forms people 'must' or 'should' use – more rigid expressions than Lowth's preferred 'ought to'.[37] He repeatedly uses the words 'proper' and 'propriety'. Yet Priestley has a generosity of tone that is not evident in Lowth's *Short Introduction*, and he says with a kind of genial resignation that 'Language partakes much of the nature of *art*, and but little of the nature of science'.[38]

Johnson, Lowth and Priestley had different values, but their endeavours contributed to a change in the idea of what it meant to use English. The experience involved a new self-awareness. Uniform pronunciation, it was felt, could empower a sense of shared British identity. All the while, of course, the drive towards uniformity had the effect of highlighting the diversity of accents and the divisions within society. That diversity is a subject to which we shall return. But first it is time to move to a different arena, and, by way of introduction, I dangle two reported remarks of Johnson's: 'I am willing to love all mankind, except an American', and 'Sir, they are a race of convicts, and ought to be thankful for any thing we allow them short of hanging.'

9 O my America,
my new found land!

From Thomas Paine to Shredded Wheat

In 1752 a writer in the *Gentleman's Magazine* mentioned 'a fair American' and then explained that 'by an American I do not mean an Indian, but one descended of British parents born in America'.[1] The clarification is striking. To a British audience at that time, the definition of an 'American' was hazy. The term had once been used exclusively of native American Indians, before becoming blurred by its use – as in the *Gentleman's Magazine* – of the descendants of British settlers. However, during the Seven Years War of 1756–63 British views of American life sharpened; native American Indians fought alongside the British against the colonists, and it became more common to apply the label 'American' not to the indigenous peoples, but to the rebellious white colonial subjects. This new denomination reflected a change in the political climate.

The revolution that achieved American independence in 1776 was a challenge to British language as well as to British government. Until that challenge emerged, there was no notion of British English; British English was just called English. The move for American independence began not only as a war of words, but as a war about words. On the American side, figures such as Samuel Adams and Daniel Dulany, inspired by their reading of John Locke's political writings, complained bitterly of the abuse of words by their geographically remote masters. Reviewing their efforts, Thomas Gustafson has described how this led to 'a rejection of the King's English for a new discourse . . . more faithful to common sense and the language of nature' and ultimately to 'the toppling of a mother tongue . . . to achieve a new science of politics'.[2] Some of the keywords in these arguments were *liberty, equality, taxation, tyranny* and *representation*, and these repeatedly animated public orations, sermons and pamphlets.

It is significant that Benjamin Franklin, one of the architects of American statehood, was a printer and newspaperman, for the printing press was as important as any other weapon in the American revolution. Before the violence, there was rhetoric. Writing sowed the seeds of revolution, and it brought together stories about the injustices of British rule. The American revolutionaries used a language that was fundamentally the same as that of the people they fought – by no means a norm of revolutions – and preliminary arguments about the rights of the American people were presented in pamphlets and newspaper articles that could be read by both parties.

The writings of James Otis, Richard Bland, John Dickinson and Thomas Jefferson expressed a growing sense of crisis in the 1760s and '70s. The discussion of this crisis often used the word *rights*, and the understanding of that word was shaped by John Locke's *Two Treatises of Government* (1689). Locke had argued that all people have the right to liberty and property, as well as suggesting that governments that do not nurture the public good can be replaced. The Declaration of Independence would eventually enshrine Locke's principles; rather than being a sudden thunderbolt of political imagination, it was the culmination of a series of documents presenting American grievances and aspirations. It was also the apotheosis of the revolutionaries' eloquent campaign of persuasion and proclamation.

The fiercest exponent of American rights was Thomas Paine. A native of Norfolk, Paine emigrated to America in 1774, having in his first thirty-seven years failed at pretty much everything he had tried – even at being a tobacconist. Yet less than two years after his arrival he published *Common Sense*, a demand for American independence which sold in excess of 150,000 copies within three months. Paine fought passionately for the American cause, and *Common Sense* was hugely influential, not least because its insistent style was so different from the familiar language of political argument. 'We have it in our power to begin the world over again,' he wrote. 'The birth-day of a new world is at hand . . . Let the names of Whig and Tory be extinct; and let none other be heard among us, than those of *a good citizen*,

*an open and resolute friend, and a virtuous supporter of the RIGHTS of
MANKIND and of the FREE AND INDEPENDANT [sic] STATES
OF AMERICA.'*³

Fifteen years later, in his *Rights of Man*, Paine could reflect on
events and say, 'The American constitutions were to liberty, what a
grammar is to language.' In creating liberty, the role of constitutions
is to 'define its parts of speech, and practically construct them into
syntax'.⁴ Paine sees language as a means of achieving political repression. 'The punyism of a senseless word like *Duke*' is divisive; the existence of titles 'contract[s] the sphere of a man's felicity', and he 'lives
immured within the Bastille of a word, and surveys at a distance the
envied life of man'.⁵ Paine carved a passage through the fog of political grandiloquence. The vocabulary of the established political order
was made to look preposterously antique.

A politically independent United States needed to claim its
linguistic independence, and this process began before Paine entered
the fray. An anonymous author in 1774 proposed the foundation of
an American Society of Language, claiming that 'The English
language has been greatly improved in Britain within a century, but
its highest perfection, with every other branch of human knowledge, is perhaps reserved for this LAND of light and freedom. As
the people through this extensive country will speak English, their
advantages for polishing their language will be great, and vastly superior to what the people in England ever enjoyed.'⁶ These words
appeared in a letter addressed 'To the Literati of America'. It may
well have been written by John Adams, later to be the second
President of the United States.

Whoever the author was, he was reflecting on more than 150 years
of American English. Many of the people who sailed to America saw
their journey as an opportunity to forge a distinct identity. They
brought with them the pronunciations and vocabulary of their day,
which, in their new environment, survived linguistic changes that
were happening back in Britain. The result was a form of English
that struck British observers as archaic. Besides this, their use of English
was shaped by contact with native American Indians, as well as with
other settlers who spoke French, Dutch, German or Spanish. Their
new circumstances gave rise to new experiences and behaviours. Today,

if we compare the vocabularies of British English and American English, we see obvious differences in areas such as food, schooling, transportation, wildlife, shopping and basic household articles. These began early.

The first person to comment in print that a word meant different things on the two sides of the Atlantic was John Josselyn in 1663, when he noted that in America the noun *ordinary* meant a tavern, whereas in England it denoted a boarding house. Later commentators saw a large and growing difference between the two forms of the language, and saw also regional disparities within the American word-stock. In the 1750s Benjamin Franklin remarked on the existence of expressions that were peculiar to one colony and unintelligible to others; he was a Bostonian transplanted to Pennsylvania and spoke from his own awkward experience.[7]

The word *Americanism* was coined in 1781 by John Witherspoon, a Scot who had thirteen years previously arrived at Princeton to be president of the Presbyterian College of New Jersey. The idea that such a thing existed was older. Settlers in America had been adding to the English language since the early seventeenth century, borrowing terms and coining new ones to denote their new ways of life. H. L. Mencken, in his huge book *The American Language*, declares that 'The early Americans showed that spacious disregard for linguistic nicety which has characterized their descendants ever since'. He mentions as examples of this their turning 'verbs into nouns, nouns into verbs, and adjectives into either or both'. Meanings altered, some words held on far longer than they did in Britain, and Americans revealed a 'superior imaginativeness . . . in meeting linguistic emergencies'.[8] The differences attracted comment. In 1754 Richard Owen Cambridge proposed that Johnson's *Dictionary*, the publication of which was looming, should be supplemented with a list of terms peculiar to the American colonies. No supplement appeared, but Johnson did define *currency* as 'The papers stamped in the English colonies by authority, and passing for money' – a nod to what was then an American term, used by Benjamin Franklin as long ago as 1729. Those hoping for an exhibition of the disparities in vocabulary had to wait until 1816, when John Pickering published the first book-length collection of Americanisms. Examples of his haul included *backwoodsmen, to deputize, to graduate* and *package*. Pickering was not celebrating these words. Instead he was trying to narrow the gap between British and American forms of English, by providing a guide to the words that might prevent a British reader from making sense of an American book. He was explicit that Americanisms were not part of 'correct English'.

Travellers observed not only the words unique to America, but also an American style of speech. In 1796 Thomas Twining noted that 'An American speaks English with the volubility of a Frenchman'.[9] British visitors frequently remarked on the strange accents and surfeit of profanity they heard there. Mencken notes that *bloody* and *bugger* have not in America been the indecent terms that they long were in Britain, and quotes Jonathan Boucher, an English clergyman writing home from Maryland in 1759, who observed that visitors were forced 'to hear obscene conceits and broad expressions, and from this there are times w[he]n no sex, no rank, no conduct can exempt you'.[10] Then again, the reverse applied; prosperous Americans visiting Britain were alarmed by the noxious vulgarism of working-class Londoners and bemused by the clipped diction of their social betters.

Conscious of the potential for a fragmented America, Benjamin Franklin saw mass education as the key to achieving what he called 'the happiness both of private families and of commonwealths' – a united community. Beginning in the 1730s, he addressed this by developing subscription libraries, improving news services, exhorting his countrymen to build academies, suggesting social innovations such as the idea of 'generalized reciprocity' (summed up in the expression 'pay it forward'), and popularizing science. Language was important in all of this: America was to be Eden, not Babel.

The early American settlers had used in the classroom textbooks published in England. Thomas Dilworth's *A New Guide to the English Tongue* (1740) was, in the second half of the eighteenth century, the most widely used spelling book on both sides of the Atlantic. Its first American printing was by Franklin, and more than a hundred editions printed before 1800 have survived. The temper of Dilworth's book is careful and boring, and generations of schoolchildren defaced the frontispiece portrait of him – a phenomenon to which Dickens alludes in *Sketches by Boz*. Dilworth included sentences to be transcribed by young students, and these were decidedly moralistic: 'It is a commendable Thing for a Boy to apply his Mind to the Study of good Letters', 'Pride is a very remarkable Sin', 'Personal Merit is all a Man can call his own', 'Riches are like Dung, which stink in an Heap; but being spread abroad, make the Earth fruitful'.[11]

In time, it became clear that imported models such as Dilworth's were inadequate. A home-grown scheme of education in English was needed. Perhaps, indeed, the very fabric of the language needed re-fashioning. In 1780 John Adams argued before Congress that an institution be set up 'for refining, improving, and ascertaining the English language'. Two of the three verbs were Swift's from nearly seventy years before; Adams pictured an American Academy. A Congressional commission scotched the idea – surely it was not the job of polit-icians to mandate people's choice of language? – but the debate continued. Crucially, there was disagreement about where the national standard should be sought. In one camp were those, like Adams, who emphasized the need for linguistic independence from Britain; Adams even went so far as to suggest that a special tax be imposed on British dictionaries. In the other camp were figures such as John Pickering, who argued that English in America should be protected in order to stop it diverging from the norms of British usage.

The status of English as the language of the emergent nation was not assured. At the time of the revolution, English was the first language of rather less than half its people. Spanish and French were in wide use. In Pennsylvania the majority spoke German. Today the only speakers of Pennsylvania German are small communities of Amish and Old Order Mennonites, numbering perhaps 80,000. In the 1750s, though, Benjamin Franklin noted with alarm that English-speakers were outnumbered in that state. Unsure of the country's linguistic future, Thomas Jefferson advised his daughters to become skilled in languages besides English. Benjamin Rush, like Jefferson and Adams a signatory of the Declaration of Independence, urged a full embrace of multilin-gualism. Politicians stressed the importance of liberty: to insist on the primacy of English was exactly the kind of monarchical attitude that the revolutionaries had fought to shrug off. Beginning in the 1790s, America's silver coins bore the motto 'E pluribus unum' – 'Out of many, one' – which suggested political unity while also acknowledging the diversity of the elements from which this unity was being assembled.

In practice, that diversity was often treated in cavalier fashion. The nineteenth-century expansion of the United States was achieved through land purchases but also through war. It is easy to speak briskly of the purchase of the Louisiana territory from the French and much later of Alaska from the Russian Empire, the incursions into Florida, the cascade of westward settlement into Oregon, the annexing of Texas, and the acquisition of land from Mexico, without considering the impact of such events on the people whose homes lay in these territories. Easy, furthermore, to acknowledge but not scrutinize the agonies involved in the seizure of Indian lands and the large-scale importation of slaves. Tellingly, the Bureau of Indian Affairs was from 1824 to 1849 part of the government's Department of War, and Andrew Jackson, the seventh President, in 1830 began a policy known as 'Indian removal'. The term 'Manifest Destiny', coined by John O'Sullivan's *Democratic Review* in 1845, memorably suggests the expansionists' sense of entitlement. The article that announced it spoke of Mexico as an 'imbecile', and triumphantly declared that annexing Texas and California was the fulfilment of a grand scheme to 'overspread the continent allotted by Providence for the free development of our yearly multiplying millions'. Victory was inevitable: 'The Anglo-Saxon foot is already on its borders. Already the advance guard of the irresistible army of Anglo-Saxon emigration has begun to pour down upon it, armed with the plough and the rifle.'[12]

Amid the expansion of the Union, English was never accorded official status. Instead it fell to individuals to reinforce its position. The most significant player was Noah Webster, an indefatigable campaigner for a national language – an American English that would exemplify American independence. For Webster, a man as patriotic as he was bookish, the canonization of American English also promised to recapture the spirit of excellence that he felt English had lost during the previous century or so of fashion and foppery.

Webster was a descendant of William Bradford, who had governed the Plymouth Colony from 1621 to 1651, and of John Webster, who had briefly governed Connecticut in the 1650s. Nonetheless, he saw himself as an example of the pious striver who rises to fame despite humble beginnings. This was not grossly inaccurate – for instance, his father had needed to mortgage the family farm to pay for him to be prepared by a tutor for his entrance to Yale – but Webster cultivated fine myths about himself. A committed Anglophobe, he insisted that his main intention was to promote the honour of his own country. His writings suggest that he was at least as eager to promote himself. In March 1784 he wrote to Samuel Adams, then recognized as one of America's chief political visionaries, opening his letter with the words: 'The importance of this communication will, I flatter myself, be sufficient apology for the freedom I take of writing to a gentleman with whom I have not the honor of an acquaintance'.[13]

The desire to outstrip other language experts galvanized Webster. He wanted to improve on the efforts of Samuel Johnson, Lindley Murray and Thomas Dilworth. Murray above all was a goad: Webster's contempt for him and conviction that Murray was forever stealing his ideas inspired him to ever more fastidious exertions, which bordered on the paranoid. He published essays and pamphlets denouncing Murray – some of them pseudonymous, and repetitive – as well as placing advertisements in newspapers to promote his own efforts, giving his books to schools, using agents to act for him, and energetically delivering public lectures in his apparently squeaky voice.[14]

But first Webster smacked down Dilworth. Although his *A Grammatical Institute of the English Language* (1783–5) was little more than a reworking of Dilworth's *A New Guide to the English Tongue*, Webster made a point of trashing Dilworth's book, damning it as 'most imperfect' and full of 'monstrous absurdities'. Dilworth's exposition of grammar, he claimed, was 'worse than none' and 'calculated to lead into errour'. 'The only circumstance that renders it tolerably harmless, is that it is very little used and still less understood.' Dilworth's vice is to found his grammar 'entirely upon the principles of the *Latin* language'.[15]

In his numerous subsequent publications Webster rammed home what he considered his revolutionary credentials. His *Dissertations on the English Language*, published in the year of the French Revolution and dedicated to Benjamin Franklin, was a collection of the lectures he gave during a thirteen-month tour of his country in 1785 and '86. Earnest and occasionally amusing, it reflected his wide knowledge of existing theories and his capacity for pugnacious controversy. Webster trumpeted his democratic philosophy, declaring that

'The *general practice* of a nation is the rule of propriety'.[16] He cast himself as a heroic figure, a defender of his people's rights, massively different from the British philologists who doled out laws in the manner of tyrants. 'The people are right,' he averred, and 'common practice is generally defensible'.[17] Yet Webster was no meek describer of American usage; he had his own clear ideas, coloured by his New England background, of how it should be codified.

Webster was deeply concerned with spelling. He set out the basics in *A Grammatical Institute*, the first part of which was issued in a revised edition, with the catchier title *The American Spelling Book*, in 1787. This became known as the 'Blue-Backed Speller', on account of its blue cover. Over the next forty years, roughly ten million copies of it were printed; only the Bible sold in comparable quantities, and eventually its sales totalled 100 million. Webster presented his ideas for reform in an appendix to his *Dissertations*, proposing to do away with superfluous or silent letters – the *a* in *bread*, the *i* in *friend* – and amend spellings to clarify pronunciation – *key* becoming *kee*, *believe* becoming *beleev*, and *arkitecture* superseding *architecture*, for example. He preferred *laf* to *laugh, tuf* to *tough*, and *blud* to *blood*. Words derived from French should lose their French look: *oblique*, for instance, should be *obleek*, and *machine* should be *masheen*.[18] Later, he suggested other revised spellings, including *ieland* instead of *island* (the latter was 'an absurd compound ... found only in books') and *bridegoom*, which was preferable to *bridegroom* ('a gross corruption or blunder') on the grounds that the Saxon root was *brydguma*, a compound of the words for 'bride' and 'man'.

Many of Webster's other modifications were taken up. He was unhappy to see English words 'clothed with the French livery' and defiled with superfluous letters. It is thanks to Webster that users of English no longer write *public* with a *k* at the end, are consistent in ending 'agent substantives' such as *tailor, conqueror, donor* or *censor* with *-or* rather than *-our* (exceptions are *saviour* and the comparatively little-used *paviour*), write *cider* rather than *cyder*, and tend to prefer *connection* to *connexion*. Among the spellings he introduced that have not caught on outside North America but have become standard there are *ax, jewelry* and *theater*. He can also be credited with the well-known American preference for *color, odor, humor* and *labor*. His quirkier ideas notwithstanding, Webster has to rank as one of the most successful reformers of spelling.

Webster spent most of his adult life studying language and preaching about it. The culmination of this was his two-volume *An American Dictionary of the English Language*, published in 1828. Building on the earlier *A Compendious Dictionary of the English Language* (1806), in which he had recorded 5,000 words undocumented in existing dictionaries, his *American Dictionary* cemented his reformed spellings. It also represented his attempt once and for all to supersede the authority of Dr Johnson. The Englishman's writings, and his *Dictionary* especially, were ubiquitous in America by the end of the eighteenth century, and doubtless quite a few of those who consulted the *Dictionary* noticed the absence of the words *America* and *American*. Whereas Webster held Murray and Dilworth in contempt, he had respect for Johnson. But he was at pains to replace Johnson's vision of English with his own American vision.

Achieving this was less a matter of eradicating all trace of Johnson than of amending and expanding his efforts. So, Webster offered detailed definitions, but some of these were lifted straight from Johnson, and, although a smattering of his illustrative quotations came from books by American authors, he mainly followed Johnson's selection of authors. Like Johnson, he imbued his dictionary with morality. His particular brand of Christianity was strongly in evidence, as it was five years later when he published a translation of the Bible, principally notable because of his decision to expunge 'vulgarities': he removed the words 'womb' and 'teat', altered 'fornication' to 'lewdness', and replaced 'give suck' with 'nourish'.

An American Dictionary of the English Language was not an immediate success. At $20 it was beyond the reach of many who would have liked to own it. Soon, too, there came a rival publication. This was the work of Joseph Worcester, a native of New Hampshire who had assisted with the production of Webster's dictionary and had gone on to publish an abridgement of it, before in 1830 producing his own *A Comprehensive Pronouncing and Explanatory Dictionary of the English Language*. Aimed mainly at schoolchildren, it was notable for its careful guide to how words should be sounded; unlike Webster, who simply favoured the prevailing style of New England, Worcester recognized variations in pronunciation. He had many supporters, because he was less preoccupied with etymology, provided nicely condensed definitions, and seemed more moderate and less prescriptive. Improved versions of the 1830 dictionary followed in 1846 and 1860. The former defined over 83,000 words, which was 13,000 more than Webster; the 1860 dictionary defined 104,000. Moreover, Worcester was scrupulous about acknowledging his debts to the many lexicographers who had preceded him. Others were more relaxed about such matters: one devious London publisher, Henry Bohn, went so far as to publish Worcester's dictionary while presenting it on the title page as 'compiled from the materials of Noah Webster' and printing on the spine both names – with Webster's first.

When Noah Webster died in 1843, the Springfield firm of George and Charles Merriam took over the Webster brand, determined to keep it alive. The success of Worcester inspired them to bring out updated versions of *An American Dictionary of the English Language*. The competition was good for the public: better dictionaries were produced. In 1864 an extensively revised edition of Webster by a German philologist, Carl Mahn, included 3,000 pictorial illustrations. By then Worcester was eighty: there was little chance of his trumping this new work, and when he died the following year the victory for Webster's camp was sealed. The Webster dictionary of 1864 was very different from the one presented in 1828. But it preserved his name, while Worcester's faded into obscurity.

Although *An American Dictionary of the English Language* ranks as Webster's most impressive achievement, his key statements regarding his mission were made early in his career. In *A Grammatical Institute* he declared, 'This country must in some future time, be as distinguished by the superiority of her literary improvements, as she is already by the liberality of her civil and ecclesiastical constitutions.' He condemned Europe as 'grown old in folly, corruption and tyranny', and argued that 'It is the business of *Americans* to select the wisdom of all nations, as the basis of her constitutions . . . [and] to diffuse an uniformity and purity of *language*, – to add superiour dignity to this infant Empire and to human nature.'[19] In the *Dissertations* Webster stated, 'As an independent nation, our honor requires us to have a system of our own, in language as well as government. Great Britain, whose children we are, and whose language we speak, should no longer be *our* standard; for the taste of her writers is already corrupted, and her language on the decline.'[20] This image of a parent-child relationship was an important part of the rhetoric of the American revolution: the child was acting to throw off the control of a despotic parent, but, once this was achieved, the self-styled Sons of Liberty recast themselves as Founding Fathers.

In his dictionary Webster defines *Americanism* as 'an American idiom'. Before that, though, he identifies what he takes to be its primary sense: 'The love which American citizens have to their own country, or the preference of its interests.' Webster's most enduring achievement was to tighten the connection between the English language and 'American-ness'. He stimulated visions of this connection, too. Emily Dickinson claimed that her copy of *An American Dictionary of the English Language* was for a long time her only companion, and was impressed by the idea that the words she found there were bundles of energy, as well as by Webster's sense that verbs were the great drivers of self-expression. In Herman Melville's *Moby-Dick*, Webster's dictionary is rather differently treated. It is described as an 'ark', but the narrator states that when it has been necessary to consult a dictionary 'I have invariably used a huge quarto edition of Johnson, expressly purchased for that purpose; because that famous lexicographer's uncommon personal bulk more fitted him to compile a lexicon to be used by a whale author like me.'

The distinct characters of the dictionaries compiled by Johnson and Webster were discussed in a work that encapsulated the period's mania for grammatical wrangling. This was *The Grammar of English Grammars*, published in 1851 by Goold Brown, a native of Rhode Island. Its title is a clue to its scale and density: 1,028 closely printed pages, the fruits of three decades spent immersed in grammatical exercises. Brown is the sort of writer who takes acid pleasure in pointing out the grammatical lapses in Shakespeare. He condemned Webster as a friend of illiteracy, and claimed that Webster's notions of grammar were fit only to be despised. He is also responsible for the enduring notion – discussed by Dr Johnson, though not observed by him in practice – that one shares something *between* two people, but *among* more than two.

If Webster embodies what we might call the schoolmasterly tradition in American English, and if Goold Brown is the king of the fault-
finders, Walt Whitman is the most eloquent advocate of a more fluid,
experimental approach. This is nicely exemplified in his poetry by an
apparent addiction to the present participle – a 'springboard' he uses
to enable 'physical and intellectual mobility'.[21] Many of his poems
begin in this way, with a word such as 'starting', 'chanting', 'singing'
or 'facing'. As a poet Whitman is orator, actor, egotist, egalitarian –
flush with himself, flush with his Americanness. Yet when he writes
explicitly about the language which he uses to dramatize his thoughts,
he reveals a tension with which we are all too familiar: on the one
hand he is keen to celebrate the elasticity of English, yet on the other
he wishes to reform the language and render it more precise. Sump-
tuously unsystematic, Whitman relishes the freedoms of language but
proposes to circumscribe them.

Starting around 1856, Whitman kept a scrapbook of jottings about
English and other languages. This included words he relished or found
intriguing (*monolith*, *centurion*, *vendetta*), morsels of history, observations
on pronunciation, and a dig at Webster's 'stiff-necked obstinacy'.[22] At
one point he writes, 'Johnson's Dictionary First pub. 1755 (was this
first good dictionary of English?).' He later answers the question: 'O
no.'[23] He criticizes Lindley Murray, too. These men's apparently narrow
views of the language left little room for the vitality and voluntari-
ness of imaginative writing.

Between 1855 and 1860 Whitman collected notes for a lecture he
never in fact gave, the subject of which was 'the growth of an American English enjoying a distinct identity'. An essay on American slang,
published in 1885, continued his interest in how 'words become vital-
iz'd'. Slang, he thought, was 'the lawless ... element ... behind all
poetry' and also 'an attempt of common humanity to escape from
bald literalism'. Whitman wished to bring into literature a previously
undocumented language of everyday life and labour, for 'around the
markets, among the fish-smacks, along the wharves, you hear a thousand words, never yet printed in the repertoire of any lexicon.' The
result, as we already begin to see in this sentence, is an affection for
lists. Whitman's writing suggests their musical quality, breaking the
boundary between prose and poetry, and he saw lists as a tribute to

something he believed essentially American – the honour of hard work and practical labour.[24] Whitman's vision of American English is of a language incorporating many voices, many idioms and many images of his country.

This is most fully articulated in *An American Primer*, which Whitman wrote in the 1850s. There he asserted that 'The Americans are going to be the most fluent and melodious voiced people in the world – the most perfect users of words'. As if to prove this, he wrote fluently and melodiously of how 'In America an immense number of new words are needed, to embody the new political facts . . . stating all that is to be said in modes that fit the life and experience of the Indianian, the Michiganian, the Vermonter, the men of Maine – also words to answer the modern, rapidly spreading, faith, of the vital equality of women with men . . . Words are wanted to supply the copious trains of facts, and flanges of facts, arguments, and adjectival facts, growing out of all new knowledges.' He promised, 'Never will I allude to the English Language or tongue without exultation. This is the tongue that spurns laws.'[25]

In their different ways, Whitman and Webster were groping towards a national language. American English and the debates surrounding it proved a meeting place for expressions of democracy, pragmatism and poetry. Whitman approves the copiousness of American English – its breadth and inclusiveness, its expansion, its fecundity. When he looks to the future he sees the rottenness of political language giving way to a choir of different voices, many of them emerging from hitherto neglected places. He says that 'The nigger dialect furnishes hundreds of outré words, many of them adopted into the common speech of the mass of the people' and 'The nigger dialect has hints of the future theory of the modification of all the words of the English language, for musical purposes, for a native grand opera in America.'[26] His use of the now odious word *nigger* should not distract us from his prescience in seeing the important role of black Americans in shaping American English.

Whitman was in fact a favourite author in the lyceums where elocution and rhetorical instruction helped increase black literacy. The first African-American society for self-improvement was probably the African Union Society at Newport, Rhode Island, founded in 1780.

Similar societies in New York and Philadelphia organized circulating libraries, concerts and scientific lectures. Their membership was in some cases exclusively male, but Philadelphia's Gilbert Lyceum was the first of many societies to admit both men and women. On the plantations, among black slaves, there was what Ralph Ellison would later call 'free-floating literacy', aided by preachers and Christian missionaries. During the Civil War of 1861–5, camp life fostered the art of debating and communal education. There were newspapers specifically aimed at the black troops, and after the Civil War ended some black workers in factories were able to hear newspapers and novels performed by lectors. Towards the end of the century there was a flowering of black self-help literature, with titles such as *Sparkling Gems of Race Knowledge Worth Reading*, and there was also a vibrant African-American press, inspired by the example of Frederick Douglass and the abolitionist newspapers he produced in the 1840s.[27]

Where Whitman sought to see all the voices of America as part of a single opera, where Douglass argued that the abolition of slavery could be achieved by working within the existing political system and using strong language rather than new language, and where Alexis de Tocqueville in his *Democracy in America* (1838) simply played down the idea that American speech contained great variety, the distinct strands of American English were exaggerated in the arguments that led up to the Civil War. This was a conflict in which notions of the American national character were at stake, and the two sides highlighted their linguistic differences. Both professed to be fighting for freedom, but each mocked the other's idea of what this meant. Significantly, the very name of the conflict was contentious, and remains so. The Civil War is still known to some Southerners as the War of Northern Aggression, and less provocatively as the War for Southern Independence. The War Between the States has also achieved some currency. Most of the names for the conflict manifest a clear point of view: Southerners have referred to it as the Defence of Virginia, Northerners as the War of the Rebellion. Moreover, the two forces were known by many different names – the Northerners were the Union, Yankees, the National Armies and Federals, while the Southerners were Rebels, Dixie and the Confederacy; in epitome, Billy Yank and Johnny Reb – and they gave different names to the battles they fought.

At the same time, as in any war, there developed a vibrant mili-tary slang. Soldiers 'amused the enemy' – that is, kept them occupied without going so far as to provoke a full-blooded battle – and 'saw the elephant' – in other words, gained experience of combat. Spies were euphemistically known as 'guides', lice as 'crumbs', inexperi-enced soldiers as 'veal'. A man described as 'going down the line' had actually slunk off to a brothel (where he risked picking up what were known as 'diseases of indulgence'), while 'to fire and fall back' was slang for vomiting. A significant part of Civil War slang had to do not with fighting, but with avoiding it. Many soldiers 'played off' – pretended to be sick, feigned tactical confusion, or simply deserted – when there was a strong chance of physical confrontation. There were numerous words for the shirkers: they were 'stragglers', 'skulkers', 'sneaks', 'coffee-coolers', 'bummers', 'whimperers'. Very few of the combatants had previous experience of war. They entered it light-heartedly, flourishing their good humour, yet with a sense of duty. Soon their attitudes changed. The linguistic legacy of the Civil War includes the words *carpetbagger*, *bull-doze*, *ante-bellum*, *double-quick* and *reconstruction*, as well as some striking euphemisms – the war was known as 'the late unpleasantness', and slavery as a 'peculiar institu-tion'.

In the period leading up to the Civil War, the word *disunion* had conjured up nightmares of factionalism. It was brandished threat-eningly – and accusingly. After the war, America was described in new terms. The word *union* was tarnished by its association with *disunion*, by its heavy use in the rhetoric of the North, and by its implication of a voluntary organization rather than something perpetual and indissoluble. As a result, *nation* replaced it. The shift was clear in the speeches of Abraham Lincoln; in his inaugural address in March 1861 he repeatedly invoked the Union and did not speak of the nation at all, whereas by the Gettysburg Address in November 1863 the position had reversed.[28] An attractive story, popularized by the historian Shelby Foote, is that before the Civil War one said, 'The United States are flourishing', whereas after it this changed to 'The United States is flourishing'. The reality is a little less neat. Only in 1902 did the House of Representatives' commission looking into legal revisions assert that in all official documentation the United States should be treated as singular. But the story nicely presents the role of language in reintegration. Grammar, as well as vocabulary, can mark changes in ideology.

One of the main changes that followed the Civil War was America's development into an urban society. Of course, this did not happen rapidly. But by the time of the 1920 census the United States was officially urban; the majority of its citizens lived in towns and cities. Between 1880 and 1920 the percentage of Americans living in cities nearly doubled.[29] As America celebrated its progress in the closing decades of the nineteenth century, political advances were less highly extolled than those in education, manufacturing and the exploitation of the country's natural resources. Chicago, rapidly emerging as the second largest American city, seemed to embody the new spirit. In his novel *Sister Carrie* (1900), Theodore Dreiser likened Chicago to 'a giant magnet, drawing to itself . . . the hopeful and the hopeless'. The city's magnetism, and the country's, was dramatized by the World's Columbian Exposition, staged in Chicago in 1893. This set out the wares of American prosperity: besides a hugely impressive display of electrical exhibits, visitors were introduced to Shredded Wheat, Juicy Fruit gum and Quaker Oats, as well as the first Ferris wheel and, thanks to Thomas Edison's Kinetoscope, moving pictures. The Columbian Exposition proved that the city was the new 'frontier'. Its motto, 'I will', hinted at an American future that would be deeply concerned with globalizing the nation's good image.

This good image has managed to travel widely: many have pictured – and still do picture – America as a land of opportunities and discoveries, enthusiasms and inventions, in love with success and endlessly supportive of aspiration, with a coolly and deliberately formed constitution that provides for equality, liberty and that most seductive of possibilities, the pursuit of happiness; a land of skyscrapers and wildernesses, jazz and rock music, cheerleaders and marching bands, blue jeans, soft drinks and dusty old baseball mitts. But it is matched by a bad image: of America as a land of rampant gun culture, hyperbole, synthetic pleasure, flag-waving militarism, obese donut-munchers, candyfloss sentimentality and religious fundamentalism, besotted with the idea of itself, and determined to foist its goods and its values on the whole of the rest of the world.

American English is treated as a repository of these attributes. It is stereotyped by speakers of British English as twangy and slangy; British English by Americans as cold and emasculated. The distinctive characters of the two forms are easily felt but hard to describe. There are differences in some spellings, pronunciations, everyday metaphors, greetings and the way people are addressed, the past tense of 'to get', the use of certain adverbs such as *directly* and *immediately*, the acceptability of particular exclamations and expletives, the preferred interjections (compare 'bloody hell', 'crikey', 'bugger me', 'not a bit of it' and 'hear, hear' – all British in flavour – with the palpably American 'uh huh'), and so on.[30] No one reading this book will be oblivious to this.

For all the obvious continuities between British and American Englishes, it is, unsurprisingly, the divergences that are remarked on. H. G. Wells wrote in *Mankind in the Making* (1903), 'People come upon ideas that they know no English to express, and strike out the new phrase in a fine burst of ignorant discovery. There are Americans in particular who are amazingly apt at this sort of thing. They take an enormous pride in the jargon they are perpetually increasing – they boast of it, they give exhibition performances in it, they seem to regard it as the culminating flower of their continental Republic – as though the Old World had never heard of shoddy.' Lest anyone think his hostility is directed mainly at Americans, Wells says, 'Let me assure them that, in our heavier way, we in this island are just as busy defiling our common inheritance. We can send a team of linguists to America, who will murder and misunderstand the language against any eleven the Americans may select.'[31]

One modern study of American English, by Zoltán Kövecses, suggests specific properties that make it noticeably different from British English: it is economical, regular, direct, democratic, tolerant, informal, prudish, inflated, inventive, imaginative and 'success-and action-oriented'.[32] While it probably can't be all these things at once, we can see here the legacy of Webster among others. More fundamentally, we can see the effects of a people forging for themselves a new world.

10 The long shadow
of Lindley Murray

The 'positive beauty' of pedantry
... and of slang

Noah Webster's influence in America was matched in Britain by that of Lindley Murray, a key figure so far mentioned only in passing. Murray was an American, who arrived in Britain under strange circumstances. From inauspicious beginnings, his writings rose to a position of almost freakish importance. Charles Monaghan, who has looked closely at Murray's sales figures, reports that his books shifted around 14 million copies in the first half of the nineteenth century. Only Webster sold more – and that by a margin of a few per cent. Murray's *English Reader*, a selection of prose and poetry, sold more than 6 million copies in America in the period up to 1850, despite containing not a single passage by an American author.[1] Yet whereas Murray was challenged in America by Webster, in Britain for a time he had no serious rival as a grammarian.

Lindley Murray's most significant work was his *English Grammar*, published in 1795. During the 1790s the production of grammar books reached industrial proportions. The market was crowded, yet each new volume was presented with a flourish of self-promotion. Writers tackling grammar, though they tended to insist on their ability to remedy old misunderstandings, were in fact comically obsessed with spotting one another's tiny errors, and often appeared torn between nostalgia for a more elegant Classical past and a desire to push forward into a brave new world of cool enquiry.[2]

Murray was not the only writer on language to enjoy great success in Britain at this time. John Walker's *A Critical Pronouncing Dictionary* went through more than a hundred editions between 1791 and 1904; its 547 'principles of English pronunciation' – for

instance, that '*Gigantic* has the *i* in the first syllable always long' and
'*S* is sharp and hissing at the end of the monosyllables *yes, this, us, thus, gas*' – were a triumph of scrupulous dogmatism, which led to
his being canonized in the popular imagination as 'Elocution Walker'.[3]
But Walker's subject matter was different from Murray's; the two
men were not in direct competition. Most other books about
language faded into oblivion: of Thomas Spence's *The Grand Repository of the English Language* (1775), a highly original guide to the
language aimed at 'the laborious part of the people', only two copies
survive. And there are other works of the period that look, to the
modern eye, utterly bizarre: a representative example is *The Way to
Things by Words, and to Words by Things* (1766), an attempt by John
Cleland, better known to posterity as the author of the erotic novel
Fanny Hill, to retrieve the ancient Celtic language.

The success of Lindley Murray, unlike that of Robert Lowth,
had little to do with socially advantageous connections. Murray was
born in Swatara, Pennsylvania, of mixed Irish and Quaker stock,
and served an apprenticeship to a Philadelphia merchant, before
practising law in New York and experimenting with the production of salt on a farm in Long Island. In 1784, shortly before he
turned forty, he moved to Britain. He was familiar with life there,
having spent some time in London in the late 1760s and early 1770s;
his family had at that time been developing a business partnership
with a London trader, Philip Sansom. Now, though, he relocated
for good. Murray later alleged that he made the move for the sake
of his health. However, it seems that the real reasons he left America
were grubbier. In 1775 the family business was guilty of illegally
importing goods – including eighty-four bolts of Russia duck, a
sailcloth – into New York, and an attempted cover-up turned public
opinion against the Murrays. Over the next few years, during the
American War of Independence, their London connections made
them targets for patriot intimidation, and Lindley Murray became
the scapegoat for their shadier transactions. This was a calculated
move to deflect attention from their main agent, his father Robert;
Lindley's removal to Britain probably helped quell accusations that
the whole Murray family was irrevocably loyalist in its sympathies,
enabling them to hold on to their business interests at a time when

many loyalists' properties were being confiscated. A reluctant exile, Murray settled in Holdgate, near York, where there was a community of Quakers. He would later claim in his memoirs that Yorkshire had been recommended by his doctor. This is doubtful, and, rather than enjoying improved health in his new home, he gradually succumbed to a number of ailments, including severe rheumatism.[4] For the remaining forty-two years of his life, he led a sedentary existence, cultivating some of the habits of an English gentleman.

Murray's career as an author of instructive books about language began successfully. The *English Grammar* was written for the benefit of the girls at Trinity Lane School in York, of which his wife Hannah was a proprietor. It went through more than fifty editions in its first thirty-seven years. Beginning with the fifth edition in 1799, it was published in London as well as in York, an abridged version having been issued in London the previous year. Murray followed *English Grammar* up with several more successes. His compact and neatly printed *English Spelling-book* of 1804, 'calculated to advance the learners by natural and easy gradations', had gone through forty-four editions by 1834. Murray's publications also found significant audiences abroad; the *English Grammar* was translated into numerous languages, including Russian, Spanish, French and Japanese, and its English editions were widely reprinted, from Dublin and Belfast to Calcutta and Bombay. A version for the blind was printed in New England in 1835, and John Betts of the Strand, a firm otherwise known mainly for its collapsible portable globe, produced a board game called 'A Journey to Lindley Murray's'.

The success of Murray's *English Grammar* had nothing to do with originality. Heavily reliant on the writings of Robert Lowth, as well as on Hugh Blair's *Lectures on Rhetoric*, it drew accusations of plagiarism. To counter this charge, Murray in later editions gave details of his sources. He never made much pretence of having new ideas. Others grammarians saw their role similarly, presenting themselves as compilers, not original thinkers. One contemporary, Peter Walkden Fogg, apologized for plundering much of his material from other books – 'my character in this undertaking is a mixture of the author and collector' – and then suggested rather oddly that his predecessors 'have been plagiarists to me', before claiming for himself 'the mitigating merit of Robin Hood, who took from the rich and gave to the poor'.[5]

For Murray, selectiveness was essential. Yet he could be steely in his prescriptivism; much of what he took from Lowth he stiffened, establishing rules where Lowth had registered tendencies. The central pillar of Murray's book is the section on syntax. This sets out twenty-two fundamental rules. For instance, Murray repeats Lowth's argument about double negatives; they 'destroy one another, or are equivalent to an affirmative'. He also states, none too elegantly, that 'All the parts of a sentence should correspond with each other, and a regular and dependent construction, throughout, be carefully preserved'.[6] Just occasionally he arrives at a rule with less certainty, as when he explains that 'We say rightly, either "This is the weaker of the two;" or "The weakest of the two:" but the former appears to be preferable, because there are only two things compared.'[7] Sticklers will agree with the final judgement, but will be surprised to see Murray allow 'The weakest of the two' as well.

Murray imagines a connection between proper syntax and moral rectitude. His names for what he considers the two fundamental principles of syntax are 'Concord' and 'Government', and when he explores the criteria of good writing, he emphasizes purity, propriety, precision, the 'unity' and 'strength' of sentences, and 'perspicuity', a quality previously stressed by Priestley and now characterized by Murray as 'positive beauty'. By 'purity' he says he means 'the use of such words or constructions as belong to the idiom of the language which we speak, in opposition to words . . . not English'. 'Propriety' involves avoiding 'low expressions' such as 'topsy turvy' and 'hurly burly'; ensuring we omit no words that are needed to make our sense clear and 'in the same sentence, avoid using the same word in different senses'; steering clear of baffling technical terms and ambiguities as well as 'unintelligible words and phrases' more generally; and avoiding 'in our words and phrases . . . all such as are not appropriated to the ideas we mean to express'. The perspicuous writer 'frees us from all fatigue of searching for his meaning', and his 'style flows always like a limpid stream, where we see to the very bottom'.[8]

Like Lowth, Murray displays errors, but the examples tend to be of his own invention, rather than lifted from famous authors. He is insistent about the difference between *will* and *shall* – frequently mixed up, so Noah Webster alleged, by the Irish and the Scots. '*Will*, in the first person singular and plural, intimates resolution and promising,' he writes, and 'in the second and third person, only foretells'. He gives as an example of the former, 'I will reward the good, and will punish the wicked', and of the latter, 'You or they will have a pleasant walk.' He then explains that '*Shall*, on the contrary, in the first person simply foretells; in the second and third persons, promises, commands, or threatens.' He exemplifies this with the sentences 'I shall go abroad' and 'They shall account for their misconduct.' Finally, '*Would*, primarily denotes inclination of will; and *should*, obligation.'⁹ As we know, these distinctions were not original to Murray, having been drawn by Wallis and by Lowth. But Murray made them stick. He also popularized spelling rules, such as 'Words ending with *y*, preceded by a consonant, form the plurals of nouns . . . by changing *y* into *i*; as, spy, spies', 'those words, which end with double *l*, and take *ness*, *less*, *ly* or *ful* after them, omit one *l*, as . . . skilful', and '*able* and *ible*, when incorporated into words ending with silent *e*, almost always cut it off; as cure . . ., curable . . . : but if *c* or *g* come before *e* in the original words, the *e* is then preserved; as, change, changeable; peace, peaceable'.¹⁰

Murray's work was often criticised – William Hazlitt being a notable detractor, partly because he had his own grammar textbook to boost – and was also satirized, notably in Percival Leigh's *A Comic English Grammar* (1840), which is full of ludicrous examples and analogies. There was also a parody, *The Comic Lindley Murray* (1871), which abridged his grammar and replaced his serious examples with frivolous ones. But to several generations of English-speakers Murray's name was synonymous with grammar. It appears in Dickens more than once. In *Little Dorrit* Mr Pancks the reluctant rent collector wonders, 'Is any gentleman present acquainted with the English Grammar?' The people gathered around him in Bleeding Heart Yard (in London's Clerkenwell) are 'shy of claiming that acquaintance'. The 'English Grammar' in question is undoubtedly Murray's. There was doubt, though, over whether Dickens himself knew the work well; a review by Thomas Cleghorn of *Martin Chuzzlewit* slammed him for barbarous grammar that 'offends the shade of Lindley Murray'.[11]

In the opening chapter of *Uncle Tom's Cabin* Harriet Beecher Stowe condemns Haley the slave-trader because of his 'gaudy vest' and 'flaunting tie' before concluding: 'His conversation was in free and easy defiance of Murray's Grammar, and was garnished at convenient intervals with various profane expressions, which not even the desire to be graphic in our account shall induce us to transcribe.' In *Moby-Dick* this semi-precious volume is studied by Pip, the genial black boy who looks after the *Pequod* when the others go out whaling; he hopes to improve his mind. The most memorable reference to Murray is in George Eliot's *Middlemarch,* set at the time of the 1832 Reform Bill. In that novel Mrs Garth, a former schoolteacher, is representative of her age in cherishing Murray's writings: we are told that 'in a general wreck of society [she] would have tried to hold her "Lindley Murray" above the waves'. Defective grammar, Mrs Garth believes, prevents a person from gaining the attention of the world. Murray's books are ideal for her purposes as she doles out education while making pies in her kitchen; they are specifically intended for the use of learners who have not had much formal education.

Lindley Murray's conservative dogma percolated through nineteenth-century ideas about grammar. For instance, he resisted the idea that there could be different yet equally valid forms of usage; in his eyes, one form had always to be preferred. There were a few exceptions: he was prepared to accept both 'expert in' and 'expert at', and 'He was never seen to laugh' was considered neither better nor worse than 'He never was seen to laugh'. But his doctrine was that the rules of usage should not allow choice. He insisted on what he called 'clearness', yet did not define what he meant by this, and in much the same way urged subjective notions of 'graceful' or 'elegant' expression. He cleaved to an ideal of the true 'nature' of language, which he did not expound.[12] In one of his more risibly inexact moments he asserts that 'Sentences, in general, should not be very long, nor very short'.[13] His writing has a quality of *littleness* – in striving for a proud certainty he is sometimes comic. Things that now seem strange would not have surprised his contemporaries. Today we would be startled to be told that it is 'harsh' to use the relative pronoun *who* when speaking of a child – as in 'A child who likes swimming' – for the reason that 'We hardly consider children as persons, because that term gives us the idea of reason and reflection'.[14]

In his memoirs Murray says of the *English Grammar* that 'the approbation and the sale which the book obtained, have given me some reason to believe, that I have not altogether failed in my endeavours to elucidate the subject, and to facilitate the labours of both teachers and learners of English grammar'. In making this statement, he reiterates the 'special regard' he has always given to 'the propriety and purity of all the examples and illustrations'.[15] Murray did a huge amount to reinforce the connection between sound grammar and virtue, and at the same time to reinforce another connection: between mistakes and vice.

Considering the temper of Murray's writing, it may come as a surprise that he has nothing to say about slang. One feels confident that he would have dismissed it as a disgraceful aberration. But *slang* would not have meant much to him. The *OED*'s first citation for this word in the sense 'language of a highly colloquial type' is from 1818. As a term for the special vocabulary of a group of disreputable people, it appears in 1756. Previously what we now think of as slang had been known as *jargon*, *cant*, *lingo* or – less commonly – *speciality*. Alexander Gil, writing in 1621 in support of a phonetic spelling system, had condemned the 'cant speech' of 'the dirtiest dregs of the wandering beggars'; he described their language as 'that poisonous and most stinking ulcer of our state', and argued that it would not go away 'until the magistrates have its authors crucified'.[16]

Jargon, originally a term for the chattering of birds, was used censoriously by Hobbes, Swift and Johnson. It signified the language peculiar to professions – and, less commonly, to cliques and particular ethnic groups. But only one substantial and wide-ranging view of the subject had been produced. This was the work of Francis Grose, the son of a rich Swiss jeweller, who in 1785 had published *A Classical Dictionary of the Vulgar Tongue*. There had, it was true, been compilations of slang as long ago as the sixteenth century; one early collection appeared in Thomas Harman's *A Caveat or Warening for Common Cursetors* (1565), which its author was able to put together as a result of about twenty years' ill health, during which he would interview any beggar who appeared at his door. It was Grose, though, who made this kind of compendium a credible department of lexicography. He argued, too, that the abundance of English slang was a reflection not of the nation's corruption, but of its liberty: 'the freedom of thought and speech, arising from, and privileged by our constitution, gives a force and poignancy to the expressions of our common people, not to be found under arbitrary governments.'[17]

The noteworthiness of Grose's work lies partly in its almost clairvoyant interest in what we might now call popular culture. *A Classical Dictionary of the Vulgar Tongue* was the fruit of a considerable amount of reading and also of numerous nocturnal trips from his favourite Holborn tavern into the nearby slums – accompanied by Batch, his manservant, and later by another friend he called The Guinea Pig. In the *Dictionary* Grose explains about three thousand words. Among these are items of jargon used by soldiers and sailors, prostitutes and pugilists, tailors and tradesmen. But Grose is not just a collector of pleasing oddments; he argues that slang is central to the life of language, and notes how quickly the language of the street finds its way into politics, as well as into the prose of people writing for magazines.

It will be apparent by now that language plays a central role in establishing our relationships with other people, and this is especially true in the case of slang. For slang, more than any other kind of language, creates solidarities. Slang is a kind of sport; Otto Jespersen remarked that like all other sports it essentially belongs to the young. Slang is playful. It also feels quick. 'I fancy I do like slang,' says Lily Dale in Trollope's *The Small House at Allington* (1864). 'It's so slow, you know, to use nothing but words out of a dictionary.' Words undictionarized are considered smart and snappy; they have yet to be tamed. In the TV series *Buffy the Vampire Slayer*, which aired from 1997 to 2003, a highly original form of teenage slang becomes one of the weapons deployed by the eponymous heroine; it enables her to survive, and, in an intriguing development of traditional vampire stories, her words are the sharpest stakes she can use against her adversaries. Of course, to turn the idea on its head, there is something just a little ridiculous about people in the vanguard of this kind of usage. The desire to appear up to date, often evident in an obsession with looking and sounding young, can be to others a source of mirth or embarrassment.

Walt Whitman likened slang to belching ('eructation', he called it), but it's a very revealing kind of belching. The slang we use says a lot about who and what we want to be. Social groups have their particular dialects: electricians have an argot that is largely incomprehensible to the initiates of a college fraternity, and vice versa; the jocks and the burnouts in a high school have discernibly different specialized vocabularies; a jeweller talks about gems and their settings in a manner unlike that of a professional thief; and there are kinds of jargon familiar only to mariners, truckers, bankers and gamers. 'Chicken salad' means quite different things to a snowboarder and a chef. In Charlotte Brontë's novel *Villette* (1853) the narrator Lucy Snowe comments that 'the strange speech of the cabmen . . . seemed to me odd as a foreign tongue. I had never before heard the English language chopped up in that way.' Choppedup English is, according to your perspective, conveniently brisk, gibberish or a kind of poetry. Inasmuch as it's the last of these, it is the people's poetry – a creative expression of a group dynamic. In the 1950s David Maurer wrote *Whiz Mob*, a book-length study of the specialized language of American pickpockets. Their argot was rich. Picking a person's pocket outside a bank was known as a 'jug touch'; skilful, shrewd pickpocketing was reckoned to depend on 'grift sense'; an especially deft and fast-moving practitioner was a 'lightning tool', while the more ruthless operators who worked public conveniences were known as 'crapper hustlers'. Perhaps all this sounds a bit James Ellroy: to an outsider, talk of 'donickers', 'dinging the poke' and 'double duke frames' seems almost gratuitously obscure. But this esoteric language is subtle and detailed, and reveals something of the pickpocket's psychology – his cult of finesse, his unexpectedly proud professionalism, his equation of grifting with sex. It's with good reason impenetrable.

One leading lexicographer of slang, Jonathon Green, reflects on his work in the field and finds that 'in comparison with the Standard English lexis its vocabulary covers a tiny waterfront, but in what depth: 3,000 drunks, 1,500 copulations, 1,000 each of penises and vaginas'. These words are usually 'coined at society's lower depths, and make their way aloft'. He characterizes slang as a target, as 'resolutely human', as 'welcoming of the crassest stereotyping', as Falstaffian, and as 'the great re-inventor'.[18] While editing this chapter I was on a London bus and was treated to a panorama of slang at its most discussibly bizarre, which bore out Green's description. Treated, or subjected – but really both, for I was at once fascinated and appalled as two teenage boys attempted to outdo each other in itemizing really grimy terms for having sex. Many were new to me, and when they were done I felt enlightened more than sullied.

This suggests why dictionaries of slang are popular: we turn to them partly in order to arm ourselves, but mainly because they help us understand what seem to be the deformities of the world around us. Actually, slang dates quickly, and much of what we will find in a slang dictionary is dusty stuff: instead of helping us practically, a book of this kind will end up on a shelf within arm's reach of the loo. Readers of Francis Grose's dictionary were, I think it's safe to say, more likely to be amused or scandalized than enlightened by the information that when somebody spoke of 'one who uses, or navigates the windward passage' he meant 'a sodomite', and that a dildo was 'an implement, resembling the virile member, for which it is said to be substituted, by nuns, boarding school misses, and others obliged to celibacy'.

While Grose the antiquarian was sniffing out such details, his son (also Francis) was serving in the American War of Independence. In 1791 the younger Grose travelled to Australia to be the Lieutenant Governor of New South Wales. He soon replaced his ailing superior, Arthur Phillip, who had founded the convict settlement at Sydney; at the point where he took over, there were 4,221 Europeans in New South Wales, and 3,099 of these were convicts. The contrasting lives of father and son evoke the broadening horizons of English. The elder Francis Grose noted the prevalence among thieves of the word *bloody*; half a century later Alexander Marjoribanks, depicting life in New South Wales, identified it as one of the leading British exports. Marjoribanks was moved by the experience of hearing a bullock driver utter the word *bloody* twenty-five times in a quarter of an hour to reflect that the man, with 'ten hours for conversation' each day, would in fifty years use it more than 18 million times.[19]

The work done by Murray and the elder Grose suggests two very different approaches to language that would occupy arbiters of English usage in the century that followed: a determination to issue conservative and moralistic prescriptions, and an appetite for describing the language in all its hues. The experiences of the younger Grose and of Alexander Marjoribanks offer an alternative vista: towards the development of English on continents where it had previously been unknown, and its role in forming the identities of new communities.

In addition, Marjoribanks's little calculation was a step towards the word *bloody* being consecrated as an Australian national treasure. When in 1898 Edward Ellis Morris received an honorary doctorate from the University of Melbourne in recognition of his recent *Austral English: A Dictionary of Australian Words, Phrases and Usages*, students at the university were so piqued by the absence from this volume of *bloody* that they staged a mock degree ceremony in which a gowned figure appeared lugging a tome labelled 'The Great Australian Adjective'.[20]

11 The pedigree of nations

Language, identity and conflict

Lindley Murray was one of life's anthologists, content to pick other men's flowers. Yet at the same time as he was doing this, original theories of English and its uses were burgeoning. Arguments about the language were becoming, to a striking degree, explicitly political. The appetite for a standard of English usage, which we might reasonably associate with a desire for political stability, was in some quarters a vestige of radicalism.

Concern for the state of the language is, as I have suggested, always bound up not just with practical missions, but also with social or political agendas. In the 1790s it became normal to think that a challenge to the existing structures of power could be achieved through literary and linguistic endeavours. The period was marked by a special awareness of the relationship between language and nation. This was shaped to a significant degree by the revolutions in America and France. Amid the rise of nationalist feeling in Europe, the idea of language as a badge of identity – not just *our* togetherness, but *their* lack of it – became customary. This was not a new idea, but the conscious attention it received was a fresh development.

One agitator who combined political iconoclasm with philological investigations was John Horne Tooke. His anti-authoritarianism took many forms, but included campaigning for parliamentary reform, distributing copies of Thomas Paine's *Rights of Man*, and advertising to raise money for the widows of American soldiers killed by British troops. Most important, though, was Tooke's attempt to set language on a more democratic footing. He rejected conventional grammar. His book *The Diversions of Purley* – the first part of which was published in 1786, though the work was not completed till 1805 –

used etymology in an attempt to demystify the often abstract language of politics. It scraped away the extraneous matter with which important words had over time become coated.

Tooke's radical thesis was that all language can be traced back to nouns and verbs. Whereas Johnson, Lowth and Lindley Murray referred to nine distinct parts of speech, Tooke stripped grammar down, in the belief that language begins in the material world and in actions. 'The first aim of Language,' he writes, 'was to *communicate* our thoughts: the second, to do it with *dispatch*.'[1] Perhaps he recalled the characters in *Gulliver's Travels* whose mission it was to eliminate from language all parts of speech except nouns. In his personal life Tooke appreciated quick communication of feelings, even wishing that when women were pleased with what he said they would simply purr.[2] The brevity he favoured had practical benefits, and the idea that words were fundamentally the names of sensations earned him many disciples.

There were strong links between Tooke's studies in etymology and his politics. He prepared a second edition of the first part of his work while in prison on a charge of high treason; his crime had been to argue the need for constitutional change, and in his work on language he analysed the vocabulary of political authority. His first-hand experience of legal process had sharpened his sense of the relationship between injustice and the professional cant of lawyers. He belongs to a tradition of thinkers, including John Locke and Jeremy Bentham, who have posited that there can be no liberty without an intelligible language of law and politics. Intelligible legal and political language creates accountability; the people who are affected by legislation can understand it and engage with it. Tooke was a key mover in the Society for Constitutional Information, which sought to bring about parliamentary reform.[3]

Tooke's main achievement lay in marrying philology and philosophy. His ideas were interesting, but his blunders numerous, and his influence retarded the development of English philology, insulating it from the new Continental scholarship of (among others) Jacob Grimm. In the early part of the nineteenth century, philology enjoyed a vogue among creative writers; Samuel Taylor Coleridge and William Hazlitt were among those enthusiastic about Tooke, believing he had penetrated the clutter of polite refinement and seen language in its primitive state. Hazlitt on the title page of his 1810 grammar book 'for the use of schools' indicated that 'the Discoveries of Mr Horne Tooke . . . are for the first time incorporated'. This particular enthusiasm did not last long, but there was a general excitement about all that English seemed to make possible: the traffic of goods and ideas between Britain and its far-flung dominions, the cementing of a national consciousness, and the scope for creating the sort of ideal, civil, standard language that Germans call a *Hochsprache*. It also represented the exchange of radical ideas through private correspondence, the reconstitution of literary genres, the magic of impure speech and dialect, and the liberty – intellectual, political, imaginative – of an unfettered vernacular.

In the 1790s William Wordsworth was one of those who, like Tooke, saw in the French Revolution a portent of radical change in Britain. When he visited Paris in 1791, he pocketed a little piece of the ruined Bastille – a souvenir of his visit and a symbol of French radicalism. Through his friend Samuel Nicholson, a member of the Society for Constitutional Information, he was exposed to the thinking of some of Britain's most passionate agitators for political reform. Later he would reassess his attitude to the French Revolution, but early in his career events in France convinced him of the need to construct a new literary language, which would be a means of nationalizing poetry.

Wordsworth's manifesto was the preface to *Lyrical Ballads*, the collection he and Coleridge published in 1798. There he made it clear that he was breaking with the aristocratic tradition in English poetry. In the preface to the second edition, two years later, he declared that he was providing readers with 'a selection of language really used by men'. Arguing that a poet must be 'a man speaking to men', he suggested the power of poetry to improve social conditions and reverse the general degradation of public taste. 'The primary laws of our nature' are discernible in 'low and rustic life', and in taking as his subject this neglected area of existence he believed he had found the source of 'philosophical language'.

The language of the poems in *Lyrical Ballads* does not fulfil the promises of the preface. But Wordsworth and his contemporaries did create a new literary language. In the Romantic period English literature stopped trying to copy the literature of Latin and Greek, and asserted its independence. However, as this happened, literary language no longer seemed able to represent the language of the nation.[4] Instead of something solid and accessible, there were new and confusing enthusiasms for the vibrancy of dialect, obsolete words, archaism, lushness, haphazard borrowing from other languages, casually bad grammar and bursts of emotion. In Wordsworth's work, there is everywhere the looseness of improvisation and invention. The emergence of Romantic poetry was the moment when novels ceased to be an upstart form, becoming instead the everyday furniture of the national literature. Meanwhile poetry was increasingly treated not as a staple of the public conversation about culture, as it had been for most of the eighteenth century, but as an enigma. Wordsworth preached community without achieving it. But his idea that refashioning literary language was a means of redistributing property suggests the spirit of the times: the old authorities, in matters of both language and law, were deemed obscure; the invention of a new common language could liberate the people; and the true genius of the nation lay in its everyday, untutored eloquence.

If we look at the history of the word *nation*, we find that it was first used to signify an ethnic group, not a political one. Its Latin root conveyed ideas of birth, descent and race – issues of breeding, not of conviction. But since the seventeenth century the noun *nation* and its kindred adjective *national* have been employed as emotive, unifying terms. A nation is, in Benedict Anderson's crisp definition, 'an imagined political community', and it is 'imagined as both inherently limited and sovereign'. Why 'imagined'? 'Because the members of even the smallest nation will never know most of their fellow-members, meet them, or even hear of them, yet in the minds of each lives the image of their communion.'[5]

To feel that one is part of a certain nation is to subscribe to an invention. The invention is not a lie, yet it is, as Anderson emphasizes, an imagining – a function of an aspiration, psychological rather than material. This is not to say that it is something small; often the national attachments that people feel have a religious quality, and it is no coincidence that the rise of nationalism in Europe in the eighteenth century coincided with a decline in religion. Nationalism was not a direct replacement for religion, but was the product of other changes that had slowly been eating away at the old certainties. For instance, the rise of printing and of printed reading matter had facilitated the spread of religious propaganda, which had destabilized religious communities, and it had also established different (and secular) communities – of readers.

It is easy to say that this kind of national sentiment is now the stuff of nightmares, where once it was a dream. But really it is double-sided: it binds peoples together, hoisting them out of little local allegiances and creating the fertile possibilities of a shared public life, yet it also encourages a collective antipathy to other peoples. There is no sense of nationality without a sense also of rivalry. It may with some justice be argued that promoting the idea of a nation's unity has the ironic effect of emphasizing the divisions that fester among its inhabitants. Leaving this aside, though, it is clear that the pleasures and rewards of national feeling are inseparable from a capacity for hostility and violence. A society that maintains an army does so in the belief that there are some things more precious than life itself.[6] Those 'things' are the principles of one's nationhood – for which, in the twentieth century especially, millions have been prepared to die, or have been forced to. Such principles are every day flagged all around us. Part of this is literal: national flags are displayed. But we are surrounded also by badges of national identity – to many of us unobtrusive, familiar and reassuring. A lot of these are what the social scientist Michael Billig calls 'invented permanencies'. These are notions that feel as though they have always existed but have in fact been created far more recently than we imagine.

National identity is anchored by a sense of shared experience: we share our past, it seems, and so we share our future. (Of course, *we* is a vexatious pronoun – troublingly corporate, subsuming varieties of experience and imposing a collective morality. But it's also convenient.) Languages are obvious indicators of what we share and of our difference from other peoples. The sociologist Michel Foucault observed that the modern era witnessed a change in the understanding of language: its function was no longer 'imitation and duplication', but instead a presentation of 'the fundamental will' of the person who speaks it or writes it – and indeed of the will that 'keeps a whole people alive'.[7] One idea that has been prevalent since the nineteenth century is that the speakers of a language should mark out for themselves a homeland in which that language can be supreme. Eager to stir up German resistance to Napoleon, the philosopher Johann Gottlieb Fichte argued more than two hundred years ago that wherever a separate language is found, a separate nation exists. Another German, Johann Gottfried Herder, claimed that every people was shaped by the food it ate and the soil upon which it lived; there were rivers and mountains separating different nations, yet also, he noted thankfully, distinct languages and characters.

This kind of idyllic vision of a national language has tended to include the less picturesque business of suppressing minority languages. National languages are examples of invented permanencies. French is an interesting case in point, for until the nineteenth century people from one part of France typically had difficulty understanding those from another. At the time of the French Revolution, the country's fringes were dominated by other languages: Breton, Basque, Flemish and Alsatian. Other languages thrived: Lyon was 'a hive of micro-dialects'. As late as 1880, not much more than a fifth of the population professed itself comfortable speaking French.[8]

In a famous lecture delivered in 1882 at the Sorbonne, the philosopher Ernest Renan asked, '*Qu'est-ce q'une nation?*' A Breton by birth, and on his father's side of solid Celtic stock, Renan argued that nationality was a matter of conviction more than of ethnicity. The sense of a nation is something created in the present by human will and buoyed by a shared sense of past glories. It also, said Renan, involves some forgetting. To paraphrase Benedict Anderson, no sharp change in consciousness can be achieved without a measure of amnesia. Part of the fantasy of nationhood is an incomplete, mistaken or wilfully selective impression of history. By the same token, when we speak of English, which it is both convenient and satisfying to do, we are pretending that it is something robust and long-lived, unyielding rather than porous. We think of our variety of English in this place and in the present; other times and places are ignored, and we project an illusion of English's permanence. But our ideas of languages as formally constituted entities are not very old, and it is nationalism that has created these ideas.

Today it is usual for a nation to be based on political rather than ethnic unity. The European Union is the most striking example of a project in which peoples who in the past have fought horrifically bloody wars have integrated into a community which is both political and economic. Euro banknotes, tellingly, do not have lots of words printed on them, the way pound and dollar notes do. As an instrument of European political and economic union, they mark a shift from statements such as 'In God we trust' or 'In the monarch we trust' to a new, implicit act of faith: 'In money we trust'.[9]

Nevertheless, within the EU there are bitter conflicts between languages. These tend to manifest themselves as arguments about the right to speak a language in a particular place. In Spain, the position of Castilian is challenged by Catalan, which is spoken not only in Catalonia, but also in the Balearic Islands and the Comunitat Valenciana. Euskara, commonly known as Basque, has official status alongside Castilian in the Basque Country around Bilbao, but for radical Basque nationalists this is not enough. In Belgium, there is a tension between Flemish and French, particularly in the contested Brussels-Halle-Vilvoorde arrondissement. If we look further afield, in recent history there have been struggles for language rights – to give but a few examples, some of them still very much live issues – by the Gagauz in Moldova, Croatians in Austria's Burgenland, Kurds in Turkey, Maoris in New Zealand, Sámi in Norway, the Qua in Nigeria, Hungarians in Slovakia, Albanians in Macedonia, Tamils in Bangalore, and Russian-speakers in Ukraine.

Arguing for the right to use one's mother tongue can be a means of expressing a range of cultural and social grievances. Marc Shell, a distinguished scholar of comparative literature, observes that 'many wars that we used to call simply "religious" or "nationalist" turn out . . . to have been "linguistic" as well'.[10] It is worth noting that, whatever quaint ideas we may have to the contrary, most contact between speakers of different languages is discordant, not harmonious. In fact, wherever more than one language is used, conflict of some kind is inevitable. In such a society, a particular language will tend to be used by the dominant social group. Those who are outside this group can easily be identified by their use of a different language and can be discriminated against because of it. Where there is an official national language, people who have no command of it are likely to have difficulty accessing services provided by the state.[11]

When there are conflicts over language, they are waged *through* language: as statements, threats, denials, demonstrations. This has the effect of reinforcing the two sides' positions: the dominant group uses its own language, while the minority group, attempting to assert its case, must either use the dominant group's language (a deeply uncomfortable manoeuvre) or use its preferred language and risk incomprehension or simply being ignored.

Within such conflicts, people are killed for speaking the 'wrong' language; their linguistic preference, which is difficult to mask, prompts accusations of disloyalty, separatism and treason. It is easier to change your political allegiance than to change your language, and also easier to cover up your religious faith (or lack of it). A single word, mishandled, can betray you. The concept of a *shibboleth* encapsulates this. In chapter 12 of the Book of Judges in the Bible, the following verses appear:

> And the Gileadites took the passages of Jordan before the Ephraimites: and it was so, that when those Ephraimites which were escaped said, 'Let me go over'; that the men of Gilead said unto him, '[Art] thou an Ephraimite?' If he said, 'Nay', then said they unto him, 'Say now Shibboleth': and he said 'Sibboleth': for he could not frame to pronounce [it] right. Then they took him, and slew him at the passages of Jordan: and there fell at that time of the Ephraimites forty and two thousand.

From this story comes the idea that the pronunciation of a particular word marks whether one belongs to a certain group. In World War II, American soldiers used the word *lollapalooza* as a means of catching out Japanese spies who were posing as Filipinos or indeed as Americans. Its *l* sounds were difficult even for Japanese who were confident in English.

Being put to the test in this way is rather like being handed a live grenade – an unusual example of the cliché that 'Words are weapons'. The best writers renew the force of this line. John Bunyan suggested that the Ten Commandments were cannons firing upon the soul. For Robert Burton in *The Anatomy of Melancholy*, 'A blow with a word strikes deeper than a blow with a sword.' Swift wrote of 'the artillery of words', Percy Bysshe Shelley's Prometheus likened the Furies' speech to 'a cloud of winged snakes', and of course Hamlet promises to 'speak daggers' to his mother Gertrude. We can use words to force unpleasant thoughts on other people. It is with good reason that in the metaphysics of many religions the holiest of believers retreat into speechless solitude and the soul ultimately ascends from the material world into silence.

One of the most significant thinkers in this area is Thomas Hobbes, who argued that words have allowed people to behave antagonistically. For Hobbes, language is a transformative invention, a technology that makes it possible to reason, but it also makes monsters of us, amplifying our desire for power and glory, and causing us to advertise this publicly. To be able to speak is to convert private desires into public ones, and thus to engage in the complex and unpleasant business of jockeying for position as we seek to satisfy our desires. We talk not just about the present, but about the future too, and this primes us with anxiety.[12]

Consider, for instance, the tendency of news reporting to present all stories as straightforwardly antagonistic: East versus West, terror-ists versus governments, black versus white, tradition versus modernity. These are crude binary distinctions. But crude binary distinctions are easy to grasp and enable the most attention-grabbing coverage; the altogether greyer business of what we might call The Truth just isn't easy to package. Truth is not its own ambassador. 'War' is itself a term that constitutes what are actually quite diffuse and disparate activities: we speak of 'nuclear war', a full-scale form of which has never happened), the 'war on terror', terrorism itself as a type of war, civil wars and guerrilla wars, holy war, the sex wars, the culture wars and – yes – language wars. War is the failure of communication; it happens when communication is exhausted or impossible, and the rhetoric of war crystallizes tensions and antipathies, turning debatable issues into hard positions.

Furthermore, success in war legitimizes the identity of the successful. A historical example: Great Britain was a slippery entity in the eighteenth century, created by the Act of Union in 1707, but came to seem more real and less disparate through its victories in wars abroad, especially with France. We determine who we are by emphasizing who we are not. Actually, war may buttress the losers' sense of identity, too. Conflict creates easy-to-see distinctions between 'us' and 'them', and on each side this bolsters unity – or rather, a mindfulness of unity.

It is relevant to our thinking about nations that the names we give things instantiate our perceptions of division, not real divisions. For when we speak of nations, uttering their names, we divide geographical and social continuities into pieces. There are historical reasons for the divisions, and the boundaries are defined geographically and in most cases linguistically. But the constructs that result are fragile. Putting faith in the durability of one's national language is a strategy for holding one's own arbitrary or fragile domain together, and this is one of the reasons why even small threats to a language can feel so harmful.

12 Of fish-knives and fist-fucks

The discreet charisma of Victorian English

'The Victorian age will not go away,' writes the historian Lawrence James. It lasted more than sixty years and 'produced a social and moral environment that has not entirely disappeared . . . Whenever Britain undergoes one of its periodic fits of moral introspection, the codes and certainties of the Victorian middle class are invoked, either in admiration or in horror.'[1] The period began with political unrest, passed through a prosperous 'age of equipoise' and culminated in a mixture of bold scientific progress, pomposity, nervous pessimism and a loss of imperial confidence. To the reign of Queen Victoria, from her accession as an eighteen-year-old in 1837 to her death in 1901, we can attribute a large portion of the myth of Englishness – that compendium of invented traditions and pruned historical verdure used by the English to present themselves to the rest of the world. I say 'English' rather than 'British' advisedly, for Britishness is a set of qualities less romantically imagined. Many Victorian thinkers displayed an antiquarian preoccupation with defining and lionizing Englishness, and the England of Queen Elizabeth conveyed an especially seductive image of national pride and power. They cleaved to the Elizabethan idea that controlling the resources of English was the basis of a strong nation. We can also trace to the Victorian age the origins of many of the attitudes to English usage that are prevalent today.

A brief survey of that era and its spirit will help anatomize those attitudes. Many of the period's linguistic legislators were responding not so much to real and immediate problems as to issues that had become ingrained in polite imagination. Victorian doctors derived most of their income from treating imaginary complaints, and thus it was with many of the doctorly types who sought to remedy the defects

143

of Victorian English. English changed less in the nineteenth century than in any century since the Norman Conquest, but even when language change is not dramatic people perceive it as such. The fortunes of the language, and of society, were compulsively discussed.

The word *Victorian* is usually associated with primness and propriety. In the Supplement to the *Oxford English Dictionary* published in 1986, part of its definition is 'prudish, strict; old-fashioned, out-dated'. To this we might add 'reticent'. In Henry James's *The Portrait of a Lady* (1881) Isabel Archer, who is an American, makes the bracing remark that 'An Englishman's never so natural as when he's holding his tongue.' When this was not possible, the Victorian Englishman had recourse to euphemism: *masturbation* was referred to as 'peripheral excitement', a *limb* was sometimes a 'lower extremity', and a *prostitute* was a 'fallen woman'. Another word to avoid was *trousers*. Nouns such as *emolument* and *honorarium* sanitized dirty talk of money. The journalist and social reformer Henry Mayhew recorded the job title *pure-finder* to describe someone whose daily work consisted of collecting dog shit that was then used by tanners.[2] Mayhew documented the lives of London's poorest citizens, and claimed to be transcribing exactly what he had heard. But the poor people he depicts rarely swear or blaspheme; their real speech has been edited. Verbal evasions were central to the Victorian public consciousness. A typical relic of that age, which I recall vividly from childhood, is the tendency when carving a turkey or chicken to ask people whether they want 'white' or 'dark' (or 'brown') meat, rather than mention the bird's breasts and legs.

There were other fundamental Victorian virtues and vices – often linked. Lawrence James provides a good overview, highlighting the energy, practicality and work ethic of the Victorian middle class, as well as the period's commercial bustle and (in opposition to it) escapist medievalism, its mass production and urban regeneration, self-congratulation and urge to improve the rest of the world. There was a culture of public works and civic spirit, a concern with developing the national infrastructure, a desire for permanence and public symbols of permanence, a combination of modern building materials with backward-looking aesthetics, and a devout belief in the sovereignty of the market. Industrialization and urbanization went hand in hand, bringing disparate groups of people together as never before.

Family life was exalted. You cannot read Victorian literature without sensing how important it had become. G. M. Young wrote in his classic *Victorian England* (1936) of 'the Victorian paradox – the rushing swiftness of its intellectual advance, and the tranquil evolution of its social and moral ideas', and suggested that the age's 'advance . . . in all directions outwards' was possible because it began from 'a stable and fortified centre'.[3] The fortified centre of family life was, in both literal and figurative terms, a place to keep spotlessly clean. Especially in the 1870s, as knowledge about germs increased, sanitation became a cause for anxiety. Poor drainage and inadequate ventilation were demonized. Modernity meant creating new systems for flushing away pollution. Where the real filth proved worryingly ineradicable, relief could be achieved by getting rid of verbal filth. Yet as prudery and squeamishness propelled the editing and policing of English, acts of rebellion and subversion multiplied. Then as now, disgust and desire tended to mingle. Pornography thrived, and there were writers delighted to produce salacious works for an audience of enthusiasts. *Lady Pokingham, Or They All Do It* is one striking example, a novel dating from 1880 which is full of deflowerings and orgies, and *My Secret Life*, a very long, repetitive and startlingly explicit erotic memoir, provides the *OED*'s first citations for *fist-fuck, frig, fuckee* and *randiness*. It is tempting to characterize the Victorian age as schizophrenic, and the combination of outward respectability and inner squalor appears again and again.

Though often viewed as an age of laissez-faire, the Victorian period saw ambitious law-making. Much of this involved revising existing legislation: one result was the expansion of the middle-class bureaucracy – a caste of literate law-givers who formed a significant part of the new bourgeoisie that glorified machines, record-keeping, printed documents and neat mechanical procedures. (The notion of 'lawyer's slang' emerges in the early nineteenth century.) The urge to mark boundaries and create mechanisms of control was evident in the treatment of language. During the nineteenth century the number of English-speakers globally almost quintupled, from 26 million to 126 million.[4] More than a thousand grammars were published in Britain, and perhaps as many as eight hundred in America. English became a university subject with the opening of King's College London, in 1831; boosted by Matthew Arnold, it took off in the 1850s when applicants for civil service posts in India started being examined in English language and literature. It is telling that the rise of English as an academic discipline was associated with training adolescents and young adults for bureaucratic careers.

Literacy improved significantly, and, thanks to better and cheaper printing techniques, a drop in the cost of paper and the abolition in 1861 of the tax on paper, there was more to read – magazines, newspapers and cheap books, including a wealth of writing aimed specifically at children. From the 1850s public examinations, controlled by the universities, helped set the previously chaotic schools system in order. Whereas previously a minority of working-class children had attended school, from 1870, when the Elementary Education Act was passed, schooling for children aged between five and twelve was compulsory, and throughout the United Kingdom that schooling had to be conducted in English. By 1880 English literature had become the most popular subject in schools – albeit with an emphasis on memorizing extracts.[5] In passing, it is worth recalling how many noted figures of the nineteenth century did not go to school: examples include John Ruskin, George Eliot and John Stuart Mill, while those who had very little schooling include Dickens, Darwin and Disraeli.[6] One of the features of late-nineteenth-century education, besides an optimism about eliminating illiteracy and the various evils with which it was associated, was the propagation of a national tradition that transcended local identity and was clothed in the rhetoric of conservatism and a kind of romantic xenophobia.

But the central problem of Victorian English was class. The title page of Young's *Victorian England* displays the Victorian maxim 'Servants talk about People: Gentlefolk discuss Things'. How alien that now seems: we all talk about people, perhaps more than is good for either us or them, even if we also talk more than ever about 'things'. Yet throughout the nineteenth century the things one talked about and the ways one talked about them were symbols of status; the eighteenth-century equation of linguistic and moral propriety became a fact of education. The result was an oppressively limited style of conversation. The enthusiastic epithet was one of its conspicuous features. Disraeli joked that English appeared to consist of only four words: '*Nice, jolly, charming* and *bore*, and some grammarians add *fond*'.[7] Class was more fluid than we may imagine: movement from one level up to the next was achievable. The erosion of traditional class barriers created self-consciousness and uncertainty; as old markers of class became less secure or even disappeared, attention to language as a source of information about people's social standing became more intense. Many of the most derided articles of Victorian life – the words as often mocked as the things they denoted – were the paraphernalia of the new middle classes: serviettes and tea-cosies, fish-knives and napkin rings, flounces and trimmings. The upstart Veneerings in Dickens's novel *Our Mutual Friend* are identified through their 'bran-new' belongings: furniture, horses, carriage, pictures, and even their baby. They see people only in terms of their roles. Dickens shifts into the present tense when describing their behaviour, as though to emphasize its shallow modernity, and the name he chooses for them hints not just that their glossiness is mere varnish, but also that their empty acquisitiveness might be a sinister (venereal) disease.

The noun *class* is defined in Thomas Blount's *Glossographia*, a 1656 dictionary of 'hard words', as 'an order or distribution of people according to their several Degrees'. A hundred years later it is often used in discussions of social structure. But it is in the nineteenth century that the word comes alive – to denote the system of social divisions, and by the end of the century to suggest 'distinction' or 'high quality'. Increasingly, it involves a range of judgements about status. The *OED* shows 'class interests' (first attested in 1828), 'class morality' (1833), 'class feelings' (1839), 'class prejudices' (1850), 'class grievance' (1852), 'class system' (1877), 'class barrier' (1889) and 'class conflict' (1898). Class shifted from being something that was accepted as having a basis in fact to being a matter of popular debate. And as this happened, crucially, concerns about correctness shifted from a focus on grammar to an obsession with vocabulary and pronunciation. Where Dr Johnson had written of 'solecisms' and 'barbarisms', in the nineteenth century the terms of criticism became 'socially loaded', with an emphasis on 'vulgarism', 'slang' and 'etiquette'.[8] Beginning in the 1830s, there was a spate of publications about the last of these; whereas the old conduct books had focused on the individual, these new titles constructed the idea of polite people as a class and emphasized social standing rather than moral behaviour.

For William Cobbett, the division between those who knew grammar and those who did not was a mainstay of the class system: the poor were taught no grammar and as a result were condemned to lives of unlettered servility. He wrote *A Grammar of the English Language* in the hope of enabling the working classes to protect themselves from abuse. At the same time he ridiculed authority figures, providing specimens of false grammar from the writings of Dr Johnson and examples of nonsense from a speech by the king. He labelled Noah Webster a 'toad'.[9] He laid into Lindley Murray and pounced on errors in Hugh Blair's lectures. One of his more striking ideas is that one should always write spontaneously, using the first words that come to mind, and resisting the temptation to recast one's thoughts. It was a mistake, he claimed, to slow down in order to make a deliberate choice of words; that would lead to artificiality.

Cobbett's Grammar was remarkable in its purpose rather than its material. His representation of grammar was conventional, but he insisted that grammatical knowledge could liberate working men from a group he called the 'borough-tyrants'. In his newspaper *The Political Register*, he wrote of his desire in presenting a work of grammar to create 'numerous formidable assailants of our insolent, high-blooded oppressors'.[10] As far as numerousness was concerned, he succeeded; the book sold 100,000 copies in the fifteen years following its publication. But it was not adopted in schools, and, although it was admired by self-taught working men who appreciated its political bent, it seems that its price (2s 6d) deterred many of those Cobbett had hoped would acquire it. Instead his audience was mostly lower middle class.[11]

When Cobbett's son James Paul reworked the Grammar for a fresh edition, published in 1866, his changes reflected a different kind of sensitivity about class. He added a section in which common pronunciation mistakes were pointed out and corrected. His father had thought such matters unimportant. James Paul, who was sixty-three by the time he revised his father's work, had had half a century of exposure to attitudes that he, unlike his father, had not been able to ignore. Faults in speech, he wrote, 'are the most offensive, because they happen to be those which so frequently cause, with the hearer, a presumption of "vulgarity" in the pronouncer'.[12]

In recognizing the likelihood of this presumption, James Paul Cobbett saw the degree to which the language of class and status had become imbued with morality. An interesting example of this is the word *villain*. In the fourteenth century it had meant something like 'simple-minded yokel'; by the early nineteenth, though sometimes used playfully, it denoted a criminal – and typically an important one, as in a play or a novel. The adjective *vulgar*, which from the fourteenth to the seventeenth centuries meant before all else 'ordinary', began to have the senses 'plebeian' and 'unrefined' around 1550 and 1650 respectively; these became much more common in the nineteenth century, especially to describe not just 'vulgar' behaviour, but the people who exhibited it. In that period, too, emerged the adjectives *vulgar-minded* and *vulgar-looking*. *Rascal* was a term for a member of the lowest social class – and for a common soldier – before it began to be used of people lacking principles. *Ignoble* was in the fifteenth and sixteenth centuries used of people who were not of noble birth; beginning in the 1590s, and increasingly thereafter, it signified baseness and dishonour, and by the Victorian period using it in the older sense was a consciously old-fashioned gesture. *Beggar* is another word that has made this journey from being merely descriptive to being emotive, and *wretch* denoted an exile hundreds of years before it became a term of contempt. C. S. Lewis neatly summed up this phenomenon as 'the moralization of status words'. It began long before the age of Dickens and Disraeli, but the emotive use of status words was exaggerated as an increasingly urban population advertised its distance from rustic living and its less affluent forebears.

It became normal for the more privileged members of society to dismiss those less privileged as an amorphous mass or a monstrous glut of flesh. This grew more pronounced at the beginning of the twentieth century, thanks in part to the influence of Friedrich Nietzsche's eloquently nasty condemnation of the crawling Christian rabble – an idea explored at length in John Carey's book *The Intel-*

lectuals and the Masses.[13] But nineteenth-century discussions of usage tend to emphasize the gulf between the gentleman and the commoner.

The definition of gentlemanliness was contentious. According to whose criteria you applied, it could mean maintaining a carriage, being indifferent to money matters, or having no profession. Lord Chesterfield mockingly noted in the 1750s that the word *gentleman* was applied to 'every man, who, with a tolerable suit of cloaths, a sword by his side, and a watch and snuff-box in his pockets, asserts himself to be gentleman, swears with energy that he will be treated as such, and that he will cut the throat of any man who presumes to say the contrary'.[14] Chesterfield borrowed from French the word *etiquette* to speak of a code of manners not directly connected to morals. In one of his letters he suggested that a man of the world should be a chameleon. Doing the right thing was less important than doing as others did. With regard to language, this meant being smoothly conformist. One should not speak of oneself, but should fit in with one's group. 'Avoid singularity,' he cautioned.

Where morals were concerned, the opposite position to Chester-field's was that of Samuel Richardson, whose novels resembled conduct books. In *Sir Charles Grandison* (1753–4) Richardson envis-aged a succession of situations in which his protagonist had the opportunity to prove himself a gentleman. Richardson portrayed a kind of eighteenth-century Christ, a paragon of benevolence. Gran-dison is a man of honour but also of commerce – devoted to his family and to promoting marriage, forever resolving conflicts and bringing harmony to the lives of others, admired by women and held in universally high regard. One of his stated virtues is that 'He never perverts the meaning of words'. Yet his use of language is animatedly sentimental, and Richardson's French translator Prévost found it necessary to tone down this excess.

Both Richardson and Chesterfield informed the Victorian notion of gentlemanliness. But while Richardson was cherished mainly by female readers, Chesterfield was the more common model for male ones – an important divergence. The latter's detachment of propriety from ethics was wonderfully convenient: it made being 'proper' so much easier. The *Spectator* essays of Joseph Addison and Sir Richard

Steele were also highly valued; their nineteenth-century audience, reading them a century and more after they were composed, noted the restraint they counselled. It was decorous but also cunning. Addison declared the essays 'calculated to diffuse good Sense through the Bulk of a People'. In fact, they suggested one should be an actor in the theatre of daily life. Reading other people's gestures was a crucial part of this, and so was interpreting the fabric of one's environment. Steele had previously advised in *The Tatler* that 'the Appellation of *Gentleman* is never to be affixed to a Man's Circumstances, but to his Behaviour in them'. Often in *The Spectator* there is close attention to particular words, such as *good-breeding* or *conversation*, and the behaviours they imply are discussed. Ideals of conduct are suggested by repetition of these terms, and they become a kind of shorthand for a code of comportment. In Victorian arguments about English, such repetition is a substitute for examining the truth.

In Victorian Britain gentlemanly conduct was variously defined, but always involved the idea of exclusivity – of keeping the ungentlemanly at arm's length. John Ruskin suggested that 'the *essence* of a gentleman' is that he 'comes from a pure *gens*, or is perfectly bred. After that, gentleness and sympathy, or kind disposition and fine imagination'.[15] In *The Book of Snobs* (1848) William Makepeace Thackeray provides a definition that is effectively an article of faith:

> What is it to be a gentleman? Is it to be honest, to be gentle, to be generous, to be brave, to be wise, and, possessing all these qualities, to exercise them in the most graceful outward manner? Ought a gentleman to be a loyal son, a true husband, and honest father? Ought his life to be decent – his bills to be paid – his tastes to be high and elegant – his aims in life lofty and noble? In a word, ought not the Biography of a First Gentleman in Europe to be of such a nature, that it might be read in Young Ladies' Schools with advantage, and studied with profit in the Seminaries of Young Gentlemen?

One of Thackeray's projects was to redefine gentlemanliness, in a way that reflected a shift in the balance of power that occurred during his lifetime (1811–1863): from the landowners to the new middle classes. Thackeray thought that the middle classes should reject the example of their social superiors, rather than modelling themselves on it. Yet as the ideal of gentlemanliness became entrenched, so the word itself became awkward. It was a yardstick, but it was also a form of trap. Harold Laski, in an essay published in the 1930s on 'The Danger of Being a Gentleman', reflected on the anti-democratic and anti-intellectual nature of gentlemanly conduct; the gentleman Laski pictured was a leisured amateur, unimaginative, accustomed to command, and narrow in his social loyalties.[16]

The Victorian gentleman was judged on his inner qualities as well as his outward bearing, and those inner qualities were inferred from his language. In *Basil* (1852), Wilkie Collins's first novel of modern life, a character's speaking 'pure English' leads to his being imagined 'a gentleman'. Pronunciation was a key part of this perceived purity. In one of his later novels, *I Say No* (1884), the flighty wife of a manservant asks a woman to whom she has just been rude, 'Do you notice my language? I inherit correct English from my mother – a cultivated person, who married beneath her. My maternal grandfather was a gentleman.' And in the more celebrated *The Woman in White* (1859–60) there is Pesca, an Italian professor who 'prided himself on being a perfect Englishman in his language, as well as in his dress, manners, and amusements'. He has 'picked up a few of our most familiar colloquial expressions' and sprinkles them in his conversation 'whenever they happened to occur to him, turning them, in his high relish for their sound and his general ignorance of their sense, into compound words and repetitions of his own, and always running them into each other, as if they consisted of one long syllable'. The man who considers himself 'a perfect Englishman in his language' is a stock comic figure: to be correct is one thing, but to take pride in what one believes to be one's correctness is quite another.

The 'correct English' spoken of so archly by the character in *I Say No* is, in her eyes, a marker of status. But, for Collins, her decision to draw attention to it belies this. The need for discretion about one's correctness is a symptom of the contemporary cult of the 'lady'. An anonymous publication of 1835, *Woman: As She Is, and As She Should Be*, argued that 'Whatever nature or law may have denied women, art and secret sway give them all'. The author claimed that women were 'glorified with a false worship' and had an 'unwholesome liberty'. 'Mental strength is not the gift, nor can it be the glory of the woman,' it was claimed, and 'it is to her no legitimate source of public or even private influence.' Creating an ideal of ladylike behaviour was a means of remedying this: women were 'by no means to be left in darkness, as regards wholesome knowledge', and should be trained in 'conversation with sensible men, and the virtue of listening'.[17] As a term for a woman having the characteristics of high social standing, *lady* is a phenomenon of the middle decades of the century, accompanied by *ladydom*, *ladyhood*, *ladyish* and *ladykind*. Today many find the word *lady* an absurd relic of a less enlightened past, but it holds on, a little mistily. As the author of a *Reader's Digest* style guide dating from 1983 justly notes, it is 'so full of social overtones and built-in gender assumptions that no one can prescribe rules of its usage for others'.[18]

For a Victorian lady, the key concern was voice. Among the qualities considered desirable in a female voice were elegance, correctness, purity and refinement. Efforts to explain these were patchy, but clear articulation was essential, as was a carefulness about emphasis and breathing. In *Jane Eyre* (1847), one of the novels Queen Victoria read to her husband Prince Albert (reading aloud being a necessary accomplishment among socially superior women), Miss Temple displays a 'refined propriety in her language, which precluded deviation into the ardent, the excited, the eager: something which chastened the pleasure of those who looked on her and listened to her, by a controlling sense of awe'. In *The Black Robe* (1881), Wilkie Collins comments that 'Even in trifles, a woman's nature is degraded by the falsities of language and manner which the artificial condition of modern society exacts from her.'

George Vandenhoff's *The Lady's Reader* (1862) was one of the more notable works aimed at helping young women achieve this expected artificiality. His opening words are 'Grace of speech is particularly attractive in woman'. He goes on to characterize grace in terms of 'sparkling accentuation' and 'an agreeable tone of voice'.

'Every lady,' he claims, 'should be able to take up a book of prose or poetry, and read any passage in it smoothly, intelligently, and musically, without aiming at effect or display, but in a sensible, pleasing, and graceful manner.' He continues in this vein, lamenting that while 'many ladies' can play and sing Rossini and Verdi 'with taste, elegance, and effect', there are few 'who can read aloud with clearness, sentiment, and expression'. Vandenhoff throws in a certain amount of technical material – bits about 'nasal-labials' and 'labia-dentals' – but even in 1862 many would have been loath to share his assumption that women differ from men by tending to 'stumble and confuse themselves' when reading aloud.[19] What Vandenhoff does estimate correctly, though, is the capacity of his audience to learn. Suspiciously sexist though it may sound, there is a lot of cogent modern research suggesting that women have tended to be more receptive than men to prestige forms of language. The work of Peter Trudgill in Norwich illustrates this. Trudgill makes the point that men have traditionally been evaluated in terms of what they do ('Oh, so you're a barrister?', 'Sheep-shearing – how interesting'), while women have been evaluated according to how they look and other markers of their status, one of which is their use of language. He argues that 'Women in our society are more status-conscious than men, generally speaking, and are therefore more aware of the social significance of linguistic variables'. Men are more likely to be influenced 'from below' and women 'from above'.[20]

Nineteenth-century novels reflect on such concerns intriguingly. Novelists capitalized on readers' familiarity with prescriptive rules and related notions about accents and dialects to position their characters precisely in the social hierarchy. In *Middlemarch* the newly rich are characterized by the gossipy Mrs Cadwallader as having an accent which is 'an affliction to the ears' and confirms that 'such people were no part of God's design in making the world'. Those who, like Mrs Cadwallader and Rosamond Vincy, sniff out the 'aroma of rank' are limited by this delicacy, even though they think it elevates them.

Dickens's characters perfectly exhibit many tics we recognize and others we sense are typical of the age. So, in *Bleak House* (1852–3) there are lawyers who leave out syllables and sometimes several words as they clip through their patter, and Dickens's prosecutors are apt to cross-examine the people to whom they speak not just in the courtroom, but beyond it. Many of those who populate his novels are defined by their catchphrases, like modern game-show hosts whose personalities are annihilated by their professional joviality. Then there are characters who embody familiar conversational mannerisms: Littimer the manservant in *David Copperfield* who uses no superlatives, Mr Chillip the doctor in the same novel whose meekness means he cannot 'throw' a word at anyone and instead gently offers fragments of speech as if proffering a treat to a mad dog, the gentlemen in *Hard Times* who 'yaw-yawed in their speech', and gouty Sir Leicester Dedlock in *Bleak House* who 'had so long been thoroughly persuaded of the weight and import to mankind of any word he said, that his words really had come to sound as if there was something in them'. We also see the snottiness with which the speech of foreigners is regarded; Cavalletto in *Little Dorrit* is mocked for his dodgy conjugations and overcooked adverbs, and the people with whom he mixes 'spoke to him in very loud voices as if he were stone deaf' – which is still the standard approach of the English when addressing people who do not speak their language.

Better known is Dickens's facility for capturing ordinary London folk's everyday speech. His deliberate and significant misspellings include *arternoon, sov'ring, tremendjous, earnins, fi'typunnote, particklery, gen'lm'n, hinfant* and *everythink*, and there is a mass of cracked syntax, among which a favourite example is Joe Gargery's line in *Great Expectations* that 'it were understood . . . and it are understood'. Now and then, when Dickens is dealing with the manglers of speech, the membrane between narrator and character is perforated. Sam Weller in *The Pickwick Papers* cannot pronounce his *v*s or his *w*s, but he can use the word *mottle-faced* (already used by the narrator – though of course Sam's not supposed to know that). Occasionally characters seem to be turning into ventriloquist's dummies, as they give forth melodramatic orations that are dense with sub-clauses and far removed from the usual register of spoken language.

Dickens as an author is forever a performer – deliberately making detours, subverting expectations, exuberantly clustering images, and exaggerating – and his reflections on language suggest that he sees it as a source and object of amusement. In *Our Mutual Friend* there are young women, the daughters of army officers, who are 'accustomed to every luxury of life (except spelling)', while in *Nicholas Nickleby* the brutal Squeers says confidently that 'A horse is a quadruped, and quadruped's Latin for beast, as everybody that's gone through the grammar knows, or else where's the use of having grammars at all?' Where indeed? Characters in Dickens express aversions to the words *plunder* and *must* (as in 'I reckon you must do it'); *barber* is condemned as a dishonourable poor relation of *hairdresser*. But Dickens also has fun at the expense of larger phenomena of the age. The Circumlocution Office in *Little Dorrit* parodies the prolix absurdities of Victorian administration. In *Oliver Twist* he includes some of the 'flash' language of the criminal underworld; struck by Dickens's evocation in that novel of squalor and vice in all their colour, the teenage Queen Victoria recommended it to Lord Melbourne. He was far from smitten, objecting to the novelist's depiction of pickpockets, coffin makers and other things he did not wish to see in either life or art. Melbourne was a relic of the previous age; Victoria noted in her diary that he pronounced *Rome* and *gold* as *Room* and *goold*, and she therefore thought he might be the best person to explain to her the difference between *who* and *whom*.[21]

A greater historical range is found in Thackeray, who illuminates questions of language in a thoroughly knowing fashion. He frequently alludes to the changes in linguistic standards over the preceding century and a half. In *The History of Henry Esmond* (1852), which is set at the end of the seventeenth and beginning of the eighteenth centuries, he creates a pastiche of that period's style that is at once amusingly archaic and perfectly natural. He carefully uses obsolete words and period slang to evoke his setting, employs some antique spellings, and indeed comments that 'spelling was not an article of general commodity in the world then'. In *Catherine*, which also has an early-eighteenth-century setting, he notes that 'People were accustomed in those days to use much more simple and expressive terms of language than are now thought polite; and it would be dangerous to give, in this present year 1840, the exact words of reproach which passed between Hayes and his wife in 1726.' Characters' accents, spelling and handwriting are forever being used to place them socially: one aristocratic lady 'wrote like a schoolgirl of thirteen', while another 'breaks the King's English, and has half a dozen dukes at her table'. In the nineteenth century new terms of reproof for bad handwriting included the adjectives *spidery, scrawly, cramped, shaky, stiff, niggling* and *unreadable*, which added considerably to the existing stock – *illegible, foul, scribbled, scrabbled* and *loose*. Bad script was, implicitly, the result of bad posture, and it comes as little surprise to find that an important article for the nineteenth-century penman (or *penwoman* – a word first attested in 1747) was blotting paper.

In *The Newcomes* the Anglophile French aristocrat Florac aspires to be the perfect English squire: 'In conversation with his grooms and servants he swore freely – not that he was accustomed to employ oaths in his own private talk, but he thought the employment of these expletives necessary as an English country gentleman.' Always a commentator on his fictional creations, Thackeray offers numerous asides on this theme. So, for instance, 'rich baronets do not need to be careful about grammar, as poor governesses must be', and in speech the true 'distingué English air' consists of 'dawdling'. To be a gentleman or a minor aristocrat was to articulate oneself in a manner both incoherent and inconsequential. Thackeray was not the first, and certainly not the last, to spot that some of the linguistic habits most derided when practised by the working classes were nonetheless common among those near the top of the social pyramid. In a book entitled *The Vulgarisms and Improprieties of the English Language* (1833), W. H. Savage commented, 'we know many who would feel ashamed of a false quantity in Greek or Latin that are absolutely incapable of reading with propriety an English newspaper.'[22] In his novel *Mr Scarborough's Family* (1883), Anthony Trollope writes of the Belgian government official Grascour, 'He would only be known to be a foreigner by the correctness of his language.' Compare this with the judgement of the American critic Harry Thurston Peck in the 1890s: 'The speaker and writer who is always spick and span in his verbal dress . . . may perhaps be an "educated" man; but his education is, in all probability, a very superficial one, for he is not sufficiently educated to be on easy terms with his education.'[23]

Marie Corelli, the author of a string of best-selling melodramas, presents a different angle. One of her characters is described as 'taking a fantastic pleasure in . . . bad grammar' (his own), while in another novel she satirizes 'Miladi in Belgravia, who considers the story of her social experiences, expressed in questionable grammar, quite equal to the finest literature'. Corelli thought of herself as a purifier of language, inheriting the spirit though not the design from the man whose illegitimate child she was: the Scottish poet Charles Mackay, author of *Extraordinary Popular Delusions and the Madness of Crowds* (1841). Mackay's attitude to English was most fully expressed in *Lost Beauties of the English Language* (1874), in which he asserted that 'Old English . . . is a passionate rather than an argumentative language; and poets, who ought to be passionate above all else . . . should go back to those ancient sources'. He was intent on reviving archaic words, arguing that English literature 'might advantageously borrow from the language of the people'.[24] The sort of words he wanted to bring back were *trendency*, 'a strong deviation'; *flaucht*, 'a flash of lightning'; and *whommle*, 'to turn over clumsily and suddenly'; but also *lodestar*, *chancy* and *afterword*, which do not look strange now.

For Mackay, a good style was one that exploited the full resources of English, the defining character of which was 'vitality'. Style was understood as an expression of soul. Towards the end of the century, quantitative methods of analysing style came in: T. C. Mendenhall's essay 'The Characteristic Curves of Composition' was published in *Science* in 1887, and a technical approach to stylistic analysis was separately developed by Lucius Sherman. Yet to most of us style remains a matter of effects and impressions, not of calculations: when we classify it, we use descriptive labels. These are hardly definitive. Francis Bacon drew a distinction I rather like between the 'magistral' and the 'probative' – the authoritative and dogmatic, on the one hand, and the testing and investigative, on the other. A more modern view, set out by Walker Gibson, is that modern prose, in America at least, is always tough or sweet or stuffy. We may find a distinction being drawn between the organic and the ornamental, or between the expository and the argumentative. More simply, the formal is contrasted with the informal. The adjective 'colloquial' labels a kind of writing that resembles the spoken word.[25]

Changing attitudes to style had much to do with the rise of the newspaper and the periodical. In 1700 there had been no daily paper in London; by 1811, there were fifty-two.[26] Provincial weeklies had also sprung up during this period. Some of these publications featured pronouncements about style, and, beginning around 1750, reviewers in specialist literary magazines made a point of criticizing what they considered bad English, exerting a surprisingly large influence as they did so. But more significant than the achievements of critics was a fundamental alteration in writers' conception of what they were doing – especially with reference to factual prose. By the end of the eighteenth century, writers of pamphlets and news pieces were increasingly convinced that nice diction and honesty were not at all the same. This view matured in the nineteenth century. Between 1836 and 1880 the number of British newspapers rose from 221 to 1,986, and the reporting of news, though sometimes melodramatic, was typically carried out in a corporate style that was precise, pure and informative.[27] All the while other beliefs about style flourished: there were advocates of soulfulness, athleticism and 'virile' bluntness. Of a character in Trollope's *The Eustace Diamonds* (1871–3) it is said, 'He had escaped from conventional usage into rough, truthful speech', and it was not unusual to make this equation between roughness and truth. Thomas Paine's *Rights of Man* was regarded as a founding work here, beginning a tradition of radical writing that dispensed with the meretricious colour of adjectives and adverbs. In fact, Paine's style is not exactly plain. He belongs to a somewhat different tradition, in which political writers deplore the rhetorical embellishments of their adversaries, claiming that these demonstrate the hollowness of their arguments, yet gild their own writing with many of the devices they profess to loathe. Nonetheless, Paine's writing was regarded as an exemplar of unadorned enlightenment.

The conversational style in English prose was championed by William Hazlitt, who argued that any author whose works could not be read aloud was scarcely fit to be read at all. Writing in the 1820s, Hazlitt railed against vulgarity, affectation and the monotony of academic tracts. He criticized the lack of variety in Johnson, arguing the need for greater flexibility and pressing the case for what he called 'familiar style', a form of writing free from mean-ingless pomp, pedantic flourishes and stilted theatricality; such a manner, idiomatic and relaxed yet tactful, would be suited to 'the real purposes of life'. (A similar approach had of course been promoted by Wordsworth and Coleridge in *Lyrical Ballads*.) Hazlitt cleaved to the principle that good writing should serve the reader, making use of plain words and straightforward modes of expres-sion. A further principle of style, as important now as then, is that it should be suited to one's subject. In many circumstances one's writing can and should convey one's personality, but sometimes the personal should be suppressed, out of a sense of gravity or tact.

The poet Matthew Arnold spoke up for a laconic style, calling it 'Attic prose'. By 'Attic' he meant writing like that of Plato – direct, restrained, concise. Instead of theatrical sincerity he desired an accessible simplicity. As Jason Camlot explains, 'One of the most familiar arguments forwarded by Victorian theorists of style . . . was that writing made available to the English public should work to unite all of its readers and thus consolidate the English as a people'.[28] For those who wanted to achieve that solidity, the language advo-cated by Hazlitt did not seem apt, but neither did one full of frills and curlicues.

Thomas Kington Oliphant, a Scottish grandee, published in 1873 a remarkable book entitled *The Sources of Standard English*. Its surprising character is dramatically established on the opening page, where the author says, 'There are many places, scattered over the world, that are hallowed ground in the eyes of Englishmen; but the most sacred of all would be the spot . . . where our forefathers dwelt in common with the ancestors of the Hindoos, Persians, Greeks, Latins, Slavonians, and Celts – a spot not far from the Oxus'.[29] When Kington Oliphant has completed a 320-page history of the 'advance' of the language, he surveys 'good and bad English in 1873'. He identifies the following ills: the middle class's 'amazing love of cumbrous Latin words', the 'Babylonish speech' of hack journalists, the 'long-winded sentences' of clergymen, and the tendency to 'daub stucco over the brick and the stone' – by which he means the importation of foreign terms to supplement the Anglo-Saxon word-stock.[30] The last of these is the subject to which we now turn.

13 'Our blood, our language, our institutions'

Purism and the comforts of ignorance

In his novel *The Fixed Period* (1882) Anthony Trollope imagines a former British colony called Brittanula, where all citizens are removed when they turn sixty-seven to an institution called The College. A year after their 'deposition' at The College, they are meant to proceed to the next stage – 'departure'. This is a euphemism for their being killed. When one character hears the taboo word *murder* and complains that it is 'very improper', he is met with the down-to-earth response that 'English is English'. It's a familiar type of statement: it looks like a tautology, but we grasp that the first 'English' means something different from the second, and we understand it to be another way of saying 'Don't be so fussy'. If we think about the sentence more closely, though, we may unpack more complex meanings: one is, 'The English that people actually use is what we should accept as the language's standard form'; another, 'The English language has qualities and properties that disclose the English national character'.

'English is English' is a striking line to find in a novel by Trollope, a writer perennially concerned with the performance of Englishness and the enjoyment of property. Owners, in Trollope, are unusually apt to be absent-minded; they are happy to let others get the benefit of their possessions. A recurrent theme is the way the bonds of ownership and also of nationality are taken for granted.

Trollope and Kington Oliphant introduce us in different ways to one of the great arguments of the Victorian age, which was about the true character of the English. Specifically, their true racial character. In 1841 Thomas Arnold, giving his inaugural lecture as Regius Professor of Modern History at Oxford, claimed that Anglo-Saxon history was modern. 'We, this great English nation,' he declared, 'whose race and language are now overrunning the earth from one end of it to the other, – we were born when the white horse of the Saxons had established his dominion from the Tweed to the Tamar. So far we can trace our blood, our language, the name and actual divisions of our country, the beginnings of some of our institutions. So far our national identity extends.'[1] The theme, a revival of the seventeenth-century arguments of Camden and Verstegan, became prevalent, and found especially vivid expression in John Mitchell Kemble's *The Saxons in England* (1849). Kemble, who had studied under Jacob Grimm and had immersed himself in analysing the Teutonic languages, argued that an account of 'the principles upon which the public and political life of our Anglosaxon forefathers was based, and of the institutions in which those principles were most clearly manifested' was 'the history of the childhood of our own age, – the explanation of its manhood'.[2] The triumphalism of Arnold and Kemble was contested, but it was widely repeated, as well as being rather mournfully echoed in America by Elias Molee in his *Plea for an American Language, or Germanic-English* (1888), and it is in the arguments of this period that current obsessions about the purity of English are rooted.

Thomas Arnold's son, Matthew, mocked those of his contemporaries who gorged on fantasies of the Anglo-Saxon age. He called them 'Teutomaniacs'. There were plenty of them, eager to claim that the English were an unmixed race of Germanic origin, and eager also to play down the historical influence of the French. According to the most fervent, all the crucial elements of Englishness were established long before 1066, and everything that had happened since was bastardization. The historian Edward Augustus Freeman – who had been beaten by Matthew Arnold to a scholarship at Balliol College, Oxford – was the most vehement exponent of this view, but it was his pupil J. R. Green who found the largest audience. Green's hugely successful *A Short History of the English People* (1874) began with the statement that 'For the fatherland of the English race we must look far away from England itself ... [to] what we now call Sleswick, a district in the heart of the peninsula which parts the Baltic from the Northern seas'.[3] Green was not a straightforward Teutomaniac, but he captured the period's passion for the Anglo-Saxon. His fanciful, emotive style meant his account of 'the people's history' caused a sensation, and for fifty years it was the standard popular history of England.

These historians were not primarily concerned with language, but they stirred up the national memory, inspiring nostalgia for an Anglo-Saxon past that was robustly embodied in the vocabulary of Old English. No one articulated that nostalgia better than the poet William Barnes. As Philip Larkin pointed out, Barnes looks rather like a successful version of Thomas Hardy's worshipper of learning, Jude Fawley: born into a family of impoverished Dorset farmers, he secured his first job as a clerk in a solicitor's office by virtue of his neat handwriting. Thanks to vigorous self-education he was able to flourish as a schoolmaster, and in due course he became a successful lecturer on historical and literary subjects. As philology became his chief focus, he began to speak out against the foreign textures of what he called 'book English', arguing instead for a return to the simplicity of Anglo-Saxon. His poetry, appropriately rustic in subject matter and vocabulary, won him many admirers – Hardy for one, but also Robert Browning, Gerard Manley Hopkins, and even Matthew Arnold.

Barnes preferred *wheelsaddle* to *bicycle* – a detail quoted by Hardy in his obituary of Barnes in 1886 – and *nipperlings* to *forceps*. More alarming, perhaps, was his suggestion that *leechcraft* was better than *medicine*. But not all his proposals were shunned: it was Barnes who revived the Old English term *Wessex*, steeped in associations with paganism and Saxon kingship, and we can see a Barnesian flavour in the use of *foreword* and *handbook* instead of *preface* and *manual*.

Wessex is more often associated with Hardy than with Barnes, and the author of such works as *Under the Greenwood Tree, Far from the Madding Crowd* and *The Return of the Native* appears to be among the most poetically nostalgic figures of the period. Yet in the 1890s he recoiled from romanticizing the past. Immersed as a child in the songs and rituals of rural Dorset, Hardy was sensitive in his own writing to the delights of a rustic orality. But he also recognized the stigma that attached to it. In Hardy's Wessex, language is a source of anxiety. At times of crisis, characters relapse into usage they have tried to leave behind. Hardy pictures archaisms as dangerous mementoes; they link us to our losses. So, in *The Trumpet-Major* (1880) the hot-tempered yeoman Festus Derriman is described 'dropping his parlour language in his warmth', while the heroine, Anne, disappoints her mother because of the 'readiness' with which she 'caught up some dialect-word or accent from the miller and his friends'. In *The Well-Beloved* (published as a serial in 1892) the innocent Avice Caro has been brought up in a manner calculated 'to teach her to forget all the experiences of her ancestors; to drown the local ballads by songs purchased at the Budmouth fashionable music-sellers', and the local vocabulary by a governess-tongue of no country at all'. In *Jude the Obscure* (1895) the schoolmaster Gillingham uses the odd dialect word 'lumpering' while talking to his fellow teacher Phillotson, and Hardy feels the need to editorialize: 'Though well-trained and even proficient masters, they occasionally used a dialect-word of their boyhood to each other in private.' In *Tess of the d'Urbervilles* (1891) he parenthetically explains that Tess's mother habitually speaks dialect, while Tess herself, 'who had passed the Sixth Standard in the National School under a London-trained mistress, spoke two languages: the dialect at home, more or less; ordinary English abroad and to persons of quality'.

Hardy grasped that trying to perpetuate the obsolete and obsolescent requires an act of forgetting that is almost a kind of sickness. Far from subscribing to William Barnes's revivalism, he opined that 'Purism, whether in grammar or in vocabulary, almost always means ignorance.' The addicts of Anglo-Saxonism might care to consider the possibility that the language they cherish – a hybrid of the several languages brought to Britain in the fifth century by the Angles and the Saxons (as well as by the Frisians and the Jutes) – was itself far from pure. Its Proto-Germanic source had been coloured by contact with other tongues – including, quite possibly, that of Phoenician adventurers.

No such awareness modified the arguments of the composer and virtuoso pianist Percy Grainger (1882–1961), an athletic Australian who took a keen interest in Norwegian dialects and old English folk songs. It may well be that Grainger knew nothing of William Barnes's writing, but he shared Barnes's love of a kind of bygone language more poetically immediate than 'book English', and his most memorable project was championing what he called 'blue-eyed English'. The Anglo-Saxons, he insisted, had had blue eyes, and all imports into the language since their time had debased the Anglo-Saxon stock. Grainger was serious about eradicating foreign words, but his blue-eyed prose is hardly pretty: readers will tire quickly of *joy-quaffed* standing in for *enjoyed*, *othery* ('different'), *tone-tool* ('instrument') and the especially absurd *thor-juice-talker* ('telephone'). Moreover, Grainger hardly helped his cause by being an enthusiastic advocate of flagellation, racial separatism and incest.

Barnes and Grainger were creative amateurs. For a professional perspective on purism at the end of the Victorian period we can turn to Thomas Lounsbury, Emeritus Professor of English at Yale University (or, as the title pages of his books state, 'in Yale University'), who writes in *The Standard of Usage in English* (1908) of 'phrases borrowed from foreign tongues, especially from the French' that 'replace and drive out the genuine vernacular'. Emotive words – Lounsbury plainly sees this is a loss. He goes on to say that 'the history of language is the history of corruptions', yet makes the point that 'a return to what is the theoretically correct usage would seem like a return to barbarism'.[4]

'Theoretically correct' is generous. To hanker after the very distant past is grotesque; it denies progress and misunderstands the essential dynamism of language. The world's languages are forever rubbing up against one another, and as they do so they alter. Items from one language enter another. The more of us there are on this planet, and the more we travel, the more this will happen. The most extreme kind of alteration is, of course, death. Every two weeks a language becomes extinct. Around five hundred of the world's roughly six thousand languages have fewer than a hundred speakers, and it is fair to say that more than half our languages are moribund. A language disappears because the people who speak it die – victims of conflict, political oppression, sickness or a cataclysm such as an earthquake – or because their culture is swamped by another, more powerful one – perhaps because of urbanization or thanks to the long reach of the commercial media. Sometimes abandoning one's language can be a survival strategy. When we speak of the death of a language, we mean the end of its being spoken. If written records are preserved, we may be able to revive it. But in practice, with the exception of Hebrew, extinct languages have not come back to life.

Some see a reduction in the number of languages as convenient. According to this view, in an ideal world there would be just one language – theirs. The result would be a return to the perfect condition that supposedly existed before Babel. This is naïve. Global peace will not be achieved by humanity's sharing a single language, and no one language provides a mechanism fit to convey all the complexity of human thought. Languages other than our own suggest different ways of understanding the world. Moreover, the death of languages has high costs: in the short term we lose some of the knowledge accumulated by their now departed speakers, and in the longer term the creativity and vitality of our own language diminish. Maintaining the diversity of languages supports a complex ecosystem, a richness akin to the genetic variety that is essential to evolution.

Purists are possessive: they are tremendously proprietorial not only about the correctness of what they say, but also about the myriad examples they have corralled of other people's gaffes and atrocities. They especially like to trot out specimens of vocabulary that they find offensive. In the 1550s Thomas Wilson could parody an ambitious clergyman's use of such spurious words as 'domesticall' and 'Archigrammarian'; a hundred years later Peter Heylin relished listing the 'uncouth' words in a recent history of the reign of Charles I, including some that we now use a good deal ('complicated', 'relax') and others that we don't ('accalladoes', 'anomabous'); and Addison wrote in *The Spectator* about a soldier whose 'Modern Military Eloquence' meant that his father, reading one of his letters home, 'found it contained great news, but could not guess what it was'.[5] Purists continue to do this sort of thing. Of course, in their eyes the faults they find are matters of eternal verity, not personal taste. But much of what is now considered pure was once regarded as barbarous. Purists exult in their resistance to change not because they have a rigorous understanding of the relationship between language and time, but because they are heavily invested in the status quo – or, more often, in a fantasy of the status quo. References to the 'mother tongue' are telling: for language as for women, purity has traditionally been represented as the ideal.

A dislike of borrowed words can be presented as a preference for simplicity. Borrowings, so the argument goes, confuse people. They make documents hard to understand. They obfuscate the truth – of the scriptures, for instance. But purists in their hostility to imported terms fail to keep pace with the changing realities of the world around them. Although some borrowings are whimsical, most are not. A borrowed word answers a need; rejection of a word is in many cases also the rejection of a phenomenon.

As the example of Percy Grainger shows, the purist's nostalgia can have a sinister edge. In his book *On the Death and Life of Languages* the French scholar Claude Hagège makes the point that purism is often the mark of a language in decline; those who use a language in a ritualistic fashion, or express a finicky concern for traditions even though their command of them is far from perfect, are defensive zealots who 'want to give themselves the illusion of full competence by artificially maintaining a stringent norm that runs counter to the healthy image of life'.[6]

Purists are people who want you to do things their way. At their best, they are well-informed and their arguments are carefully constructed. The Society for Pure English, founded in 1913 by the poet Robert Bridges and quickly joined by an assortment of other distinguished literary figures including E. M. Forster and Thomas Hardy, published a series of tracts between 1919 and 1947. The SPE Tracts are impressively scholarly. The project began from an enlightened position: democracy was a watchword, and there was a policy of not interfering with 'living developments'. Yet the SPE's name was a promise of failure. Societies 'for' anything are almost always busily defiant in the face of massive and irreversible realities. And 'Pure' in this case came to mean 'Traditional'. By the 1930s the SPE was preoccupied with such things as defending the honour of English from American invasions, and its efforts were being likened to those in the political sphere of Europe's ascendant Fascists.

There is a purism of a different and smaller kind, which begins – and often also ends – with the protest that a word is not being used in its true etymological sense. The idea is that we should treat words as they were treated in the language from which we derived them. But do we really believe that a candidate should be dressed in white, that being meticulous means feeling beset by fears, or that a sycophant must be someone who reveals the whereabouts of figs? A real stickler for etymology would be required, absurdly, to claim the truth of these definitions.

Many other words have 'etymologically pure' senses that are now lost to most English-speakers. I can remember being told as a child that my reference to a dilapidated stable was incorrect, because only things made of stone could truly be called 'dilapidated'. I can also recall being instructed that *to decimate* meant to kill one person in ten. This procedure had been practised in the Roman army, where among a unit that had committed some offence one man in ten, chosen by lot, would be clubbed or stoned to death. It did not stop with the passing of Imperial Rome; in his account of the Battle of Stalingrad, Antony Beevor describes a Soviet divisional commander lining up cowardly riflemen and shooting every tenth man in the face until his pistol was emptied.[7] However, *to decimate* is now commonly used to mean something more like 'to kill or destroy a significant part of something or some group'. Opportunities to employ the verb in its Latin sense are rare, and pretending that this is the only permissible sense is a denial of reality. *To decimate* has been used not just of killing, but also of taxation and in mathematics, since the seventeenth century, and has been employed 'loosely' for a couple of hundred years at least.

Sometimes the etymologies to which such heed is paid are in any case bogus. Those who suggest that *till* should be written with a single *l* imagine that it is a contraction of *until*, but in fact *until* was originally spelled *untill* and is a thirteenth-century intensification of the much older *till*. Something similar happens with *none*. I tend, through force of habit, to treat *none* as though it is singular: 'None of us is going on holiday soon.' Occasionally this results in what seems quite ungainly phrasing: 'I'm making extra mince pies even though none is likely to be needed.' The idea that *none* takes a singular verb stems from the misconception that *none* is a contraction of *not one*. The popularity of this belief can be traced to Lindley Murray. But in fact *none* is closer to *not any*. The *OED* explains,

'Many commentators state that *none* should take singular concord, but this has generally been less common than plural concord, especially between the 17th and 19th centuries.' It is perhaps worth noting that Robert Lowth uses plural verbs with *none*.

Such professions of etymological fidelity are the fictions of people who claim history as their justification without having troubled to check what the history is. This type of purism often involves manipulating the past, rather than understanding it. More broadly, purism is an emotional commitment, which betrays insecurity and usually results in insensitivity. As for the purists' attempt to repel lexical invasions, it's a repression of life itself. For now, as for all the recorded past, languages are able to cross-pollinate, and as they do so the achievements, visions, philosophies and memories of different cultures interfuse, enriching our expressive resources and making our experience more intricate.

14 Organizing the Victorian treasure-house

Schemes of correctness, large and small

The most redoubtable guardians of proper English are never the grand theorists. Instead they are the defenders of morality. Swift, Lowth and Priestley were all clerics, but their piety was exceeded by the unordained high priests of Victorian correctness.

For a large part of the nineteenth century one of the leading moralists in print was Henry Butter. A follower of the teachings of the Swedish Christian mystic Emanuel Swedenborg, Butter was a prolific author of instructional volumes. His popular titles included *The Etymological Spelling Book* and *Butter's Reading and Spelling in Easy Gradations*. He also addressed himself to impressionable young people in books such as *Maiden, Prepare to Become a Happy Wife* and *Is the Pleasure Worth the Penalty?* The latter was meant for young men and afforded 'a common-sense view of the leading vice of the age'. In *What's the Harm of Fornication?* Butter expanded on the subject, condemning young men's appetite for 'riotous enjoyment, which they mistakenly fancy to be happiness'. Extramarital sex was guaranteed to 'insanely pervert them to the destruction of their health'.[1] Butter is interesting because he so clearly sees moral teaching and language training as related activities. His volumes on one subject tend to include advertisements for those on the other.

The 1860s witnessed a public quarrel between two of the most strident arbiters, Henry Alford and George Washington Moon. Alford was a piously evangelical man. At the age of eight he had written a 'history of the Jews', and at ten a sermon setting out 'what looking unto Jesus means' and 'when we ought to look unto Jesus'. By the time he published a series of articles about the state of English in 1863, under the title *A Plea for the Queen's English*, he was Dean of Canterbury, an established poet and the author of several popular hymns. In these pieces, which appeared in the magazine *Good Words*, Alford worried about 'manly' English's dilution: nothing appeared to upset him more than the 'bespanglement' of English with words imported from other tongues, and he condemned the taste for 'flimsy' foreign terms as morally disgraceful. He fretted about the dropping of *h*s and intrusive *r*s (as at the end of the word 'idea', say), as well as about journalese, the inflated language used in prayer books for children, the prevalence of embarrassing nicknames, the 'false glitter' of borrowings from French, 'terrible' or 'horrible' words (examples being *desirability* and the verb *to evince*), the correct way to pronounce *cucumber*, bad spelling in regional newspapers, and Americanisms – the last of these characterized as typical of a people guilty of 'reckless exaggeration' and a 'blunted sense of moral obligation and duty to man'.[2] Other criticisms were focused closer to home: 'I never knew an English man who misplaced "shall" and "will"; I hardly ever have known an Irish-man or a Scotchman who did not misplace them sometimes.' He added that 'it is strange to observe how incurable the propensity is'.[3]

George Washington Moon was a Fellow of the Royal Society of Literature, who over a period of roughly forty years made it his business to vituperate about eminent figures' errors of language, morality and religious conviction. Born in London to American parents, he forged a career out of arguing with those who dared to offer pronouncements about English usage. His response to Alford's pieces for *Good Words* was initially published as *A Defence of the Queen's English*. When Alford gathered the pieces in a book he called *The Queen's English*, the title of Moon's volume now sounded like an endorsement of Alford rather than an attack, so Moon punchily rebranded it as *The Dean's English*.

Alford was not the first writer Moon clobbered, nor the last. Another of his books had the title *The Bad English of Lindley Murray and Other Writers on the English Language*, and attributed to Murray an 'almost malicious pleasure' in the confusions caused by his rules of grammar.[4] Moon was explicit that he was paying Murray back for the pain he had suffered as a child when forced to learn his grammatical rules by rote. But it was the squabble with Alford, a living target who could answer back, that attracted widespread notice.

Moon addressed himself to Alford in the form of a long letter which, although signed 'Yours most respectfully', was larded with disrespect. He argued that 'Great writers may make or may mar a language. It is with them, and not with grammarians, that the responsibility rests; for language is what custom makes it; and custom is, has been, and always will be more influenced by example than by precept.'[5] Moon, incidentally, is one of the few authorities to be explicit in saying that one should never begin a sentence with *And*.

Of the two, Alford is the more representative, a self-professed amateur who characterized his writings as a collection of 'stray notes'. As a rule, people who tell you they are offering a hotchpotch of stray notes are really peddling what they hope are big ideas. False modesty is not an accident, but an assault strategy. Typical of this movement with its surreptitious moralism (and xenophobia, to boot) was the best-selling *Enquire Within Upon Everything*, which sold 592,000 copies between 1856 and 1877.[6] It contained a wealth of information about household management, and dropped in on such thorny linguistic issues as the use of hyphens and the imperfections of regional usage. Indeed, a list was provided of 'examples of provincial dialects [that] will be found very amusing'.[7] This sturdy volume – advertised as offering guidance on how to cure a headache or bury a relative – set down 256 'rules and hints for correct speaking'. 'Rules and hints' suggests just how flaky its rules could be. Apparently, one should not say 'If I am not mistaken'; it is better to say 'If I mistake not'. 'Two couples' is an unacceptable locution; the proper form is 'four persons'. 'Instead of "Handsome is *as* handsome does," say "Handsome is who handsome does."' 'Instead of "It is raining very *hard*," say "It is raining very fast."' And 'He must not do it' is inferior to 'He needs not do it' – never mind the difference in meaning. Not everything in the list looks wrong-headed. One can hardly complain about the instruction that instead of 'I enjoy bad health' one should say 'My health is not good'.[8] But it is surprising that the author thought it acceptable to talk about one's health at all.

Enquire Within Upon Everything also had great fun – or what its author thought to be great fun – at the expense of a woman called Mrs Alexander Hitching. This woman, supposedly the author's neighbour, had 'a most unpleasant habit of misusing the letter H to such a degree that our sensitive nerves have often been shocked when in her society'. She was therefore known to the world as Mrs Halexander Itching.[9] Sensitivity to the opinions of one's neighbours, be those opinions real or imagined, is one of the most exasperating features of daily life; it creates anxiety, and inspires us only to a tawdry homogeneity. Among Mrs Hitching's sniffy coevals, sneering at people who misplaced their *h*s was common. This was fairly new: the habit had not been stigmatized until the second half of the eighteenth century, and it seems it was Thomas Sheridan who created sensitivity about the matter. John Walker had been especially forceful in condemning this 'vice', which he thought was most common in London. Now there was even a little sixpenny manual entitled *Poor Letter H*, presented as the work of the abused letter itself, which sold more than 40,000 copies in the ten years following its publication in 1854. Though hardly a success on the scale of *Enquire Within*, it was still indicative of the snobberies and anxieties occasioned by English usage. It was read mainly for amusement, not instruction. Its sales led others to try to cash in; Charles William Smith in 1866 produced a similar volume with the somewhat unfortunate title *Mind Your H's and Take Care of Your R's*. Smith thought English was 'perhaps, the most ill-spoken language in the world', and he found the blurring of the 'fine, manly sound' of the letter *r* 'more worthy a monkey than a man'.[10]

This one easily observable detail of pronunciation created what I think of as a 'toxic binary': if you got it right, you were not guaranteed acceptance, but if you got it wrong you could count on being a pariah. It is far from clear when *h*-dropping began. In 1880 Alfred Leach published *The Letter H: Past, Present, and Future*, in which he wondered, 'Why has H-dropping been made the butt of ridicule in the present century only?'[11] Leach does not reach back far enough, but he was right to speak of 'ridicule', and such ridicule persists: in Britain, whether a person pronounces *h*s is still a significant shibboleth. Leach comes up with a startling image on this matter, claiming that 'As the chemist employs a compound of sulphur in order to decide by the reaction whether a substance belongs to the group of higher or of baser metals, so does society apply the H-test to unknown individuals, and group them according to their comportment under the ordeal'.[12]

This contrast is a theme of Victorian fiction: the 'two nations' formed by different backgrounds and 'ordered by different manners' that are depicted by Disraeli (these words are his), Dickens and Elizabeth Gaskell.[13] In *David Copperfield,* Uriah Heep strategically drops his *h*s to confirm how "umble' he is, and the behaviour of this grotesque figure must have influenced some readers to cling on to the letter, though ideally without going as far as the likeable servant Sam Weller in *The Pickwick Papers,* who adds *h*s in inappropriate places. In 1869 Alexander Ellis, a prolific scholar of phonetics, found that 'at the present day great strictness in pronouncing *h* is demanded as a test of education and position in society'; in 1890 the Oxford scholar Henry Sweet wrote that the pronunciation of the letter served as 'an almost infallible test of education and refinement'.[14] Of Sweet, it is perhaps sufficient to say that he was the main model for Henry Higgins, the professor of phonetics in George Bernard Shaw's *Pygmalion.* But it is hard to mention Ellis without noting some of his many eccentricities: he weighed himself both dressed and undressed every day, always carried two sets of nail scissors and a selection of tuning forks, and wore a greatcoat with twenty-eight pockets, which he called Dreadnought.

These are not just whimsical details. Ellis needed the tuning forks for his study of the pitch of musical instruments, and his work in comparative musicology fed into his thinking about language. The twenty-eight pockets of his greatcoat allowed him to organize the manuscripts and notes he liked to carry. Ellis was in all things systematic, and in his pursuit of his masterpiece, a five-volume analysis of English pronunciation, this was vital. In its opening chapter, he makes the following statement: 'Spoken language is born of any two or more associated human beings. It grows, matures, assimilates, changes, incorporates, excludes, develops, languishes, decays, dies utterly, with the societies to which it owes its being. It is difficult to seize its chameleon form at any moment . . . The different sensations of each speaker, the different appreciations of each hearer, their intellectual growth, their environment, their aptitude for conveying or receiving impressions, their very passions, originate, change, and create language.' He goes on to say that 'a uniform system of spoken sounds cannot extend over a very large district'.[15] Ellis's writing is marked not by the rigid certainty of his peers, but by descriptive-

ness and an emphasis on the difficulty of reaching clear-cut conclusions. 'Writers on phonetics,' he comments, 'are too apt to measure
the pronouncing powers of others by their own.'[16] He is doubtful
about his predecessors' notions of right and wrong. In a long note
he comments on John Walker's condemnation of 'unwritten
language', observing that 'it is not . . . the speakers that are in fault
in obeying and carrying out the organic laws of speech and word
formation', but rather 'those stiff-necked, pedantic, unphilosophical,
miserably-informed, and therefore supremely certain, self-confident,
and self-conceited orthographers who . . . maintain that though their
rules must be right, it is only the exceptions which prove them'.[17]

This sense of the absolute as something fragile, and of the value
of avoiding *ex cathedra* statements about delicately shaded matters,
was not shared by many of Ellis's contemporaries. In 1855 a London
publisher brought out a volume entitled *Never Too Late to Learn:
Mistakes of Daily Occurrence in Speaking, Writing, and Pronunciation,
Corrected*, which drew attention to more than four hundred everyday
blunders and their remedies. Some of these now seem strange. 'I
propose going to town next week' should apparently be 'I *purpose*
going to town next week', and we also learn that in speaking of
Gibbon's 'Rise and Fall of the Roman Empire' we ought to
pronounce *rise* so that it rhymes with *price*, although really it would
be better not to speak of it at all, since the title of Gibbon's book
was *The History of the Decline and Fall of the Roman Empire*.[18] The
following year a New York firm released an expanded version, in
which the number of flubs had increased to five hundred.

Edward Gould's *Good English; or, Popular Errors in Language* (1867)
is typical of the fierce certainty of the nineteenth-century amateur.
It identified a deterioration in English over the preceding twenty-
five years. An American, Gould mentions the popularity of Alford in
the United States, but while he finds 'great value' in parts of the
Dean's English, he also accuses him of 'bad faith' and inconsistency.
George Washington Moon's counterblast is, however, 'a masterpiece'.[19]
Gould's real interest is not in Moon and Alford, but in what he labels
'misused words'. He is particularly exercised by reference to 'a couple
of days', 'a couple of dollars', and in fact any so-called 'couple' where
the items in question are not 'fastened, chained, joined, linked,

connected together'. I can remember being gently reproved as a child for saying 'a couple' in reference to a number greater than two, but Gould's concern is of a different nature. He believes we would be better off talking about 'a pair of dollars' and 'a brace of days'. He suggests, too, that we often say 'a few' where really we mean 'a many'.[20]

No one better represented the American position on such matters than Richard Grant White, a native of Brooklyn who was a distinguished editor of Shakespeare and a noted cellist. In 1871 he published *Words and Their Uses*, a book full of complaints about 'newspaper English', the inadequacy of dictionaries, and 'words that are not words'. He even included a section of Briticisms – 'There is a British affectation in the use of some . . . words which is worthy of some attention' – and gave as an example the British use of the verb *to ride* only in terms of going 'on horseback, or on the back of some beast less dignified and comfortable', where an American might speak of riding in a carriage. 'English,' he argued, 'is an almost grammarless language', and 'In English, words are formed into sentences by the operation of an invisible power, which is like magnetism.'[21]

It is in his discussion of 'words that are not words' that Grant White seems most similar in temperament to today's snipers. *Enthused* is a 'ridiculous word . . . in vogue in the southern part of the United States', *gubernatorial* is a 'clumsy piece of verbal pomposity [which] should be thrust out of use', *practitioner* is 'an unlovely intruder, which has slipped into the English language through the physician's gate', and so on.[22] Nine years later came a sequel, *Every-Day English*, in which he tackled among other things Americanisms, spelling, and the 'enfeebling' effect of a fastidious concern with verbal elegance. He also targeted common misusages, opining that 'Some of the most ludicrous mistakes in language that are made are to be seen where they are likely to do the most harm – in the street railway cars'.[23]

Another American, Thomas Embley Osmun, writing under the pseudonym Alfred Ayres, published *The Verbalist: A Manual Devoted to Brief Discussions of the Right and Wrong Use of Words* (1882) and *The Essentials of Elocution* (1897). Osmun was not one to speak softly. In the first of these books he occupied himself with what he liked to call 'gross vulgarism'. For instance, answering the question 'How do you do?' with the word 'Nicely' was 'The very quintessence of popinjay vulgarity' and signing a letter off with 'Yours, &c.' was a mark of being 'ignorant and obtuse' – 'Few vulgarisms are equally offensive'.[24] *The Essentials of Elocution* presented chapters on subjects such as 'Deportment' and 'The Pause – Its Importance'. Ayres fancied himself a social commentator, remarking on the disastrous effects of mumbled sermons on church attendance, and claiming that lawyers' diction tends to be better than actors'.

On both sides of the Atlantic, newspapers and magazines played a leading part in the crusade for better English. In the 1870s, the *New York Times, New York Evening Post, Chicago Tribune* and *Boston Daily Advertiser* were all significant platforms for conservative comment on language. In Britain the role belonged above all to *The Times*; its writers were conscious of the paper's status as a journal of record, and letters to the editor frequently addressed its failure to uphold linguistic standards. Thus the issue of 14 February 1872 contains a letter from one E. K. Karslake, a barrister, complaining about the word *cablegram*, applauding the paper's leader writers, and then discussing etymology – with detailed reference to Greek – as well as suggesting that a telegram 'sent by a submarine cable' might be called a 'thalassogram', which is 'not unpleasant to the ear'. In the next column there is a letter from J. T. of the Athenaeum which laments the 'prevalent delusion that it is easy to write good English': 'the mere act of rewriting, with intent to improve, is a wonderful solvent of the haze which usually accompanies first conceptions', and 'the submergence of the individual in the committee, which finds so much favour under Constitutional Governments, is a serious drawback as regards good composition'.[25] Items of this kind were common in *The Times*, and they were given considerable space.

In the later stages of the nineteenth century, there was among serious writers on language a move towards surveying usage. This began with a significant effort to organize English vocabulary, which seemed huge and unruly. Scientific terminology was one area of dense growth. Another was the arts. There was more professional jargon and a richer lexis of fashion. As the horizons of the English-speaking world expanded, the word-stock did so too. The use of prefixes and compounds increased, as did other means of forming new words: clipping (*gym*), blending (for instance, *chortle* from *snort* and *chuckle*), deriving verbs from nouns (*to reference, to package*), and so on.[26] Enthusiasts characterized these masses of new vocabulary as armies, while sceptics muttered about ill winds and foul streams.

Among those who busied themselves with classifying the welter of verbiage was Peter Mark Roget, a distinguished physician who was the son of a Swiss pastor. The first edition of his *Thesaurus of English Words and Phrases, Classified and Arranged So as to Facilitate the Expression of Ideas and Assist in Literary Composition* – or, to give it its shorter name, *Roget's Thesaurus* – was published in 1852. The concept was not new, but Roget's presentation, with its five-level hierarchy, was pleasing. It won a large audience, and by 1879 thirty-five editions had appeared. Roget's masterpiece of taxonomy is an example of a kind of achievement all too common in the history of reference works and books on language: admired for its practical usefulness, applauded for its theoretical soundness, yet used rarely by most who own a copy.

There was a much bigger project to come. The Philological Society, founded in 1842, identified serious weaknesses in existing dictionaries. In 1857 it set up a committee to collect words and idioms that had not previously been registered. Two papers presented to the Society that year by Richard Chenevix Trench laid the foundation for the opus that would become the *Oxford English Dictionary*, a comprehensive record of English vocabulary that improved significantly on the deficiencies of Johnson's work and Webster's. Initially the new dictionary was expected to be a supplement to these volumes, but it became clear that something greater than this was needed. It would be compiled on historical principles. The effectiveness of this approach had been shown by Charles Richardson's *A New Dictionary of the English Language* (1837), which attempted a factually correct history of every word it contained. The creators of the *OED* saw that each word's life had to be documented: all senses had to be included for all words, even obsolete ones. Real work did not get under way until 1878 when Oxford University Press took over the project and then agreed to pay for James Murray, the president of the Philological Society, to be its editor. The first part of the *OED*, 352 pages long, appeared on 29 January 1884, and the last in April 1928, thirteen years after Murray died of heart failure. Its dozen finished volumes comprised 15,487 pages, and five years later there came a thirteenth volume, rounding up omissions.

One of James Murray's most enduringly useful ideas was that English vocabulary has no definite limits. Its 'vast aggregate' of words is like the 'nebulous masses familiar to the astronomer, in which a clear and unmistakable nucleus shades off on all sides, through zones of decreasing brightness, to a dim marginal film that seems to end nowhere'.[27] You can see the core of English well enough, but you cannot see its circumference. Whoever compiles a dictionary has to draw the line somewhere: this is a matter of policy, however, not an exactly scientific calculation. Murray was a descriptive lexicographer, but even the work of a hardcore descriptivist is an abridgement. Nevertheless, the *OED* was alive to the range of English as no previous dictionary had been, and Murray's origins in rural Roxburghshire, where his formal schooling ended at fourteen, must have shaped his sense of what English was; in editing the *OED*, he was providing an account of the nation's history, and his Scottish roots made it clear to him that this had multiple centres and was as much about the provinces and rural communities as about London and other big cities.

The history of the *OED*'s title is vexed. Murray chose at first *A New English Dictionary Showing the History of the Language from the Earliest Times*. Benjamin Jowett, the energetic but also meddlesome Vice-Chancellor of Oxford University, sneakily altered this in proof to *A New English Dictionary Written so as to Show the Continuous History of Words*. Murray was appalled, but attempted a compromise: *A New English Dictionary on a Historical Basis*. It was the view of more than one of his associates that this should read 'an Historical Basis'. The title eventually changed again – to *A New English Dictionary on Historical Principles, Founded Mainly on the Materials Collected by Members of the Philological Society*. From 1895 it was commonly known as the *Oxford English Dictionary*, which was the title under which it would be reissued in 1933.

Murray presented himself as a collector, and the *OED* as an arrangement of facts rather than as a narrative. But the finished product is not just an inventory; it has some of the bias of a story. The first edition of the *OED* pays more attention to literary texts than to non-literary ones, treats medieval writings patchily, provides really good coverage of scientific vocabulary only for the nineteenth century, and indeed overall treats that period and the late sixteenth century more thoroughly than the two hundred years in between, though the representation of sixteenth-century vocabulary is incomplete.[28] Moreover, it pays scant attention to one of the great new developments of the nineteenth century: the working-class newspaper, a radical type of publication that explained to its readers the reasons for their poverty. The *OED* was a stunning achievement, and its reception was warm, but, even as its supposed inclusiveness caused anxiety about a collapsing of the divide between good and bad Englishes, there was much that it did not disclose about the range and colour of English vocabulary.

It seems a happy coincidence that the *OED*'s first cited user of the unusual words *interlinguistic* ('intermingling in speech') and *lexiconize* ('to compile a lexicon') is the novelist George Meredith. For few other Victorian authors write as sharply about linguistic self-consciousness. Though now little read, Meredith was once celebrated as the last of the great Victorian men of letters. His perspective on English was that of a man capable of seeing it as an outsider would, and in this he was lastingly influenced by the period he spent as a teenager at school in Neuwied, near the German city of Koblenz.

Meredith relishes hyperbole, and so do his characters. In his political novel *Beauchamp's Career* (1874) he has one of his female leads, the cold and jealous beauty Cecilia Halkett, reflect that 'between the vulgarity of romantic language and the baldness of commonplace . . . our English gives us no choice', for 'we cannot be dignified in simplicity'. The idea of choice is one that Meredith emphasizes. He frequently pursues the question of what English affords its users and fails to afford them, and attitudes to English usage are often also an index of attitudes to class and gender. In *The House on the Beach* (1877) a young woman's unsuitability as a match for a much older man is summed up thus: 'She's sharp on grammar, and a man mayn't like that much when he's a husband.' In *Lord Ormont and his Aminta* (1894) a character observes that 'There'll be a "general rabble tongue," unless we English are drilled in the languages we filched from.' Of an uneducated woman in *One of our Conquerors* (1891) Meredith writes, 'her English was guilty of sudden lapses to the Thameswater English of commerce and drainage instead of the upper wells'. Most memorable is the journalist Rockney in the author's early, unfinished *Celt and Saxon* (posthumously published in 1910), who is said to have his hand 'upon the national heart' on account of 'his art of writing round English, instead of laborious Latinised periods: and the secret of the art was his meaning what he said. It was the personal throb.' Meredith was sensitive to his age's difficulties with meaning what it said, and in celebrating the intimacy of a 'personal throb' he was inviting the innovations of literary modernism, an artistic escape from repression into stylistic autonomy.

The literature of the 1920s, astonishing in its innovations, was produced by writers born in the 1880s: Virginia Woolf, James Joyce, Ezra Pound, T. S. Eliot. Their precision was also an act of destruction. In Woolf's first novel, *The Voyage Out* (1915), the main character is Rachel Vinrace, whose life initially seems hemmed in by convention. We are told that 'her mind was in the state of an intelligent man's in the beginning of the reign of Queen Elizabeth'. Yet she wants to break free, and we see this in her reading: she goes for Meredith, but above all consumes 'modern books, books in shiny yellow covers'. As she travels to South America on a ship that belongs to her father, she emerges into the full glare of modernity. At one point she imagines being 'flung into the sea, to be washed hither and thither, and driven about the roots of the world – the idea was incoherently delightful'. *The Voyage Out* is Woolf's ominous imagining of the evaporation of Victorianism and its replacement by a more fragmented, visionary culture. When Rachel reads, 'the very words of books were steeped in radiance' and 'seemed to drive roads back to the very beginning of the world'. Not for the moderns the old view of Francis Bacon that intellectual life becomes sick 'when men study words and not matter': Woolf's novel imagines, with some prescience, a new age preoccupied with words and symbols, in which philosophical questions are likely to be linguistic, and in which, too, the struggle of the individual to find a voice – to find a language in which to live – becomes paramount.

15 The warden of English

Henry Watson Fowler and Modern English Usage

The recovery of Victorian values, such as thrift and self-reliance, has repeatedly been espoused by British politicians, notably Margaret Thatcher in the 1980s. But, as I have suggested, those values have never really needed recovering, because they have never gone away. They have survived in the daily lives of men and women who, unlike Rachel Vinrace, have found nothing delightful in the incoherence of modernity.

One of the most influential of these has been Henry Watson Fowler, described by his obituarist in *The Times* as 'a lexicographical genius' possessed of 'a crispness, a facility, and an unexpectedness which have not been equalled'.[1] Small, energetic and eccentric, Fowler was a schoolmaster for two decades before he chose a second career as a freelance writer, and he was close to fifty by the time he published *The King's English* in 1906. Fowler originally proposed as its title 'The New Solecist for Literary Tiros', and the finished volume – on which he collaborated with his brother Francis, usually known as Frank and a keen grower of tomatoes – is stocked with examples of 'conspicuous' solecisms, which serve as illustrations of 'how not to write'. Many of the blunders were culled from newspapers, and many from Victorian novels (Marie Corelli gets a hard time over her affection for ugly adverbs such as 'vexedly' and 'bewilderedly', Thackeray for mixing up 'which' and 'that'). The Fowlers were not men to mince their words. 'There are certain American verbs,' they stated, 'that remind Englishmen of the barbaric taste illustrated by such town names as Memphis'. They argued that 'a very firm stand ought to be made against *placate, transpire,* and *antagonize,* all of which have English patrons'. Quite what the Fowlers

182

had against Memphis is not recorded. But they are keen on strong pronouncements. Recognizing that *fall* is more vivid than *autumn*, they comment, 'we once had as good a right to it as the Americans; but we have chosen to let the right lapse, and to use the word now is no better than larceny.'

The most celebrated statement of the Fowler brothers' vision occurs on the book's first page, where 'general principles' for the good writer are succinctly set down. One should aim always 'to be direct, simple, brief, vigorous, and lucid', and this principle 'may be translated into practical rules': one must prefer 'the familiar word to the far-fetched', 'the concrete word to the abstract', 'the single word to the circumlocution', 'the short word to the long', and 'the Saxon word to the Romance'. It is significant that the Fowlers call these 'practical rules'.

Although *The King's English* sold quite briskly, and the brothers together produced *The Concise Oxford English Dictionary*, the reputation of Henry Fowler is far greater than that of Frank, and rests on *A Dictionary of Modern English Usage*, which he wrote alone. Published in 1926, it sold 60,000 copies in its first year. In time it came to be known simply as 'Fowler', and for more than half a century it influenced British ideas of English usage more than any other book. It continues to have plenty of admirers.

At a time when scholars of language were embracing the descriptive method of lexicography, Fowler was prescriptive. Yet although *A Dictionary of Modern English Usage* was backward-looking when it came out – certainly not 'modern' – it was not revised until the 1960s. We can gauge its temper from the fact that Fowler at one time wanted to call it 'Oxford Pedantics'. Devising titles was not one of his strengths. But while some parts of *A Dictionary of Modern English Usage* possess an air of both Oxonian grandeur and submolecular pedantry, others manifest a striking reasonableness. He is much more flexible in his thinking than many of his admirers have seemed to imagine. For instance, he says it is acceptable to use *whose* of inanimate objects – 'These are designs whose merits I appreciate', instead of 'These are designs the merits of which I appreciate'. Many would demur, but Fowler enjoyably comments that 'good writing is surely difficult enough without the forbidding of things that have historical grammar, & present intelligibility, & obvious convenience, on their side, & lack only – starch.'[2] We may smile at his aversion to *parlous* ('a word that wise men leave alone') and at his informing us that *dialogue* is 'neither necessarily, nor necessarily not, the talk of two persons', but we are more likely to nod in agreement when he describes as 'pompous ornaments' the words *beverage* and *emporium*, suggests that the pronunciation of *hotel* with a silent *h* 'is certainly doomed, & is not worth fighting for', observes that 'shortness is a merit in words' and 'extra syllables reduce, not increase, vigour', and insists that when we say *sausage roll* the emphasis should be on *roll*.[3] His affection for the ampersand (&) seems, in contrast, oddly fetishistic.

One of Fowler's better-known judgements concerns split infinitives: 'The English-speaking world may be divided into (1) those who neither know nor care what a split infinitive is; (2) those who do not know, but care very much; (3) those who know & condemn; (4) those who know & approve; & (5) those who know & distinguish.' The second group, with whom you may be painfully familiar, are guilty of 'tame acceptance of the misinterpreted opinion of others' and 'subject their sentences to the queerest distortions' to escape split infinitives. Characteristically, Fowler finds a really 'deafening' split infinitive with which to appal us: 'Its main idea is *to* historically, even while events are maturing, & divinely – from the Divine point of view – *impeach* the European system of Church & States.' But he establishes, just a touch grandly, the principle that 'We will split infinitives sooner than be ambiguous or artificial.'[4]

Fowler is not a systematic grammarian. Rather, he has good intuitions, and he examines his intuitions. His great concern is 'idiom' – 'that is idiomatic which it is natural for a normal Englishman to say or write'. We can see problems here: what is 'a normal Englishman', for instance, and what are we to make of that almost throwaway 'say or write'? Fowler's impression of idiomatic usage appears to be based on statements extracted from a variety of nameless informants. One suspects they were not numerous. Fowler favoured the example of southern, male English-speakers, and it is clear that he trusted above all his own judgement. 'What the wise man does,' he writes, 'is to recognize that the conversational usage of educated people in general . . . is the naturalizing authority.'[5]

'Educated people in general' were a group he could not hope to canvass in much depth, but there was always one 'wise man' he could consult immediately.

Despite his moments of pomposity, and for all his carping about the wicked ways of sports journalists and children, Fowler has lasting appeal. Plenty of people have found it hard not to admire someone who can dismiss the use of *frock* rather than *dress* as a 'nurseryism', state without explanation that *pixy* is better than *pixie*, and say that *salad days* 'is fitter for parrots' than for human speech'.[6] There's a savviness, too, when he notes the habit of using inverted commas to apologize for slang.

A great deal of what Fowler advises has not been adopted: we do not say, as he proposed, *flutist* rather than *flautist* or *contradictious* rather than *contradictory*. From the vantage point of the early twenty-first century, many of his positions look like lost causes. Those who continue to revere him do so because they would like to climb inside Fowler's little world. The idea of Fowler, even if not the reality of what he wrote, is part of that nimbus of Englishness that includes a fondness for flowers and animals, brass bands, cups of milky tea, net curtains, collecting stamps, village cricket, the quiz and the crossword, invisible suburbs, invented traditions and pugnacious insularity. All these are areas where a love of detail goes hand in hand with firmly held opinions. Even the seemingly innocent brewing of a hot drink can be a subject of passionate debate.

Among Americans, Fowler has wielded little influence. Instead the big beasts policing the jungle of usage have proved to be Strunk and White, two men whose names have been etched in the minds of several generations of American high-school students. *The Elements of Style*, originally conceived by William Strunk in 1918 as a pamphlet for distribution to students at Cornell University, was expanded by his former student E. B. White – author of the delightful children's book *Charlotte's Web* – and published with his name alongside Strunk's in 1959. *The Elements of Style* has many fans. It contains some unimpeachable advice ('Be clear', for instance), but a great deal of what it has to say looks quaint now. Is 'six persons' preferable to 'six people'? Does the instruction 'Use the active voice' mean one should never use the passive? Are we really

THE LANGUAGE WARS

supposed to accept the imperative 'Write with nouns and verbs, not with adjectives and adverbs', when it is followed by the claim that 'The adjective hasn't been built that can pull a weak or inaccurate noun out of a tight place' – a sentence that contains three adjectives?[7] *The Elements of Style* has two obvious virtues: brevity and a low price. It has sold more than ten million copies, and has earned some astonishing tributes, the most unlikely of which include a ballet and a song cycle for tenor and soprano – accompanied by, among other things, a typewriter and a banjo. Its continued success owes much to a refusal to be modern; its simplicity seems reassuring although, as with so much that masquerades as simplicity, it is really a cover for imperiousness.

In American publishing, there has since 1906 been *The Chicago Manual of Style*. Currently its section on grammar is the work of Bryan Garner, a Texan lawyer who is also the author of *A Dictionary of Modern American Usage* and the founder of the H. W. Fowler Society. There are numerous other guides to usage, marketed by their publishers as presenting practical solutions to real problems and promoting confidence. But the irony of what I'll call Fowler-love permeates the whole province of usage guides: the people who are most interested in books of this kind are those who need them least.

One of the strengths of Fowler, which makes him well worth revisiting, is his diagnosis of human conditions. In articles on subjects such as 'pride of knowledge', 'worn-out humour', 'irrelevant allusion' and 'popularized technicalities' he deals with matters no less common now than they were in 1926. One category that seems especially useful is 'genteelism', which he defines as 'the rejecting of the ordinary natural word that first suggests itself . . . and the substitution of a synonym that is thought to be less soiled by the lips of the common herd'.[8] The genteel do not speak of bad smells, but rather of unpleasant odours; and instead of being a lodger and going to bed, one is a paying guest and one retires. Expanding on Fowler, Eric Partridge in his book *Usage and Abusage* calls words of this kind 'elegancies'. His list of examples includes 'connubial rites', 'floral tribute', 'mine host', *impecunious, remuneration, bosom, nuptials, veritable* and *umbrage*. These are 'the "literary and cultured English"

186

of those who, as a rule, are neither literary nor cultured'.[9] Partridge's book was published in 1947, and more than sixty years on most of these words are used ironically or playfully. But we recognize the nature of his targets. Fowler for his part stresses that it is wrong to think that words of this kind can never be used. However, their use should not in his view, or in Partridge's, be automatic. That way lies tweeness.

The point about genteelism is that it indicates primness and snootiness rather than any real dignity of thought and character. This disparity between people's reasons for using genteelisms and the reactions genteelism achieves was given memorable expression in the 1950s by Nancy Mitford. In 1954 Alan Ross, a professor at Birmingham University, wrote an article entitled 'Linguistic class-indicators in present-day English', which appeared in a Finnish scholarly journal. Mitford read it and quoted from it in a piece she wrote for the magazine *Encounter*. This and a simplified version of Ross's original article were reprinted in *Noblesse Oblige*, a collection intended as 'an enquiry into the identifiable characteristics of the English aristocracy'. *Noblesse Oblige* demonstrates Mitford's love of 'teases', and its mischievous statements ruffled the feathers of many readers. Ross's contribution attracted particular interest, mainly because it distinguished in detail between 'U' (upper class) and 'non-U' practices. So, for instance, it is non-U when addressing an envelope to place the name of the house in inverted commas ('The Old Rectory', Little Slumberscombe), to sound the *l* in *golf* or in the name *Ralph*, and to speak of a *serviette* rather than a *table napkin*.

A central feature of the usage denigrated by Fowler, Partridge, Ross and Mitford is hyperurbanism, although they do not use this word. This is a form of hypercorrection – which is the name for a mistake made in the course of trying to avoid a mistake or something perceived to be one. Hypercorrection is a significant factor in language change; eventually the 'wrong' form used by someone striving for what he believes to be a prestige form is used so often that it becomes acceptable. The more specific phenomenon of hyperurbanism involves avoiding what is believed to be a 'low' mistake and using a supposedly classier word or pronunciation, although in fact the result is nothing of the sort. Examples include

'between you and I', the erroneous use of *whom* ('Whom are you?')
and saying 'haitch' rather than 'aitch' because of a fear of dropping
one's *h*s.

'Between you and I' causes fits of indignation. It is condemned
as an ignorant effort at elegance. When the *Harper Dictionary of
Contemporary Usage* was published in 1975, the experts consulted did
not agree about much, but fell over one another to condemn this
form of words. It was deemed unacceptable in written English by
98 per cent, and by 97 per cent in speech. W. H. Auden pronounced
it 'Horrible!', Anthony Burgess quipped that it was okay 'only when
"Give it to I" is also used', and the whimsical poet and legendary
Harvard fund-raiser David McCord was moved to exclaim, 'Flying
catfish: NO!!!'[10] The condemnation of 'between you and I' began
in the nineteenth century. As we saw in the opening chapter, these
words occur in *The Merchant of Venice*, and in seventeenth-century
drama they appear in confidential exchanges, as when Lady Froth
in Congreve's *The Double-Dealer* says, 'Between you and I, I had
whimsies and vapours.' Mark Twain wrote 'between you and I' in
his letters. It's hardly the new-fangled perversion that its critics
believe.

One reason, I suspect, that people say 'between you and I' is the
feeling that *you* and *I* belong together. This is not a subliminal
message, but an observation about people's use of 'you and I' as if
it is not a pair of pronouns yoked by a conjunction, but a single
indissoluble unit. You-and-I belong together, and if we're together
the world belongs to you-and-I. Additionally, many people are
confused by the experience, early in life, of being corrected after
making a statement such as 'You and me are friends'. Being drilled
to say 'You and I are friends' has the effect of cementing the attrac-
tion between *you* and *I*.

Reactions along the lines of 'Horrible!' explain why people feel
anxious about their English. And while authors such as Fowler and
Partridge may be of some use to those who are tormented by the
possibility of making mistakes that might cause others to exclaim
(or think) 'Flying catfish', there is a well-established market for more
direct and pragmatic guides. In newspapers and magazines I have
many times seen an advertisement that poses the question: 'Shamed

by your English?' This is one of the more recent versions of an oft-repeated formula. Variants include 'Stop Abusing the English Language' and 'Are YOU ever overheard making mistakes like these?'

For roughly half of the last century the leading advertiser in this field was Sherwin Cody. 'What Are YOUR Mistakes in English?' reads one of Cody's sales pitches. 'They may offend others as much as these offend you.' The text promotes the Sherwin Cody School of English in Rochester, New York, and claims that Mr Cody, 'perhaps the best known teacher of practical English', has 'patented a remarkable device which will quickly find and correct mistakes you unconsciously make'. Originally a journalist and poet, Cody was an advocate of self-improvement, the contemporary of other evangelists in this field such as Charles Atlas and Dale Carnegie; his 'remarkable device' was a home-study course – somewhat disappointing, given that the words inspire thoughts of a tiny machine or prosthetic contraption – which consisted of weekly booklets that taught 'expression' on Mondays, spelling on Tuesdays, punctuation on Wednesdays, grammar on Thursdays, and finally conversation on Fridays.

Cody's approach is now intriguing mainly because of its home-spun character. In his Monday lessons on expression he encouraged his students to rehearse the stories of their lives. By way of example he recounted his own story, ranging from 'My Earliest Recollections – the Storms and Fires in Nebraska' via 'The Early Education of a Country Boy' to 'The Heaven and Hell of Love'. He also emphasized his own success.[11] The result was pleasantly accessible, literary rather than technical – Cody followed nineteenth-century American writers such as Emerson in speaking of books as a means of self-education. But the way he presented his material was narrow; what he billed as the development of one's mental life was to be achieved, apparently, in just fifteen minutes a day. His course contained little grammar and lots of examples, explicitly linking ownership of a toolkit full of nice phrases to professional and material advancement. The danger here was that mastery of language was made to seem like a box of tricks.

The writings of H. W. Fowler and Sherwin Cody are hugely different. But people have turned to them for broadly similar reasons.

Anxieties about one's English typically begin with being told that one has violated a particular rule – more likely a principle or a convention, though it will have been presented to us as rock-solid. In his book *The Devil's Dictionary*, that bitingly cynical provocateur Ambrose Bierce defined *grammar* as 'A system of pitfalls thoughtfully prepared for the feet of the self-made man, along the path by which he advances to distinction.'

A moment ago I broke what I in my schooldays was led to believe was just such a rule. I can remember being taught, when I was seven or eight years old, never to begin a sentence with *And* or *But*. I can also remember the same English teacher telling me that it was unacceptable for me to have called a character in a short story Jonathan. I was young and impressionable, and the rule about not opening sentences with *And* or *But* stuck with me for about a decade, when I began to violate it gleefully.

Having been told as a schoolchild that the habit of starting sentences with *But* or *And* was new and faddish, it came as a surprise to me when much later I encountered King Alfred's ninth-century prose, which positively favours this feature. Any rhetorical gambit will, if overused, begin to seem crass, and a piece of writing in which a large number of sentences begin with a conjunction may strike us as crudely conceived. However, the fusspots provide no such argument. As Kingsley Amis pointed out in *The King's English*, his complement to Fowler, modern 'grammatical martinets' often have no actual knowledge of grammar. But they like the *idea* of grammar because they see in its structures a model of how they would like society to be – organized and orderly, governed by rules and a strict hierarchy.

16 'Speak that I may see thee'

Of dialects and diction

Fowler gives guidance about the pronunciation of troublesome words. In many cases his preferred pronunciation differs from today's norm. For instance, he advises that *waistcoat* should be 'weskut' and that the *i* in *vertigo* should be long. Remarkably, though, he has little to say about dialects. There are passing comments, as when he mentions the different regional names for the bluebell, but where one might expect a separate entry on the subject he directs us to his discussion of jargon. There the question of dialect is dealt with in a single unmemorable sentence: '*dialect* is essentially local; *a dialect* is the variety of a language that prevails in a district, with local peculiarities of vocabulary, pronunciation, & phrase'.[1]

Many of Fowler's fans must have been disappointed by his reticence. Surely he ought to have had something trenchant to say? One explanation is that he felt he lacked the required academic expertise. In the last third of the nineteenth century the study of English dialects, previously little more than a byway of local history, had become academically respectable, and its crowning achievement was Joseph Wright's *The English Dialect Dictionary* (1898–1905). This six-volume publication showed the kind of effort it took to cover the domain. Additionally, Fowler would have been influenced by the policy of James Murray since he admired the *OED* and Murray's methods. The *OED* admitted dialect forms only up till 1500; its introduction stated that dialect words 'require a method of treatment different from that applicable to the words of the literary language'. Fowler may simply have chosen to steer clear of them.

Studying and mapping dialects calls for a great deal of philological dexterity. Many people have been moved to wonder what the point of all the effort is. This is an area in which the disjunction between what happens in universities and what happens outside them is palpable. In the public sphere, dialects are routinely demonized. It is common to treat 'dialect' as though it is somehow opposed to 'language' – as an enemy of language rather than as a part of it. The negative connotations of the word are bound up with false notions: that dialect, like hell, 'is other people'; that dialects are the result of people's failed attempts to govern their language properly; that they are deviant forms of correct speech and writing, rather than having their own distinct patterns and features; and that they are only used by the socially disadvantaged. This is not something uniquely English. Denmark is a good example of a country where dialects have traditionally not been valued. By contrast, in Germany some dialects enjoy considerable prestige.

In any discussion of the subject, it is essential to clarify that accent and dialect are different. Both words were first used in the sixteenth century, when some authorities began to argue that there was such a thing as correct pronunciation. Accent is only one feature of a dialect, which is a variety of language that also differs from other varieties in its vocabulary and grammar. Moreover, while a dialect has its own slang, it is wrong to say that dialects are slang.

Regional features mostly disappeared from written English in the fifteenth century, but they endured in the spoken form. Studying them is a specialized discipline. However, many of us are apt to behave as though we are experts in the field. The narrator of H. G. Wells's novel *In the Days of the Comet* (1906) describes a character who tells a story 'in an Anglian accent that sounded mean and clipped to my Staffordshire ears'. Statements of this kind betray our tribalism. There are, as we all know, pronunciations that are local – not necessarily local to a geographical place, but possibly local to a social group. In Virginia Woolf's *To the Lighthouse* (1927), Mr Ramsay's children notice as he talks to the local sailors 'the little tinge of Scottish accent which came into his voice, making him seem like a peasant', and Woolf's other novels are full of references to accents – some characters are ashamed of theirs, and when one, a Yorkshireman, 'increased his accent as if he were proud of it', we pick up in the cool puzzlement of 'as if he were proud of it' the author's sense that this is ridiculous.

For the most part, people do not *choose* to use particular accents or indeed dialects. Clive Upton, a leading scholar of English dialects, explains that 'far from being in free variation, available to be chosen at will, [they] have social meaning'.[2] That social meaning is emotionally charged. William Labov, who founded the discipline of sociolinguistics, published in 1963 a study of the different styles of speech he had heard in Martha's Vineyard, an island off the Massachusetts coast. Once a centre of whaling, Martha's Vineyard has for more than a hundred years been a popular destination for vacationing New Yorkers. Labov perceived that, as if to distinguish themselves from the visitors, many permanent residents unconsciously exaggerated the local accent. Young people who expected to leave the area after completing their education noticeably adopted the speech habits of the mainland. Meanwhile, those who planned to stay spoke like the middle-aged fishermen who were the most stubborn defenders of the island's independent character. They did this intentionally and – yes – with pride. In the sixties, Labov also analysed the speech of salespeople at department stores in New York. He found that at Saks Fifth Avenue those on the higher floors, where the goods were more expensive, were unlikely to drop their *r*s. At Macy's the men who stocked the shelves all dropped some of their *r*s ('Toidy-toid Street'), whereas the staff who walked the floors rarely did so.[3]

All widespread languages exhibit regional variation. There are large and obvious differences in the pronunciation of different Englishes. The English spoken in Canada is perceptibly different from that in Liberia; a Canadian and a Liberian might have some difficulties understanding each other. Within English-speaking countries there is variation, too. Many people regard Australian English as uniform, and embrace Anthony Burgess's line that 'Australian English may be thought of as a kind of fossilised Cockney of the Dickensian era.'[4] But there are discernible differences – certainly discernible to many Australians, if not to most outsiders – between the accents of Sydney, Adelaide and Hobart, to name only three cities. Equally, it is received wisdom that one Canadian cannot tell where another is from merely by listening to him, but there are differences in pronunciation, as well as in vocabulary, between the

English spoken in Newfoundland and that used in British Columbia, and there is some divergence between, for instance, that of Quebec and southern Ontario.

In America, there are clear differences – as between the accents of, say, eastern Connecticut and the Dakotas, or Wisconsin and Mississippi. In John Steinbeck's novel *The Grapes of Wrath* (1939) the Oklahoma folks claim they can barely understand anything said by a woman from Massachusetts. The present range of accents on the East Coast reflects differences established before American independence. These were partly the result of the varied origins of the successive waves of settlers who arrived there in the seventeenth and eighteenth centuries: Puritans from East Anglia made their home in Massachusetts, farmers and artisans from the south and west of England in Virginia, Quakers from the Midlands in the Delaware valley, and families from Scotland, Ireland and the north of England in Pennsylvania, Georgia and the country in between.[5]

Other factors were involved in shaping American accents and, more generally, dialects. The dialect of the Hudson Valley area shows the influence of Dutch. Some of the differences between eastern and western New England are the result of the early eastern residents depending on the sea for their livelihood; the dialect of eastern New England has a distinctive nautical element. There are also, as a result of geographical barriers to change, pockets of insularity where new forms have failed to make much impression. While it is a myth that people in the Appalachian Mountains or on the Outer Banks of North Carolina speak Elizabethan English, their local dialects do contain relic forms that have disappeared everywhere else. As one travels west, the main dialect areas become larger; when settlers fanned westward in the nineteenth century, their dialects mingled and differences were levelled. The story is of course more complex than these few sentences suggest, but regional variation in the United States, while less intense than in Britain, is a commonly observed fact of life, and when people who use different dialects meet, it is likely that each party will feel that the other speaks strangely. Statements about others' poor use of language – the drawling of Southerners, the *r*-less preciousness of Bostonians, the easily caricatured accent of New Yorkers (mainly outside Manhattan) in which *dog* becomes 'doo-og' – are much more frequent than statements about people using it well.

Within Britain there are big disparities. Daniel Defoe noticed some of these in his *Tour thro' the Whole Island of Great Britain* (1724–6), commenting on the 'boorish' Somerset dialect and the jarring *r*s in Northumberland. Local features have often been used for literary effect, as by Shakespeare, Hardy, D. H. Lawrence and Henry Green; and for comic effect, as in the joke about a Northumbrian landlord who stops a poacher, saying, 'You do realize there's no shooting here?', and is met with the response, 'Shootin'? Aa's nivver oppened me mooth!'

In *Pygmalion*, Henry Higgins asserts that 'You can spot an Irishman or a Yorkshireman by his brogue. I can place any man within six miles. I can place him within two miles in London. Sometimes within two streets.' George Bernard Shaw was paying tribute to the skills of the best phoneticians. Later, beginning in the 1960s, these skills would receive more publicity when a specialist in the field, Stanley Ellis, brought just this kind of expertise to bear on criminal investigations, most notably the case of the Yorkshire Ripper. Besides acknowledging scholarly skill, Shaw was reflecting on the many different accents audible in England, and he was making fun of the deep English sensitivity to the minute differentiating features of class and background. With good reason he observed in the preface to *Pygmalion* that 'it is impossible for an Englishman to open his mouth without making some other Englishman hate or despise him'.[6] That Shaw saw this as a two-way street is apparent in the pained reaction of Alfred Doolittle, Eliza's dustman father, when Henry recommends him as a lecturer on moral matters: 'I'll have to learn to speak middle-class language from you, instead of speaking proper English.'

It is tempting to imagine that Shaw's view was more accurate then than it is now. But I am not sure this is the case. Still, it is hard to imagine a respected university professor writing today, as Thomas Lounsbury did in 1904, that 'there is a body of English words certain pronunciations of which every cultivated man the world over recognizes at once as belonging to the speech of the uneducated', and stating that for the purposes of his view of the subject 'it is the usage

of the educated body alone which is assumed to be under consideration'. As for those whose pronunciation betrays 'social inferiority
if not . . . vulgarity', Lounsbury alleges that 'the most saddening thing
. . . is the hopelessness of their situation. For them there is no relief
in sight'.[7] We may also frown at *How Should I Pronounce?*, a book
published in 1885 by William Phyfe, in which he writes: 'We
are told that, in the days of ancient Greece, so critical were the
Athenians that if an orator mispronounced a single word, they
immediately hissed him . . . The accuracy of the citizens of Athens
is greatly to be admired.'[8]

While hostility to particular accents appears to have a long history,
the story is not straightforward. In the fourteenth century Chaucer
made fun of northern accents in 'The Reeve's Tale'; some scribes
copying his works, which circulated in manuscript, failed to spot
his intention and corrected what they took for mistakes, and others,
it seems, added extra touches of northern dialect to help along his
jokes. Writing at around the same time, John Trevisa, a Cornishman,
expressed concern about the 'scharp, slyttyng, and frotyng' speech
of Northerners, which he attributed to their proximity to 'strange
men and aliens' and distance from the centres of royal power. When
Shakespeare wanted to show Edgar in *King Lear* transformed into
a country beggar he put in his mouth pronunciations that a contemporary audience would have recognized as South-Western: *zwaggerd*
rather than *swaggered*, *vortnight* for *fortnight*, and *chud* instead of 'I
would'.

In the sixteenth century the leading authorities, though concerned
that people should cleave to a single written standard, accepted that
accents would vary. The first printed mention of a 'broad' accent is
in 1532; 'strong' accent is not found until the nineteenth century,
though in the seventeenth century one's accent could be said to
possess 'tang'. Comments on people's styles of speech had more to
do with manner than with regional background: in the age of Shakespeare, for instance, you could have been *mellifluent*, *gold-mouthed*,
tongue-gilt or *nectar-tongued*, but also *fumbling*, *maffling*, *babbling*, *snuf-
fling* or *snaffling*. In *As You Like It*, Orlando encounters Rosalind in
the Forest of Arden; she is in disguise, pretending to be a saucy
native of the woodland, but Orlando finds her manner of speech

incongruous and observes, 'Your accent is something finer than you could purchase in so removed a dwelling.' Rosalind's explanation is that 'an old religious uncle of mine taught me to speak' and he 'was in his youth an inland man'. The exchange would have struck a chord with a contemporary audience increasingly aware of the gap between rustic and urban modes of speech.

In a guide for poets published in 1589 the ambitious critic and expert orator George Puttenham tellingly advised using the language spoken at the King's court 'or in the good townes and Cities within the land'; he warned against that used in ports and frontier towns or 'in Universities where Schollers use much peevish affectation' or 'in any uplandish village or corner of a Realme, where is no resort but of poore rusticall or uncivill people'. Puttenham suggested that one should avoid imitating the speech of craftsmen and carters, poets such as Chaucer whose language 'is now out of use with us', 'Northern-men' – by which, he explained, he meant anyone who lived north of the River Trent – and the 'far Westerne'. Good English, he felt, was spoken only within a sixty-mile radius of London.[9] One of the interesting features of Puttenham's advice is the implication that a standard form of English had not yet infiltrated the area north of the Trent. The sixty-mile rule in fact meant avoiding forms used anywhere much beyond Cambridge. He even specifically mentioned the good quality of the English used in Middlesex and Surrey.

Others echoed Puttenham's preference for a southern form of the language, but voiced different antipathies. In 1619 Alexander Gil, a grammarian and London headmaster whom we have previously encountered as a critic of the cant of 'wandering beggars', mocked the rustic talk of people in Somerset, who sounded to him as though they were speaking an entirely separate tongue. A few years earlier, Richard Rowlands Verstegan had told the story of a London courtier writing 'to a personage of authoritie in the north partes, touching the training of men and providing furniture for warre'. The courtier 'willed him among other things to equippe his horses', and the letter's recipient was baffled by the word *equippe*, wondering if it was something to do with 'quipping' or 'whipping'. In the end he sent a messenger back to London 'to learne the meaning thereof'.[10]

The emphasis on London is not surprising. Political and commercial power had been concentrated there since the Middle Ages. No other town in the British Isles approached it in importance, and in the sixteenth and seventeenth centuries it was growing much faster than other major European centres such as Paris, Venice, Naples and Madrid. People were pulled to London, by higher wages and greater opportunities (thanks especially to its central role in the trade in woollen cloth), but were also pushed towards it by falling standards of living elsewhere. The period between 1580 and 1640 saw a dramatic increase in population, and the city had the highest level of literacy nationally, as well as being a seedbed of medical and scientific innovation.[11] Whether or not London English genuinely was the purest form of the language, the repeated assertion of its refinement and purity enhanced its status.

As foreigners and country folk were drawn to London, guides to the norms of its language were needed. When Ben Jonson produced his Grammar, it was intended, according to its title page, 'For the benefit of all Strangers'. Jonson's powers of observation meant he could see the true variety of usage, and he brought together some of his insights in his commonplace book, posthumously published in 1641 as *Timber, or Discoveries Made Upon Men and Matter*. 'Speech,' he noted, 'is the instrument of society,' and 'Custom is the most certain mistress of language, as the public stamp makes the current money.' The best-known statement in *Timber* is 'Language most shows a man: "speak that I may see thee."' Less well-known is the way Jonson then expands on this: 'It springs out of the most retired and inmost parts of us, and is the image of the parent of it, the mind. No glass [i.e. mirror] renders a man's form or likeness so true as his speech . . . Would you not laugh to meet a great counsellor of state in a flat cap, with his trunk-hose and a hobby-horse cloak, his gloves under his girdle, and yond haberdasher in a velvet gown furred with sable? There is a certain latitude in these things by which we find the degrees.'[12]

Jonson is right: it is significant not only that pronunciation and accent vary, but also that we notice others', that we may be teased or admired on account of our own, and that a mode of speech considered deficient is likely to affect a person's social mobility. Our awareness of the differences informs stereotypes: we hear a certain accent, associate it for traditional and largely artificial reasons with particular patterns of behaviour, and are surprised and even unhappy if our expectations are not borne out. When we appraise people's accents, though, we are less aware of our prejudices than of the degree to which the way they speak affects their intelligibility to us and distracts us from their meaning and purpose. Of course, sometimes we claim people are unintelligible when really we are refusing to make the effort to understand them.

In *The Spectator* in 1711 Joseph Addison could claim, 'The Sounds of our *English* Words are commonly like those of String Musick, short and transient' and 'rise and perish upon a single Touch', whereas 'those of other Languages are like the Notes of Wind Instruments, sweet and swelling'. That same year the grammarian James Greenwood asserted that 'the *English* do . . . thrust their Words forwards, towards the outward part of the Mouth, and speak more openly; whence the Sounds become also more distinct. The *Germans* do rather draw back their words towards the hinder part of the Mouth, and bottom of the throat; whence their Pronunciation is more strong. The *French* draw their Words more inward towards the Palate, and speak less openly . . . So the *Italians*, and especially the *Spaniards* speak more *slowly*; the *French* more *hastily*, and the *English* in a middle way betwixt both'.[13] This contains some truth, but it is symptomatic of a tendency for prejudice about national character to be dressed up as phonological insight.

The transition to finding variety of pronunciation embarrassing seems to have taken place in the half-century after Addison was writing. Dr Johnson believed that the best pronunciation was that which most closely followed the way a word was spelled, and Lindley Murray echoed him. It does not require much effort to see how inadequate a belief this is, and others sought to treat pronunciation with more conviction. This involved making qualitative judgements. As early as 1650 one Balthazar Gerbier had published a lecture on 'The Art of Well Speaking'. As a genre, this kind of publication took off with John Mason's *An Essay on Elocution* (1748), and the word *elocution* now began to be used in its modern sense.

The most notable authority on the subject was Thomas Sheridan.

Originally both an actor and a theatrical manager, he was beset by financial and digestive problems, and in his forties he tried to reposition himself as an expert on language and education. In 1762 he brought out a series of lectures on elocution; Robert Dodsley was one of those involved in the publication. Sheridan adopted a tone of authority that his predecessors had not managed. He believed that 'vicious' habits of pronunciation were acquired from nurses and favourite servants, and that speaking dialect was a 'disgrace'. When later he produced a dictionary, he claimed that as recently as the reign of Queen Anne, in the first decade of the century, spoken English had been in a state of perfection. His beliefs were taken seriously, although a less than perfect advertisement for his methods was the persistence – despite considerable efforts on his part – of his daughter Betsy's Irish accent; even his socially ambitious son, the playwright Richard Brinsley Sheridan, was mocked by the novelist Fanny Burney for pronouncing *kind* as though it rhymed with *joined*. Still, his public lectures were hugely popular, and he earned a great deal from them. It would have cost a young clerk a quarter of his weekly salary to go on one of Sheridan's courses, and it was possible for there to be 1,600 students enrolled at any one time. A single course may have made Sheridan the equivalent of £150,000 in today's money.[14]

Sheridan's main success, says Lynda Mugglestone in her history of English accents as social symbols, lay in creating a set of beliefs about habits of speech. He could not bring about wholesale reform, and many of his individual recommendations came to nothing, but he created a new consciousness about pronunciation.[15] His work advanced an idea of a standard or proper English accent. He believed a standard accent would enable greater social equality. His contemporary James Buchanan, a Scot, suggested in *An Essay towards Establishing a Standard for an Elegant and Uniform Pronunciation of the English Language* (1766) that a standard accent would reconcile the peoples of England and Scotland: 'To carry this truly momentous design into proper execution, cries aloud for the helping hand of every man of sense; particularly when he considers that he will be . . . removing national prejudice, which has too long subsisted, and been chiefly fostered betwixt the two kingdoms from their different forms of speech!' A single form of pronunciation will create 'much more benevolent and generous ties than that of a political union', and 'nothing is so likely to effect and thoroughly rivet' what he calls the 'most lasting bonds of brotherly love and affection!'[16]

One popular scheme of elocution was presented by William Enfield, a friend of Joseph Priestley. In 1774 he published *The Speaker*, a chunky anthology of literary extracts, presented under generic headings such as 'On Sincerity' and 'The Origin of Superstition and Tyranny'. With this publication he intended to 'facilitate the improvement of youth in reading and speaking'. In Enfield's view, articulation should be 'distinct and deliberate', pronunciation 'bold and forcible', the 'height' of one's voice should have 'compass and variety', words ought to be pronounced 'with propriety and elegance', a word of more than one syllable should be stressed consistently, the most important words in any sentence should be emphasized, and one's pauses and cadences should have plenty of variety. Furthermore, it was good to 'Accompany the Emotions and Passions which your words express, by correspondent tones, looks, and gestures'.[17] The principles he sets out here hardly amount to a system, but the success of *The Speaker* demonstrated the rise of public speaking as an accomplishment expected of educated young men.

In 1811 Anna Laetitia Barbauld, who had been friendly with Enfield during the time they both lived in Warrington, published *The Female Speaker*, which extended instruction in this art to young women. Barbauld's anthology suggests the different oratorical skills expected of women and manifests 'a more scrupulous regard to delicacy in the pieces inserted' as well as a 'choice of subjects more particularly appropriate to the duties, the employments, and the dispositions of the softer sex'.[18] Its subjects include 'Female Economy', 'Qualities requisite in a Wife' and 'Dissipation of the rising Generation'.

However, the most influential figure in the field was John Walker. He described in detail the pronunciations that he recommended, using numerals to indicate the different stresses on a word's syllables – a method introduced by William Kenrick's *A New English Dictionary* (1773). Aware that usage was variable, Walker argued in the preface to his pronouncing dictionary that the London style of pronunciation was the best. Its superiority was in part a matter of possessing more 'courtesy'. Besides this, London was the British capital and, to an even greater degree than in the reign of Queen Elizabeth, the seat of political and cultural influence, so its pronunciations were already 'more generally received'. This advantage meant, however, that Londoners who pronounced English poorly were 'more disgraced by their peculiarities than any other people'. Consequently, 'the vulgar pronunciation of London, though not half so erroneous as that of Scotland, Ireland, or any of the provinces, is, to a person of correct taste, a thousand times more offensive and disgusting'.[19]

17 Talking proper

Noticing accents, noticing tribes

John Walker's indictment of offensive and disgusting London pronunciation was frequently repeated in the nineteenth century. It became a commonplace, and one person who felt its effect was the poet John Keats. Incorrectly believed by his contemporaries to have been born in Moorgate at a coaching inn where his father was the ostler, Keats was hounded for his pronunciation, both actual and implicit. He faced particular condemnation for rhyming words that to his ear sounded alike but to others seemed different. One example was his decision to rhyme *thoughts* and *sorts*, and his notion of *r* sounds earned him the censure in *Blackwood's Edinburgh Magazine* of the reviewer John Gibson Lockhart, who accused him of 'loose' versification and 'Cockney rhymes'. The critic Leigh Hunt condescendingly called him 'Junkets', on the grounds that this was how the supposedly Cockney poet pronounced his own name.

At that time the word *Cockney* had for over two hundred years been an abusive term for a Londoner; some had worn it as a badge of pride, inviting further abuse. In the early seventeenth century John Minsheu suggested an etymology for the word, telling the story of a young Londoner who went with his father to the country and, having been informed that the sound a horse made was 'neigh', wondered, when he heard a cock crow, 'doth the *cocke neigh* too?' According to Minsheu, the word had ever since signalled someone 'raw or unripe in Country-men[']s affaires'.[1] It was Minsheu, moreover, who defined a Cockney as one born within sound of Bow Bells.

It is not just in Keats that we find evidence of past pronunciation; in general, poetry is a good source of this kind of information. Poems draw our attention to words that once rhymed

203

but no longer do so, and also to words that only some believed to rhyme. When Christopher Marlowe writes, 'Come live with me and be my love / And we will all the pleasures prove', we infer that in the sixteenth century *love* and *prove* had a similar sound. More concentrated evidence can be found in rhyming dictionaries. Joshua Poole's *The English Parnassus* (1657), subtitled 'A Help to English Poesie', rhymes *aunt, chant* and *grant* with *ant* and *pant* as well as with *want*, while Elisha Coles in *The Compleat English Schoolmaster* (1674) suggests that the *oo* sound is equivalent in *boot, nook* and *could*. When Shakespeare rhymes *clean* with *lane*, or when one of his many puns suggests that he pronounced *reason* and *raising* similarly, we may be tempted to wonder whether this is evidence of a Warwickshire accent. But the evidence is much weaker than that for the London accent of John Keats.

It is easy not to give any thought to the way eminent figures in the past spoke. In most cases the evidence is limited. It may surprise us that Mrs (Elizabeth) Beeton, author of the celebrated *Book of Household Management* (1861), is believed to have had something close to a Cockney accent and that Jane Austen, associated by many with polite refinement, is thought to have had a rustic Hampshire burr. Looking further back, we know that the explorer Sir Walter Raleigh, an Elizabethan favourite, was mocked for his 'broad Devonshire' speech, but he seems to have felt no anxiety on account of it, and it proved no obstacle to success. In the nineteenth century, as class sensitivity sharpened, commentary on accents took on a new pointedness. Sir Robert Peel, who twice served as Prime Minister in the 1830s and '40s, retained throughout his life traces of a Staffordshire accent, which was mocked by Disraeli. William Gladstone had traces of a Lancashire accent, and, while this did not prevent his being Prime Minister four times between the 1860s and '90s, it allowed his critics to stress that he was no gentleman.

To speak of someone using a 'regional' dialect is to mark oneself as a speaker of standard English, and in Britain the habit of unreflectingly doing this begins in the eighteenth century. But standard British English, the native form used by an elite comprising perhaps a tenth of the population, is itself a (social) dialect. Its 'standard' nature is hard to define and is not regulated by an official body. In reality, a language is a parcel of dialects. When I talk about the 'regional', it is with a heavy awareness that this is a fiction. All usage is regional; it is just that some regions are less readily identified, and others are more assertively stigmatized.

There are many people who delight in regional accents and vocabulary, revelling in the Lincolnshire term *water whelp* for a dumpling or the Durham *shig-shog* for a seesaw. This is hardly novel; in 1674 the naturalist John Ray published a collection of English words 'not generally used' and recorded with pleasure items such as the Cumbrian *towgher* (a dowry) and the Suffolk term *puckets* for a caterpillar's nest.[2] Most people who use local words of this kind do so without giving the matter any thought. Do you lay the table or set the table, speak of someone being cross-eyed or boss-eyed, refer to an armpit or an armhole, curse or cuss, pronounce *Tuesday* as if there were a *j* in it or not? Very likely, you know which you do but have not examined how this relates to where you were brought up or where you now live.

Some people are incurious or simply lack self-consciousness. Others sneer at particular regionalisms because they believe their own usage superior. As we have seen, they crassly equate usages that differ from their own with stupidity, separatism, a lack of skills, insecurity and obstinacy. This applies particularly to regional variations in grammar. These are considered unacceptable in most schools and many places of work, but they are frequently heard in informal situations. You might come across the demonstrative 'Good as gold, that there thing was' in rural Devon, what's known as a 'double modal' in some people's Scots ('I didnae think he'll dae it, but I suppose he might could'), verb forms with an unexpected final *s* in urban Sydney ('They were watching television so we gits on the floor and we crawls in my bedroom'), an emphatic adverbial *done* in the Southern states of the US ('You didn't know about it until it was all done planned and fixed'), or in the Appalachian Mountains an *a*-prefix in a statement such as 'He just kept a-beggin' and a-cryin' and a-wantin' to go out'.[3] Sometimes a single word can perform a different function from the one it usually achieves, in a way that will strike an outsider as strange. Misunderstandings may result. There is a story (apocryphal?) about a Yorkshireman who, drawing up at a level crossing in his car, saw the sign 'Wait while the red light flashes' and, when the light flashed, crossed and was crushed by an oncoming train. In Yorkshire *while* can mean 'until'.[4]

Here is George Sampson, a crusading South-East London teacher, writing in the 1920s about what he perceives as the divisiveness of regional variation: 'The country is torn with dialects . . . Enthusiastic "localists" cling to their dialects . . . The untutored speech of the multitude does not necessarily represent the unspoiled freshness of a beautiful patois.' He goes on to say that 'Standard English need not be fatal to local idiom. Where a dialect is genuinely rooted it will live; where it is feeble but curiously interesting, it may be kept artificially alive by enthusiasts; where it has no real reason for existing it will perish, as all provisional institutions will perish.' Sampson's notion that people keep dialects alive the way they might preserve a favourite old houseplant is doubtful. Dialects are not decorative. As for the conventional form of the language that he proposes as the medium for all school instruction, 'There is no need to define standard English speech. We know what it is, and there's an end on't. We know standard English when we hear it just as we know a dog when we see it.' Sampson goes on to discuss what he considers the tragedy of education: in London 'the elementary school boy takes out of school at fourteen, unmitigated and unimproved, the debased idiom he brought into it at seven, and even in that he is but semi-articulate . . . The first healthy impulse of any kindly person confronted with a class of poor, inarticulate children should be to say . . . "I must teach you how to speak like human beings."'[5]

Contrary to what Sampson imagines, standard English as we know it is a construct. In the nineteenth century it was promoted by educators, patriots and pedants (three groups not mutually exclusive). In truth, it might better have been dubbed prestige English, since those who boosted it were keen to congratulate themselves while condemning most of society for not being able to speak their own language properly. Standardization has general benefits, but often it has been practised not so much in the interests of the public at large as in those of the small authoritarian group who have enthroned their English as the best English. Yet, to flip things around, I could argue, as Thomas Sheridan did, that a standard form of

English is a means of bringing about that great chimera, a classless society. In recent decades, this tension has been central to political debate about how English should be taught in schools: is the teaching of standard English a means of reinforcing the existing class structure, or does it offer children from less privileged backgrounds a passport to freedom? On both sides, disdain masquerades as right-mindedness; the argument is a variation on the familiar contest between the prescriptive and descriptive schools.

The *idea* of a standard form of the language really being a prestige form was of course not new in the nineteenth century. But in that period scholarship crystallized the standard form, often through inaccurate statements about non-standard forms, such as the assertion (in 1900) by Henry Sweet that 'Most of the present English dialects are so isolated in their development and so given over to disintegrating influences as to . . . throw little light on the development of English, which is more profitably dealt with by . . . [studying] the educated colloquial speech of each period'.[6] Standardization always involves passing judgement on the value of variant forms, and mostly this judgement is briskly negative. One of Sweet's inheritors, H. C. Wyld, alleged that the pronunciation of what he called the Received Standard was 'superior, from the character of its vowel sounds, to any other form of English, in beauty and clarity', possessing 'a sonorous quality' and 'greater definiteness of sound'.[7] This was really a fantasy, and Wyld's notion of an easy, unstudied kind of pronunciation, springing from a gracious tradition, was a paean to what he thought of as upper-class manliness.

Nineteenth-century British novels abound with comments about what are perceived as regional deviancies, and about their charms. For the novelist, dialect was a convenient way of suggesting the richness of a local culture. Sir Walter Scott is an especially detailed recorder of dialect forms, but they are on display in at least some of the works of all the period's major writers of fiction – in Emily Brontë's *Wuthering Heights* and George Eliot's *Adam Bede*, for instance. In Wilkie Collins's *The Moonstone* (1868) one of the novel's many narrators – or is it Collins himself? – loudly draws our attention to the fact that he has chosen to 'translate' one character 'out of the Yorkshire language into the English language', adding that, since even an 'accomplished' listener has trouble understanding her, 'you will draw your own conclusions as to what your state of mind would be if I reported her in her native tongue'.

At Christmas 1858 Dickens published in his magazine *Household Words* a story entitled 'A House to Let', written by him and three others. In the chapter written by Elizabeth Gaskell, the Lancastrian salesman Mr Openshaw pictures smart Londoners 'lounging away their days in Bond Street, and such places; ruining good English, and ready in their turn to despise him as a provincial'; he delights in addressing his son 'in the broadest and most unintelligible Lancashire dialect, in order to keep up what he called the true Saxon accent'.

This business of true Saxonism is familiar from an earlier chapter, and Gaskell had written about it before. In *North and South* (1855), her fictional portrait of the social effects of industrial change, the mill owner Mr Thornton, a man for the most part shy of talking about himself, says, 'I belong to Teutonic blood; it is little mingled in this part of England to what it is in others; we retain much of their language; we retain more of their spirit; we do not look upon life as a time for enjoyment, but as a time for action and exertion.'

Charles Reade's Christie Johnstone in the 1853 novel of that name 'came to London with a fine mind, a broad brogue, a delicate ear; she observed how her husband's friends spoke, and in a very few months she had toned down her Scotch to a rich Ionic coloring, which her womanly instinct will never let her exchange for the thin, vinegar accents that are too prevalent in English and French society'. Reade has a number of pointed things to say about language, usually uttered as asides but with real tartness. The Anglo-Saxon forms are 'the soul and vestal fire of the great English tongue', yet one of his characters, contemplating a certain monosyllablic word ('a stinger' – i.e. 'fuck') considers it 'a thorn of speech not in her vocabulary, nor even in society's'. Noting one character's incorrect usage, Reade writes, 'Lucy's aunt did not talk strict grammar. Does yours?'

Among twentieth-century English novelists George Orwell, who scrupulously described himself as 'lower upper-middle class', is especially sensitive to these matters. When Dorothy Hare in *A*

Clergyman's Daughter (1935) looks for lodgings in the shabbier parts of South London, 'Her ragged clothes and her lack of references were against her, and her educated accent, which she did not know how to disguise, wrecked whatever chances she might have had. The tramps and cockney hop-pickers had not noticed her accent, but the suburban housewives noticed it quickly enough, and it scared them in just the same way as the fact that she had no luggage had scared the landladies.' In his non-fiction book *The Road to Wigan Pier* (1937) Orwell remarks, 'In a Lancashire cotton-town you could probably go for months on end without once hearing an "educated" accent, whereas there can hardly be a town in the South of England where you could throw a brick without hitting the niece of a bishop.' From his own point of view this was beneficial: in Lancashire 'your "educated" accent stamps you rather as a foreigner than as a chunk of the petty gentry; and this is an immense advantage, for it makes it much easier to get into contact with the working class.' In addition, 'If social stratification corresponded precisely to economic stratification, the public-school man would assume a cockney accent the day his income dropped below £200 a year. But does he? On the contrary, he immediately becomes twenty times more Public School than before. He clings to the Old School Tie as to a life-line.'

In his long essay 'The English People', written in 1944 but not published until 1947, Orwell diagnosed a number of problems in the use of English, claiming that 'The language of the BBC is barely intelligible to the masses' and that 'English working people . . . think it effeminate even to pronounce a foreign word correctly'. Yet since the First World War an 'important section of society' had consisted of the 'nearly classless'. Its habits of speech were changing English. Arguing that 'the great weakness of English is its capacity for debasement', Orwell asserted that its 'deadliest enemy' was the 'dreary dialect' of political speeches and news bulletins. The result was a condition of decadence.[8] He sensed an increasing detachment between the affluent and the working classes. The fabric of society was changing: one aspect of this was the growth of an artificial middle-class manner of speech, and another was the erosion of some of the most poetic, historically resonant local language.

This had been anticipated by Joseph Wright. His great dialect dictionary was the fruit of a programme of research and publication initiated by the English Dialect Society, founded in 1873. Tellingly, once the Society had turned its findings over to Wright, it promptly disbanded, on the understanding that its work was done. Wright felt the same: in the future, dialect would be less copious. But he and the EDS were wrong. The Survey of English Dialects, conducted under the direction of Harold Orton in the 1950s, confirmed that the picture had changed since the time of Wright and the EDS – and was remarkably complex. The work continues, now under Sally Johnson and Clive Upton, and will have to keep being enlarged.

Dialects have long been regarded as an unsexy area for research. Traditionally, the study of English has concentrated on its development towards a standard form, and narratives outside this central story have been given little space. Pertinently, some of the most distinguished books about regional English usage have been produced by foreigners, fascinated by matters that to many natives have seemed merely parochial – or rather mucky. For instance, a study of the dialect of Pewsey in Wiltshire was published in 1903 by a Swede, John Kjederqvist, whose main sources of information were a middle-aged plumber and the 'worst speakers' in the local schools, and a substantial 1905 thesis on the dialect of West Somerset was the work of Etso Kruisinga, a Dutchman. Then again, the twentieth century's most substantial scholarly grammars of English were the work of Hendrik Poutsma, another Dutchman, and Otto Jespersen, a Dane.

The 'worst speakers' are a subject of great interest. It helps make this interest sound respectable if we use a different adjective. But 'worst' is how we tend to think of them. Discussion of what is worst implies that we have an idea about what is best – a prestige form of speech that will be labelled 'standard', though it has never been practised by the majority. People who use standard English allege that those who fail to do so lack linguistic ability, but in reality people using stigmatized forms of English may have complex abilities as speakers – incomprehensible to many observers, but powerful among their peers. Furthermore, testing of people's linguistic abilities tends to focus, for obvious reasons, on events that happen in the classroom or in interviews, rather than on spontaneous expression.[9]

One can speak standard English without a standard accent. But standard English has such an accent: it is widely known as Received Pronunciation (RP). This has tended to be associated, especially in the minds of its critics, with public (i.e. private) schools. Daniel Jones, who promoted the term, suggested in 1917 the alternative name Public School Pronunciation. But the name RP prevailed. Jones was not the first to refer to it; John Walker had written of 'received pronunciation' in 1774, and Alexander Ellis in 1869, but it was Jones who gave it those telltale capitals.

The stigma of a non-standard accent was renewed in the last quarter of the nineteenth century, at a time when the influence of Britain's public schools was growing. The leading public schools, and the many new ones established between 1840 and 1870, preached the virtues of individualism while inculcating, through their rules and hierarchies and customs, a strong sense of the importance of institutions. Many of them were foundations of long standing, but now their influence magnified, and they were organized into a 'system', partly through the Headmasters' Conference (begun in 1869), but mainly through the interactions of their pupils on the sports field and in other arenas. The result was a new caste, the 'public school man', whose education imbued him with certain attitudes and assumptions, among which was an idea of how one should speak. 'Imbued' is not too strong a word; boarding schools differed from day schools in the scope they allowed for establishing and steadily reinforcing patterns of behaviour. The culture and character of the public schools were advertised and celebrated to a remarkable degree in newspapers and magazines, in stories and annuals, and in other sectors of the education system. The answer to the question 'Where were you at school?' influenced whether one gained admission to clubs, coteries and indeed jobs. In the 1880s and '90s, inspectors monitoring the use in schools of government money began commenting on the value of lessons that taught pupils to lose their picturesque provincial accents and move towards a standard pronunciation. In 1898 the government's department of education prescribed a method of teaching pupils how to sound their vowels.[10]

With the creation of the British Broadcasting Corporation in 1922, radio became an important medium for the diffusion of RP. Within three years of its foundation, the BBC was reaching as many as 10 million listeners with its broadcasts.[11] The influence of these, and later of the BBC's television broadcasts, was strong, encouraging the belief that acquiring RP was a means of social advancement. For many, exposure to the English of the BBC was a means of remedying their deficient speech – whether they had arrived at this perception on their own or had been nudged towards it. For others, of course, it caused resentment; accents other than RP seemed to be used mainly for comic effect. Only in the 1960s did the BBC begin to feature many presenters who did not use RP.

In fact, there is more than one kind of RP. One distinction that it is possible to draw is between the 'marked' and 'unmarked' forms. The marked form, which one hears less and less, is a more obvious sign of a person's being blithely upper class even than a signet ring engraved with a coat of arms. This isn't merely 'talking proper', but 'talking posh' – which is regarded as an affectation. It is noticeable that the younger members of Britain's Royal Family and many of today's aspiring politicians strive to avoid marked RP, for fear of being considered aloof or fusty.

Since the 1960s a new kind of standard has been emerging. In 1984 David Rosewarne, a phonetics expert, labelled it 'Estuary English' – a reference to the estuary of the River Thames, in Essex and Kent. The development of Estuary English has involved working-class and lower-middle-class accents shifting slightly in the direction of RP, while RP and accents close to it have levelled downwards. Characteristics of Estuary English include the intrusive linking *r* sound one hears between *idea* and *of* in 'the idea of going', the smearing of the *l* sound so that it is more like a *w* in words such as *milk* and *bundle*, and 'yod-coalescence', which creates the impression of a *j* in words such as *Tuesday* and leads to *dew* and *Jew* being pronounced the same way.

For now RP, rather than Estuary English or some other variant, gets taught to non-native speakers. But there is a move to change this. Given the increasing paucity of RP speakers, it might for practical purposes make more sense to teach foreign learners a different accent. Certainly, some non-native speakers are stunned to discover, on arrival in Britain, that the RP accent they have cultivated is considered by many native speakers to be superannuated and embarrassing.

In London, where I live, an increasing number of young people, from a variety of ethnic backgrounds, speak what's come to be known as Multicultural London English. This street dialect is replacing what George Steiner called 'the thick twilight of Cockney speech'.[12] It is intriguingly free from institutional influence – indeed, from the influence of adults. Its distinctive features include Afro-Caribbean cadences, vocabulary absorbed from a wide range of sources (Jamaican Creole, certainly, but also Bengali, Hindi, Urdu, Romani and various African Englishes) and a relentless use of question tags, of which *innit?* is one of the less confrontational examples. The question seeks confirmation yet can also be a challenge.

One of the features that seems likely to have inspired Steiner's image of Cockney's 'thick twilight' remains: the glottal stop – or, to give it its fuller name, the voiceless glottal plosive. It is something you hear every day if you live in London, and indeed if you are in Glasgow or Barbados, Newcastle or New York, but you will hear it less in the English spoken in Australia or southern Ireland. It occurs when the space between the vocal cords completely closes, followed by a pop that is like a little explosion. You hear it when the *t* disappears in *mountain* or *quality*, in the word *uh-oh*, and more exaggeratedly when you cough. The absence of the glottal stop has traditionally been a marker of RP, although some RP speakers do occasionally use glottal stops.

There now appear to be fewer accents in Britain than there were a generation ago. There is a pattern of supra-regionalization: in populous areas which are socially mixed, differences between minor local varieties are fading. This happens as speakers unconsciously reach a kind of accommodation, in which they converge on a new variety of speech that preserves distinctive regional features but bears few marks of affiliation to the smaller, close-knit communities of their grandparents. One of the reasons for this is the decline of industry and farming; today's school-leavers are less likely than previous generations to go into jobs which are tightly linked to local traditions and identities. However, while mobility within regions has greatly increased in the last fifty years, larger regional ties are strong. The homogenization of British life – the sameness of high streets and shopping malls, the pervasiveness of the most popular entertainment – means that accents and dialects provide precious opportunities for people from different areas of Britain to assert their distinctiveness. Precious, that is, because so many traditional marks of distinctiveness have gone.

When people express their identity through accent, the effect is powerful. I am fond of David Crystal's observation that this is because 'the voice – unlike, say, distinctive clothing, facial features, or orna-ments – is perceptible around corners and in the dark'.[13] As Anne Karpf comments in her illuminating book on the subject, the human voice 'bridges our internal and external worlds, travelling from our most private recesses into the public domain, revealing not only our deepest sense of who we are, but also who we wish we weren't. It's a superb guide to fear and power, anxiety and subservience, to another person's vitality and authenticity as well as our own.' We milk it for information, and our interpretation of voice reflects our acoustic capacities.[14] The ways we talk remain, to a perhaps terri-fying degree, significant.

18 The Alphabet and the Goddess

Literacy, gender and sexist language

It is common to associate the use of a stigmatized dialect with illiteracy. Victorian writers on education equated 'provincial', 'incorrect' or 'improper' pronunciation and choice of words with ignorance and indeed often with basic mental deficiency. This is wrong. But in any case, questions of literacy and its absence need unpacking.

The word *illiterate* used to mean 'unlettered' – that is, having no acquaintance with writing. Now it is used as a synonym for *stupid*. The degree of social judgement it entails has led to the rise of *pre-literate* and *non-literate*, terms intended to diagnose rather than condemn. We also hear about the 'functionally illiterate'; the term denotes people who can read and write, though not well enough to cope with life's everyday requirements. Hysterical comment, especially in the US, presents functional illiteracy as a disease threatening to eat away the very core of society. It is not easy to define, but a report in the *Guardian* in July 2007 suggested that in the UK there are approximately 100,000 functionally illiterate school-leavers every year.[1] The problem is worse elsewhere. An article in the *Jamaica Observer* in April 2010 suggested that while the official literacy rate in Jamaica is 89 per cent, 'about half of the population are functionally illiterate'.[2]

Language is primarily speech. 'Writing,' asserts the linguist John McWhorter, 'is just a method for engraving on paper what comes out of our mouths.'[3] He does not mean to belittle writing – which is, after all, the medium in which he is making this point – but rather to affirm an important truth: speech came first. McWhorter's position, largely orthodox, is that the written word is a substitute for the spoken one, and is artificial. Writing using an alphabet is one of the technologies that enhance life. But it is a technology that has existed for not much more than five millennia, and most of the languages that have been spoken in the history of humanity have not been written down. Although alphabetically arranged dictionaries may make it look as though it must be the other way round, genetically we are primed for talking, not for writing. Yet statements about language before the invention of writing – which is to say, statements about more than 100,000 years of language use – are speculative.

Actually, it is not quite accurate to state that writing is merely a way of recording what comes out of our mouths. Writing has distinctive features – particular functions and forms that speech does not have. Moreover, while speech certainly influences writing, writing also influences speech. But whereas it is common to think of writing as a way of representing speech, in fact both speech and writing are realizations of the fundamental system that is language.

We tend to accept that the written word is permanent and the spoken word short-lived. While it is true that the things we say cannot be deleted, and they linger in other people's memories longer than we may find it comfortable to imagine, the spoken word does not leave a tangible residue. The grandeur of the written word is often conceived in architectural terms: it is planned and highly structured and balanced. By implication, speech lacks style: spontaneous and ephemeral, it is without control and technique. Yet in reality all sentences, whether written or spoken, are complex actions. You may reasonably say, 'I can think of a sentence that isn't at all complex', but even that sentence is the product of intense electrical activity in your brain, transmitted via the cranial nerves to your vocal apparatus. This apparatus includes your lips and teeth, your nasal cavity, the apex and blade and back of your tongue, your windpipe, your hard palate and soft palate, the alveolar ridge into which your upper teeth are fixed, your vocal cords, your diaphragm and your lungs.

The notion of literacy is bundled up with other ideas: imagination, self-awareness, an 'inner life', the power of reason, choice, moral judgement, modernity. Fundamentally, though, literacy is understood to mean 'writing' – the ability to understand and create written materials. Although systems of writing have existed at least since the fourth millennium BC, the modern concept of literacy begins with the development of the printing press using movable type. As I have suggested, the growth of European print culture, which began in the fifteenth century, had many important effects. First of all, it changed the way people read: the activity of reading became personal and silent, and as a result became quicker. Furthermore, print culture made the book not so much an utterance as an object. Knowledge became quantifiable; works of literature were increasingly written from a fixed point of view.[4] Print stabilized the idea of the past. In due course, probably towards the end of the seventeenth century, the keeping of printed records and the codification of laws – rendering knowledge and values as objects – created the idea of a public. In the present we can see the ways in which printed writing aids education, administration and discipline. Literacy, as embodied in printed written language, is crucial to the systems we use to order our lives.

Imagine being part of an entirely oral culture. Let us say your language is called Frimpo. The utterances of Frimpo-speakers leave no trace. People do not look things up. Instead of abstract definitions, you favour reference to your own experience: if I ask you to tell me what a flower is, you'll show me a flower rather than speculating about floweriness. Complex thoughts can be assembled only through communication with others, and mnemonics are essential to ensure that these thoughts are preserved. Your mnemonic needs probably influence the way you organize your more complicated thoughts; you may well use verse, and failing that will use rhythm as an aid to recall. You like drawing parallels. Epithets cluster around objects. Certainly, you and those around you are sensitive to the power of words. Compared to someone in a literate culture, your thoughts are very deeply influenced through sound. All Frimpo words are sounds and only sounds, and they seem to possess magical properties. Names are vitally important; they give you power over the world. Traditions are also crucial. Objectivity is unlikely; you need to stay close to what you know, and you react to the world in a communal, participatory fashion. Empathy is a key part of your social life.[5] The structure of Frimpo words is complex, too. When English-speakers write their language down, they leave spaces between their words. Very long words look strange when surrounded by much smaller words. Because Frimpo is never written down, there is no such sense of the oddity of long words; fusions of words are common. You probably have little contact with people who speak other languages or dialects, so there is less pressure on your language – less pressure, for instance, to become more simple. Frimpo illustrates the principle that isolated societies have languages fraught with archaism and oddity, whereas those societies that can be described as developed or sophisticated have languages that are comparatively simple in their mechanics.

When a people learn to write, huge changes happen. It is usual to think these changes are uniformly positive – we might encapsulate them in the convenient word 'progress' – but there are certain costs. Listening skills diminish. Power tends to be consolidated in the hands of an authoritarian elite. This was famously highlighted by the anthropologist Claude Lévi-Strauss, who, after spending time with the non-writing Nambikwara people of Brazil, concluded that writing served a sociological function rather than an intellectual one: namely, to increase the authority of those who can write at the expense of those who cannot. (Lévi-Strauss argued that this held true invariably, but counter-examples – such as the democracy of Periclean Athens – are available.) It is certainly the case that literacy is exploited by those who possess it. This may seem obvious, but it explains why the gap between written and spoken usage has been insisted on so earnestly: a punctilious, formal, systematic written language supports the mechanisms of officialdom and allows the educated to further their particular interests. When people in positions of authority express anxiety about the decline of this literacy – and about the rise of a different 'street-level' usage, which they may well struggle to recognize as a competing literacy – they offer an insight into their sense of entitlement and enfranchisement and into their incomplete yet urgent grasp of the precariousness of their superiority.[6]

Writing may commonly be linked to personal power and achievement – from scratching down our names as nursery-school children to producing business documents as adults – but it is also linked, because of our experience of writing as part of our education, with punishment, humiliation and submission – a test, a drama, a means of limiting our existence.[7] Feminist scholars have argued that writing is inherently patriarchal, and that it compromises the power of women in society. Leonard Shlain, in a highly original study of the conflict between word and image, posits that 'a *holistic, simultaneous, synthetic* and *concrete* view of the world are the essential character- istics of a feminine outlook; *linear, sequential, reductionist* and *abstract* thinking defines the masculine'. We are all, suggests Shlain, endowed with the capacity for perceiving the world in both these ways, but the invention of the first alphabet tipped the balance of power between men and women in favour of men. 'Whenever a culture elevates the written word,' he argues, 'patriarchy dominates.'[8] He suggests that the benefits of literacy have made it easy to overlook ways in which literate culture has caused the brain's left hemisphere – which is wired to process content rather than form, be analytical and discriminatory, accomplish skilled movement, and specialize in the retrieval of facts – to be prized at the expense of the right – with its greater capacity for generating non-logical feelings, deciphering images such as facial expressions, perceiving form rather than content, and processing information in its entirety instead of breaking it down.

Claims about the lateralization of brain function are not without controversy. Yet the subject, especially as condensed by Shlain, serves as a point of entry into the vexed question of the relation- ship between gender and language. Of the linguistic battles being waged today, those to do with gender are among the least tractable. The pioneers of feminism, from Mary Wollstonecraft to Simone de Beauvoir and beyond, have focused on language because it has enabled them to devise strategies for achieving liberty, to empha- size the inequitable history of who has been permitted to write or speak, and to highlight unfair practices and submerged meanings. Efforts of this kind continue, in mundane contexts and in momen- tous ones.

Traditional images of the sexes make much of their different linguistic abilities and tendencies: women are voluble and ought to be silent, men swear a lot and should be kept out of the nursery lest they contaminate children with their foul talk, women shrink from profanity, men are less tentative in their style of speech, and so on. It was once normal to suggest that women should be denied a full education in language because knowledge of such matters might put their health at risk. Around 1530 Richard Hyrde published a translation from the Latin of Juan Luis Vives's recent *The Instruction of a Christian Woman*. It included the claim – from which Hyrde himself demurred – that if women were exposed to the eloquence of Latin and Greek writing it was likely they would 'fall to vice, upset their stomachs, and . . . become unstable'.[9] For two centuries after this, although some like Hyrde voiced scepticism, there persisted a suspicion that women were not robust enough to deal with the hard business of grammar. Samuel Hartlib, arguing in the 1650s for educational reform, worried that women did not have the strength to survive the rigours of the classroom.

The perception that grammar is a sort of physical challenge has a long history. It can be traced back at least as far as Greek methods of tuition in the fourth century BC, which had a strong physical basis. The 'trivium' taught in medieval places of learning – consisting of the study of logic, rhetoric and grammar – was an exploration of the word, but like all ways of teaching the mind about the mind it had its grittily mechanical dimension. In the fifth-century writings of Martianus Capella, which were central to the medieval doctrine of the trivium, Lady Grammar was depicted carrying her specialized tools in a box; the western entrance to Chartres Cathedral shows her brandishing a bouquet of birch-rods. Grammar and trauma were closely associated: knowledge was achieved through the sort of coercion that left marks.

During the period in which Richard Hyrde was working, and until the late eighteenth century, the limits of what men expected women to accomplish were set out in conduct books. These manuals, mostly written by churchmen, prescribed correct forms of individual behaviour. One example was *A Godly Forme of Householde Government*, published in 1612 and attributed to John Dod and Robert Cleaver. It differentiated the duties of husbands and wives. Husbands should supply money and provisions, deal with other men, be skilful in talk and be entertaining; wives should be careful in their spending of money, talk with few, take pride in their silence and be solitary and withdrawn.[10] These attitudes were old; in Sophocles's play *Ajax*, written in the fifth century BC, the hero is presented as saying that silence makes a woman beautiful, and his wife Tecmessa sniffs that this is a hackneyed line.

The idea that men should be loquacious and women quiet is linked to the common assumption among men that women talk more than they do – memorably summarized in Byron's couplet in *Don Juan*, 'I have but one simile, and that's a blunder, / For wordless woman, which is silent thunder'. Women's alleged garrulousness, which in the eighteenth century was held responsible for the prevalence of bad grammar (and for other, specific crimes, such as a surfeit of adverbs), is today regarded with scepticism by experts. Yet when the old myths resurface, they are enthusiastically publicized. In 2006 Louann Brizendine, a professor of psychiatry at the University of California in San Francisco, scored a commercial success with a book entitled *The Female Brain*, in which she claimed that 'Men use about seven thousand words per day. Women use about twenty thousand'. She expanded on this by saying that 'women, on average, talk and listen a lot more than men' – some readers will instinctively agree – and that 'on average girls speak two to three times more words per day than boys' – now we are in more dubious territory – before asserting that 'Girls speak faster on average – 250 words per minute versus 125 for typical males'.[11] These figures were not the product of research, and Brizendine's sources leave something to be desired; one source for her first statistic is *Talk Language*, a self-help book by Allan Pease, author of such works as *Why Men Don't Listen and Women Can't Read Maps*. Authoritative studies suggest that the disparities between the conversational speech rates of men and women are small, and that the 7,000/20,000 dichotomy is baloney.[12] But Brizendine's 'findings' were widely reproduced.

It has become common to argue that there is no such thing as fixed gender identity. Instead gender is a performance. Gender seems self-evident, but it is really an accomplishment – 'embedded so thoroughly in our institutions, our actions, our beliefs, and our desires, that it appears to us to be completely natural'.[13] Every functioning gene in a man's body is found in a woman's also (and vice versa), with the exception of the gene that determines whether we are male or not. The maleness gene is like a switch, which activates or deactivates certain other suites of genes, but men and women depart from identity of design only with regard to the physiology of reproduction and some related problems.[14] Of course, this is not a trivial departure. Our relationships, the ways in which we socialize, our attitudes and our wants are shaped by biological fact. However, physiological difference is supplemented from the moment of our birth ('It's a boy!', 'It's a girl!') by rituals, commentary and received wisdom that cause us to grow up in distinct ways. In the long term, this may seem to guarantee the continuity of biological reproduction – whether it actually does so is questionable – but it also perpetuates social patterns in which the female is expected to be passive, cooperative and nurturing, while men are expected to be active, competitive and aggressive. We speak of 'the opposite sex', and in countless smaller ways reiterate this opposition.

Most men and women are aware, both in the workplace and in their personal lives, of communication problems that appear to arise because of differences between the sexes. The typical male observation – and I am aware of the crudeness of this generalization – is that women are too emotional, while women – the same caveat applies – are apt to find men too authoritarian. In her book *Genderflex*, Judith Tingley identifies certain differences: women 'express to understand', 'support conversation' and 'talk to connect', whereas men 'express to fix', believe 'conversation is a competition' and 'talk to resolve problems'.[15]

The American linguistics professor Deborah Tannen has written several popular books about differences between the conversational styles of men and women. Her explanations elicit frequent nods of assent and the occasional moment of fervid irritation. The irritation often stems from the uncomfortableness of the truths she illuminates. Tannen's writing is based on research and scrupulous observation, not on a wily sense of her own innate rightness. She notes that in young girls' conversation the main commodity that is exchanged is intimacy. Indeed, it is something the girls barter. By contrast, boys barter status. She also shows how indirectness in women's talk can be not defensive, but a means of creating rapport. At the same time she is careful not to say that all women are indirect, and she points out that in some communities male indirectness is highly valued while women practise a comparatively artless style.[16] Tannen's main contention, though, is that boys and girls grow up in different subcultures; these establish different conventions of interaction, one area of which is the use of language.

Others have argued that the differences between the languages of men and women have come about because men have relentlessly dominated women. Language has been a mechanism for repressing women. This view has led some feminists to call for a new, utopian female language, a fabricated alternative to the present state. A more conservative kind of activism involves language planning: documenting sexist language practices, and amending language to make it more symmetrical in its representation of men and women.

Sexist bias has long been evident in such disparate domains as children's books, assessment in schools and universities, the reporting of rape cases and the treatment of psychiatric disorders. More obvious to all is the hostile vocabulary applied to women's sexual appetites: a woman who is promiscuous or even just flirtatious will be flayed with abuse (*slut*, *slag*, *whore*, and so on), but there is no equivalent vocabulary of disapproval for men who behave in this fashion. *Love rat* is perhaps as close as we get. Try also to think of male equivalents for such terms of half-enraptured denigration as *pricktease*, *temptress*, *siren*, *sexpot*, *jezebel*, *jailbait* or *femme fatale*, or indeed for equivalents to *pussywhipped* and *cuntstruck*. We hear far more about nymphomania than about the male form of 'hypersexuality', namely satyriasis. There are abundant terms of endearment and appreciation for women and children, and far fewer for men; this says more about the nature of the appreciation than about the nature of those being appreciated. There are many words and expressions that present women as commodities; you can still read, for instance, about women being 'married off'. Men are sometimes forced into arranged marriages, but the language used of this is not dehumanizing. We also see gratuitous modifiers: someone is described as a 'lady doctor' or a 'male nurse', implying norms (male doctors, female nurses) that are outmoded. Even apparently innocent terms such as *girl* and *lady* are more heavily sexualized than their male equivalents.

Dictionaries, particularly those aimed at schoolchildren, long represented male and female sexuality in different ways: there was more about male genitals, and these were identified as sexual, whereas female genitals tended not to be. The penis was described as being used for copulation, whereas the vagina was identified as a sort of channel or canal, and the clitoris was presented as a 'rudimentary' little version of the penis.[17] This kind of thing is uncommon now. But the habit of denying or circumscribing female sexuality remains.

Men have historically monopolized the naming of the world's phenomena, and until the modern era they dominated formal education – both as providers and as recipients. The first woman to make a palpable contribution to the study of English was Bathsua Reginald, who around 1616 collaborated with her father, a London schoolmaster, on a system of shorthand, and nearly sixty years later, under her married name Bathsua Makin, published *An Essay to Revive the Antient Education of Gentlewomen*, in which she complained with enjoyable vigour about the deficiencies of William Lily's system of grammar.

The first Grammar of English to be written by a woman was probably Ann Fisher's *A New Grammar* (1745). The wife of a Newcastle printer, Fisher had nine daughters and ran a school for young ladies. *A New Grammar* shows her determination to move away from modelling English usage on Latin; she is critical of existing grammars, suggesting that they are of limited use to teachers. She also came up with the original strategy of confronting readers with examples of what she called 'bad English', which they were then expected to correct. The innovation, as we know, became popular.

Several female grammarians followed Fisher. The most successful of them was Ellin Devis, who initially published her work anonymously, but soon acknowledged her authorship. *The Accidence; or First Rudiments of English Grammar* (1775) was 'designed for the use of young ladies' – a first – and went through eighteen editions in the fifty-two years after it appeared. Devis, a teacher in Kensington and then in Bloomsbury, combined moral and grammatical guidance in her concluding 'Maxims and Reflections'. Her name became a touchstone for female educationalists and others interested in promoting women's education. Erasmus Darwin, for instance, set up a school in Ashbourne in Derbyshire where two of his daughters, Susanna and Mary, did the teaching, and two, Emma and Violetta, were among the first students. His published plan of how young women should be educated made specific mention of Devis, and other programmes aimed at girls suggested using Devis's *The Accidence* alongside Lowth's *Short Introduction*.

Devis is an intriguing figure, but Ann Fisher is historically more remarkable. She is interesting partly because of her argument that Latin, rather than being the ideal model for English, was inferior to it. English's lack of inflections made it more manageable. Unlike her contemporaries, she did not insist on Latin grammatical terminology. However, inasmuch as her name is now known, it is for a different reason. For it was Fisher who promoted the convention of using *he*, *him* and *his* as pronouns to cover both male and female in general statements such as 'Everyone has his quirks'. To be precise, she says that 'The *Masculine Person* answers to the *general Name*, which comprehends both *Male* and *Female*; as, *Any Person who knows what he says*'.[18] This idea caught on. Since then it has been attributed to another grammarian of the day, John Kirkby, but Kirkby nabbed the idea from Fisher. The convention was bolstered by an Act of Parliament in 1850: in order to simplify the language used in other Acts, it was decreed that the masculine pronoun be understood to include both males and females. The obvious objection to this – obvious now, even if it was not obvious then – is that it makes women politically invisible.

It is not unusual to hear a sentence like the following: 'If someone asks to spend the night on your sofa, you'd be rude to send them packing.' A common objection to this is that *them* is plural, whereas *someone* is singular. However, this use of *them* gets round a problem we today take seriously. Until quite recently, it would have been considered standard to write, as Fisher and Kirkby would have encouraged, 'If someone asks to spend the night on your sofa, you'd be rude to send him packing'. But this would now widely be considered sexist. It's not hard to understand why: you cannot see *he*, *him* or *his* without thinking of a male. The inclusive alternative, which

I often use, is 'he or she'. (In the 1850s a lawyer by the name of Charles Crozat Converse proposed *thon*. Other suggestions have included *ha* and *heer*.) Employed repeatedly, though, 'he or she' sounds clunky. In 1880 Richard Grant White pronounced, 'The fact remains that *his* is the representative pronoun . . . To use "his or her" in cases of this kind seems to me very finical and pedantic.'[19] It's easy enough to exemplify his point: 'If someone asks to spend the night on your sofa, you'd be rude to send him or her packing, and you should give him or her every chance to make himself or herself comfortable, perhaps even furnishing him or her with a spare duvet and a towel for his or her morning ablutions.' Two of the alternatives – defaulting to *her* rather than *his*, or switching arbitrarily between the two – feel arch. Hence the quick fix: 'If someone asks to spend the night on your sofa, call them a taxi and pay their fare home.'

Often it is alleged that *everyone* equals 'every one', and that therefore it should be matched with not only a singular verb, but also singular pronouns. Imagine that John and Christine run camping holidays for teenage boys on their remote island. If Christine picks the teenagers up on arrival and John then comes along with essential equipment, we might say, 'Christine met everyone off the boat before John arrived with their tents.' The convention requires us, however, to say that 'Christine met everyone off the boat before John arrived with his tent'. This phrasing could invite doubts about John's motives for running the camping holidays. The use of *their* in this instance is not slovenly; rather, it removes ambiguity.

Wielding *they*, *them* and *their* in this way has a much longer history than is generally recognized. It was practised by Shakespeare – 'And every one to rest themselves betake' in his poem *The Rape of Lucrece* – and by Chaucer, as well as by a host of others that includes Lord Byron, John Ruskin, George Eliot, Henry Fielding, Jonathan Swift, Lord Chesterfield, Lewis Carroll and Dr Johnson. We end this chapter's rapid journey here, with something apparently minor, because it is in arguments over such small details of everyday English that we most often come into contact with big issues of cultural bias or suffocating tradition, and because, too, it suggests that some usages regarded as illiterate are really acts of discretion.

19 Modern life is rubbish

Facing up to language 'as it is'

Reporting in the early 1980s on the 'critical condition' of English, the combative theatre critic John Simon lamented the effects on it of the 'four great body blows' dealt to education: the student rebellion of 1968, the notion that 'language must accommodate itself to the whims, idiosyncrasies, dialects, and sheer ignorance of underprivileged minorities', 'the introduction by more and more incompetent English teachers . . . of ever fancier techniques of *not* teaching English', and the rise of television, a 'word-mangling medium that sucks in victims . . . perniciously'.[1] Simon is unusual only in the burning vehemence of his expression. Decline was the main theme of twentieth-century comment on English. As scholarly understanding of language in general and this language in particular grew massively, aided by developments in technology, the gap widened between academic views of English and everyday ones. In trade books and in the mainstream media, the state of English was endlessly lamented. Meanwhile professional linguists pursued technical matters that had ever more technical names: among the different branches of linguistics, for instance, emerged schools variously labelled computational, generative, cognitive, integrational, contrastive, and stratificational.

The seeds were sown in the nineteenth century, in an area that at first looks unlikely – the comparative study of languages. The scientific understanding of languages and their relationships, articulated by William Jones and Franz Bopp, changed how language was imagined. As Edward Said wrote in his classic study *Orientalism* (1978), 'the divine dynasty of language was ruptured definitively' and language became 'less a continuity between an outside power and the human speaker than an internal field created and accomplished by language users among themselves'.[2] The scientific turn shifted the emphasis from statements about what ought to hold true to an examination of language *as it is*.

Popular writers on language felt the rush of modernity. It became conventional to think about the future of English and to imagine ways of securing that future. I have already several times cited H. G. Wells: best known today for his visionary scientific fiction, he often wrote non-fiction about the future, in which he made forecasts, discussed the challenges of modernity, and urged his readers to embrace a new vision of the world – republican and rational. His fantasies, whether cast as fiction or non-fiction, tended to be played out against the familiar landscape of southern England, and he frequently considered the role of English in the future. He speculated, for instance, that by 2000 'the whole functional body of human society would read, and perhaps even write and speak, our language'.[3]

Wells's most sustained discussion of the subject is in his book *Mankind in the Making* and is worth quoting at length. Wells is not now a fashionable figure, and sometimes he expressed himself in a way that offends modern sensibilities, but his prescience and perceptiveness are arresting.

> There can be little or no dispute [he writes] that the English language in its completeness presents a range too ample and appliances too subtle for the needs of the great majority of those who profess to speak it. I do not refer to the half-civilized and altogether barbaric races who are coming under its sway, but to the people we are breeding of our own race – the barbarians of our streets, our suburban 'white niggers', with a thousand a year and the conceit of Imperial destinies. They live in our mother-tongue as some half-civilized invaders might live in a gigantic and splendidly equipped palace. They misuse this, they waste that, they leave whole corridors and wings unexplored, to fall into disuse and decay. I doubt if the ordinary member of the prosperous classes in England has much more than a third of the English language in use, and more than a half in knowledge, and as we go down the social scale we may come at last to strata having but a tenth part of our full vocabulary, and much of that blurred and vaguely

understood. The speech of the Colonist is even poorer than the speech of the home-staying English.[4]

Wells felt that his contemporaries tended to 'speak a little set of ready-made phrases', could write English 'scarcely at all', and read nothing except 'the weak and shallow prose of popular fiction and the daily press'. He lamented,

> One is constantly meeting, not only women, but men who will solemnly profess to 'know' English and Latin, French, German and Italian, perhaps Greek, who are in fact – beyond the limited range of food, clothing, shelter, trade, crude nationalism, social conventions and personal vanity – no better than the deaf and dumb. In spite of the fact that they will sit with books in their hands, visibly reading, turning pages, pencilling comments – in spite of the fact that they will discuss authors and repeat criticisms, it is as hopeless to express new thoughts to them as it would be to seek for appreciation in the ear of a hippopotamus. Their linguistic instruments are no more capable of contemporary thought than a tin whistle, a xylophone, and a drum are capable of rendering the Eroica Symphony.

One problem, he felt sure, was the poor quality of teacher training: 'Too often our elementary teachers at any rate, instead of being missionaries of linguistic purity, are centres of diffusion for blurred and vicious perversions of our speech.'[5]

Though he expressed himself in arresting terms, Wells's vision of a widely diffused and poorly maintained English was not uncommon. Progressives put forward radical ideas for streamlining the language's international form. The most significant of these was the work of a psychologist, C. K. Ogden, who in the 1920s conceived and developed what he called Basic English. 'Basic' was a felicitous acronym for British American Scientific International Commercial. Ogden, an entrepreneurial pacifist whose interests included collecting masks (and wearing them), envisaged 'an auxiliary international language comprising 850 words arranged in a system in which everything may be said for all the purposes of everyday existence', and by 1939 he had published more than two hundred titles demonstrating what he had in mind. Strongly influenced by the philosophy of Jeremy Bentham – even going so far as to acquire and wear his ring – Ogden was especially taken with Bentham's idea that verbs impede meaning, and he invested two years working towards a core stock of just eighteen essential English verbs.[6] The practical aspect of the scheme had a moral motivation; Ogden's frequent collaborator, the literary critic and theorist I. A. Richards, felt that the lack of an international language led to individual countries' insularity, which in turn led to conflict.

There was a good deal of support for Ogden's proposals, especially during the 1940s when Winston Churchill championed the cause. A Basic English Foundation was set up with a grant from the Ministry of Education, Basic English was taught in more than thirty countries, and Ogden grudgingly accepted £23,000 in return for assigning his copyright to the Crown. But interest dropped off sharply in the 1950s. Typically, there was a feeling that, even if Basic English proved a success, it posed a danger: it was seen as threatening to constrain not just language, but thought. Ultimately, it failed because of the widespread suspicion that it lacked range and expressiveness (it wasn't even possible to say 'Good evening' or 'Thank you'), was clumsy and open to parody, and was too deeply coloured by Ogden's personal world-view, and also, crucially, because of the longueurs of British bureaucracy and a lack of sustained political or institutional support. Ogden retreated into the narrow life of a garrulous clubman, and by the time he died of cancer in 1957 the demise of Basic English was certain. Recently, though, it has been revived by Wikipedia; Ogden's Basic is the model for the Simple English version of the online encyclopaedia.

In America, institutions strove to promote a more realistic sense of how English was used and how it might be used in the future. The American Philological Association was founded in 1869, and there followed the Modern Language Association in 1883, the American Dialect Society in 1889, the National Council of Teachers of English in 1911, and the Linguistic Society of America in 1924. These bodies contributed to a new scholarly idea of correctness, grounded in the mapping of actual usage.

One of the most influential figures to emerge from American academia during this period was George Philip Krapp, who in *Modern*

English (1909) asked, 'What is good English?' Stressing the importance of living speech, he argued that the laws of English arise from
the ways in which the language is used, rather than originating in
theory. Questioning the existence of any such thing as a standard
form of English, he delighted in the notion of the language constantly
being refreshed. Krapp repeatedly acclaimed the idiomatic life of the
language, which he saw as something lying within its users.

Krapp's work inspired theorists of education such as Charles Carpenter
Fries to advocate a new style of teaching that would focus on the practical business of using English. Eventually this led to the publication in
1952 of *The English Language Arts*, a report by the National Council
of Teachers of English which argued for a change in the way English
was taught in schools and colleges: instead of emphasizing rules and a
negative view of language, teachers should offer 'positive insights'. *The
English Language Arts* was 'a benchmark for a half-century of growing
liberality in attitudes towards usage'.[7] Its relativism was dismissed by
traditionalists such as Jacques Barzun, who criticized what they saw as
the report's central message that change was invariably improvement –
though in fact the report offered no such maxim.

Mounting tension between traditionalists and liberals found
dramatic expression in the controversy surrounding *Webster's Third
New International Dictionary*, which was published in September 1961.
Its editor, Philip Gove, stressed that it would impose no artificial
notions of correctness. It certainly represented a sharp deviation
from the practices of the lexicographer whose name it bore. Although
the edition was billed as 'Utilizing all the experience and resources
of more than one hundred years of Merriam-Webster dictionaries',
beneath its traditional packaging lay new thinking. Gove insisted
that lexicography should be descriptive, not prescriptive. Consequently, *Webster's Third* would sparingly apply status labels to different
types of usage. The previously popular label 'colloquial' was
discarded. *Webster's Third* had virtues – a high level of scholarship,
including greatly improved etymologies, and crisp layout – but the
descriptive approach provoked acerbic criticism, and Gove was
instantly demonized.

There were some positive assessments, but many bruising ones.
The editors of *Life* magazine complained that it was typical of 'the

say-as-you-go school of permissive English' and came close to abandoning 'any effort to distinguish between good and bad usage –
between the King's English, say, and the fishwife's'.[8] The *Atlantic
Monthly* headed its coverage with the words 'Sabotage in Springfield'. The *New York Times* parodied the dictionary's inclusiveness: 'A
passel of double-domes at the G. & C. Merriam Company joint . . .
have been confabbing and yakking for twenty-seven years . . . and
now they have finalized Webster's Third New International Dictionary,
Unabridged, a new edition of that swell and esteemed word book.'
A later item dubbed the new edition 'Webster's Third (or Bolshevik)
International'.[9] It was not just the newspaper writers who derided
the efforts of Gove and his team. Two decades after the publication
of *Webster's Third*, John Simon, never one to mince his words, called
it 'seminally sinister'.[10] And in Rex Stout's 1962 detective novel
Gambit the hero, Nero Wolfe, feeds the pages of this 'intolerably
offensive' work into a fire. The reason for this topical gesture? *Webster's
Third* fails to uphold the distinction between *imply* and *infer*. Since
the two volumes comprised more than 2,700 pages and cost $47.50,
Wolfe's was an expensive and time-consuming expression of disgust.

Strikingly, the traditionalists perceived *Webster's Third* as being
actively unpleasant rather than just passively so. Its greatest offence,
in the eyes of many, was its alleged acceptance of *ain't*. According
to the *Toronto Globe and Mail*, the 'embrace of the word "ain't" will
comfort the ignorant, confer approval upon the mediocre, and subtly
imply that proper English is the tool only of the snob; but it will
not assist men to speak true to other men. It may, however, prepare
us for that future which it could help to hasten. In the caves, no
doubt, a grunt will do.'[11] Comment of this kind was widespread.
The language of outrage was white-hot. In the *New Yorker*, Dwight
Macdonald described as an 'incredible massacre' the removal of many
of the entries that had graced the previous edition. Others resented
not only the desecration of the past, but also the generous welcoming
of the present. *Webster's Third* was considered a product of the dope-
smoking counterculture.[12] The approach of Gove and his colleagues
to their subject matter resembled the non-evaluative method of
Alfred Kinsey's work on sexual behaviour, and, according to the
Jeremiahs, like Kinsey's reports *Webster's Third* was a licence for

depravity. It was, in short, evidence of the disintegration of civilized existence.

Besides the descriptivism there were plenty of specific features of the new *Webster's* for critics to deplore. Why, they wanted to know, were there illustrative quotations from the Broadway stalwart Ethel Merman and the baseball player Willie Mays? Merman was quoted to illustrate the verb *to drain*: 'Two shows a day drain a girl.' Why were brand names such as *Kleenex* presented without an initial capital? Just one headword in the entire dictionary was given a capital letter: *God*. There were complaints about the dropping of much of the encyclopaedic material that had been available in the previous edition; for instance, readers could no longer find in the pages of *Webster's* details of the names of the twelve apostles. But the real fuss was over the absence of value judgements. The message was simple: if a dictionary bearing the name of America's greatest lexicographer could not be counted on to condemn loose usage, we might as well start preparing for the end of days. Ironically, at the very time that *Webster's Third* was being launched, Merriam-Webster was printing advertisements, in popular magazines such as *Life*, promoting the idea that 'Good English is a *must* for success in high school and college!' and claiming that 'This ability develops quickly with regular use of a personal copy of Webster's New Collegiate'.

Examining *Webster's Third*, the image presented by its critics turns out to be inaccurate. When I look up *irregardless*, the inclusion of which had caused the *Life* reviewer to complain bitterly, I see it is labelled 'nonstand', i.e. not standard usage. *Ain't* is not exactly 'embraced', either. It is described as 'disapproved by many and more common in less educated speech'. A graver problem, in truth, results from Gove's requirement that each definition be a single sentence. Thus *tocopherol* is 'any of several pale yellow fat-soluble oily liquid phenolic compounds that are derived from chroman and differ in the number and locations of methyl groups in the benzene ring, that have antioxidant properties and vitamin E activity in varying degrees, that are found in the dextrorotatory form esp. in oils from seeds' – and that is only about a quarter of the full, one-sentence definition. A personal favourite is *door*: 'a movable piece of firm material or a structure supported usu. along one side and swinging on pivots or hinges, sliding along a groove, rolling up and down, revolving as one of four leaves, or folding like an accordion by means of which an opening may be closed or kept open for passage into or out of a building, room, or other covered enclosure or a car, airplane, elevator, or other vehicle.' Reading this, I feel I know less about doors than I did before.

The revulsion against the new *Webster's* found its most sustained expression in *The American Heritage Dictionary of the English Language.* James Parton, the president of the American Heritage Publishing Company, initially tried to buy up shares in the Merriam Company and suppress *Webster's Third.* Then he changed his angle of attack, and the result was *The American Heritage Dictionary*, which appeared in 1969. Its publishers made much of their responsibility as custodians of the English language and of American culture. Emphasizing how seriously they took this role, they set up a panel of one hundred distinguished arbiters – a number later enlarged – to comment on key matters of usage. The list of names is intriguing. In my 1976 copy, it includes the broadcaster Alistair Cooke, Peter Hurd (identified as a painter and cattle-rancher), film critic Pauline Kael and the feminist writer Gloria Steinem. Ethel Merman did not make the cut. Flicking through a copy of *The American Heritage Dictionary*, one occasionally finds statistical information about the panel's views. For instance, we are told that 99 per cent disapproved of 'ain't I?' in written English 'other than that which is deliberately colloquial' and that 84 per cent thought it unacceptable in speech. *Bus* as a transitive verb ('We need to bus these children to school') is 'an almost indispensable term', acceptable in formal writing to 91 per cent of the panel. 'Rather unique' and 'most unique' are not accepted by 94 per cent.

Webster's Third has outlived the controversy that greeted it, but *The American Heritage Dictionary* is also popular, and it embodies the widespread hostility to descriptivism. That a descriptive approach to language is the academic norm serves only to intensify the disgust felt by conservatives. Since the 1960s the study of language has played an increasingly important part in American academic life, embracing (not always very comfortably) the different interests of logicians, anthropologists and humanists. The activities of scholars in these fields are the butt of much everyday humour. Pop grammarians exploit public insecurity about the use of language and public misgivings about the abilities of scholars to provide sensible guidance. Meanwhile the scholars themselves complain about a society that does not honour their work.

American universities have been the test bed for new ideas about the role of language in everyday life – specifically, its capacity to perpetuate unfairness and injustice. Advocates of political correctness have sought to amend the language of academic study, of campus life, and of the wider public. The rise of political correctness was one of the defining phenomena of the late 1980s and early 1990s. The phenomenon is with us still, though it operates less overtly than it did in its heyday. As its open-ended name suggests, it consists not of a single solid principle, but of a range of activities which can be split into two areas: describing and questioning. In the first of these areas, PC manifested itself in the form of verbal hygiene – a new, preferred terminology for speaking of minorities such as homosexuals, as well as in new ways of talking about teaching, learning and the curriculum. In the second area, it involved casting doubt on received notions of history, artistic merit and appropriate public behaviour.

Promoted in the interests of sensitivity and the redistribution of cultural capital, often by sixties radicals who had internalized their outrage and become pillars of academe, PC was initially, as Geoffrey Hughes writes in his history of it, 'a basically idealistic, decent-minded, but slightly Puritanical intervention to sanitize the language by suppressing some of its uglier prejudicial features'.[13] But it was soon demonized by the political right as an exercise in sanctimonious relativism and leftist prickliness. To its sponsors, it was 'a healthy expansion of morality' (the phrase is Noam Chomsky's); to its detractors, a sickness depleting the very idea of freedom.

Significantly, the debate over PC consisted not so much of the proponents and opponents trading invective, as of PC's enemies first hotly publicizing the issues and then dousing them with the icy water of ridicule. The opponents of PC saw themselves as a minority, when they were nothing of the sort. Though the label 'politically correct' had been in use for almost two hundred years, it gained currency in the eighties chiefly because conservatives adopted it to sum up the new enforced orthodoxies they were eager to disparage. The most acerbic critic of PC was Robert Hughes (no relation of

Geoffrey), whose book *Culture of Complaint* (1993) diagnosed 'the fraying of America'. Hughes savaged the 'fake pity' of political discourse, an entire culture's 'maudlin reaction against excellence', feminism's 'abandoning the image of the independent, existentially responsible woman in favour of woman as helpless victim of male oppression'.[14] Language was key. 'We want,' Hughes wrote, 'to create a sort of linguistic Lourdes, where evil and misfortune are dispelled by a dip in the waters of euphemism.' The 'affected contortions' of PC could do nothing to heighten civility and understanding.[15] Instead, believed Hughes, they led to a loss of reality.

The inherent problem of PC was, and is, that it seeks to extend people's rights while at the same time curbing their freedoms. Instead of fostering respect for variety (of people, of cultures, of experiences), it stresses differences: we are not to think of the common good, but instead must recognize a growing number of special social categories. This contributes to the increasing atomization of society: shared experiences and values are regarded not as things to cherish, but as reflections of constraint, evidence of the oppression of the individual and his or her particularity.

The basic intent of PC has been to draw attention to submerged social ills. Deborah Cameron argues that the largest threat it poses is to 'our freedom to imagine that our linguistic choices are inconsequential'.[16] Certainly, although some manifestations of PC are bovine, it is instructive to be shown that the names we give to things – to people – can reinforce prejudices. But negative attitudes precede negative names, and reforming language in the interests of equality is not the same thing as accomplishing equality. The niceties of PC allow us to applaud our own sensitivity while evading the redress of real evils. PC represents a return to linguistic prescriptivism (and proscriptivism), sponsored by those who would otherwise see themselves as progressives and natural descriptivists.

20 Unholy shit

Censorship and obscenity

Political correctness is an invitation to practise self-censorship: to conform to a model of fairness. This brings us to the larger issue of what we are not permitted to say, what we are discouraged from saying, and what we elect to say only in very particular circumstances.

Censorship has a long history, and so does opposition to it. Indeed, it is the practice of policing what people are allowed to say that creates opportunities for subterfuge. The main concern of censorship is smothering ideas, yet because language is the vehicle of ideas censorship has often seemed to be above all else an attempt to muffle language or extinguish it. You can jail a person, but not an idea. There are two forms of censorship. One is interference in advance of publication – by the state or by some other authority such as the Church. The other is action after publication: lawsuits and financial penalties.

In Britain it is the Crown that has usually taken responsibility for censorship. Henry VIII published a list of banned books in 1529, and in 1545 the first permanent Master of the Revels was appointed, with responsibility for licensing playhouses and approving the works staged there. Later this role passed to the Lord Chamberlain, whose responsibility for theatrical censorship continued until 1968. There is also a tradition of self-appointed moralists: early ones included William Prynne and Jeremy Collier, who attacked the decadence of the theatre in the seventeenth century; the type is perhaps best represented by Mrs Grundy, a character mentioned in Thomas Morton's play *Speed the Plough* (1798) who embodies the idea of bourgeois propriety and is name-checked in novels by Dickens, Thackeray and Dostoevsky.[1] The moralists' indignation is always no more than a step away from intolerance, and part of it stems from the conviction that the authorities should do more to repress profanity and depravity.

It is well known that whole books have been suppressed on the grounds of obscenity: for instance, *Lady Chatterley's Lover* in Britain, the United States and Australia, and, less famously, a guide to euthanasia called *The Peaceful Pill Handbook* in Australia and New Zealand. Sometimes, too, a regime has outlawed literature on polit-ical grounds. A current example is North Korea, where the arts are expected to instruct people in socialism; educated North Koreans are unlikely to have read anything published outside their own language or before 1948.

More often there have been small acts of suppression. Parts of books have been cut or amended to avoid causing offence, and certain books have been kept out of schools. Hugh Lofting's *Doctor Dolittle* titles have been purged of words such as *coon* and *darky* – favourites of Dolittle's pet parrot Polynesia. Ray Bradbury's novel *Fahrenheit 451*, which has been interpreted as an indictment of censor-ship, was expurgated for distribution in high schools; among other things, an episode describing fluff being removed from a navel was changed to a description of ears being cleaned. J. D. Salinger's *The Catcher in the Rye* was widely banned in schools in the 1960s and '70s; in 1960 a teacher in Tulsa, Oklahoma, was fired after assigning the book to a class of sixteen-year-olds. The American Civil Liber-ties Union reports that the most challenged books in the 1990s included *Huckleberry Finn* (because of its use of the word *nigger*) and J. K. Rowling's *Harry Potter* novels (because they allegedly teach witchcraft). Common reasons for challenges are allegations that books contain 'sexually explicit' material and 'offensive language' or are unsuited to the age group to which they are ostensibly addressed.[2]

Probably the most celebrated example of censorship in English is Thomas Bowdler's *The Family Shakespeare* (1818). As its subtitle announced, this edition of Shakespeare's plays omitted any words that 'cannot with propriety be read aloud in a family' – stripping away anything sexual, yet retaining the violence. The edition was Bowdler's completion of work done by his sister Henrietta Maria; ungenerously, the title page omitted her name, though it did advertise his position as a Fellow of the Royal Society. Bowdler was also a member of what became the Society for the Suppression of Vice. His text, in which vice was diluted rather than completely effaced, led to his being accused in one review of having 'castrated' Shakespeare and of having 'cauterized and phlebotomized him'.[3] But *The Family Shakespeare* was popular, and went through five editions in twenty years. (Less well-known is Bowdler's attempt to do the same thing with Gibbon's *Decline and Fall of the Roman Empire*, from which he excised 'all passages of an irreligious or immoral tendency'.) The verb *to bowdlerize* has passed into everyday English vocabulary.

By contrast, an atmosphere of the alien clings to the title of John Milton's *Areopagitica* (1644) – a work often claimed as a pioneering defence of free speech, although it would be more accurate to call it a wartime defence of the freedom of the press from government interference. The name of this tract is an allusion to the Areopagus, a hill where the Court of Athens met in the fourth and fifth centuries BC. Maybe we should read something into the fact that the name Milton chose for his defence of a free press remains so obscure. We may find many acts of censorship ridiculous, especially when we reflect on them from a distance yet the defenders of free expression are often thought of as superfluous bores, or are simply forgotten.

Sometimes a single word can cause outrage. George Bernard Shaw wrote several plays that, while apparently apolitical, addressed controversial issues; of these the best-known is *Pygmalion*, in which Shaw pokes fun at the social purity movement. For a bet, Henry Higgins transforms the Covent Garden flower-seller Eliza Doolittle into a 'princess', which chiefly involves purifying her pronunciation. This is also, covertly, an attempt to ensure her moral probity. At the start of the play Eliza is mistaken for a prostitute – a matter dealt with obliquely, but not obscurely – and in learning a more refined style of speech she reduces the chances of this kind of thing happening in the future. However, the refinement is robotic, and there are moments when she escapes from it, expressing her true personality in vivid terms. One of these exercised the press. Before the first performance on the London stage of *Pygmalion*, the *Daily Sketch* warned that 'One word in Shaw's new play will cause sensation'. Its preview continued: 'It is a word . . . certainly not used in decent society. It is a word which the *Daily Sketch* cannot possibly print.' The word was *bloody*. On 11 April 1914, the first night of the run, Eliza's use of it did indeed cause a sensation: in the theatre there was a stunned silence followed by more than a minute of hysterical laughter. Newspapers responded with dramatic headlines such as 'Threats By Decency League'. Both *bloody* and *pygmalion* became catchwords of the moment. Shaw made a statement that was printed in the *Daily News*: 'I have nothing particular to say about Eliza Doolittle's language . . . I do not know anything more ridiculous than the refusal of some newspapers (at several pages' length) to print the word "bloody", which is in common use as an expletive by four-fifths of the British nation, including many highly-educated persons.'[4] Almost a hundred years on, news media continue to play an ambivalent part in censorship, reporting events that have caused scandal, and often thereby drawing attention to acts or statements that might otherwise have gone largely unnoticed.

The practice of censorship is closely linked to the concept of taboo – behaviours that are prohibited or strongly inhibited by the belief that they are improper, and things that are considered unfit for mention because they are sordid or sacred. The first recorded use in English of the word *taboo* – usually said to be of Tongan origin – is in Captain Cook's 1777 account of his Pacific voyage. Sigmund Freud gave the word greater currency. In paying attention to the social role of taboo, he noted that we can feel guilty not just about things we have done, but also about our wishes (even subconscious ones). He identified this 'creative' kind of guilt as an important part of the machinery of our psyche, and went so far as to suggest that swearing, easily dismissed as mere catharsis, is an expression of wishes that exist below the threshold of consciousness, conveying a primal disgust.

We frequently censor ourselves. I may sweeten a salty anecdote when relating it to a friend's parents, or modify the way I talk about religion when I am with someone I know is a believer. While there is nothing that is at all times taboo for all people, we typically restrict or suppress parts of our vocabulary for fear of violating common taboos. This may well feel not like fear, but more akin to reverence or courtesy.

The words and expressions most tabooed in English-speaking society are to do with sex, excretion, ethnicity and religion. Elsewhere there have been other prohibitions. Bandits in Republican China did not use the names of animals they considered dangerous. The linguist Leonard Bloomfield reported that a Cree Indian would not mention his sister's name. In Japan, taboo terms are known as *imi kotoba*; at a wedding, one is expected to avoid using a common verb meaning 'to repeat', because it hints at the idea of divorce and remarriage. The Zuni of New Mexico will not use the word *takka*, meaning 'frogs', on any ceremonial occasion. Traditionally, Faroese fishermen refrain from using the word for knife (*knívur*), and, in the Yakut language spoken in parts of the far north of Russia, the word for a bear is avoided.

For most readers of this book, though, the four taboo subjects I have mentioned will be to the fore. In Britain until the 1960s the use in print of *fuck* or *cunt* could result in prosecution. Speech, of course, has been a different matter. Michel de Montaigne observed in one of his essays that the words most rarely or warily spoken are among those most readily recognized. There is justice in this, but in the English-speaking world the rarity and wariness are doubtful. William Hazlitt had it right when he remarked that the English are 'rather a foul-mouthed nation'. I don't think of myself as a heavy swearer, but elsewhere in the English-speaking world – except in Australia – I seem to pass for one, as taboo terms trickle from my lips.

The reaction these words provoke is caused more by the words themselves than by the things they denote. Far fewer people will be upset by the word *vagina* than will be appalled to hear the word *cunt*. Very few will be disconcerted by a reference to *sexual intercourse*. It's also, I think, worth briefly reflecting that swearing, besides often expressing strong feelings and relating to taboos, is not on the whole to be taken literally. Consider, for instance, the statement 'I got fucked by my boss in my annual review'. Or 'Fuck me!', which is an expression of surprise more often than an invitation. Yet the associations of sex with physical force, pain and exploitation –

concentrated in the quick invasive aggression of *fuck* – are present here.

Shit is, undoubtedly, a different matter. The word does not seem to have bothered readers in the fifteenth century, when Caxton used it in a translation of *Aesop's Fables*. By the eighteenth century, attitudes had clearly changed. It seems safe to assume that English-speakers by then were a little less intimately acquainted with their dung than Caxton's contemporaries had been. Some dictionaries of the period were squeamish, and others less so. In Nathan Bailey's *Dictionarium Britannicum* (1730) there is no entry for *shit*, but *shitten* ('beshit, fouled with Ordure') is there and so is *to shite*, which is 'to discharge the Belly; to ease Nature'. (Bailey also registers *cunt*, but evasively defines it only as '*pudendum muliebre*'.) Johnson includes none of these words. Moving forward, in the first edition of the *OED shit* does appear, labelled 'not now in decent use'.

It has been suggested, by Steven Pinker among others, that slang words for effluvia are unacceptable in precise relation to the unacceptability of emitting – or eliminating – those effluvia in public. Accordingly, *shit* is worse than *piss*, which is worse than *fart*, which is worse than *snot*. The various slang words for semen are probably somewhere between *shit* and *piss*. It is no coincidence that the substances that most disgust us are the most dangerous. Faeces is a powerful vector of disease, whereas snot carries less hazardous infections. There are ways of referring to faeces that infantilize or medicalize it – *doo-doo*, for instance, and *stools* – and these neutralize our disgust. But *shit* does no such thing and is offensive because it arouses our disgust and connects us, subconsciously, to disease. It seems plausible that, the further we are (or believe ourselves to be) from shit in our daily lives, the more the word appals us, because it insinuates something feculent back into a world we think we have made clean and safe.

Undoubtedly, too, even if on an intellectual level we accept that the connection between sounds and meanings is arbitrary, we feel otherwise. Steven Pinker explains that 'most humans . . . treat the name for an entity as part of its essence, so that the mere act of uttering a name is seen as a way to impinge on its referent'. Confronted with a taboo word such as *shit*, the part of one's brain known as the amygdala experiences a surge in metabolic activity: 'The upshot is that a speaker or writer can use a taboo word to evoke an emotional response in an audience quite against their wishes.'[5]

George Orwell writes in *Down and Out in Paris and London* (1933):

> The whole business of swearing, especially English swearing, is mysterious. Of its very nature swearing is as irrational as magic – indeed, it is a species of magic. But there is also a paradox about it, namely this: Our intention in swearing is to shock and wound, which we do by mentioning something that should be kept secret – usually something to do with the sexual functions. But the strange thing is that when a word is well established as a swear word, it seems to lose its original meaning; that is, it loses the thing that made it into a swear word.

Less than twenty years after the first London production of *Pygmalion*, Orwell notes, 'No born Londoner . . . now says "bloody", unless he is a man of some education. The word has, in fact, moved up in the social scale and ceased to be a swear word for the purposes of the working classes. The current London adjective, now tacked on to every noun, is ——. No doubt in time ——, like "bloody", will find its way into the drawing-room and be replaced by some other word.' No prizes for guessing what —— stands for. In *Nineteen Eighty-Four* (1949) Julia strikes Winston as natural and healthy because she cannot mention the Party 'without using the kind of words that you saw chalked up in dripping alley-ways'; Orwell avoids saying which words she uses in order to shock by implication, and perhaps also to avoid committing himself to a view of what might prove shocking in the future.

Fuck is the dirty prince of English vocabulary – aggressive, flamboyant, versatile, awkward. As Jesse Sheidlower's book *The F-Word* enjoyably illustrates, it not only has a vast number of applications, but also is prolific: here's Robert Louis Stevenson writing in a letter about a *fuckstress*; here's a character in a Philip Roth novel using the verb *guaranfuckingtee*; and here's Eric Partridge in his *Dictionary of Slang and Unconventional English* explaining that a *Dutch fuck* is the act of lighting one cigarette from another.

Until quite recently, dictionaries have treated *fuck* with caution. In Britain, the word appeared as early as 1598 in John Florio's Italian-English dictionary, in the definition of the Italian verb *fottere* – 'to iape, to sard, to fucke, to swive, to occupy' – and in cognate forms under *fottarie* ('fuckings'), *fottitrice* ('a woman fucker'), *fottitore* ('a fucker'), *fottitura* ('a fucking') and *fottuto* ('fuckt'). The verb *to fuck* was listed in Bailey's *Dictionarium Britannicum* as 'a term used of a goat; also *subagitare feminam*', and found its way into John Ash's *New and Complete Dictionary of the English Language* (1775). But then *fuck* disappeared from lexicographic view. After the second edition of Ash in 1795, where it is labelled 'a low vulgar word' and defined as 'to perform the act of generation, to have to do with a woman', *fuck*'s next appearance in a general English dictionary was in 1965, when a definition was presented in the *Penguin English Dictionary*. No general American dictionary contained *fuck* until it appeared in *The American Heritage Dictionary* in 1969. For all its alleged permissiveness, *Webster's Third* did not include the word. Less surprisingly, neither did the original *OED*. When the entries for the letter *F* were being put together in the 1890s, it had been omitted; by the 1920s, when the editors had made it as far as *W*, the word *windfucker* – the name of a type of kestrel – was considered fit for inclusion. *Fuck* got its own entry when the *OED*'s first supplementary volume was published in 1972.

When the American scholar Allen Walker Read published an article about the word in 1934, his chosen title was 'An Obscenity Symbol', and he managed by various circumlocutions not once to use the offending term. In 1948 Norman Mailer, preparing his novel *The Naked and the Dead* for publication, amended every instance of *fuck* to *fug*, on the insistence of his publisher. The wisecracking Dorothy Parker, meeting her fellow author, allegedly joked, 'So you're the young man who can't spell *fuck*.' (In some accounts it was not Parker, but the sexually adventurous screen star Tallulah Bankhead. Mailer denied that it happened at all.) Elsewhere the word was printed with asterisks in place of its second, third and sometimes also fourth letters; the practice had begun in the early eighteenth century. It was not used in the *New York Times* until 1998, and then only in the context of the Starr Report into alleged misconduct by President Clinton. Many newspapers continue not to print the word. In other media the equivalent of this reticence is the bleep. The practice of bleeping out profanities on television began in the 1960s, and *fuck* was not heard in mainstream American cinema until around 1970.[6] Yet in Martin Scorsese's *Casino* (1995) *fuck* is in one form or another said about four hundred times, a figure surpassed by Gary Oldman's *Nil by Mouth* (1997) with 428.[7]

If you suspect that *fuck* is more common than it used to be, you may well be right. The decline of religion in much of the English-speaking world may help to explain why *fuck* appears where a religious expletive would once have been effective. Unrestrained language seems to attend unrestrained behaviour. Steven Pinker notes that 'Sexual language has become far more common since the early 1960s, but so have illegitimacy, sexually transmitted infections, rape, and the fallout of sexual competition, like anorexia in girls and swagger culture in boys. Though no one can pin down cause and effect, the changes are of a piece with the weakening of the fear and awe that used to surround thoughts about sex and that charged sexual language with taboo.'[8] Though Pinker is no conservative in matters of language, this argument, phrased more angrily, is perfectly suited to becoming a weapon in the arsenal of reactionary commentators.

There are circumstances in which saying *fuck* creates a momentary solidarity even between people who would normally be offended by the word. If I call you a 'fucking idiot' you will be unimpressed, but if I drop a hammer on my foot, I may well exclaim 'Fuck' or 'Shit', and very few will disapprove. Besides being cathartic, my exclamation has the effect of reassuring anyone who has just seen what has happened; it is a sign of my normality, much less disconcerting than silence, and I am acknowledging my incompetence. If I drop the hammer on the ground rather than on my foot, I am more likely to exclaim 'Whoops'. My performance in this case is milder, and there is no need for catharsis, but the purpose of the exclamation is the same: I am still drawing attention to the fact that this mishap was unintended – and subconsciously, or semi-consciously, I am keen not to be thought of as someone who goes around dropping hammers.

Fuck, it should be emphasized, was not the only word to be deliberately omitted from the first edition of the *OED*. The absence of *cunt* is not surprising, though the issue of whether or not to include it was vigorously discussed. But the comparatively innocent *condom* did not make it either. James Dixon, a surgeon who was a valued contributor to the *OED*, was startled by the word when he came upon it in print – or rather, startled by the existence of the item itself. He told James Murray that it was 'a contrivance used by fornicators, to save themselves from a well-deserved clap'. It was 'too utterly obscene' to be included in the *OED*. It seems that Murray concurred.[9] *Clap* was labelled 'obsolete in polite use', despite recent evidence to the contrary.

In the opposite camp there were, and of course still are, those who think there is no such thing as an obscene word. Their strategy, usually, is to administer shock treatment. One of the prime movers in this was George Carlin, whose comedy often contained social commentary and observations about language. In Carlin's sketch 'Seven Words You Can Never Say on Television' – which appeared on an album he released in 1972 and led to his arrest when he performed it in Milwaukee – the words in question are *fuck*, *cunt*, *shit*, *piss*, *cocksucker*, *motherfucker* and *tits*. These words were not in fact banned; there was simply an informal understanding that they should not be used. Carlin dubbed them the 'heavy seven', joking that their use will 'curve your spine'. His real point was that there were 'no bad words', only 'bad thoughts' and 'bad intentions'.[10] Carlin's aim was to question people's capacity for taking offence. What made certain words more shocking than others? He later expanded the list, adding *fart*, *turd* and *twat*. Was *fart* acceptable, or was it bad? Wasn't it, after all, just *shit* without the mess? In 1978 the Supreme Court ruled that the sketch was 'indecent but not obscene'. Yet, as Jack Lynch notes, 'Carlin's list became the *de facto* standard of what really couldn't be said on the public airwaves. It's a strange paradox that a foul-mouthed champion of free speech should have been instrumental in writing the law prohibiting those same words.'[11]

In Britain, the law relating to obscenity has been in place since 1857, modified in England and Wales by two further Obscene Publications Acts in 1959 and 1964. The 1959 Act states that 'an article shall be deemed to be obscene if its effect . . . is, if taken as a whole, such as to tend to deprave and corrupt persons who are likely, having regard to all relevant circumstances, to read, see or hear the matter contained or embodied in it.' (For these purposes an 'article' is anything 'containing or embodying matter to be read or looked at or both, any sound record, and any film or other record of a picture or pictures'.) However, the publisher of an 'article' cannot be convicted if publication 'is justified for the public good on the ground that it is in the interests of science, literature, art or learning, or of other objects of general concern'. The contradiction here is hardly inconspicuous: can things that 'tend to deprave and corrupt' really be 'justified for the public good'? And how are we to assess or indeed define the experience of being depraved and corrupted?

Anxieties about obscenity lie behind a lot of humour, which tends to deal with sex, violence and society's ritual practices. Jokes help us grapple with our distastes and mistrusts: of our bodies, our desires, our apparent superiors and people who seem to menace our lives' equilibrium. Typically, jokes expose a gap between what we expect and how things turn out; humour is liberating because it momentarily makes the real world seem surreal and because it briefly gives us a chance to reflect on the fears implicit in our daily existence. 'The genius of jokes,' writes the philosopher Simon Critchley, 'is that they light up the common features of our world.'[12] They pique our distaste, making us uncomfortable and at the same time making us question this uncomfortableness.

Lenny Bruce is an important figure here. Unusually for a comedian, Bruce did not tell jokes. His rhythm was typically that of a conventional stand-up comedian – set-up, delay, punchline – and his subject matter (despair, destruction, the truth) was of a kind that has frequently been mined by comics, but Bruce's profanity took the form of an abstract jazz performance rather than a studious progression. Bruce wanted his audiences to be shocked by the things that were really wrong – not by four-letter words, but by the inequalities and depravities of society. Why was it unacceptable to depict sex (something most of us practise) in a film, yet acceptable to depict murder? A crucial part of his act lay in demystifying the language conventionally deemed obscene. Bruce used the phrase 'yada yada yada' to sum up the endless torrents of blather spouted by the moral majority.

It probably now seems bizarre that Bruce was in 1961 arrested for using the word *cocksucker* during a routine at San Francisco's Jazz Workshop. Twenty years later Meryl Streep won an Oscar for her performance in *Sophie's Choice*, in which she uttered this very word. We have become inured to hearing it – and to hearing what would generally be considered far worse. Still, the use of so-called bad language is likely to provoke complaint when it happens in a context where it seems especially inappropriate. When the singer Madonna presented the Turner Prize for contemporary art in 2001, she successfully outraged many by exclaiming, on live television and before the nine o'clock 'watershed', the words 'Right on, mother-fuckers!'

Although *motherfucker* is regarded as outstandingly obscene in its condensed expression of Freud's Oedipal theory, today the term most likely to cause shock is *nigger*. When first adopted in the sixteenth century – from French, Spanish or Portuguese, though ultimately its source was Latin – it was used neutrally, without obvious hostility and contempt. That changed in the late eighteenth century, and there is no mistaking the tone of Byron's 'The rest of the world – niggers and what not' (1811) or Henry Fearon's reference in *Sketches of America* (1818) to 'the bad conduct and inferior nature of niggars [*sic*]'. The word is fatally linked to white supremacy and slavery. Although it has different levels of toxicity according to who is using it, nobody can now free it from its long history of derogatory connotations. The popularization of the hip-hop endearment *nigga*, which the rapper Tupac Shakur improbably claimed was an acronym for Never Ignorant and Getting Goals Accomplished, and what might be called its neutralized and generalized use as an equivalent of *guy* or *man*, have only complicated reactions to the original word. Black people's use of *nigga* or indeed *nigger* as a form of address is not a unique example of an insult being recast as a badge of honour; the Christian movement known as the Quakers adopted that nickname for their movement – more formally called the Religious Society of Friends – in order to neutralize what was at first a term of derision.

Sensitivity about *nigger* has led to the avoidance of the unrelated adjective *niggardly*. In 1999 David Howard, who worked in the mayor's office in Washington DC, used the word during a meeting. Rumours circulated that he had used a racist epithet: Howard resigned his post, conceding, 'I should have thought, this is an arcane word, and everyone may not know it.'[13] Because *niggardly* sounds as though it derives from *nigger*, it is tainted. Knowledge of the two words' different etymologies is no protection against those for whom their sounds are simply too close for comfort. There are other words one can use instead of *niggardly* that will cause no offence. Patricia O'Conner and Stewart Kellerman suggest that 'Somebody who uses it is in effect telling his audience: "I'm smarter than anyone who's dumb enough to get mad." '[14] Well, maybe. But I suspect most people who use *niggardly* do so without the snooty premeditation this implies.

The episode involving David Howard was not the first time that *niggardly* had caused controversy, and there have been similar rows since, as when a student at the University of Wisconsin made a formal complaint about a professor's discussion of the word's use by Chaucer. *Niggardly* is a pejorative word, and was in the four-teenth century, though of course Chaucer knew nothing of *nigger*. The negative import of *niggardly* makes its similarity to *nigger* both plausible and likely to give offence. I suspect that many people hear it as *niggerly*. I am pretty confident that *niggardly* will fall out of use. But will that be the end of it? What of *niggling* or *snigger*? Or *denigratory*?

There has been more than one campaign to have *nigger* removed from American dictionaries. Yet a dictionary that registers usage rather than policing it must include *nigger*. Called upon in 1936 to explain why the *OED* gave 'cheat' as one of the meanings of *Jew*, the Oxford University Press's representative Kenneth Sisam wrote, 'I should like to explain that our dictionaries aim at explaining actual usage and do not attempt to form moral judgements'.[15] In 1972 a businessman from Salford brought an action against the

OED's publishers, claiming that the definition in question was defamatory. He lost the case in the High Court because he was unable to meet the law's requirement that he show the offending words 'referred to him personally or were capable of being understood by others as referring to him'.[16] Words and disagreeable senses of words are hard to kill off, and prohibition is a form of encouragement.

Abuse moves with the times. Call a woman a *witch* and you'll cause offence, but four hundred years ago the charge would have had graver implications. Witch-hunts do in fact still happen – notable recent examples have occurred in Kenya and the Gambia – but for most people in English-speaking countries belief in witchcraft seems archaic. Insults work by attacking our points of greatest vulnerability: the things about which we feel awkward, certainly, but also the things about which we know others feel awkward. A few years ago, when a teenage boy on a train said to me, as his mother looked on blithely, 'Fuck off, you bald cunt', my reactions were complex: I was amused by his brazenness but also struck by the realization that, even though I was reconciled to the fact of having lost a good deal of my hair, this was how I was seen by others – not as a man, cuntish or otherwise, but as a bald man. Typically, insults give narrow names to aspects of us we would wish to be treated in a more complex fashion. They place us in categories to which we may indeed belong, but they insist on those categories at the expense of judging us more roundly. Personally, I would sooner be called a *cunt* than a *coward* or a *thief*, because to be called either of the latter is to be an object of focused moral disapproval. That said, someone who calls me a *cunt* is more likely to want to thump me.

Coming up with an original insult demands a great surge of creativity. Swearing can be extraordinarily expressive. However, most of the time it is formulaic. For the person doing the swearing, what matters is the performance of excess; injuring the target may not be important at all. The most obvious kind of formulaic abuse consists of ritual insults – the 'flyting' of sixteenth-century Scottish poets, the African-American tradition of ribald trash-talk (sometimes called 'the dozens'), the orchestral banter of teenagers just about anywhere. Insults of this kind are not true – 'Your momma drink rainwater', 'You got shit for brains' – but sting because for a moment they make us part of a piece of theatre over which we have no control.

Obscenity invades every area of our lives, however much we do to try and repel it. Fear of the obscene is expressed in networks of vigilance such as campaigns for public morality. Legislation about obscenity persists, and calls for its extension are frequent. But the fascination of the forbidden is irresistible, and obscenity can seem the nucleus of English eloquence. The English were once labelled '*les goddams*' by the French; since the 1960s they have been '*les fuck-offs*', and among the many benisons of English-speaking culture is that snarling expletive, a two-word anthem for the Anglosphere.

21 'It's English-Only here'

The trouble with hyphens

The basic psychology of legislating language is that it allows us to believe we can control our destiny. When language appears no longer to be something we can discipline, we suspect that wider anarchy is nigh. Politically, this connection is opportune: passing laws about language is a means of shackling the populace, and making pronouncements about it can be a quick way to mobilize patriotism and other clannish or exclusionary sentiments.

Theodore Roosevelt was a particularly deft exponent of this. 'We must have but one flag,' he pronounced in 1917, and 'We must also have but one language.' 'The greatness of this nation,' he continued, 'depends on the swift assimilation of the aliens she welcomes to her shores. Any force which attempts to retard that assimilative process is a force hostile to the highest interests of our country.'[1] Roosevelt, the American President from 1901 to 1909, believed that the English language could create unity of voice and of values. His statements might lead one to imagine that English is the official language of the United States. But in fact it has no official language. The primacy of English is assumed, not legally enshrined. The United States is unusual in not having an official language. At the time of writing, this is only the case there and in the United Kingdom, Pakistan, Costa Rica, Ethiopia, Somalia, Eritrea and Bosnia-Herzegovina. Yet if you were to ask someone casually what the official language of the UK or America is, you would likely be told 'English'.

In Britain at present the central position of English is not aggressively contested. Britain as an English-speaking unity is not so very old, and on its way to pre-eminence English has killed off other languages such as Cornish, Manx (the Celtic vernacular of the Isle of Man) and Norn in Orkney and Shetland. Consider for a moment the effects of being asked to change the language you use. When we imagine this, we picture ourselves adjusting – perhaps none too smoothly – to different behaviours. Brian Friel's play *Translations*, written in 1980, depicts this in an Irish setting. The action takes place in County Donegal in 1833: we follow a detachment of English soldiers who are part of an Ordnance Survey team anglicizing Gaelic place names, and their work illustrates the significance of names in framing people's perceptions of the land. The belief that Gaelic is somehow responsible for Irish savagery, superstition and sententiousness dates back at least to the sixteenth century, when Henry VIII asserted that it was sufficient grounds for compelling the Irish to speak English. (When he declared himself king of Ireland in 1541, he did so first in English and then, as an afterthought, in the language of the people he was bringing under his rule.) Friel's play dramatizes the moment when one language supplants another.

There are areas of Britain where people still use languages that were present before the arrival roughly 1,500 years ago of the Germanic settlers whose dialects became English. But while the central role of English has not been achieved without bloodshed and resentment, it is a largely uncontroversial fact, historically ingrained. Of the languages spoken in Britain today, Welsh has the most ancient roots. It now coexists in Wales with English, but its position was once precarious. Wales was incorporated into England by a series of parliamentary measures between 1535 and 1543, completing a process that had begun when Edward I invaded in 1282. The decline of Welsh began with the seizure of the English Crown by the part-Welsh Henry VII in 1485, and accelerated in the sixteenth century as English became the language of education and administration in Wales. Nevertheless, Welsh has held on, buoyed by cultural traditions such as the eisteddfod and male-voice choirs, and the Welsh Language Acts of 1967 and 1993 provided the Welsh and English languages with equal status in Wales. The resurgence of Welsh has not been painless – I can remember as a child seeing the English place names obliterated from road signs in Wales, and I understood that this was a symptom of a resentment that could sometimes be more violently expressed.

In Scotland, English arrived earlier; there were English-speaking settlers as far back as the sixth century. However, English became the *de facto* public language only in 1707 when the Act of Union joined Scotland to England and Wales. Even then, other languages were common. Scottish Gaelic, which had once been the language of most Scots, continued to hold sway in the Highlands and the Western Isles until late in the eighteenth century. The Scots language, which descended from Northumbrian Old English, had been used for official records – with some interference from English – until 1603, when James I (who was James VI of Scotland) succeeded Queen Elizabeth. In the eighteenth century a Scottish variant of standard English became the prestige form of speech, and Scots became 'essentially a curiosity, albeit sometimes a fashionable one'.[2] It is now not officially recognized, although in late 2009 the Scottish parliament unveiled a Scots version of its website, while Scottish Gaelic has recently enjoyed a degree of official recognition that may well increase.

In Ireland, as Friel's play *Translations* suggests, the situation is rather different. Ireland is not part of Britain, although in my experience some otherwise knowledgeable people seem to consider this an eccentric statement. The details of Irish history are too complex to digest here. The first English-speakers to settle there arrived in the twelfth century, but it was only in the seventeenth century that Irish resistance to English plantation gave way. By the following century, the use of Gaelic was 'a marker of rural, Catholic poverty' whereas English was associated with 'Protestantism, ownership, and the towns', although some towns 'had a sizeable Gaelic-speaking working class until well into the nineteenth century'. Gaelic was to a large degree abandoned in the nineteenth century, but from the 1890s it was promoted as a minority language.[3] For present purposes, it is enough to say that Gaelic has in Ireland an appreciable symbolic value; that there is a distinct Irish English with its own grammatical features, vowel sounds, stresses and vocabulary; that Irish English exists in several different forms; and that, these facts notwithstanding, English is spoken by very nearly everyone in both the Republic of Ireland and Northern Ireland.

By contrast, in America, where the English language has been present for a much shorter time and the volume of immigration has been much greater, the issue of English's precedence is alive and is becoming incendiary. With characteristic foresight H. G. Wells wrote in 1903, 'In the United States there is less sense of urgency about modern languages, but sooner or later the American may wake up to the need of Spanish in his educational schemes.'[4]

The US Bilingual Education Act of 1968, twice amended to be more specific, made provision for students with limited ability in English to receive education that catered to their extra needs. The 1964 Civil Rights Act, which outlawed racial segregation in schools and the workplace, also provided for non-English-speaking students' language needs. But observation of events in Canada caused anxiety about where this might lead. During the 1960s militants in Quebec attempted to establish a breakaway French-speaking nation. In 1970 the Front de Libération du Québec, which had for seven years struggled to assert its hostility to what it identified as Anglo-Saxon imperialism, kidnapped the province's labour minister Pierre Laporte and strangled him to death when the Prime Minister, Pierre Trudeau, would not give in to their ransom demands. The Canadian parliament voted by an overwhelming majority to invoke the War Measures Act of 1914, which had never been used in time of peace. Events in Quebec were apparently symptomatic of a new wave of guerrilla action; the linguistic desperadoes, inspired by Che Guevara and Fidel Castro, were turning to terrorism to advance their philosophy of 'Small is beautiful'.[5] In the wake of the period's riots and acts of terrorism, French was recognized as the official language of Quebec in 1974; its position was cemented by the so-called Loi 101 of 1977, which among other things guaranteed the rights of all people in Quebec to conduct their business activities in French, be served and informed in French in their capacity as consumers, and be taught in French. Many Americans fretted about something similar happening in their own country, but with Spanish rather than French the ascendant language.

In 1981 Samuel Ichiye Hayakawa, a Republican Senator who was a critic of bilingual education, introduced a bill to amend the US Constitution to declare English the nation's official language. Hayakawa had been a university professor of English, and had written a great deal about language. He was a whimsical, elusive figure, yet

also a stubborn one. The bill foundered, but following his retire-
ment two years later Hayakawa helped set up US English, a lobby
'In Defense of Our Common Language'. Its advisory board included
Walter Cronkite and Arnold Schwarzenegger. While the mooted
English Language Amendment has not yet succeeded, individual
states have made their own declarations of the primacy of English.
The first to do so was Louisiana as long ago as 1812; the move was
made in the hope that it would gain the state admission to the
Union. But following Hayakawa's revival of the issues, the 1980s
and '90s witnessed a flurry of similar declarations, as well as the
emergence of other lobbying organizations. At present twenty-eight
states have made English official. These moves are seen by their
advocates as reaffirmations of patriotic feeling, and by their opponents as insulting and coercive repressions of America's many cultural
minorities.

The lobby for conformity has tended to prevail over the promoters
of diversity. In 1998, for instance, 70 per cent of voters in Alaska
approved an initiative to make English the official language of their
state.[6] Attitudes in other states are not significantly more moderate.
The notion of making provision for other languages commonly
triggers anti-immigrant sentiment and expressions of economic insecurity. There are obvious incentives for immigrants to learn English,
which suggests that legislation to make the status of English official might really be superfluous. But support for an 'English-Only'
policy is robust. Implicit in this is the belief that there is such a
thing as an 'American identity', to which people who live in America
must subscribe. The notion that a range of identities might happily
coexist is shunned. Monolingualism has many costs – economic,
educational, cognitive – but is supported in the name of national
security, political stability, the preservation of a collective morality
and harmony between different ethnic groups, as if it is inevitable
that people wishing to use languages other than English will practise terrorism, sedition, depravity and racist hatred. No matter that
within diversity there can be a fundamental unity. No matter that
America was born in a spirit of inclusiveness and has at no point
in recorded history been truly monoglot.

As the English-Only movement has gathered momentum, op-

position has crystallized. Organizations such as the Mexican American Legal Defense and Educational Fund have put forward a case
for language rights to prevent members of minorities being disenfranchised. MALDEF's website explains that it 'recognizes that
learning English is critical to participating in, contributing to, and
succeeding in American society', but believes that 'English-only and
Official English laws do nothing constructive to advance the important goal of English proficiency. Laws that interfere with or under-
mine the government's ability to communicate quickly and effectively
are simply bad public policy.'[7]

The greatest American linguistic controversy of the last century
centred on this issue of linguistic diversity. It began in Oakland, a
city in California of about 400,000 people, a few miles east of San
Francisco. A port with a history of shipbuilding, it was once recognized mainly as the birthplace of the cocktail known as a Mai Tai
and for its baseball team, the Oakland Athletics. But in December
1996 this ethnically diverse community became newsworthy for a
different reason: the Oakland School Board passed a resolution that
African-American students be instructed in their 'primary language'
– to wit, Ebonics, which was described as having its origins in 'West
and Niger-Congo African language'. Most Americans had never
heard of Ebonics. The issues were familiar to those who had followed
a story almost twenty years before, in which the parents of students
at an elementary school in Ann Arbor, Michigan, sued the local
School Board for failing to teach them to read. Teachers had wrongly
identified the students, who were used to speaking a non-standard
form of English at home, as having learning difficulties. (As so often,
non-standard was thought to be the same as substandard.) But
whereas the talk then had been about Black English, now there was
a crisply affirmative name for this language. That name had been
coined by Robert L. Williams, a professor at Washington University in St Louis, in 1973.

The Oakland School Board's decision fuelled a nationwide argument. Plenty of loud and poorly informed commentators decried
the idea of institutional support for what they saw not as a language,
nor as a dialect, but simply as a corrupt and base type of English.
In the *New York Times* Brent Staples sniped at the cabal of 'academic

theorists, lushly paid consultants and textbook writers all poised to spread the gospel', a creed which meant that 'time that should be spent on reading and algebra gets spent giving high fives and chattering away in street language'.[8] The Board's plans met with so much hostility that they had to be shelved.

Ebonics is now usually referred to by the name African-American Vernacular English – most scholars consider it a form of English showing African influence, and thus a dialect, rather than a separate language – and the debate continues. Apologists argue that black students will achieve higher levels of literacy and proficiency in standard English if their own vernacular is recognized; critics dismiss this as a grotesque manifestation of 'affirmative action'. Explicit in this debate are anxieties about race and educational justice; implicit in it are feelings of shame and resentment about the past humiliation and enslavement of black Americans. There persists what one scholar in the field identifies as 'a dominant culture which describes African-American speech as bad, uneducated, unintelligible, etc., while wantonly imitating and celebrating its wit, creative vitality, and resilience'.[9] It is worth emphasizing that the most stinging scorn for African-American mass culture is often expressed by middle-class African Americans.

The English language's position in America is not under threat. It benefits America to have citizens who are proficient in languages besides English. Furthermore, from my British vantage point, it seems that the unity of America is grounded not in a shared language, but in shared ideals. The success of America has had a great deal to do with its pluralism and the mobility of its populace. Nevertheless, to say these things is to invite furious contradiction. The confrontation over language policy in America looks sure to become more fierce. Its resolution, or indeed the failure to resolve it, will indicate what kind of country twenty-first-century America is set to be.

At the start of this chapter I cited Theodore Roosevelt's vision of an America with one flag and one language. Two years earlier, in 1915, he had talked dismissively of what he called 'Hyphenated Americans'. This was a familiar theme. 'There can be no fifty-fifty Americanism in this country,' he had declared at the Republican Convention in 1906.[10] Roosevelt was speaking against the background of a decade (1900–1910) in which more than eight million immigrants arrived in the United States. Woodrow Wilson, when he was President a decade later, would repeat the line, saying, 'I think the most un-American thing in the world is a hyphen.'

Neither Roosevelt nor Wilson imagined that immigration would continue on this scale. But it has. For instance, between 2000 and 2005 there were roughly eight million immigrants to the US. A century after Roosevelt's rhetoric, the hyphens he abhorred are flourishing. The Hyphenated American – the Chinese-American, Mexican-American, Italian-American, Greek-American, African-American, and so on – is everywhere. Yet the hyphen is a symbol of tension rather than of a truly comfortable pluralism. The novelist Toni Morrison has remarked, 'In this country American means white. Everybody else has to hyphenate.'[11] As Morrison's words indicate, the hyphen suggests an uneasy accommodation, a life lived either side of the hyphen rather than truly across it. It is for this reason that the hyphen's position in these hybrid terms is under threat. Increasingly now, it is dropped when the compound term is used as a noun, though kept when it is used as an adjective. Prior to this paragraph, that is the practice I have observed.

This brings us, by an unlikely route, to the question of the more general status of the hyphen. A mark that has always been used capriciously, the hyphen is plainly not a letter, but it does not really function as punctuation either. It has two purposes: to connect two or more words as a compound, and to divide a word for typographical convenience or to show its distinct syllables. Many a reader has been thrown by a poorly managed word-break: *leg-end* rather than *legend*, and such bewildering items as *une-lectable* and *poig-nant*. Compounding also needs to be handled carefully. Hyphens are used in compounds to avoid a triple consonant (*egg-gathering*, *still-life*), to avoid a double or indeed triple vowel (*bee-eating*), where one of the words contributing to the compound contains an apostrophe (*bull's-eye*, *will-o'-the-wisp*), where the compound consists of a repetition or of conflicting elements (*ha-ha*, *sour-sweet*), when denoting a colour (*pale-bluish*), as an aid to pronunciation (*knee-deep*, *goose-step*), in compound words built on other compounds where there is only one stress (*great-grandfather, south-southeast*), and usually in compounds where the second part is an adverb or a preposition (*passer-by, go-between*). Improvised compounds also tend to be hyphenated: *young-boyish, honey-tempered*.[12] Compound words express something different from what is signified by their component parts. A great-grandfather is clearly different from a 'great grandfather', and if I describe someone as young-boyish it is not quite the same as saying he is young and boyish.

In practice, though, all of this is handled without method or conviction. In 2007 the editor of the two-volume *Shorter Oxford English Dictionary*, Angus Stevenson, eliminated about 16,000 hyphens from a new edition of the work. 'People are not confident about using hyphens any more,' he said. 'They're not really sure what they're for.' As Charles McGrath explained in a piece for the *New York Times*, the casualties were most of the hyphens hitherto used to link the halves of compound nouns: *fig-leaf* and *hobby-horse* were fractured into *fig leaf* and *hobby horse*, while in other cases – *crybaby, bumblebee* – the previously semi-detached halves of words were squeezed together. Traditionally the hyphen had 'indicated a sort of halfway point, a way station in the progress of a new usage'. Shakespeare was a hyphenator, introducing compounds such as *fancy-free* and *sea-change*. Modern graphic designers dislike them, though. The hyphen can be useful, as McGrath points out: 'A slippery-eel salesman . . . sells slippery eels, while a slippery eel salesman takes your money and slinks away.' But much of the time hyphens are an affectation; he likens them to spats, and reflects that amid the modern uncertainty about hyphenation a good many of us have been putting our spats on incorrectly.[13]

The hyphen, it seems, is in decline. This may sound improbable: after all, we are continually encountering new hyphenated compounds. Increasingly, though, the hyphen suggests something temporary and contested. When stability is achieved, the hyphen goes. The slow demise of the hyphen is not merely a matter of orthographic nicety or typographical felicity. Rather, it has a political dimension.

22 The comma flaps its wings

Punctuation: past, present and future

From the troublesome hyphen, it is but a short step to those other specks and spots so enticingly described by Pablo Picasso as the fig leaves hiding literature's private parts. Punctuation is a subject that arouses strong feelings. A misused semi-colon or stray comma will cause some people the same violent distaste that I might feel on witnessing, say, a puppy being tortured. John Simon, expatiating on the decline of literacy, writes about the 'peculiarly chilling' confusion of quotation marks and apostrophes by the *Los Angeles Times*.[1] The British journalist Victoria Moore reports that, seeing 'martini's' and 'classic's' on a cocktail menu, she was 'caught up in a spasm of punctuation-rage' and 'asked the poor waitress what those two utterly extraneous apostrophes were doing there'. The result: 'I momentarily lost my thirst.'[2] There are even – no joke – punctuation vigilantes, who scamper around blotting out rogue apostrophes and rejigging punctuation – signs and advertisements being their favourite targets. The 2009 film *Couples Retreat*, in which 'retreat' was a noun rather than a verb, invited such attention.

One generally accepted idea about punctuation is that it indicates the flow of speech – or the intonation that should be used in performing a text. Before it was called *punctuation*, it was known as *pointing*, and it has also been referred to by the names *distinction* and *stopping*. Originally, the main purpose of punctuation was to guide a person who was reading aloud, indicating where there should be pauses and stresses. Punctuation is thus like a musical score. But it renders the music of speech imperfectly, and it is limiting to think of it merely as a way of transcribing the features of speech.

The first book in English concerned solely with punctuation was an anonymous treatise which appeared in 1680. It was not until

1768 that James Burrow became the first author to put his name to a work on the subject, and Joseph Robertson's *An Essay on Punctuation* of 1785 was the first treatment to achieve popularity. 'The art of punctuation is of infinite consequence in WRITING,' states Robertson.[3] Really, though, it is the finite consequences of punctuation that make it valuable.

The role of punctuation is to enhance the precision of our meaning. It clarifies syntax: '"The bonobo," said the zookeeper, "enjoys penis fencing"' is in an important way different from 'The bonobo said the zookeeper enjoys penis fencing', and punctuation signals the difference. The units of sense are presented. We are provided with an apparatus that helps create understanding between writers and readers. A useful summary is provided by Walter Nash: 'Punctuation . . . makes *sense* and projects *attitudes*.'[4]

Occasionally the omission of punctuation is championed by creative or contrary figures; well-known examples are the poets ee cummings and Guillaume Apollinaire. Poets like to knock the familiar frames of language sideways in order to suggest interesting incongruities. T. S. Eliot spoke of verse as its own system of punctuation, in which the usual marks are differently employed. Another kind of maverick argues that marks such as commas are aesthetically unclean and introduce false partitions between ideas. Usually, though, punctuation is an accessory of creativity. What is the difference in meaning between 'After dinner, the men went into the living room' and 'After dinner the men went into the living room'? According to the *New Yorker* writer James Thurber, the magazine's legendarily punctilious editor Harold Ross thought the comma after 'dinner' was a way of 'giving the men time to push back their chairs and stand up'.[5] Does this seem laughable? Personally I find it both delightful and credible. Punctuation can achieve subtle effects, and thinking about the effect of punctuation on one's readers is a far from trivial part of any kind of writing.

H. G. Wells's Mr Polly is one of literature's non-punctuators. Made to read the catechism and Bible 'with the utmost industry and an entire disregard of punctuation or significance', he is said to specialize in 'the disuse of English'. In *A Midsummer Night's Dream* the 'rude mechanical' Peter Quince mangles the prologue to a play he is performing with his associates; the watching Duke of Athens remarks, 'This fellow doth not stand upon points' (meaning by 'points' the text's marked punctuation), and his bride Hippolyta, the Queen of the Amazons, comments that 'he hath played on this prologue like a child on a recorder; a sound, but not in government'. Hippolyta's is a nice summary, and indeed punctuation is like government in that, while you need enough of it to keep order, it is quite possible to have too much.

For many readers, thoughts of punctuation will call to mind *Eats, Shoots & Leaves*, a book published in 2003 by the popular journalist and broadcaster Lynne Truss. Subtitled 'The Zero Tolerance Approach to Punctuation', and seemingly impelled by Truss's hatred of rogue apostrophes and slapdash emails, *Eats, Shoots & Leaves* is presented as a sane corrective to the madness of the modern world. In her second paragraph Truss describes a 'satanic sprinkling of redundant apostrophes' – a reference to a sign at a petrol station that reads 'Come inside for CD's, VIDEO's, DVD's, and BOOK's'. Her horror is one most of us probably share, but the choice of the adjective 'satanic', which at first seems jaunty, begins to feel more pointed as Truss's rhetorical questions swarm across the page. She proposes that 'sticklers unite', but admits that 'every man is his own stickler'. This makes her conviction that 'we should fight like tigers to preserve our punctuation' hard to go along with.[6] For whose is 'our punctuation'? And, in any case, isn't this notion of preserving it rose-tinted, falsely imagining a happy age of consummate comma use? Geoffrey Nunberg, an American commentator on language and politics, pithily defines the book's spirit as 'operatic indignation' and says, of Truss's brand of fussiness, 'It's like hearing someone warn of grave domestic security threats and then learning that he's chiefly concerned about Canadian sturgeon-poaching on the US side of Lake Huron'.[7] While readers were presumably not expected to act upon the suggestion that abusers of the apostrophe be hacked to death on the spot and buried in unmarked graves, it was clear that Truss intended to win converts.

But converts to what, exactly? 'We are like the little boy in *The Sixth Sense* who can see dead people,' Truss writes, 'except that we can see dead punctuation.' This 'dead punctuation' is 'invisible to everyone else – yet we see it *all the time*. No one understands us seventh-sense people.' A few pages later she delights in the idea that good use of punctuation is a courtesy: 'Isn't the analogy with good manners perfect? Truly good manners are invisible.'[8] So, correct punctuation is invisible, but errors of punctuation are constantly visible?

If this seems merely weird, a deeper problem is that *Eats, Shoots & Leaves* is unexpectedly sloppy and inconsistent. In a caustic review in the *New Yorker*, Louis Menand pointed out the many deficiencies of Truss's writing, and observed, 'The main rule in grammatical form is to stick to whatever rules you start out with, and the most objectionable thing about Truss's writing is its inconsistency. Either Truss needed a copy editor or her copy editor needed a copy editor.' Commas appeared in unexpected places, causing confusion. A rule about the semi-colon was announced, then flouted. Sometimes punctuation was absent where it was needed; Menand used as an example the statement 'You have to give initial capitals to the words Biro and Hoover otherwise you automatically get tedious letters from solicitors.' Truss, he suggested, was a Jeremiah full of dire warnings and angry harangues, addressing herself to the sort of people 'who lose control when they hear a cell phone ring in a public place'.[9] As David Crystal comments of Menand's review, 'This is one kind of zero tolerance being eaten by another.'[10] Behind Truss's sulphurous complaint lies a laudable belief that children should receive a better education in the use of written English. But she draws attention to the failure of education rather than putting forward a remedy. I doubt that many of the hundreds of thousands who have read *Eats, Shoots* have become more confident punctuators as a result. The book's success has had a great deal to do with the existence of a large number of people out of love with modern living.

As Lynne Truss's writing illustrates, the punctuation mark that inspires the most searing arguments is the apostrophe. Uncertainty about its correct use leads to overcompensation. You've seen this sort of thing: 'Fresh Iceberg lettuce's', 'Who's turn is it?', 'He say's he's got a cold.' The apostrophe has been amusingly described as 'an entirely insecure orthographic squiggle'.[11] It is, as this implies, often seen but rarely heard – 'a device for the eye rather than for

the ear', which after a period of fairly stable use in the late nineteenth and early twentieth centuries is 'returning to the confusion
from which it but recently emerged'.[12] Promoted by the Parisian
printer Geoffroy Tory in the 1520s, the apostrophe first appeared in
an English text in 1559. There is a reference to it in Shakespeare's
Love's Labour's Lost, and it is used in the 1596 edition of Spenser's
The Faerie Queene, but it was rare before the seventeenth century.[13]
Initially it was employed to signify the omission of a sound in a
text (usually a printed play). Then it came to signify possession, as
can be seen in the Fourth Folio of Shakespeare's works in 1685,
and its possessive use was confined to the singular. But writers' decisions about where to locate it in a word were haphazard, and in
the eighteenth century its use became erratic. Some authors used
it in the possessive plural, but authorities such as Lowth insisted this
was wrong. John Ash's *Grammatical Institutes* takes the same position,
and Ash says that the possessive use of the apostrophe 'seems to have
been introduced by Mistake'.[14] However, there were others at that
time who, in a fashion that will incense many sticklers today, used
it to form plurals; in 1712 the typographer Michael Mattaire
suggested, for instance, that the correct plural of *species* was *species's*.
The apostrophe's correct use was vigorously debated by grammarians throughout the eighteenth and nineteenth centuries. As this
brief account of the apostrophe indicates, punctuation comes and
goes, and its history is more complicated than we may assume. A
sketch of that history follows.

Early manuscripts had no punctuation at all, and those from the
medieval period reveal a great deal of haphazard innovation, with
more than thirty different punctuation marks. By the time of Chaucer
legal documents contained few punctuation marks, if any, and among
lawyers there is still a culture of minimal punctuation, as anyone
who has muddled through a British property contract will have
seen. The modern repertoire of punctuation emerged as printers in
the fifteenth and sixteenth centuries, rather than reproducing the
marks they saw in the manuscripts from which they worked, moved
to limit the range of marks. Printers worked with the craftsmen
who cut their costly type-punches to create pleasing fonts, and, as
more of these became available, a hierarchy of typefaces developed.

The shapes of punctuation marks were fixed, and so were their functions.

The period, now usually called a full stop, is Greek in origin and was in wide use by the fifteenth century, though its role was ambiguous until the seventeenth. Commas were not employed until the sixteenth century; in early printed books in English one sees a virgule (a slash like this /), and the comma seems to have replaced this mark around 1520. Writing *circa* 1617, Alexander Hume could suggest, somewhat surprisingly, that when reading aloud one pronounced the comma 'with a short sob'.[15] Colons were common by the fourteenth century. The semi-colon, apparently introduced by the Venetian printer Aldus Manutius in 1494, was rare in English books before the early seventeenth century, when its exponents included Ben Jonson and John Donne. Hyphens, discussed at the end of the previous chapter, were initially used only when a word was split between two lines of writing; Ben Jonson, a meticulous user of punctuation marks, was one of the first authors to use them in compound words. Dashes became common only in the eighteenth century, and were far more popular in French. Samuel Richardson, who printed his own works, popularized the em-dash with his novel *Clarissa* (1748).[16]

Exclamation and question marks were not much used until the seventeenth century. Ben Jonson referred to the former as admiration marks, and they were casually known by the names *shriekmark* and *screamer* before *exclamation mark* became standard; they too seem to have been adopted from the French. The caret, invariably known when I was a child as a 'carrot', has a long history; it has existed in its current form since the thirteenth century. There used also to be a clunky paragraph sign like this ¶, known as a pilcrow or a gallows bracket.[17] Similar in its effect was one of the oldest punctuation symbols, now little employed, a horizontal ivy leaf called a hedera: ❧

Parentheses were first used around 1500, having been observed by English writers and printers in Italian books. Manutius was one of the first to include them in the design of a font. A hundred years later they were common in the printed texts of dramas and were sometimes used to help guide readers through difficult passages in other kinds of writing (or to provide sententious comment). Over the past five hundred years they have gone by a variety of names including *braces* and *hooks* as well as the better-known *brackets*, and they have often been disparaged – by Lowth and Dr Johnson, among others. John Ash's *Grammatical Institutes* contains the marvellous information: '*A Parenthesis (to be avoided as much as possible)* is used to include some Sentence in another'.[18] Lindley Murray suggested that brackets had an 'extremely bad' effect; they were used by writers for 'disposing of some thought' for which they had not managed to find a 'proper place'.[19]

One other mark that deserves mention is the *point d'ironie*, sometimes known as a 'snark'. A back-to-front question mark, ؟ was used by the sixteenth-century printer Henry Denham to indicate rhetorical questions, and in 1899 Alcanter de Brahm, a poet, suggested reviving it. I would venture that there are two problems with using a special mark to indicate irony: the first is that it dampens the irony, and the second is that readers are likely to wonder whether the mark is itself being used ironically.

The chances of the *point d'ironie* becoming common are slim. The heavy modern use of email and text messaging is encouraging a lighter, more informal style of punctuation. New punctuation marks may find widespread popularity, but I doubt it. I think it far more likely that more punctuation marks will disappear. One candidate may be the semi-colon, which has become a sort of celebrity among punctuation marks – regarded by some as delectable, and by others as superfluous. In France there has been a noisy debate about its value. In 2008 an April Fool's joke circulated to the effect that President Nicolas Sarkozy had decreed the semi-colon should be used three times a page in all official correspondence. One critic, the satirist François Cavanna, dismissed it as 'a parasite' signalling 'a lack of audacity, a fuzziness of thought'.[20] Plenty of writers insist that it is an invaluable mark, helping to reveal relationships within their arguments, yet critics suggest that an argument that needs a semi-colon is an argument that needs recasting.

A few pages ago I referred to 'a misused semi-colon'. Now what is that? Traditionally, a semi-colon has been used to separate clauses that have a close relationship. For instance, 'The car juddered to a halt; it had run out of fuel.' A colon is used when something is to be specified: a result, a quotation, a list, a contrast. A semi-colon is like a partition, whereas a colon draws attention to what comes next. Another way to imagine the difference is to think of passing from one room into another: when we encounter a semi-colon it is as if the door between the rooms has been left half-open and we need to open it further to continue on our way, whereas a colon is akin to a door open wide, which invites us in but at the same time makes us briefly pause to see what lies ahead.

More widely lamented than the seeming decline of the semi-colon is the jeopardy of the apostrophe. I talked a moment ago about its misuse, and gave an impression of its historical insecurity. Yet the real story is its peril right now. A report in the *Daily Tele-graph* in November 2008 noted that in a poll of 2,000 British adults more than nine hundred thought, when confronted with the words 'people's choice', that the apostrophe had been incorrectly placed.[21] Apostrophes have passionate defenders, but they are undeniably a source of confusion.

In Britain, one of the main guardians is the Apostrophe Protection Society, which was founded by John Richards, a former journalist, in 2001. Its stated aim is 'preserving the correct use of this currently much abused punctuation mark in all forms of text written in the English language'. When Richards set up the Society he hoped to find half a dozen like-minded people. But, he reports, 'I didn't find half a dozen people. Instead, within a month of my plaint appearing in a national newspaper, I received over 500 letters of support, not only from all corners of the United Kingdom, but also from America, Australia, France, Sweden, Hong Kong and Canada!' Sarah Lyall, reporting Richards's crusade in the *New York Times*, quoted Jean Aitchison, Rupert Murdoch Professor of Language and Communication at Oxford University, on the apostrophe's misuse: 'Greengrocers might do it out of ignorance, but it is also being used intentionally to draw attention to what you are selling. In the informal setting you can do what you like. That's the way language works.'[22] Richards disagrees, and he was on hand in January 2009 when Birmingham City Council decreed that apostrophes be removed from local street signs. A report in *The Times* noted: 'There was anger . . . at the headquarters of the Apostrophe Protection Society in Lincolnshire.''It's setting a very bad example,' said Richards, 'because teachers all over Birmingham are teaching their children punctuation. Then they see road signs with apostrophes removed.'[23] In an accompanying article Philip Howard vilified the Council, whose decision was 'wet, cowardly, solecistic and philistine' – an example of 'linguistic vandalism', the more alarming because 'those who neglect exactness and correctitude in little things cannot be trusted with big things such as local elections and council tax'.[24] The use of *correctitude* is telling, because the word blends *correct* and *rectitude*, conflating linguistic nicety with morality.

In the US there are very few places (in fact, five) with apostrophes in their names: Martha's Vineyard is the best known. There are rather more in Britain – well-known examples are King's Lynn, Bishop's Stortford and St John's Wood – but there is no consistency – witness the place-names Kings Langley, Bishops Lydeard and St Johns. On the London Underground a particularly droll juxtaposition is that of Earl's Court and Barons Court. According to one historical explanation, Barons Court is named after Baronscourt, the Irish estate of Sir William Palliser, who developed the area, and Earl's Court takes its name from its former owner, the Earl of Oxford. This is plausible rather than provably correct.

In truth, there are not many situations in which the omission of an apostrophe can lead to real confusion. Its incorrect use can be more confusing than its neglect. To give a banal example that is for obvious reasons close to my heart, I am sometimes thrown by its use with people's names. Can I be sure when I read 'Jenkin's argument is weak' that the arguer under fire is Jenkin rather than Jenkins? Experience suggests not. Experience, that is, of reading about 'Hitching's book'.

My guess is that the apostrophe is going to disappear. One factor that may contribute to this is the preference among graphic designers for a clean, unfussy look. Walking around my home town I pass shopfronts emblazoned with the names Dixons, Barclays, Lloyds and Boots – all of which 'should' have an apostrophe. The reason for its absence in these cases is not ignorance, but rather the desire for visual crispness.

23 Flaunting the rules

On not being, like, disinterested in modern life's meaningful aggravations?

In *White Heat*, his history of the second half of the 1960s, Dominic Sandbrook notes the British affection for gardening. Its popularity can be interpreted, he says, 'as evidence of the underlying conservatism, individualism and domesticity of British life'. Britain is a densely populated and decidedly urban country; genteel, 'pseudo-rural' husbandry is a pleasant antidote to the frequent grimness of metropolitan existence.[1] The same impulses – an infatuation with verdure, so long as it is decorously managed, and a desire to keep the borders nice and neat – are present in our maintenance of language. The connection between this and gardening is an old one, made popular by Baldassare Castiglione's Renaissance best-seller *Il Cortegiano* (1528) and by Thomas Hoby's English translation of it (1561).

I have yet to come across anyone who is never irritated by other people's use of language. Some people pretend to be above this sort of intolerance, but they turn out to have their pet hates: most of us will readily admit to being irked by certain words or forms of speech. It is not always a matter of believing one's own use of language more polished; there are many who make a point of showing contempt for the patrician and the punctilious, poking fun at anything that seems old-fashioned or fey. But most pedantry runs on the fuel of self-applause, and, to an impassioned few, the question of whether one eats soup or drinks it is as urgent as any other.

It is not just inveterate fusspots who target what they see as defects in others' grammar, pronunciation, spelling, punctuation and vocabulary. In the last of these categories our assumptions are often especially supercilious, like Estella's in *Great Expectations* when she disdainfully says of Pip, 'He calls the knaves Jacks, this boy!' And we are familiar with the pattern of Pip's reaction: when he is next alone he looks at his 'common boots' and his 'coarse hands', and, though these have never troubled him before, he now sees them – and of course his less than genteel vocabulary – as 'vulgar appendages'.

By airing our grievances in public, we perform a ritual show of irritation. The naming and shaming of words that offend us is also a naming and shaming of people – or, more often, types of people – we find distasteful. An orgy of abuse may result. A sure way to start a flame war on the internet is by posting an article about one's lexical peeves. The people who take time to add their comments will, you can be confident, compete over whose peeve is the most pestilential. All the while they hyperstimulate one another's peevishness; anyone joining the fray will be confronted with many new examples of things to get upset about.

Vocabulary is a garden of delights. But all gardeners are obsessed with pulling up weeds. Thus William Zinsser, the author of a much-loved volume called *On Writing Well*, spends a good deal of time pinpointing the essence of writing badly. He decries journalese, which he suggests is 'the death of freshness in anybody's style'. Consisting of 'a quilt of instant words patched together out of other parts of speech' (that is, 'a world where . . . the future is always "upcoming" and someone is forever "firing off" a note'), it is defined by a 'failure . . . to reach for anything but the nearest cliché'.[2] A cliché is a threadbare phrase or trite expression, not a single overused word. Zinsser additionally distinguishes between 'good' words and 'cheap' ones. His own views about which words fall into these two categories are not important here. Rather, it is the existence of the categories that matters. For we are all familiar with the sensation of relishing one person's use of what we quietly believe is a good word and recoiling at another's use of what we consider a cheap one.

We have already come across Thomas Lounsbury, the eminent professor 'in Yale University'. He claims that 'Nothing is more striking in the history of language than the hostility which manifests itself at particular periods to particular words or phrases. This is a state of mind which characterizes us all, and rarely, if ever, does it affect seriously the fortune of the expression disliked.' Lounsbury cites the example of Thomas De Quincey, who was appalled by the word *unreliable* and insisted that it would be more correct to write 'unrelyuponable'. 'From that day to this,' wrote Lounsbury in 1908, 'the discussion of the propriety of the word has been constant.'[3] Many other authors have voiced highly specific revulsions. Jonathan Swift detested not just *mob*, but also *banter*. Benjamin Franklin was so offended by the use of *progress* as a verb that he wrote to Noah Webster asking him to help keep it at bay, and he was similarly concerned about *to advocate*. Samuel Taylor Coleridge reserved special loathing for *talented*. Fowler condemned *electrocution* and *gullible*. In 1877 William Cullen Bryant, editor-in-chief of the *New York Evening Post*, published a list of words he could not stomach; it included *artiste*, *pants* and *standpoint*. (Editors today make such proscriptions part of their papers' house style. I know of one who will not accept the word *iconic*, and another who disallows *whilst*.) Much further back, Edward Phillips in *The New World of English Words* (1658) expressed a distaste for *autograph*, *ferocious*, *misogynist* and *repatriation*. In venting hatred of a particular word, one may reach for arguments from etymology or logic, but typically the reaction is aesthetic and coloured by political and personal sentiment. It may stem from an aversion to a sound or to a word's associations, or because we feel the word is a mask for something terrible, or, more simply, because it denotes something that upsets us. Identifying the cause of aversion can be difficult: I know I dislike the adjective *moist*, but when I try to explain this, my reasoning sounds hollow.

Each year Lake Superior State University in Michigan publishes a list of words and phrases that its professors and students have agreed should be banished. In 1976 they threw out *meaningful* and *input*; two years later they discarded *parenting* and *medication*; and thirty years on they chose to do away with *wordsmith* and *waterboarding*. Of course, no word can ever be consigned to oblivion by academic edict; the quirky and not exactly publicity-shy folks at Lake Superior State University seem aware of this – another cherished activity on campus is unicorn-hunting; one's licence to hunt must be worn over the heart, pinned with a sprig of rosemary – but the spirit of the exercise will be appreciated by many.

Which verbal tics especially annoy you? Rhetorical questions, perhaps? Among people I know, the list of irritants includes (brace yourself for a long sentence) stock phrases and nuggets – 'at the end of the day', 'I think you'll find', 'in the final analysis', 'with all due respect' (the noun *respect* is in some, mostly political contexts an irritant in its own right), 'new and improved', 'tried and tested', 'at this moment in time', 'bear with me', 'it is what it is', 'I'm good to go', 'almost exactly', 'sum total', 'lifestyle choices', 'quality time', 'decisive factors', 'the lowest common denominator' (with the implication that this is a small number, though often it isn't – the lowest common denominator of ⅓ and ¾ is 12), 'no problem', 'in fairness', 'to be honest', 'free gift', 'workable solution', 'positive feedback', 'it is incumbent upon me', 'you don't want to go there', 'no offence, but . . .', 'can I ask you a question?', 'for your convenience', 'do you know what I mean?', 'what's not to like?' – and a number of individual words that have become wearisomely common – *synergy, sustainable, paradigm, ongoing, facilitate, empower, customer-facing, closure, process* in contexts to do with emotions and psychology ('the grieving process'), and perhaps also *context* to boot, along with *creativity, leverage, proactive, pathfinder, challenge, solution, 24/7, co-worker, user-friendly*, the emptying *situation* (compare 'There is crime' and 'There is a crime situation') and the pretentious *historic* ('This is an historic moment for Basildon'). These words and phrases are disliked because they seem devoid of meaning; they have been discoloured through overuse or through too much unthinking use, and have become fillers, formulae, dumb scraps barnacling the truth. But we can't eradicate them. The reason? It's not rocket science. And yes, dear reader, I added that one just to pique you.

Many of these words became common because they seemed capable of exalting our thoughts. If I tell you I am 'hopeful' that something will happen, you may well believe that I think it is unlikely. If I say instead that I am 'optimistic', you will have greater faith in my outlook. Such, at least, seems to be the prevailing pattern of thought. But change is afoot. *Optimistic*, a term once comical because of its association with Voltaire's buoyant and pedantic Dr Pangloss, now seems anaemic because it has become part of the rhetoric of mediocrity. It is a word many of us have ceased to take seriously. Still, not so long ago it seemed more hopeful than *hopeful*, and plenty of words are in vogue today because they are believed to maximize the flavour of what we are saying. A lot of us object to nouns becoming verbs: *task, leverage, action, transition, architect, roadmap, version, showcase*. These verbs are meant to sound cutting-edge, serious, busy and indeed business-y, but instead of conveying salt and spice they mostly seem pretentious.

In Britain, dissenters argue that the phenomenon is American in origin. This is doubtful. A more common complaint is that British English is generally being tainted by Americanisms. As I have suggested, outrage at American influence was common among Victorian defenders of British English, and its volume increased as first American silent movies and then 'talkies' conquered the British picture palace. In a piece for the *Daily Express* in January 1930, Jameson Thomas wrote that 'the talkies have presented the American language in one giant meal, and we are revolted'.[4] This type of complaint was a journalistic staple from the 1920s onward. There were supporters of American words and expressions, such as Frank Dilnot, who described them as 'like flashes of crystal' and deemed American English 'a potent and penetrating instrument, rich in new vibrations, full of joy as well as shocks'.[5] But among the British the pro-American party has always been small. Neutrality is common enough, but hostility has always made itself loudly felt.

Of the more recent claims that American English is a menace, the most sustained I have come across is Edwin Newman's 1975 book *Strictly Speaking: Will America be the Death of English?* A distinguished American broadcaster, Newman claimed, 'The United States may prove to be the death of English, but Britain . . . plainly wants to be in at the kill.'[6] Newman's suggestion that the British are apt to hop aboard every American linguistic fad still earns eager approval. Meanwhile British newspapers routinely dismiss the particular vocabulary of American English with words such as 'loose', 'annoying', 'strangling', 'obscure' or 'insidious'. There are also, so we hear, those pesky American pronunciations: putting the stress on the third syllable of *advertisement* and the second of *detail*, saying *docile* in such a way that it rhymes with *fossil*, the noticeably different sounds of *depot*, *apricot*, *tomato*, *clerk* and *missile*. There are the different spellings, too:

ax, plow, color (the Webster legacy). But most repugnant, if you believe the detractors, are the little oddities of American vocabulary: *semester, garbage can, cookie, elevator* and, perhaps worst of all, *math* instead of *maths*. Never mind that *buzz saw* is more evocative than *circular saw*. Never mind that many words once condemned as rank American-isms are now in everyday use in Britain: *lengthy, mileage, curvaceous, hindsight*. Never mind that there are more of 'them' than there are of 'us'. Never mind that American English is now the most im-portant of English's many varieties. For, no, the vital thing is to resist and indeed repel the onslaught of Americanisms because they are, you know, wrong, man.

The collectors of language peeves are annoyed by new words and by not-so-new words acquiring new meanings. The new word is a solution to a problem, but the problem may be invisible to many of us. A shift in one word's meaning involves shifts in other words' meanings; as a word acquires new layers of significance and loses others, it keeps different company. This change, too, may be hard to detect.

When we aggregate the keywords of our age, we may wince. Terms that repeatedly crop up in our public discourse that would have seemed strange and obscure to our grandparents include *media, multiculturalism, network, otherness, fundamentalism, fetish, globalization, postmodern* and indeed *discourse*. They would probably have been able to work out the meanings of such words, but would have been surprised by our frequent use of them today. Other items might simply have struck them as empty, overblown or superfluous: *celebrity, heritage, identity, mobility, communication* (as in 'communication skills' and 'interpersonal communication'), *culture* (with its flows and differ-ences, its relativity and hybridity, and its many offshoots such as *nanoculture* and *cyberculture*), *community* ('the gay community', 'commu-nity organizer'), and the emphasis on types of *experience* – for instance, the management of 'customer experience'. Then there are all the things labelled 'alternative': lifestyles, energy sources, media, therap-ies, investments, religion.[7] I am not condemning any of these words, but their prevalence is indicative of some of the principal features of our society, and each of them, as it has emerged or shifted, has proved troublesome.

A slippery word we encounter almost daily is *rights*. It is used promiscuously by the architects of international law, by advertisers, and by people who find the word 'ideals' insufficiently emotive to suit their polemical ends. Rights are usually perceived in relation to injustice: it is through the repeated failure of justice that people assemble a sense of their entitlements. But promoters of rights rarely see them as the product of a process of trial and error; instead, claims about rights are couched in the language of moral theory, often coloured by the rhetoric of religion. The word *rights* has a woolly comprehensiveness: legal, political and ethical entitlements are muddled together, and a precise evaluation of duties, responsibilities and powers is lost in the fog of unscientific hooey.

This is sometimes called semantic bleaching: a word's specific meaning is eroded and, thanks to frequent use, becomes general. The best example is probably the change in the meaning of *thing*: in Old English it denoted a meeting, especially a judicial assembly, and later it meant a piece of business, but, beginning in the Middle English period, the word was used indefinitely, becoming a convenient term for any object or matter that a person could not (or would not) particularize. Other instances are more recent. 'No word in English carries a more consistently positive reference than "creative"', wrote Raymond Williams in 1961.[8] That no longer holds true. It has become a token of humbug, an indicator of soullessness, box-ticking and narcissism. In certain contexts, mainly financial, *creative* is the equivalent of *misleading*: we have creative accountancy, for instance, and the creative pricing of products and services.

I have written the last dozen or so paragraphs knowing full well that there are bad habits of which I am guilty. One, common among non-fiction writers, is the use of what Sir Ernest Gowers in his *ABC of Plain Words* neatly called 'pushful adjectives of vague intensification'.[9] *Considerable* is the classic example: 'This is urgent' manages to convey a greater sense of urgency than 'This is a matter of considerable urgency', which sounds stuffy. Gowers might have mentioned adverbs, too. Does 'The water was very hot' evoke a stronger impression of heat than 'The water was hot'? Clearly it is meant to, but the economy of the second version seems more decisive. Whipping up great curds of *very*-ness is an ineffective strategy.

How impressed are we going to be by the assertion that 'This is very, very, very, very important'? What would an extra *very* contribute?

In truth, intensifiers are often markers not of importance, but of triviality. If something is 'a complete disaster' or 'an absolute tragedy', you can be pretty sure it is not a train crash or a devastating tornado. It is much more likely that the words *complete* and *absolute* would be omitted in these cases. 'A total catastrophe' is a footballer's blunder in the penalty box or an unsuccessful dinner party, not the destruction of an orphanage. We recognize in the extremity of some words of intensification a parodic excess.

An example of this inflationary practice that we often come across is people's use of *literally* when they mean *figuratively*: 'The guys making the presentation literally got crucified', 'He was offside by literally miles', 'My urethra is literally on fire'. Offenders use it to assure us of the veracity of their exaggerations. It is not always a marker of untruth – I may literally be pulling my hair out with anxiety, and may employ *literally* to help you interpret my meaning correctly – but it smacks of over-affirmation. This is hardly new. In *Little Women* (1868–9) Louisa May Alcott wrote of 'an out-of-door tea' that was 'always the crowning joy of the day' because 'the land literally flowed with milk and honey on such occasions'. The *OED* cites the actress Fanny Kemble's statement in her *Journal of a Residence on a Georgian Plantation*, written in the late 1830s, that 'For the last four years . . . I literally coined money.' In *Nicholas Nickleby* (1838–9) we read that Squeers 'literally feasted his eyes, in silence, upon the culprit'.

A strange form of pushfulness is the use of *like* as punctuation – as in, 'He is so, like, not cool'. *Like*, rather than achieving its usual effect of approximation or simile, here serves as an intensifier. Many people diagnose it as a tic or as an egotistical defence against being interrupted. They may also feel that the heavy use of *like* reflects the poverty of a speaker's vocabulary. It stands in for all the adjectives, verbs and adverbs of which young folks are, like, totally ignorant. Or perhaps it indicates that adjectives, verbs and adverbs no longer feel adequate to convey the mysteries of (perpetual) adolescence.

One influential commentator, Thomas de Zengotita, has argued that the rise of *like* reflects not the narrowing of vocabulary but 'the inadequacy of language in principle'. At first the proliferation of *like* conveyed 'the futility of trying to put into words what could only be known directly': now it serves 'as a kind of quotation mark . . . [and] introduces a tiny performance rather than a description'. Originally, then, this use of *like* signalled that an experience – a concert, maybe – was too special to be squeezed into the small containers of everyday words. 'Led Zeppelin were, like, completely amazing' was a sentence calculated to make it clear that 'completely amazing' was an insufficient plaudit. Later, *like* became more overtly theatrical. De Zengotita hears it being used to cue 'a "clip" displaying a message in highly condensed gestural and intonational form'. Whatever follows *like* is a riff, an impersonation, an act. This use of *like* has been called 'quotative'.

For de Zengotita, this is all part of 'the dance of the moment'.[10] He sees modern life as an extended presentation, a perpetual whirl of social showmanship. *Like*, it seems, licenses its users to be – for a moment – Method actors. That's certainly how it comes across in the 1982 song 'Valley Girl' by Frank Zappa and his then fourteen-year-old daughter Moon Unit, and it was 'Valley Girl' that brought the performative *like* to wide attention. Generations immersed in the simulations of TV are sensitive to the ironies and dramas of their every gesture.

There are other ways of understanding *like*, though. It can be seen as a form of hedging. The performance it cues may resemble a ritual of uncertainty – which, paraphrased, goes thus: 'I don't know if the next word I'm going to say is the right word. I don't want to look stupid or hasty or dogmatic, so instead of just saying the word straight out I'm going to indicate that it's here only on probation, awaiting your blessing or improvement.' Seen thus, *like* is a form of politeness.

As such, it seems to be related to another mannerism, sometimes referred to as 'uptalk' (a term coined by the journalist James Gorman in 1993). Uptalkers avoid flat assertion. Writing in *The Times* in 2006, Stefanie Marsh characterized this as 'the rise of the interrogatory statement':

My sister lives in Los Angeles, and has picked up this irritating verbal tic, 'uptalk', which means that she uses an interrogative tone even when making statements such as 'I never want to talk to you again (?)' In the old days I could pretend to listen to her on the phone while actually reading a book – I would do this by keeping one ear on her intonation and lobbing a well-placed 'in principle, I would say yes', after every one of her high notes. These days when I do that she sighs and says flatly: 'It wasn't a question, Stefanie.'[11]

In 2004, Ian Jack wrote in the *Guardian* about his eleven-year-old daughter's style of speech, in which 'odd, questioning stresses . . . settle on random words, not necessarily at the ends of sentences (if any sentences happen to be hanging around, that is)'.[12]

When I first came across this phenomenon – sometimes known by the technical yet not quite accurate name 'high rising terminal', or by the less technical and less accurate Australian Questioning Intonation – I imagined it was a mark of self-doubt. But a different and academically accepted view is that uptalk is a means of asserting control; the speaker is requiring me to confirm that I am paying attention – and perhaps even that I agree with what is being said. It may also be practised in a spirit of inclusiveness, to highlight the newness of a piece of information being presented, or to check that we are being understood and aren't falsely assuming knowledge on the part of our listeners.[13]

People who adopt these mannerisms do so for the very simple reason that patterns of speech are contagious. The use of individual words is undoubtedly contagious, too. Who hasn't had the experience of coming across a new word and then extravagantly overusing it? Sometimes, gallingly, the word is one we would profess to dislike; or we initially succeed in resisting some voguish term and then collapse into acquiescence.

As vogue words gain momentum, we may worry that unless we use them the world is passing us by. In 2007 the columnist William Safire wrote about vogue words in the *New York Times*; he cited as current examples *age-appropriate* and the expressions 'to show ankle' and 'go figure'.[14] Typically, vogue words are rampant for a while, then disappear from view. Alternatively, they stop seeming voguish and become part of the well-worn vocabulary of daily life. In 1947 Eric Partridge could cite as vogue words *blueprint, complex* as a noun, *crisis* (which he felt was 'used with nauseating frequency'), *economic* and *ego*.[15] Today, a fascination with new terminology means that something can be anointed as the latest buzzword before it has really had an opportunity to prove itself, and the pundits who pick words of the moment can go horribly wrong. In 2007, the word of the year chosen by Australia's *Macquarie Dictionary* was *pod-slurping*, a term for illicitly using a storage device such as an iPod to download data from someone else's computer, and Oxford University Press went for *locavore*, meaning someone who consumes only food produced locally. I have never heard anyone say either of these words, and have seen them written only in the context of commentators laughing at what poor choices they were. When the pundits do seem to get it right, their verdicts are disquieting. In early 2010 the American Dialect Society declared the verb *tweet* its top word of 2009. Its word of the decade was the verb *google*. Both are proprietary names, registered by Twitter and (pretty obviously) Google.

Our attitude to voguish vocabulary reflects our relationship to the newness and strangeness of developments in the world. We expect much of it to fail – to enjoy a moment's attention and then to disappear. The difficulty is knowing which parts we need to adopt or at least accept; it is hard to predict what will last, although for the most part unobtrusiveness helps a word's chances more than gaudiness. And while we may find some people's embrace of evanescent fashions embarrassing, we may also embarrass ourselves by dismissing all novelties as trinkets of the moment.

Change is always happening. It is, as wags like to point out, life's one constant. Frank Kermode counsels in his book *Shakespeare's Language*, 'We . . . need to remember how quickly the language of quite ordinary people grows strange, recedes into the past, along with other social practices and assumptions taken for granted in one age yet hard for a later age to understand.'[16] It is a curiously easy thing to forget. 'Curiously' because the evidence is all around us.

A common concern is people's failure to distinguish between superficially similar words that have different meanings: *fortunate* and *fortuitous*, for instance, or *disinterested* and *uninterested*. The distinctions here seem useful. I'll admit to being irked when I hear someone say *simplistic* when he means only *simple*. Equally, one may be niggled by the mixing-up of *imply* and *infer*, *tortuous* and *torturous*, *venial* and *venal*, *credible* and *creditable*, *regrettably* and *regretfully*, *militate* and *mitigate*, *derisive* and *derisory*, *masterly* and *masterful*, *aggravate* and *irritate*, *flout* and *flaunt*, *compose* and *comprise*, *ability* and *capacity*, *oral* and *verbal*. (The last of these perhaps requires explanation: all language is verbal, but only speech is oral.) I wince when *hysterical* is used as a synonym for *hilarious*. I am not going to have a fit of the vapours, of the kind some delicate souls claim to suffer at such moments, but I feel uncomfortable, and I tell myself that the differences between these words are important. Occasionally, confusion can give rise to unpleasantness: in my case, there was an instance a few years ago when a waitress insisted on passing on to a chef not the congratulations I intended, but something she seemed to think was the same or even better – commiserations.

The trouble is, when I fuss over the distinction between, say, *coruscating* and *excoriating*, I am faced with immediate evidence that others do not feel the same way. And history does not always support my case, for not all the supposed differences are borne out by investigation. If we accept the evidence of the *OED*, *disinterested* was used to mean 'not interested' before it was used to mean 'impartial', and *uninterested* meant 'impartial' before it meant 'indifferent'. In any case, the distinction is now slipping away, as inspection of a corpus of current usage confirms.

Geoffrey Nunberg has done some research into the changing attitudes of the usage panel of *The American Heritage Dictionary*. In 1969, 43 per cent thought it was 'acceptable' to use *aggravating* as a synonym for *irritating*; by 1988, this had gone up to 71 per cent. *Cohort*, used as a term equivalent to *conspirator* or *colleague* (i.e. of individuals, not as a collective noun), was acceptable to 31 per cent in 1969, but to 71 per cent in 1988. Yet in some cases the mood had become more conservative over the period Nunberg was considering. In 1969, *hopefully* as a 'sentence adverb' ('Hopefully, neither side will insist . . .') was accepted by 44 per cent; by 1988 the figure was 27 per cent.[17]

Several of the pairs of words I listed above have superficial similarities that lead to their being mixed up. *Flout* and *flaunt* provide an obvious example. The words are sufficiently different that we can tell them apart, but sufficiently similar for many of us to have trouble remembering which one is which. Yet often the problem is pretentiousness rather than confusion. *Disinterested* sounds more sophisticated than *uninterested*, as *fortuitous* sounds more sophisticated than *fortunate*. This concern with presenting an appearance of sophistication is related to hypercorrection, which I discussed in Chapter 15.

I can't help suspecting that most of the distinctions discussed in the preceding paragraphs are on their way out. In fact, they may already have been lost. It is disconcerting to realize that one is clinging on to something that has already withered. Yet in some cases it has never been vital. The argument against using *hopefully* is that the word means 'in a manner that is full of hope', so it should only be used of a person or group which is doing something in just that way. 'Hopefully, the jury will come to a unanimous verdict' is considered inferior to 'I hope the jury will come to a unanimous verdict' – unless we really mean that the jury is hopeful about the effects of such a verdict. This makes sense until we think about other sentence adverbs such as *accordingly, seriously, understandably, amazingly, frankly* and *honestly*. A sentence adverb presents the attitude of the speaker or author, rather than the attitude of the sentence's subject. The comma following the adverb signals this: 'Honestly, you are a total liar' leaves no room for confusion, whereas without a comma there is ambiguity.

When I was younger, one of the most common complaints I heard about any aspect of the English language was the change in the use of the word *gay*. This perfectly good equivalent to *bright* and *fun*, so the argument went, had been converted into a term – first of denigration, then of celebration – for homosexuals. Now, the grounds for complaint have changed; the word has become a throwaway insult. When in 2006 the Radio 1 presenter Chris Moyles described a ringtone as 'gay' during his breakfast show, he defended himself against charges of homophobia by claiming that it was a synonym for 'rubbish'. He was supported by the BBC. In fact, the history of the word is complicated. As early as Chaucer it had conno-

tations of lasciviousness, and by the Elizabethan period it had overtones of uninhibited hedonism. From the 1790s it acquired the sense
'living by prostitution': the gay ladies of Covent Garden were tarts,
not lesbians, and in Victorian newspapers the word appears
euphemistically in reports about brothels. Early in the nineteenth
century 'gay instrument' was a term for the penis. The association
of 'gay' with homosexuality predates the Second World War. Its
slangy dismissiveness is traced back by the *OED* as far as a novel
about skateboarding that appeared in 1978.

For many, the BBC's defence of Moyles was evidence of its decadence and impending collapse. Long regarded as a stronghold of
traditional values, a spiritual influence as well as a cultural one, it
has become a target for critics of corporate profligacy. In common
with the leading newspapers, it is endlessly berated for its lax use
of English. Lord Reith, the BBC's founder, proposed that its
announcers adopt a uniform approach to pronunciation, and an
Advisory Committee on Spoken English was set up in 1926. Its
first list of recommendations was published two years later, containing
advice on such matters as where to put the stress in *chastisement* (on
the first syllable, apparently), the preferability of *airplane* to *aeroplane*,
and the three different pronunciations of Leghorn.[18] Subsequent
volumes included guidance on how to pronounce tricky names –
chiefly those of places (Hiroshima, Uruguay) and people (Quiller-
Couch, Wemyss).

In the 1970s the BBC began to move away from a rigid uniformity. Local colour became increasingly common in its radio and TV
broadcasts. Today the BBC is one of the English-speaking world's
most conspicuous platforms for arguments about language. It is responsible for many programmes that take obvious pleasure in the variety
of English; in 2000 a series of Radio 4's *The Routes of English* included
episodes looking at the dialects spoken in Cornwall, coastal Northumberland and Brixton. The BBC also continues to stress its role as a
source of accurate, impartial journalism, and this is expected to manifest high standards of English usage. The remit of its international
arm, the World Service, emphasizes the promotion of the English
language. A large section of the British public counts on the BBC
to act as a custodian of the English language, and is disappointed if

it fails to do so. Among its senior broadcasters, John Humphrys is especially caustic about the linguistic spirit of the age. One of his pet hates is the historic present. According to Humphrys, if you are talking about social conditions in Victorian England, you need to use the past tense. You cannot make your portrait vivid by saying 'The streets teem with sweeps, musicians, shoeblacks and cabmen', because this may confuse some people, leaving them uncertain whether you are talking about then or now.

William Cobbett noted that, when thinking of time and tenses, 'we perplex ourselves with a multitude of artificial distinctions'. These distinctions have come about because 'those who have written English Grammars, have been taught Latin; and, either unable to divest themselves of their Latin rules, or unwilling to treat with simplicity that, which, if made somewhat of a mystery, would make them appear more *learned* than the mass of the people, they have endeavoured to make our simple language turn and twist itself so as to become as complex in its principles as the Latin language is'. As far as Cobbett was concerned, there were three 'times': past, present, and future. Anyone deviating from this view was being 'fanciful'.[19]

Yet we all have some experience of the plasticity of the English tense system. If I pick up a newspaper and read the headline 'Queen Mother Dies', I know that what is being referred to in the present is actually in the past – she isn't dying right now. But the headline writer uses the present tense to make the information seem more urgent and impressive. 'Queen Mother Is Dead' might be considered tactless; 'Queen Mother Has Died' sounds lumpen and banal. Alternatively, consider this: 'I am going away tomorrow.' Though cast in the present, the sentence refers to something in the future. 'When do you start your new school?' 'You are to report to reception on arrival.' 'The train departs at 6.30.' As these phrases suggest, it is a nonsense to pretend that the present tense always refers to present time.

The same applies to the future tense. Take 'You will insist on criticizing my driving'. This clearly refers to something that has already happened – several times, we gather. Meanwhile, 'Hydrogen will burn with a squeaky pop' refers to something that *always* happens.

Such examples confirm that verbs alone do not convey the sense of time. Other words will be involved. To quote David Crystal, 'the linguistic expression of time spreads itself throughout the whole of a sentence'.[20] When we read the words 'Radio broadcasting begins in 1920' we don't see the verb 'begins' and think 'My God, it's 1920!' The words 'in 1920' tell us to read 'begins' in a special way. The author who chooses to write 'begins' rather than 'began' is guilty of nothing worse than exploiting our ability to see this. He or she is striving for immediacy, not trying to mislead us.

Not just our purposes but also our circumstances affect our choice of language. This may seem uncontroversial, but before the last century it was rare to hear the matter put so explicitly. We adapt the way we express ourselves to suit our audience's expectations, or, more accurately, our expectations of their expectations. Most of us occasionally suffer from what the linguist Einar Haugen called 'schizoglossia', an anxiety about which is the right form of our language to use at a particular moment. We are guilty sometimes of strange linguistic posturing. We use one sort of language when we are in the presence of people whose status – and whose opinion of our status – we consider important: we use another with our intimates. An extreme version of this is Charles V's addressing himself to ladies in Italian and to God in Spanish. A less extreme one is my choosing to write this book in a style that from time to time includes quite technical terms; were I talking to a ten-year-old about its subject matter, I would express myself in a simpler fashion. When someone loses sight of which level of language he or she should be using, it can feel like an affront, even a violation. I would not be impressed if the vet wrote in his notes, 'Poor little kitty's botty is going "ow".' Neither would I be impressed if he said to my young daughter, 'Your cat has squamous cell carcinoma'; if he said to me, 'Your moggie's gonna snuff it, pal'; or if he said more expansively, 'Damn – I've just got cat all over the floor.'

Now and then a single word violates our sense of appropriateness. When did you last hear someone say 'That's not a proper word'? A search on the internet quickly provides me with numerous examples of terms smeared in this way: *joys, irregardless, unvalidated, aluminium, politeful, email, gotten, prioritize, extensible, cohabiting* and *splurge*. Some of these doubtless seem inoffensive to you (as some do to me), but I am confident that others will have set your teeth on edge. The 'not-proper' word achieves this in two ways: it signifies something we dislike, perhaps a substance or a behaviour, and, more than this, it brings to mind an image of a person or type of person we disfavour, whom we can recall using the word or whom we can imagine using it. You may protest, 'No, that's not it at all. I object to *irregardless* because it's illogical.' But catch yourself in the act of disapproval: you're likely to find that, rather than taking a stand on matters of etymology or logic, you have a reaction that is pointedly social. What's striking is how long many of these words have been causing irritation. *Splurge* is attested with the sense 'a sudden extravagant indulgence' as early as 1928, the much-reviled *irregardless* appears in a dictionary of American dialects dating from 1912, and the verb *to cohabit* has been around for half a millennium. *Gotten*, widely heard in America, used to be quite acceptable in Britain and survives in 'ill-gotten gains', but is mostly regarded as an American eccentricity. There is actually a distinction in American English between *got* and *gotten*: *got* signals current possession ('I've got ten dollars in my pocket'), whereas *gotten* relates to the process of acquisition ('I've gotten us tickets to the ballet'). Those who sneer at *gotten* seem oblivious to this.

There are several definitions of what a 'word' is. For something to be a word, it need not have existed a long time nor be in wide use. It may be defined as a unit of speech that can be uttered on its own to meaningful effect, or as a written sequence representing such a unit of speech. When we think about English words on the page, we think of each word having white space on either side of it but no space within. Commonly, what we call words are lexemes – abstract units of the sort that we can find in a dictionary, free forms that when spoken or written have some semantic content. To put it nakedly, words are the smallest units of language that can always stand alone as independent utterances. There are smaller meaningful units, morphemes, but they are not necessarily able to stand on their own. *Pleasant* is a lexeme, and so is *unpleasantness*, but the *un-* and *-ness* that we add to the first to make the second are morphemes.

When we use a word that is unusual, perhaps when playing Scrabble or reporting a strange thing that has happened to us, a familiar rejoinder is 'I bet it's not in the dictionary'. The first problem here concerns what is meant by 'the dictionary'. If I look in the *OED*, I shall find *rastaquouère* meaning 'a person . . . regarded as a social interloper' and *nudiustertian* meaning 'of or relating to the day before yesterday'. It also includes *puh-leeze* and *achy-breaky*. But if I look in a pocket dictionary, it is possible that a word I really use will be absent. Besides, the word under scrutiny may be new, and even in the digital age dictionaries take a while to catch up with novelty.

A dictionary is ostensibly a record of usage. This means that on the one hand it provides explanations of words we may consider undesirable, debased or spurious, and that on the other it does not cover everything, because it is impossible to keep abreast of all usage. In any case, the almost religious recourse to dictionaries is naïve. Dictionaries manifest bias. Some are pretty candid about this. For instance, the *Chambers Twentieth Century Dictionary* (1972) defines *jaywalker* as 'a careless pedestrian whom motorists are expected to avoid running down'. No dictionary, however clinically produced, is entirely untouched by human prejudice.

Change in vocabulary is easily registered. It involves not just the arrival of new words, but also the disappearance of words that were once in everyday use. On the whole we are less aware of changes in grammar. Where grammar is concerned, we are more likely to suspect that 'something is going on' than to be sure of it. I have touched already on the way *they* is increasingly used in the singular. *Whom* seems to be receding. The passive appears increasingly to be formed using the verb 'to get' and a past participle – not 'we were caught', but 'we got caught'. *Shall* as a modal auxiliary to denote future tense, particularly in the first person ('I shall see you later'), is in decline. *Less* is used where traditionally *fewer* was preferred.

With regard to the last of these, there is always someone who is irked by the sign in the supermarket that says 'Five items or less'. Shouldn't it be 'Five items or fewer'? One way round this, adopted by a supermarket where I shop, is for the sign to read 'Up to five items'. The rule that I can recall being taught is that *less* is used of bulk, but not of countable nouns: 'I do less entertaining than you because I have fewer friends.' One of the reasons for the blurriness of the distinction between *less* and *fewer* is the way *more* behaves. We use *more* with countable nouns and with non-countable ones: 'I do more entertaining than you because I have more friends.' However, in the Middle English period, *more* was used of quantities that were not being counted and the now obsolete *mo* was used where numbers were specified: one spoke of 'more butter' and of 'mo loaves', and, were I to revive the distinction, I would say, 'I do more entertaining than you because I have mo friends.' As *mo* disappeared, *more* took over both roles, and *less* copied this extension. But there were objections. The conventional distinction seems to begin in 1770 with Robert Baker's *Reflections on the English Language*. Baker was different from most of his contemporary writers on language, informing his audience that he 'quitted the School at fifteen', knew no Greek and not much Latin, and owned no books. His *Reflections* contains some statements that will have sounded odd to his peers and continue to seem so now; for instance, 'There are . . . Places, even in Prose, where for the sake of Sound, *Whom* may be used in the Nominative'. But regarding *less* he has proved influential. He claimed that the word was 'most commonly used in speaking of a Number; where I should think *Fewer* would do better. *No fewer than a Hundred* appears to me not only more elegant than *No less than a Hundred*, but more strictly proper.' 'I should think', 'appears to me': this is mere opinion, but Baker's view caught on.[21]

Amid all of this, we should be aware of the ease with which one can succumb to illusions. First of all, there is the illusion of frequency: when something happens a little, we believe we have seen the tip of an iceberg, and consequently we start to believe that it happens a lot. Then there is the illusion created by our selective attention. We are likely to notice and condemn things that are done outside our own social group, and to home in on the vices of a particular group to which we do not belong (often it's teenagers), without considering whether (a) people behave differently when we're looking at them, (b) our own social group is guilty of the misdemeanours we are so quick to scold, and (c) the corruptions within this group are rather less than the epidemic we suppose. Finally, there is what Arnold Zwicky has called the 'recency illusion' – a theme on which I have touched a few times already. We believe that something we have just noticed has only just started happening, although it may in fact be long-established.

This illusion pervades discussion of disputed pronunciations. Some words can be pronounced in two noticeably distinct ways. Spotting this, many of us claim, without supporting evidence, that one pronunciation is edging the other out, as though this is strange and new. Examples of words that receive this attention include *exquisite, economic, tissue, romance, scallop, controversy, finance, envelope, praline, either, respite, transport* and *zebra.* (The list could be much, much longer.) While the difference is in some cases one of emphasis, mostly it is to do with the sounds of vowels. It hardly seems sensible to draw strong conclusions from the fact that I say *zebra* with a short *e*. In fact, self-observation reveals that I am not consistent in the way I pronounce several of these words. Despite reflecting on it, I have not been able to make out an absolutely clear pattern in my behaviour. This much is sure, though: while in English the location of the stress in a word is not completely free, it is not fixed as it is in, say, Polish or French, and the rhythm of a sentence – the locations of our articulatory force – will affect the way we treat the words within it.

Finally, it is striking that the editors of *The American Heritage Dictionary* are responsible for a book with the title *100 Words Almost Everyone Mispronounces*. Examples include *acumen, chimera* and *niche*. If 'almost everyone' mispronounces them, it follows that almost no one pronounces them 'correctly', so perhaps the supposedly correct pronunciations are close to becoming obsolete.[22] As so often, the guardians of English are defending positions that seem already to have been lost.

24 Technology says 'whatever'

Wired life … wireless … lifeless?

It is common to blame what we might call The New Incorrectness on technology. In his book *The Gutenberg Elegies*, which investigates the impact of technology on the experience of reading, Sven Birkerts characterizes the negative effects of the information age as 'mediation, saturation, and fragmentation'. He suggests that the modern, 'connected' human is becoming weightless; 'human gravity' is being lost.[1] Birkerts decries the increasing shallowness of culture – and what he calls 'the gradual but steady erosion of human presence' and 'the ersatz security of a vast lateral connectedness'.[2] Countless others are saying the same thing: technology is changing every department of experience, and too little attention is being paid to the consequences.

When we hear the word *technology*, we probably think of computers or of what they make possible. But technology is of course rather older: examples include the wheel, the plough, and the hand axes used by our primitive ancestors more than a million years ago. The arrival of personal computers in our homes and places of work is really quite recent. I was born in 1974; I first used a computer in 1982, and first owned one soon afterwards, but did not start to work at a computer on a daily basis until about 1995. The concept of 'desktop publishing' is a mere twenty-five years old. The system of interconnected computer networks we now call the internet is older. The technologies that laid its foundation were originally developed as an aid to formal communication within the American military; the internet's precursor, the ARPANET, took its name from the US Department of Defense's Advanced Research Projects Agency and grew briskly in the early 1970s. Thanks to the development by Tim Berners-Lee of the World Wide Web, a system enabling connections between documents and services, the internet has, of course, become something very different. Berners-Lee's invention, set out in a proposal in 1989, was publicized in 1991 and began to capture real public interest two or three years later. An interesting sidelight: his original name for it was Enquire, which he explains was 'short for *Enquire Within Upon Everything*, a musty old book of Victorian advice I noticed as a child in my parents' house . . . With its title suggestive of magic, the book served as a portal to a world of information.' However, 'unlike *Enquire Within Upon Everything*, the Web that I have tried to foster is not merely a vein of information'. The vision Berners-Lee sets out is 'a society that could advance with intercreativity and group intuition rather than conflict as the basic mechanism'; the ideal Web he imagines will 'help me reorganize the links in my own brain so I can understand those in another person's'.[3]

I am writing these words on a computer, rather than in longhand. This has implications for the way I write. I use a piece of software called Scrivener, which intrudes less on my writing process than other word processing software I have owned. At least, that's how it feels. If you use a word processing program such as Microsoft Word you will be familiar with the ways in which your writing is – or can be – mediated and moderated by it. For instance, there is the spelling checker, which flags words that may be incorrectly spelled, and, according to which settings you have programmed, may even 'auto-correct' some apparent mistakes as you write. The first spelling checker on a home computer was marketed in 1980. A grammar checker was part of a package called Writer's Workbench in the 1970s; the first grammar checker for a home computer appeared in 1981, and in 1992 Microsoft for the first time included one as part of Word. People often point out the deficiencies of these utilities, but for many they have become a crutch, and users expect the software to catch their errors.

I can't remember when I first used an internet search engine, but it certainly wasn't Google. The Google search engine was launched in 1997, and now to many internet users 'search engine' means Google and nothing else. Google's unofficial slogan, suggested by Paul Buchheit who was the lead developer of their webmail service Gmail, is 'Don't be evil'. Yet in the eyes of some critics the company's pre-eminence makes it distinctly sinister – in principle, even if not in practice. The French historian Jean-Noël Jeanneney, who from 2002 to 2007 was president of the Bibliothèque nationale de France, has attacked Google's decision to digitize the holdings of a number of important British and American libraries. Jeanneney has argued that this project threatens to unleash an avalanche of English-language data on the internet, and that this could dramat-ically skew future generations' idea of the world.

Electronic media have changed the rhythms of living. Barriers to communication have been removed: information flows more freely and inexpensively (and leaks more, too), and people and organ-izations who might never before have had the chance to interact feel connected. Furthermore, we are able to shape the information we exchange: everything can be digitized, and everything that has been digitized can be transformed. We see more, we hear more, and we feel . . . *less*? The devices we now use to communicate promise greater immediacy, but they can make depth seem shallow, intimacy alien, transparency opaque. Sven Birkerts has argued that 'To repre-sent experience as a shaded spectrum, we need the subtle shading instruments of language', and without what he calls 'the refinements of verbal style' there is a risk that we may 'condition ourselves into a kind of low-definition consciousness'. He suggests that 'the knowl-edge mode now preferred in our culture is one that combines externality with a sophisticated awareness of interconnectedness. Interiority . . . and the more spiritual resonances are suspect.'[4]

Certainly one of the effects of electronic media has been to turn up the noise levels in our daily lives. Sustained attention has become more difficult. The selective process of listening is losing ground to hearing – something we cannot turn on and off. Culturally, we are programmed to understand the world in strongly visual terms – you *see* what I mean, I get the picture – and when we are bombarded with sounds our visual understanding is jarred. Notions of space are jolted, and so are our ideas of time. To put matters in stridently disturbing terms, the concept of a private mind is becoming less stable; increasingly, we participate in the functions of a collective mind, borrowing other people's subjectivity. The media scholar

Derrick de Kerckhove speaks of 'the globalization of our personal psychology' and 'our new, electronic common sense' which is 'no more within ourselves, but without'. He concludes that 'A new human is in the making'.[5] In 2006 *Time* magazine announced its Person of the Year: 'You'. The 'You' thus canonized was presented as the almighty controller of the information age. But the experience of being in control leaves many of us exhausted – physically, emotionally, socially, intellectually.

The consequences for language are palpable. In the electronic society, everything has to be accelerated. Words, which have to be used in a linear fashion, frequently cede ground to images. On the internet capital letters and verbs are apt to disappear, along with punctuation – question and exclamation marks are retained and indeed sometimes laid on extra-thick, but commas evaporate. Writing on web pages often mimics spoken forms, and the customary stability of the written word is undermined as pages are edited or vaporized. Communication is neither speech nor writing as we conventionally understand them, and it is staccato. Abbreviations are rife. At the same time there are creative misspellings and wilful, playful grammatical goofs, as well as multitudes of new words. There is more linguistic variety, a greater degree of hybridity, a faster propagation of novelties. A further, loosely related point: the credibility of websites is judged according to the way they look more than on the strength of who created them, and there is a clear difference between what may be called information literacy and the ability to evaluate the *quality* of information that's available.

There are people who speak English who have no access to the new technology, so the changes I am talking about do not affect everyone who uses the language. But the chances are that they have affected you. Developments on the internet mean that right now there are significant changes afoot in the ways we think about work, business, privacy, sex, ownership, authorship, copyright, knowledge, community, morality and indeed ourselves. In these areas our use of language is altering, and so is our idea of what 'language' means.

The notion that everything can be translated into information – or that whatever cannot has no real value – eats away at the richness of existence. In their thoughtful book *The Social Life of Information*,

John Seely Brown and Paul Duguid suggest that 'some of the attempts to squeeze everything into an information perspective recall the work of the Greek mythological bandit Procrustes . . . [who] stretched travellers who were too short and cut off the legs of those who were too long until all fitted his bed.'[6] It is a mistake to think that all of our organic experience can be crammed into hierarchical data structures.

Activity on the internet today comprises a huge assortment of informal conversations. These conversations often resemble marketplaces, and theirs is a culture in which rumour is indistinguishable from reality and in which memories are short. Whereas conversations that happen face-to-face involve subtle effects of intonation, posture, gesture and gaze, virtual conversations lack these extra layers of information. I am sure you have had the experience of being misinterpreted because a message you sent online did not convey those additional nuances. Emoticons (such as :-D to suggest a big grin) have developed as a way of making up for some of this loss, or of averting misunderstanding of one's mood and tone. But they are crude, and they are often misunderstood. In the virtual world, besides missing the non-verbal envelope in which we package our words, we lose the benefits of simultaneous feedback, the information you provide, a bit like a commentary, when I am speaking to you in person. Even if I am video-conferencing, rather than just exchanging emails or posts on a message board, elements of my non-verbal communication will be unclear.

'Communication' is coming up repeatedly here, with good reason. It is one of the keywords of our age. We are in the midst of a new literacy. There is a huge amount of writing being done, if not perhaps quite so much reading. We write a great deal about ourselves, and do so as a way of socializing. Text messages, emails, the little notes people leave on Facebook, the snippets of autobiography and comment posted on Twitter – these call for ingenuity, an ability to say a lot succinctly. They also require careful thought about appropriateness. Sometimes there is not enough forethought; we have all sent a message into the aether that we have later had cause to regret. Conversely, though, consider the number of times you have punctiliously reworded a text message or email in the interests of brevity, clarity, crispness and wit. All the while another kind of writing is booming: a new, unlimited, expository prose, seen for instance on blogs, which allows even shy people to be exhibitionists. Blogs, which are in most cases unmoderated, suit people who hold extreme views that they would have trouble broadcasting through traditional media. They empower individuals. But their content is treated differently from the content of, say, a printed magazine. In the blogosphere, it seems, writing suffers less than reading.

Online, anonymity is easy. In discussion forums this can make for a vociferousness about inflammatory issues. The feminist writer Jessica Valenti has suggested that at its worst this can mutate into 'an almost gang rape-like mentality'.[7] In our online experience, we may feel less accountable for what we say. We may also feel less accountable for what we look at. The internet is changing perceptions of what is offensive. This is not the place for an extended meditation on the way the availability on the internet of pornography is changing sexual tastes and behaviours, or indeed to comment on the other ways in which the internet has enabled new sexual behaviours. What is clear, though, is that the internet accustoms us quickly to new sights and sounds.

One of the great rewards of wired life – and of its increasingly common successor, wireless life – is rapid access to information. Another is rapid access to people. But this does have some disadvantages. Electronic communication can seem perfunctory and unappreciative, and it can be dangerously hasty. Text messaging illustrates the benefits and the drawbacks, and has become a bugbear of those who worry about the decline of English. They grouse about SMS language, in which 'u k m8' stands for 'Are you okay, mate?' and Hamlet's most famous line becomes '2b/-2b=?' Writing in the *Daily Mail* in 2007, John Humphrys condemned texters as 'vandals who are doing to our language what Genghis Khan did to his neighbours eight hundred years ago.' Their vices included 'savaging our sentences' and 'raping our vocabulary'.[8] I am reminded of Lord Reith's equally disproportionate comparison in the late 1950s between commercial television and 'smallpox, bubonic plague and the Black Death'.[9] The truth is that the majority of texters do not employ the most extreme abbreviations – the elliptical textspeak

cited by its critics – and the use of abbreviations is hardly something new. It is a myth that large numbers of schoolchildren use
these condensed expressions in their written work, and in any case
the heyday of extreme textspeak may well have passed; many phones
now have full QWERTY keyboards, and prolific texters are able to
secure cheap deals that allow them to send unlimited texts. As a
result there is less use of abbreviation than when text messaging
began, since typing messages is easier and the cost of exceeding the
160-character limit has for many users become nil. In any case, the
mangled spellings and dodgy grammar of texts are frequently deliberate. Taking delight in linguistic deviancy is not the same in fact
or in spirit as Genghis Khan's genocidal purging of 20 million
people. It is absurd to imagine that the average person sending a
text message – which is often done while half-occupied with something else – cannot distinguish between the language used for this
purpose and the language to be used in an essay or report.

Yet John Humphrys rightly detects what he calls 'an erosion of
formality'. Elsewhere he avows, 'Formality matters. It creates a space
between us that allows for a measure of independence and freedom.
Take it away and that space is open to all manner of intruders.'
Instead of formality we now tend to have 'enforced intimacy'.[10]
Real intimacy is something to cherish, but enforced intimacy, besides
being embarrassing, has the side effect of permitting a general relax-
ation of informativeness. The strenuous chumminess of TV news
reporting is a case in point. It seems to be terribly important for
us to know that the presenters in the studio are on first-name terms
with the reporters shivering or sweltering in the field, and the
public's opinions are eagerly canvassed, though they contain no
surprises – people are unhappy about a rail strike, saddened by the
death of a public figure, gutted about a football defeat, outraged by
spending cuts, bored by electioneering. All of this occupies space
that might more fruitfully be given over to exposition of the facts.

There is widespread aversion to behaviour that appears starchy.
Some of what we have done away with really was just empty ceremony, but formality is not intrinsically coercive or disagreeable, and
it can be pleasurable. Do you remember the days when you got
dressed up to go out for dinner or to the theatre? If you do, and

if you live in Britain, you're almost certainly over the age of forty. There are situations where formality creates symmetry and is equalizing rather than divisive. Yet often, if we behave formally, we are made to feel stodgy or creepy. I can remember being an object of ridicule when, in my twenties, I put on a suit and tie for a job interview. One of my interviewers made sure I could see he was wearing a pair of soiled trainers – a blazon of his liberal values. Today the formality described above will to many people seem weird. Formality in general has been relinquished. Thomas de Zengotita calls this 'the rise of the casual'.[11] In language, as in clothes, it is conspicuous. Letters I receive from strangers begin not with the words 'Dear Mr Hitchings', but with 'Dear Henry Hitchings', 'Dear Henry' or 'dear hitchings': emails from people I know just slightly are even more relaxed, opening 'Hiya H', 'hitch –' or even 'm8', though there are occasional and surprising archaisms, including the marvellous 'Respected Sir'.

Not so long ago 'Respected Sir' – used by a correspondent who had English only as his third or fourth language – would not have seemed odd. Traditional forms of linguistic politeness have fallen into disuse. Egalitarianism and terms of deference are incompatible. Prime Minister Tony Blair was mocked by traditionalists for saying 'Call me Tony', though in fact he did not utter these words; by contrast, his doughy successor Gordon Brown really did introduce himself to staff at 10 Downing Street with the instruction 'Call me Gordon'. Up until the 1970s an adult male would in many far from ceremonial situations have been addressed by his surname alone, and at my boarding school in the early 1980s I was invariably addressed in this way. Now this use of surnames rather than given names is a mark of affected stiffness or Wodehousian banter, and the affectation is usually recognized on both sides. One member of staff at the British Library, where I am writing these words, calls me 'Hitchings' rather than 'Mr Hitchings' with an archness that is, I think, a joke, though at whose expense I cannot be sure. Tellingly, some of my friends cannot spell my surname correctly, having rarely seen it written down. Contrary to what some Britons claim, Americans tend to have held on to a little more of this courtliness.

The rise of the casual manifests itself in an inability (which may be interpreted as either ignorance or unwillingness) to perceive the nuances of social situations. Politeness, that middle ground between civility and courtesy, is to a large degree a behaviour achieved through language. While it can hardly be considered dead, it has been supplanted by the vapid notion of 'respect', which combines timorous deference with a hollow mateyness – and has enjoyed some extra exposure as the name of a broadly socialist British political party. It is frequently suggested that traditional British reserve has been superseded by rudeness. We recognize, perhaps with pain but perhaps with a certain macabre relish, *Little Britain*'s Vicky Pollard and Catherine Tate's sweary grandmother with her catchphrase 'What a load of old shit!' But is the behaviour we condemn as lack of restraint and roiling incivility symptomatic of social decline? Or does it suggest something else – maybe the triumph of democracy? Whatever.

Ah, *whatever*. 'I don't really think that dress is appropriate,' says Concerned Parent. To which her child responds, 'Whatever.' Is this dismissive, apathetic, calculatedly disengaged? What's for sure is that *whatever* drives a great many people nuts. Sometimes it means something akin to 'Yes, that's what I said'; at other times it is equivalent to 'Have it your way'. Alarmists suggest that the commonness of *whatever* is an indication of a new lassitude: the headline might read, 'Young people do not care any more.' One American academic, Naomi Baron, has latched on to the ubiquity of the word, writing of The 'Whatever' Generation. She suggests that digital technology has created a nomadic culture in which people simply do not set much store by using language clearly. She also diagnoses what she calls 'the end of anticipation': we save up fewer of our experiences for discussion when we meet face-to-face. Baron suggests that the next few decades will see standards of spelling and punctuation revert to levels 'redolent of the quasi-anarchy of medieval and even Renaissance England', and that there will be 'a diminution in the role of writing as a medium for clarifying thought'. Language, she thinks, will play less of a role in marking its users' social status.[12] Baron does not insist on these predictions; they are simply 'plausible'. Yet she does argue, like Sven Birkerts, that being 'always on', perpetually connected, compromises our ability to be reflective.

We are saturated with information, and that makes it harder for us to know our selves.

We do not have to be 'always on'. But we can lose sight of this truth. A friend of mine, a workaholic writer, returned from a holiday to report that he had been unable to use his phone or connect to the internet in the remote community where he had stayed. 'It was bliss,' he told me. 'For a few days I was just me.' As he said this, his body spasmed in Pavlovian response to the cheeping of his iPhone. This disharmony is fascinating. Or perhaps I should bring into play the current smart term: not *disharmony*, but *disconnect*. When Naomi Baron pictures a world in which we do not care about language, what she's really imagining is a world where we have no idea of how to take care of ourselves.

25 'Conquer English to Make China Strong'

The globalization of English

No language has spread as widely as English, and it continues to spread. Internationally the desire to learn it is insatiable. In the twenty-first century the world is becoming more urban and more middle class, and the adoption of English is a symptom of this, for increasingly English serves as the lingua franca of business and popular culture. It is dominant or at least very prominent in other areas such as shipping, diplomacy, computing, medicine and education. A recent study has suggested that among students in the United Arab Emirates 'Arabic is associated with tradition, home, religion, culture, school, arts and social sciences', whereas English 'is symbolic of modernity, work, higher education, commerce, economics and science and technology'.[1] In Arabic-speaking countries, science subjects are often taught in English because excellent textbooks and other educational resources are readily available in English. This is not something that has come about in an unpurposed fashion; the propagation of English is an industry, not a happy accident.

English has spread because of British colonialism, the technological advances of the Industrial Revolution, American economic and political ascendancy, and further (mostly American) technological developments in the second half of the twentieth century. Its rise has been assisted by the massive exportation of English as a second language, as well as by the growth of an English-language mass media. The preaching of Christianity, supported by the distribution of English-language bibles, has at many times and in many places sustained the illusion, created by Wyclif and Tyndale and Cranmer, that English is the language of God.

The history of English's global diffusion is littered with import-

300

ant dates: the planting of the Jamestown colony in 1607; Robert Clive's victory at the Battle of Plassey in 1757, which ushered in the dominion of the British East India Company; the creation of the first penal colony in Australia in 1788; the British settlement at Singapore in 1819 and establishment of a Crown Colony in Hong Kong in 1842; the formal beginning of British administration in Nigeria in 1861; the foundation of the BBC in 1922 and the United Nations in 1945; the launch by AT&T of the first commercial communications satellite in 1962. This list is condensed. It takes no account, for instance, of the various waves of Anglomania that swept much of Europe in the eighteenth century. But it will be apparent that the diffusion of English has had a lot to do with material reward, the media, and its use as a language of instruction. A fuller list might intensify the impression of a whiff of bloodshed.

Wherever English has been used, it has lasted. Cultural might outlives military rule. In the colonial period, the languages of settlers dominated the languages of the peoples whose land they seized. They marginalized them and in some cases eventually drove them to extinction. All the while they absorbed from them whatever local terms seemed useful. The colonists' languages practised a sort of cannibalism, and its legacy is still sharply felt. English is treated with suspicion in many places where it was once the language of the imperial overlords. It is far from being a force for unity, and its endurance is stressful. In India, while English is much used in the media, administration, education and business, there are calls to curb its influence. Yet even where English has been denigrated as an instrument of colonialism, it has held on – and in most cases grown, increasing its numbers of speakers and functions.

In *A Modern Utopia* (1905), a work partly of fiction and partly of philosophical discussion, H. G. Wells describes a copy of Earth, billions of light years away, where everything proceeds rationally. As far as the language of this technocratic utopia is concerned, 'We need suppose no . . . impediments to intercourse'. The language 'will no doubt be one and indivisible', and 'I fancy it will be a coalesced language, a synthesis of many. Such a language as English is a coalesced language; it is a coalescence of Anglo-Saxon and Norman French and Scholar's Latin, welded into one speech more ample and more powerful and beautiful than either.'[2] Nine years later, in his prophetic novel *The World Set Free*, Wells returns to this subject. He imagines the world's leaders meeting in the Italian Alps in 1959. They make resolutions and establish a government to achieve 'a new common social order for the entire population of the earth'. He goes on:

> It was not until the end of the first year of their administra-
> tion and then only with extreme reluctance that they would
> take up the manifest need for a lingua franca for the world.
> They seem to have given little attention to the various theor-
> etical universal languages which were proposed to them. They
> wished to give as little trouble to hasty and simple people as
> possible, and the world-wide distribution of English gave them
> a bias for it from the beginning. The extreme simplicity of
> its grammar was also in its favour. It was not without some
> sacrifices that the English-speaking peoples were permitted the
> satisfaction of hearing their speech used universally. The language
> was shorn of a number of grammatical peculiarities, the distinct-
> ive forms for the subjunctive mood for example and most of
> its irregular plurals were abolished; its spelling was systematized
> and adapted to the vowel sounds in use upon the continent of
> Europe, and a process of incorporating foreign nouns and verbs
> commenced that speedily reached enormous proportions.[3]

I quote Wells at length because, as so often, his thinking is strange, bold and perceptive. In the early decades of the twentieth century, he was imagining what would become known as World English. That term for the concept of English as an international language, a global second language, an intellectual and commercial lubricant, even an instrument of foreign policy on the part of the major English-speaking nations, grew common only in the 1960s. It has circulated since the 1920s, though, and the idea was touched upon earlier, not just by Wells, but also by Alexander Melville Bell, who had in 1888 presented *World-English*, a scheme of revised spellings intended to help learners acquire the language that, as he saw it, exceeded all others 'in general fitness to become the tongue of the World'.[4] Robert Nares, writing in 1784, presented with no little relish a vision of

English extending prodigiously around the globe. Even before that, John Adams had prophesied that it would become the most widely spoken and read language – and 'the most respectable'.[5]

The term World English is still in use, but is contested by critics who believe it strikes too strong a note of dominance. Today World English is known by several names, perhaps the most catchy of which is Globish (though personally I think this sounds silly), a term popularized by Jean-Paul Nerrière in his book *Don't Speak English, Parlez Globish* (2004). Globish, as conceived by Nerrière, is a pragmatic form of English consisting of 1,500 words, intended to make it possible for everyone in the world to understand everyone else. It is reminiscent of C. K. Ogden's Basic English. To give a flavour of it, I shall list all the words it contains that begin with *y*: *year, yellow, yes, yesterday, yet, you, young, your, yours.* We may not miss *yeoman* or *yodel*, but what about *yawn, yell* and *youth*? Nerrière is a former vice-president of marketing at IBM, and has branded Globish a 'decaffeinated' form of English. Humour and metaphor are out. Short sentences are in. The late Palestinian leader Yasser Arafat is held up as an excellent exponent of the form. Nerrière also argues, less than convincingly, that the rise of Globish will help preserve French by minimizing the influence of caffeine-loaded English. The opposite view has been put forward by Claude Duneton, whose book *La Mort du français* (1999) predicts that French will disappear by 2050.

For Jean-Paul Nerrière the decaffeination of English is virtuous, but in the same phenomenon Edward Said has found cause for alarm. In his book *Culture and Imperialism* Said recalls his experience of visiting the English department at a university in 'one of the Persian Gulf States' in 1985. 'In sheer numerical terms English attracted the largest number of young people of any department in the university', but although the students 'dutifully read Milton, Shakespeare, Wordsworth, Austen, and Dickens' their purpose in doing so was to become expert in the lingua franca of international business. 'This,' writes Said, 'all but terminally consigned English to the level of a technical language stripped of expressive and aesthetic characteristics and denuded of any critical or self-conscious dimension.'[6] Such an approach makes the use of English a mechanical act;

it enables the basic transmission and deciphering of information, but it is intellectually stunting rather than empowering.

Nerrière's Globish is not alone. Madhukar Gogate, a retired Indian engineer, has independently come up with an idea for something he too calls Globish. It would use phonetic spellings to create what he considers a neater form of English. This could become a global language enabling links between people from different cultures. Meanwhile Joachim Grzega, a German linguist, is promoting Basic Global English, which has a mere twenty grammatical rules and a vocabulary comprising 750 words that learners are expected to supplement with an additional 250 words relevant to their individual needs.

Although these schemes may be intended in a different spirit, promoting a neutral form of English rather than one freighted with 'Anglo' values, they are part of a larger, often invisible project: to establish a community, without territorial boundaries, of people who use English; to make its use seem not just normal, but also prestigious; and to market it as a language of riches, opportunity, scholarship, democracy and moral right. This is supported economically, politically, in education and the media, and sometimes also by military force. Much of the endorsement happens covertly.[7] And as English continues to spread, it seems like a steamroller, squashing whatever gets in its way. True, it is often used alongside local languages and does not instantly replace them. Yet its presence shifts the cultural emphases in the lives of those who adopt it, altering their aspirations and expectations. English seems, increasingly, to be a second first language. It is possible to imagine it merely coexisting with other languages, but easy to see that coexistence turning into transcendence. As English impinges on the spaces occupied by other languages, so linguists are increasingly finding that they need to behave like environmentalists: instead of being scholars they have to become activists.

There have been attempts to create an artificial language for use by all the world. In the second half of the nineteenth century and then especially in the early years of the twentieth, schemes to construct new languages were numerous. Most of these are now forgotten: who remembers Cosmoglossa, Spokil, Mundolingue, Veltparl, Interlingua, Romanizat, Adjuvilo or Molog? Some of the innovators sound like remarkably odd people. Joseph Schipfer, developer of Communicationssprache, was also known for promoting means of preventing people from being buried alive. Etienne-Paulin Gagne, who devised Monopanglosse, proposed that in time of famine Algerians help their families and friends by exchanging their lives or at least some of their limbs for food, and was willing if necessary to give up his own body to the needy.

Only two schemes enjoyed success. In 1879 a Bavarian pastor, Johann Martin Schleyer, devised Volapük. It was briefly very popular: within ten years of its invention, there were 283 societies to promote it, and guides to Volapük were available in twenty-five other languages. As Arika Okrent observes in her book *In the Land of Invented Languages*, Volapük is a gift to people with a puerile sense of humour: 'to speak' is *pükön*, and 'to succeed' is *plöpön*.[8] More famous and less daft-sounding were the efforts of Ludwik Zamenhof, a Polish ophthalmologist of Lithuanian Jewish descent, who in the 1870s began work on creating Esperanto, a language without irregularities. He published his first book on the subject in 1887, summing up the language's grammar in sixteen rules and providing a basic vocabulary. Zamenhof's motives were clear; he had grown up in the ghettos of Bialystok and Warsaw, and, struck by the divisiveness of national languages, he dreamt of uniting humanity.[9] Esperanto is certainly the most successful of modern invented languages, but although it still has enthusiastic supporters there is no prospect of its catching on as Zamenhof once hoped.

Readers of this book are more likely to have heard Klingon, which was originated by Marc Okrand for the *Star Trek* films, and the Elvish languages – notably Quenya and Sindarin, modelled on Finnish and Welsh respectively – devised by J. R. R. Tolkien and faithfully used in Peter Jackson's films of *The Lord of the Rings*. A more recent example of a new artificial language is the one conceived by Paul Frommer that is spoken by the blue-skinned Na'vi in James Cameron's 2009 film *Avatar*. Where once they embodied political hopefulness in the real world, invented languages have become accessories of art and entertainment.

Today it is English, rather than any created alternative, that is the world's auxiliary tongue. There are more people who use English as a second language than there are native speakers. Estimates of the numbers vary, but even the most guarded view is that English has

500 million second-language speakers. Far more of the world's citizens are eagerly jumping on board than trying to resist its progress. In some cases the devotion appears religious and can involve what to outsiders looks a lot like self-mortification. According to Mark Abley, some rich Koreans pay for their children to have an operation that lengthens the tongue because it helps them speak English convincingly.[10] The suggestion is that it enables them to produce r and l sounds, although the evidence of the many proficient English-speakers among Korean immigrants in American and Britain makes one wonder whether the procedure is either necessary or useful. Still, it is a powerful example of the lengths people will go to in order to learn English, seduced by the belief that linguistic capital equals economic capital.

In places where English is used as a second language, its users often perceive it as free from the limitations of their native languages. They associate it with power and social status, and see it as a supple and sensuous medium for self-expression. It symbolizes choice and liberty. But while many of those who do not have a grasp of the language aspire to learn it, there are many others who perceive it as an instrument of oppression, associated not only with imperialism but also with the predations of capitalism and Christianity. (It is mainly thanks to Lenin's 1917 pamphlet about imperialism and capitalism that the two words have come to be pretty much synonymous.) The Australian scholar Alastair Pennycook neatly sums up English's paradoxical status as 'a language of threat, desire, destruction and opportunity'.[11] Its spread can be seen as a homogenizing (some would say, Americanizing) force, eroding the integrity of other cultures. Yet it is striking that the language is appropriated locally in quite distinct ways. Sometimes it is used against the very powers and ideologies it is alleged to represent. Listening to Somali or Indonesian rappers, for instance, it seems sloppy to say that the use of English in their lyrics is a craven homage to the commercial and cultural might of America.

In his book *Globish* (2010), Robert McCrum diagnoses English's 'subversive capacity to run with the hare and hunt with the hounds, to articulate the ideas of both government and opposition, to be the language of ordinary people as well as the language of power and authority, rock'n'roll *and* royal decree'. He considers it 'contagious, adaptable, populist', and identifies the fall of the Berlin Wall in 1989 as the symbolic moment that signalled the beginning of 'a new dynamic in the flow of information'.[12] McCrum sees English as performing a central role in what Thomas L. Friedman has catchily called 'the flattening of the world', the new 'single global network'.[13]

There are challenges to the position of English as the dominant world language in the twenty-first century. The main ones seem likely to come from Spanish and Mandarin Chinese. Both have more first-language users than English. But at present neither is much used as a lingua franca. The majority of speakers of Mandarin Chinese live in one country, and, excepting Spain, most Spanish-speakers are in the Americas. There is an argument that the revitalization of minority languages is good for English, because it weakens English's large rivals and thus removes obstacles to the language's spread. So, for instance, the resurgence of Catalan, Basque and Galician weakens Castilian Spanish, making it a less powerful rival to English.[14] Apologists for English invert this argument, claiming that the advance of English is good for minority languages. The inversion is spurious.

Nicholas Ostler, a linguist whose insights are often brilliantly surprising, observes that 'If we compare English to the other languages that have achieved world status, the most similar – as languages – are Chinese and Malay'. All three have subject-verb-object word order, and their nouns and verbs display few inflections. Moreover, 'the peculiarly conservative, and hence increasingly anti-phonetic, system is another facet of English that bears a resemblance to Chinese', and 'as has happened with Chinese . . . the life of English as it is spoken has become only loosely attached to the written traditions of the language'.[15] It's an intriguing link, but hardly a guide to what will happen next.

The main challenges to English may come from within. There is a long history of people using the language for anti-English ends – of creative artists and political figures asserting in English their distance from Englishness or Britishness or American-ness. For instance, many writers whose first language has not been English have infused their English writing with foreign flavours; this has enabled them to parade their heritage while working in a medium that has made it possible for them to reach a wide audience.

Two challenges stand out. I have mentioned India already; English is important to its global ambitions. The language's roots there are colonial, but English connects Indians less to the past than to the future. Already the language is used by more people in India than in any other country, the United States included. Meanwhile in China the number of students learning the language is increasing rapidly. The entrepreneur Li Yang has developed Crazy English, an unorthodox teaching method. It involves a lot of shouting. This, Li explains, is the way for Chinese to activate their 'international muscles'. His agenda is patriotic. Kingsley Bolton, head of the English department at the City University of Hong Kong, calls this 'huckster nationalism'.[16] It certainly has a flamboyant quality; one of Li's slogans is 'Conquer English to Make China Strong'. A few dissenting voices suggest that he is encouraging racism, but the enthusiasm for his populist approach is in no doubt, and it is a symptom of China's English Fever: the ardent conviction that learning English is the essential skill for surviving in the modern world.

The embrace of English in the world's two most populous countries means that the language is changing. Some of the changes are likely to prove disconcerting for its native speakers. The 'Englishness' of English is being diluted. So, more surprisingly, is its American flavour. English's centre of gravity is moving; in fact, in the twenty-first century the language has many centres. As this continues, native English-speakers may find themselves at a disadvantage. Native speakers freight their use of the language with all manner of cultural baggage. An obvious example is the way we use sporting metaphors. If I say to a Slovakian associate, 'you hit that for six', she probably won't have a clue what I am on about. Nor will an American. An Indian very likely will (the image is from cricket), but really I should choose my words with greater care. The trouble is, often I and many others like me do not exercise much care at all. To non-native speakers, quirks and elaborations of this kind are confusing. Non-native speakers of English often comment that they find conversing with one another easier than sharing talk with native speakers. Already many people who learn English do so with little or no intention of conversing with its native users. If I join their conversations, my involvement may prove unwelcome.

At the same time, native speakers of English tend to assume that their ability in this potent language makes it unimportant to learn other languages. The reality is different. British companies often miss out on export opportunities because of a lack of relevant language skills.[17] Moreover, there is a chance that a command of English will within twenty or thirty years be regarded as a basic skill for business, and native speakers of the language will no longer enjoy any competitive advantage. When polled in 2005, more than 80 per cent of people in the Netherlands, Denmark and Sweden claimed to be able to speak English. The figure was around 60 per cent in Finland, 50 per cent in Germany, 30 per cent in France and Italy, and 20 per cent in Spain and Turkey.[18] These figures can safely be assumed to have increased. They come from a study published in 2006 by the British Council, an organization set up in 1934 and today operating as an 'international cultural relations body' in more than a hundred countries. In 1989 its Director General, Sir Richard Francis, stated that 'Britain's real black gold is not North Sea oil, but the English language'.[19] That view is often played down, but the role of the British Council in promoting British English ties in with British corporate interests. Large companies such as British Petroleum (now BP Amoco) have worked with the British Council, funding educational schemes to encourage foreign nationals to learn English. This is not exactly an act of altruism. As Robert Phillipson punchily says, 'English for business is business for English.'[20] But while English is being pushed, it is also being pulled; it is the language, more than any other, that people want to learn.

The consequences are complex. Some, it would seem, are not as intended. Even as vast amounts are spent on spreading British English, the reality is that English is taking on more and more local colour in the different places where it is used. Accordingly, while the number of languages in the world is diminishing, the number of Englishes is increasing.

26 What do we do with the flowing face of nature?

Language and the shape of thought

Talking about the global spread of English and about the march of technology leads, inevitably, to speculations about the future. But what about the language's role in the immediate present? What, indeed, of the relationship between language and thought?

It is sometimes said – and it has become quite fashionable to say – that language enables us to construct reality. I might have enclosed that last word within inverted commas, for according to this view reality is a kind of fiction and much of what we hold to be true is a dream inspired by the social world we inhabit. Thus we are continually struggling to wrestle a degree of objectivity from our accustomed subjectivity, although we are hardly likely to see the struggle this way or even to see it as a struggle.

It makes more sense to say that language enables us to construct an *image* of reality. Sensory experience is like a stream, which we channel using language. To put this another way, language organizes our fluid impressions of the world. But it is not the world that we are arranging; rather, we are arranging our experience of the world. When we use language we are translating and interpreting our sensuous responses to things outside us. Language frames our experiences. It breaks experience up into pieces – a digital packaging of analogue reality. Different languages do this in different ways. We could say that each language is like a map and manifests distinct conventions about mapping. The geography of the mental territory being mapped is a constant, but it gets represented in a variety of ways.

While this mapping is an everyday occurrence, it is not a neutral one. The French philosopher Jacques Derrida has argued that 'everyday language' is far from innocent: 'It carries with it . . . presuppositions of all types', and these presuppositions, 'although little attended to, are knotted into a system'.[1] One of the more obvious examples of what Derrida is talking about is the tendency to represent the world in terms of oppositions – active versus passive, hero versus coward, good versus bad, inside versus outside, native versus foreign, edible versus inedible, male versus female. These constructions are antagonistic – which is to say, they always favour one and diminish the other. As long as we are happy to believe that experience precedes language we may not worry too much about them. But what if language contaminates the way we think and the way we feel? Is there really such a thing as 'pure' language, or are we always translating, compromising, and hypnotizing ourselves with metaphor?

It suits us in our daily lives to believe that the meanings of words have some primordial reality. We put faith in the apparent connection between language and the phenomena around us. Intuitively, this feels right. But language is a differential system. Thought, we might usefully say, is the perception of relationships – of differences.

In the field of language study, the great exponent of this view was Ferdinand de Saussure, whose ideas have been explored by thinkers across the humanities and have served as the starting point for arguments such as those of Derrida. A Swiss who could with justice claim to be a descendant of Henry VII of England, Saussure taught for a decade in Paris and then, from 1891 to 1913, at the University of Geneva. The sole book he published concerned the vowel system of Proto-Indo-European; his lasting influence can be attributed to the decision of two of his Geneva students, Charles Bally and Albert Sechehaye, to compile an edition of notes they had made in his classes and of other material gleaned while taking his course.

Saussure stresses that there is no inevitable link between the thing you are signifying and the form in which you signify it. In more concrete terms: the sequence of sounds in the word *crocodile* is no better suited to talking about the creature we know as a crocodile than any other sequence of sounds would be. The connection is arbitrary, not intrinsic. There are two fairly obvious exceptions to this principle: words made up of others that already exist and contribute to their meaning (*lawnmower, corkscrew*) and onomatopoeic words (such as *boom, clang, kerplunk* and the Latin *sussurus*, meaning 'whisper') that imitate the sounds they denote. But these exceptions aside, the principle holds: there is no inherent link between 'signifier' and 'signified'. As Shakespeare's Juliet says, 'What's in a name? That which we call a rose / By any other word would smell as sweet.'

All natural languages, rather than naming categories that exist already, enunciate their own categories. This is demonstrated by the way words change their meaning: as we know, instead of standing still, the concept that a word denotes may shift. If the relationship between words and the things they denote included some sort of 'natural connection', words would be sequestered from the effects of history. This is not how language works. As Saussure commented, a 'language is a system of pure values which are determined by nothing except the momentary arrangement of its terms'.[2] It is the influence of Saussure that lies behind modern language scholars' repudiation of the prescriptive tradition; he argued that linguistics should establish itself as a science, and indeed he achieved a scientific footing for the subject.

Language enables us to make our feelings public – accessible to others, influential. It also has another important effect: it makes us moral creatures. The link between language and morality is indissoluble. But that's not to say that it is obvious. Our system of morality is created and maintained through language. It is achieved through our (largely unnoticed) conversations with ourselves and through larger, public conversations. One simple form this takes is our statements about categories to which we say we belong, or in which we place others. This begins when we are children: the critical period for our acquisition of language is also critical for our development of social skills and moral capacities. Categories enable us to function socially. By means of categorization, language provides scope for rewards and punishments, and enables cooperation and solidarity – as well as deception. Language is recursive, allowing us to generate an infinite variety of expressions from finite resources, and morality is recursive, too, for we can moralize about an infinite number of matters and can also moralize infinitely about a single matter. What's more, we can refer to situations that are at some remove from our own, even imaginary or unreal.[3] Our ability to hypothesize, rather than being trivial, is crucial to our moral judgement.

Metaphor plays a crucial role in enabling us to engage with unfamiliar or abstract subject matter. When we talk about moral issues, we rely heavily on metaphor. It is customary to conceive of morality itself as strength and as something that sustains us. English possesses a wealth of metaphor that sets store by sincerity, justice, generosity, caring for others, listening, self-control and safety.

Let us look for a moment at some of the everyday metaphors by which we live. They tend to cluster. George Lakoff and Mark Johnson, who have studied the subject in detail, note the prevalence of 'orientational metaphors': health, control, high status and virtue are 'up', while sickness, being subject to control, low status and depravity are 'down'. Lakoff and Johnson illustrate the way we speak of an argument as a journey ('We will proceed in a step-by-step fashion', 'Do you follow?') and also a container ('The argument has holes in it', 'I'm tired of your empty arguments'), and they show how these different characterizations are compatible.[4]

Metaphors help organize our experience coherently. They vivify the abstract. Money is equated with blood; its flow is invigorating, we are flush with funds, cash is injected, liquidity gets squeezed, cash circulates, funds haemorrhage from an ailing business, and exploitative individuals (bloodsuckers?) will bleed you dry. Knowledge is to a significant degree thought of – seen – as sight, and ignorance is blindness, darkness, the condition of night. Love is, among other things, madness, conflict and a gravitational force. Sex is violence: I may not need to spell this out, but consider, for instance, the images of the *man-eater* and *lady-killer*, a large portion of the slang terms for the penis, and casual talk of a 'conquest' or 'making a pass' (the latter an image from the realm of sword-fighting). Andrew Goatly, who has written at length about the sex/violence connection, goes so far as to suggest a link between sexual metaphors and rape, observing that 'juries and judges do not recognize rape for what it is, maybe because of the tendency to conceptualize sex as violence.'⁵ We may think that such associations are long-standing and immutable, but it seems that ideology can skew our everyday metaphors. To think that everything is a commodity, that enterprise equals wisdom, that change is development: these ideas are not eternal and unquestionable, although they are often presented thus. By the same token, the metaphorical language of capitalism has intertwined itself with the metaphors we use of freedom and democracy: success is movement, freedom is movement, creativity is wealth, quality is size, ownership is identity.

Many everyday metaphors are dead, the fossilized remains of what were once original and poetic statements. Creating new ones is tricky, though: attempts often fail. We have all come across so-called mixed metaphors, which are reviled because of their clumsiness. When we experience this clumsiness, we feel that meaning has been tainted. Metaphor conveys an impression of likeness between one thing and another. Where that likeness is at its fullest, we find significance. A successful metaphor may enable a discovery. When Wallace Stevens writes that a poem is a meteor, we probably think of certain attributes of meteors that a poem could share: a poem is a sudden streak of bright light, something rare that fades within a moment of being witnessed, debris shed by a comet (the comet perhaps being inspiration), or, more trivially, something we are most likely to see – to appreciate – at night. When a metaphor is mixed, the connection is broken. Instead we see a ludicrous misalignment. If I were to write 'A poem is a meteor hammering home a poet's ideas', you would no longer value the connection I make between poems and meteors, because what follows the word *meteor* is remote from your image of what meteors are and what they do. By extending the metaphor in an inaccessible direction, I have made the whole of it preposterous. However, sometimes a metaphor can, precisely because of its dividedness or diffuseness, say something interesting about the thing described – its elusiveness, maybe – or about the way we perceive it. When Hamlet wonders if he should 'take arms against a sea of troubles', his metaphor is mixed, but we infer that he is hinting at the likely ineffectiveness of an armed solution to his troubles, which are too fluid and huge to be dealt with in this way.

We may imagine that certain emotions are basic parts of human experience: happiness and sadness, fear, surprise, disgust and rage feel as though they ought to be universal. The facial expressions which communicate feelings such as disgust, surprise and happiness do indeed seem to be biological rather than cultural in origin. But when we use language to describe emotion – as opposed to expressing it by exclaiming *wow* or *ugh* – we are cramping or grooving our feelings, and in the process we are regulating them. When we examine ourselves honestly we see that often our emotions are not entirely separate and that the distinctions we make between them are not completely clear. Language can seem like a grid dividing and compartmentalizing our feelings, and different languages do this in different ways. To take an everyday example, we may compare the ways languages articulate love. The Spanish equivalent of 'I love you' is '*te quiero*', which expresses want, whereas a Finn says '*rakastan sinua*', meaning roughly 'I love a part of you'. Alongside these, the French '*je t'aime*' sounds blithe. But if it seems at least plausible that our accustomed vocabulary has a bearing on the ways we see and feel, what of our grammar? Can it too shape our outlook?

The notion that grammar 'is' thought – that grammatical categories classify experience, and that different languages do this in different ways – was advanced by Franz Boas, a scholar best known for developing anthropology into a professional discipline, in the early years of the last century. Boas believed that a language's ways of classifying experience reflected thought rather than dictating it. His ideas were developed by one of his outstanding students, Edward Sapir, whom we briefly met in an earlier chapter. Sapir turned the argument around, claiming that we read experience according to categories that do not in fact directly correspond to it. Every language, according to Sapir, channels thought in its own way. A language's system of classification shapes the interpretation of experience. Sapir went so far as to say that no two languages were sufficiently similar to represent the same reality.

Sapir's student Benjamin Lee Whorf built on this. Besides being an enthusiastic amateur linguist, Whorf was an expert in the field of fire prevention – a somewhat ironic occupation for anyone pushing grand arguments about language. Whorf investigated examples of matters Sapir had treated only in the abstract. 'The real question,' he wrote, is 'What do different languages do . . . with the flowing face of nature in its motion[?]'[6] He suggested that the metaphors of what he called Standard Average European languages such as English imposed certain ways of perceiving relationships in space and time. These, he said, differed sharply from those evident in the Amerindian language Hopi: he claimed that in Hopi there are no words or grammatical constructions that enable direct reference to time, to the past or the future, or to the notion of something lasting, and that the language's speakers have little interest in matters such as chronology, sequence and measurable lengths of time. 'The Hopi metaphysics,' he wrote, 'imposes upon the universe two grand cosmic forms, which . . . we may call *manifested* and *manifesting*.' By contrast, 'The metaphysics underlying our own language . . . imposes upon the universe two grand cosmic forms, space and time.' He concluded that 'Every language contains terms that have come to attain cosmic scope of reference, that crystallize in themselves the basic postulates of an unformulated philosophy, in which is couched the thought of a people'. As a result 'Hopi, with its preference for verbs, as contrasted to our own liking for nouns, perpetually turns our propositions about things into propositions about events'.[7]

In a separate move that had unexpectedly lasting consequences, Whorf followed up some remarks made by Boas about the number of words North American Indians have for snow. He claimed that to an Eskimo (the preferred term now is usually Inuit) the 'all-inclusive' word *snow* 'would be almost unthinkable; he would say that falling snow, slushy snow, and so on, are sensuously and operationally different, different things to contend with; he uses different words for them and for other kinds of snow'.[8] Later authors, seduced by this notion, made specific and increasingly large estimates of the number of different words, going as high as four hundred. They also suggested that Inuit paid more attention to differentiating types of snow because they had a larger number of words for them.

The idea put forward by Boas, altered by Sapir and re-examined by Whorf, came to be known as the Sapir-Whorf hypothesis. As broadcast by anthropologists and psychologists, the argument at its simplest is that a language's distinct forms oblige its users to see reality in a particular way. That is, we dissect the world around us according to lines our language has laid down. The community to which we belong predisposes the way we interpret everything. By extension, one's behaviour may be seen as a function of the language one speaks, and there are concepts we cannot entertain because they have no names in our language. This line of thinking has been pursued by numerous researchers and writers. For instance, Alfred Bloom's work on the differences between English and Mandarin Chinese has led him to suggest that speakers of English have a greater facility for theoretical and counterfactual thinking.[9] In 2004 a journalist wrote in the *New York Times* about the Kawesqar people of southern Chile, who 'rarely use the future tense; given the contingency of moving constantly by canoe, it was all but unnecessary'.[10]

Most of this is wrong. Research indicates that Whorf's claims about the Hopi are untrue: in Hopi speech there are ways of quantifying units of time, there are grammatical tenses, and records are kept that make use of various means of measuring time. Whorf's account seems to have been a mixture of wishfulness and romantic mysticism. Alfred Bloom's findings resulted from flaws in the way he constructed his tests.[11] The *New York Times* story about the Kawesqar does not stand up. Reflecting on it, the linguist John McWhorter comments, 'Never mind that Japanese has no future markers either, and yet the Japanese hardly seem unconcerned with the future.'[12] Quite so.

We should be wary of believing that the patterns of a language's grammar reflect the patterns of its speakers' minds. Does every one of the world's more than six thousand tongues encode a distinct world-view? No. Is it significant that in German the word for a little man, *Männlein*, is neuter, or that the words for knife, fork and spoon are respectively neuter, feminine and masculine? Mark Twain quipped that 'In German, a young lady has no sex, but a turnip does. Think what overwrought reverence that shows for the turnip, and what callous disrespect for the girl.' It's a nice line, but grammatical gender is an abstract, formal concept – not tied to biological sex, and not absurd.

The claim about the number of Inuit words for snow is interesting chiefly on account of its reception. It has become one of those 'facts' that 'every schoolboy knows'. (George Orwell kept a list of these fallacies, which included the beliefs that if you tell a lie you get a spot on your tongue and that a pig will not swim for fear of cutting its throat with its trotters.) The notion that Inuit pay more attention to snow because they have more words for it seems a strange reversal of cause and effect. In any case, linguists laugh off the idea that there is a noticeably large number of Inuit snow words. It has given rise to the term *snowclone*, which signifies a well-worn phrasal template such as 'If Eskimos have dozens of words for snow, Germans have as many for bureaucracy'.[13] If they want to sound tough in their opposition to popular myth, language experts say that it is racist to swallow unverified stories about unfamiliar peoples. Yet although the wild overstatements about snow words are the exaggerations of hacks straining for effect, it does seem plausible that many Inuit encounter snow more than I do, talk about it more than I do, experience a greater range of snow-related phenomena, and may therefore have a somewhat bigger repertoire of names for types of snow, snow events and so on. This is a point astonishing in one respect only: its banality. It has nothing to do with the Sapir-Whorf hypothesis. An enjoyably sceptical combatant in the language wars, Mark Halpern, comments that 'In the minds of most observers, it is perfectly natural . . . to possess and use a large vocabulary for the most prominent concerns in one's daily life'.[14] That is all it is: a large vocabulary, not a radically different psychology.

Only in a diluted form does the Sapir-Whorf hypothesis hold true: vocabulary can affect the ways we perceive things and the ways we recall them. This partly has to do with our perceptual abilities being shaped during childhood, which happens under the influence of language. We are likely also to recognize that when we come across a new word, its novelty may be enjoyable, and, if we adopt the word, we may start overtly to identify the thing it denotes. But this is hardly a restructuring of our cognitive equipment.

When we think about the relationship between language and thought, we quickly see how large a part our choice of metaphors and indeed of individual terms plays in framing our communica-tion with others. Words have powerful associations. In part these relate to their most familiar collocations – that is, the company they tend to keep. For instance, the noun *takeover* more often appears with the adjective *hostile* than with *benign*, and *rain* will be accompanied by *torrential* or *heavy* more frequently than by *fat* or *whirling*. Collocations are an area of concern for people learning the language: to show a good command of English one needs to know that it is usual to speak of a great difficulty, a big smile and a large area, rather than of a great area, a large smile and a big difficulty. But there are associations of other kinds: those personal to us, and those fostered by society (for the most part invisibly) and redolent of magic, superstition, a primitive holiness – or its verso, horror. We think of words as having colours, faces, humours, scents – in short, character. Their accessories can sometimes seem the most important parts of them.

In the 1960s two American academics, David Palermo and James Jenkins, researched this area closely. Testing 500 children in each of the fourth to eighth, tenth and twelfth grades in Minneapolis public schools, as well as 1,000 students taking psychology classes at the University of Minnesota, with a 50/50 gender split, they focused on the first response produced by each of 200 stimulus words. Just to take a single example of their findings, I'll concentrate on *sour*. The responses show plenty of overlap – there are obvious 'association norms' – but there are striking differences. The word with which *sour* was most often associated was *sweet*; among the university students, this was the response of 232 males and 255 females. Aside from *sweet*, which was roughly five times more common a response than any other, the most frequent responses were *bitter*, *cream*, *lemon* and *milk*. *Cream* was about 50 per cent more common among females than males. None of the university students wrote *hurt*, which was by contrast the second most popular response of sixth-grade males. Younger respondents were more likely than university students to link *sour* with *bad* – and with *good*. Older ones were more likely to mention *apple*, *grapes* and *pickle*. A small number made connections with *pain* and *sweat*. Two male respondents of college age produced *whiskey* (as in a 'whiskey sour'); and three fourth-grade males offered *foot*, though no one above the fifth grade made this connection. Idiosyncratic responses which appeared only once in the entire sample included *arm, basement, English, horn, monkey, shepherds, teacher, vowels* and *work*. And surprisingly uncommon, from my point of view, were *dough, puss* and *taste* – the responses of, respectively, ten, eleven and ninety-one young people out of a total of 4,500.[15]

If the work of Palermo and Jenkins seems almost antique, a simple experiment now might involve taking a word such as *peace* and asking a few volunteers to scribble down ten other words brought to mind by this 'trigger'. When I tried this with three friends, *peace* prompted each of them to write *war* and *quiet*, but no other word appeared on all three lists. Only one included *treaty*, and only one *dove*, while the third's selection contained *pipe, grass* and *massage*. Trying again with *naked*, I found that all three wrote down *eye, ape* and *body*; two wrote both *lunch* and *aggression*; only one wrote *flame* or *ambition*; and the quirkier one-offs included *grape, rambler, fish* and *hotel*. There is nothing terribly surprising about this divergence, but it neatly demonstrates that a word can have different associations for different people. Equally, according to your vantage point and values, you and I may respond in very distinct ways to words such as *socialist* and *pudding*.

This may seem crude. It *is* crude. But it draws attention to a large problem: assumptions hide in everything we write or say. Word association tests provide evidence – incomplete, and not easily de-cipherable – of patterns of thought that are rarely articulated. Each of us contains a cognitive map, densely contoured and permanently invisible, which organizes our attitudes.

In *Nicholas Nickleby* Dickens writes, 'Spite is a little word; but it represents as strange a jumble of feelings, and compound of discords, as any polysyllable in the language.' Ralph in Edith Wharton's *The Custom of the Country* recognizes that for his mother and sister 'the word "divorce" was wrapped in such a dark veil of innuendo as no ladylike hand would care to lift.' You may have similar feelings about these words. More likely, though, there are other words that for you are especially enveloped in significance. These differences may sound innocuous, but they cause problems.

27 Such, such are the joys

Politics, George Orwell and
the English language

If you change perception, it's often alleged, you change reality. And
if you change what things are called, you can change how they are
perceived. This is true of the positioning and branding of, say, a
breakfast cereal or an insurance company, but it is also true of other
phenomena, and acts of renaming are political. Confucius in his
Analects suggests that when a politician takes up the reins of government his first task should probably be to rectify the names of things.

This is what George Orwell depicts in *Nineteen Eighty-Four*. The
citizens of Orwell's imagined dystopia – a creation influenced not
just by the spectre of Stalinism, but also by Orwell's experience of
his miserable prep school and working for the BBC – are expected
to use Newspeak, a reduced form of English which enforces civil
obedience by eliminating subtle expression and rebellious statements.
In practice, no state-enforced distortion of language can defeat
subversiveness; there will always be resistance. Nevertheless, Newspeak
is a cautionary vision of a language without history and colour.
Orwell's thinking was shaped in part by his hostility to Ogden's
Basic English; initially intrigued by Ogden's ideas, he later concluded
they were mechanical and degraded. In *Nineteen Eighty-Four* he was
not predicting the future so much as satirizing the present, and
Newspeak, which could be spoken 'without involving the higher
brain centres at all', was a satire on the gibberish of totalitarian
regimes.

It is a bland sort of alarmism to say that today Newspeak is all
around us. In reality, instead of the narrow and imperative language
Orwell imagined we have an alternative Newspeak of persuasion
and befuddlement. Newspeak paraded massive lies ('Freedom is

Slavery', 'Ignorance is Strength'), but the contemporary language that is sometimes dubbed Newspeak is really something different. It conceals its deceptions. And it grows like wisteria – hardily, invasively, twistingly, and yet all the while ornamentally. Sometimes it is roundabout and confusing; often it has the appearance of straightforwardness. Take, for instance, the word *choice*, beloved of modern politicians. It is appealing because of its connotations of freedom. Yet frequently it implies opportunity where none is available. When faced with the choices so enthusiastically heralded, we find that we are expected to pick from an array of options that are tediously similar and perhaps equally undesirable. We know what a choice is, and we like the idea in principle, but talk of *choice* in practice masks lack of flexibility – or sanitizes selfishness and unreasonableness.

We have had a tremendous amount of exposure to advertising – enough, one might think, to be able to resist its persuasive strategies – but still we are dazzled by it. And when I say 'advertising', I mean more than just TV commercials and the glossy spreads in magazines. Traditional 'interruption marketing' (a term coined by the marketing expert Seth Godin) is being supplemented by new strategies that seek to emphasize the sensuousness of products and our relationships with them. Advertising is a pervasive feature of modern living. It clutters our environment, and increasingly it seeps into places we would tend to think of as sacrosanct, such as schools. While it often addresses us directly, it also uses subliminal messages to prime our preferences. The language of advertising is coded; though typically positive, exaggerated and repetitive, its persuasiveness can be indirect. But the idea of consumption is threaded through our lives. We are consumers first, citizens second. The package matters more than the product. A particularly insidious development has been the supplanting of need by desire at the heart of our culture – or rather, the smudging of our idea of what it is to 'need' something; for 'need' has become intimately bound up with 'want'.

Re-packaging is the way to change perception: to make the merely desirable seem necessary, and also to make the undesirable less appalling. Do you, for instance, remember 'global warming'? You could hardly fail to. Now it's more often 'climate change', which is arguably more accurate – and definitely sounds less sinister. Imagine if we called it 'global heating' or 'global burn-up': for many this would seem too patently emotive, but it would foster a different kind of debate about climate, politics and the future. 'Intelligent design' sounds scientific and credible, where 'creationism' does not. (To whom, I wonder, is the intelligence being attributed – the designer, or by foxy implication the theorists who push the idea of intelligent design?) In aviation there are 'safety events', which traditionally have been called 'near misses'; in finance there is 'subprime' lending, aimed at borrowers with no credentials; in many fields there is 'standard procedure', which is a pompous way of denoting an arbitrary, probably stupid and possibly also costly way of doing something that most of us, exercising a little discretion, could briskly polish off. 'Crime' is repositioned as 'tragedy'. A much older example is the 'concentration camp'; 'death camp' would be nearer the mark. 'Ethnic cleansing' sanitizes the practice more damningly known as 'genocide'; 'extraordinary rendition', though many now understand it to mean something along the lines of 'torture by proxy', sounds like a sophisticated and important legal process; and 'torture' itself is often more nebulously presented as 'abuse'.

These are not ordinary euphemisms, designed to shield us from unpleasant odours. Normally euphemisms are exercises in discretion, which conceal from us what we actually know is there: when a friend pops off 'to powder her nose' I know she's going to excrete some waste matter, but on the whole she is not desperately keen for me to think about this, and I am happy enough to be complicit, since it means I am spared an image of her discharging this waste. However, these new pumped-up euphemisms conceal from us a truth we want to see, and they are used not out of a concern for modesty (be it mine or the user's) but out of a concern to keep sensitive or embarrassing information from flowing freely to places where it may cause dissent.

The use of the passive voice is another technique of denial; it adjusts our focus by changing the grammatical subject of a sentence. Conventionally, whatever is of greatest interest or importance in a sentence is made its subject. Consider the difference between the active statement 'We shot the protester' and the passive 'The protester was shot by us'. Then note how often in the passive version the statement is clipped short; so, instead of 'We shot the protester', one learns only that 'The protester was shot'. Even before 'by us' is removed, the focus has been shifted on to the protester (and on to the fact of his being a protester); the next step is easy, and it gets rid of the embarrassing little matter of agency. Instead of saying 'I made mistakes', the politician says that 'Mistakes were made' – a favourite formula of Richard Nixon's. A feature of this rhetorical device is its implication that the mistakes were made *by someone else*.

Besides the language of denial, there is a language of self-legitimation, in which the names things are given are used to justify the way they are treated. Not euphemism, then, and not dysphemism (which is substituting a nasty word for a pleasant or at least innocuous one), but 'dyslogy', which is the opposite of eulogy. *Terrorist*, a word which was originally a badge of honour during the French Revolution, has become a conveniently alarmist way of denoting rebels, enemies, freedom fighters, insurgents.

As Steven Poole has commented, a related and loaded term is 'terrorist suspect' (or 'terror suspect'). A *suspect* is someone who is under suspicion and is being accused, but who has not yet been found guilty. Yet by attaching the word *terrorist* to the suspect, one signals an assumption of guilt. As Poole puts it, 'the person is first defined as a terrorist . . . and only then is it grudgingly acknowledged that the basis for such a categorisation is as yet untested.'[1] Similar in effect is 'legitimate force', which justifies the use of force – perhaps to restrain a prisoner – by implying that the degree of force used was judged to be within the law at the time it was used, even though in fact any such judgement will have happened retrospectively, if at all.

Poole writes with appealing clarity about the peculiar weaponry of modern public discourse. He clearly has a following. But his reasonable voice struggles to be heard above the cacophonous orations of the public figures and popular writers he decries. We have become pitifully familiar with government-endorsed sophistry and the flatulent rhetoric of politicians and political pundits. This is not exclusive to English-speaking nations; it probably goes on everywhere.

In several of his essays George Orwell wrote about the worn-out metaphors, pretentiousness and obscurantism of political language, and he has become a touchstone for all who tackle this subject. In 'Propaganda and Demotic Speech', published in 1944, he emphasized the gulf between language as presented in political writing and language as it is used by people in their normal lives. In pamphlets, manifestos and the statements made by government spokespeople, 'clear, popular, everyday language seems to be instinctively avoided'.[2] To be effective, he argued, political language needed to be ordinary and colloquial.

Orwell returned to this subject in an essay published in *Horizon* in April 1946. 'Politics and the English Language' discussed at greater length the defects of the language used by politicians and political writers. It has become his most-cited essay. As I hope I have made clear by now, I think the two nouns in its title are inextricably linked; the first two words of the title could be considered redundant. Orwell was not the first to examine the abuse of language for political ends. Locke, for instance, saw the 'affected obscurity' and 'learned gibberish' of different sects as posing a threat to 'humane life and society', bringing 'confusion, disorder, and uncertainty into the affairs of mankind' and, if not destroying, certainly rendering useless 'those two great rules, religion and justice'.[3] But Orwell has become the person commentators and arbiters turn to when in need of crisply phrased support.

In his *Horizon* essay Orwell spoke of language as an instrument for expressing thought rather than preventing it. We are familiar with the idea that language enables us to express our thoughts, but we are attuned to the ways in which this goes awry; we are attuned also to the suggestion by the French diplomat Talleyrand that language really exists to hide our thoughts – which Søren Kierkegaard amended, claiming that many people use language to conceal the fact of their not having any thoughts. Kierkegaard's *bon mot* would have appealed to Orwell, whose focus was the way the corruption of language engendered distortions of thought. The engine of this corruption was, he argued, the political imperative to defend the indefensible: in support of grotesque or fatuous policies, the authors of political speeches and statements need to deploy a massive arsenal of euphemisms, clichés, inflations and smoke-bombs. If we express ourselves in a pretentious and obscure fashion, falling back on prefabricated phrases and decayed metaphors, we are doomed to succumb to foolish thoughts. Orwell praised the careful, the concrete, the simple. He was reviving the principles of the Royal Society, which from its foundation pressed for straightforward expression.

Orwell probably developed his views while serving in the Indian Imperial Police in Burma in the 1920s. Colonial English was steeped in overcomplicated orthodoxy. As a remedy Orwell proposed certain rules. Although superficially they are rules of language, really they are recommendations about how we should think. To simplify one's English is to free oneself from 'the worst follies of orthodoxy'. This is his code:

(i) Never use a metaphor, simile or other figure of speech which you are used to seeing in print.

(ii) Never use a long word where a short one will do.

(iii) If it is possible to cut a word out, always cut it out.

(iv) Never use the passive where you can use the active.

(v) Never use a foreign phrase, a scientific word, or a jargon word if you can think of an everyday English equivalent.

(vi) Break any of these rules sooner than say anything outright barbarous.[4]

These are not far removed from the practical rules laid down by the Fowlers. They might well have pleased William Barnes and Percy Grainger, too. But Orwell's motives are different from theirs. His main purpose is to try and ensure that there remains a language fit for reasoned political debate. The objection to the passive voice was one Orwell may well have learnt from Arthur Quiller-Couch, who demonized it in *The Art of Writing* (1916), a book he could have come across at school. It's also, incidentally, a principle that Orwell often violates – not least in this very essay, where roughly a fifth of his sentences use passive constructions. In fact, there is such a construction in his opening sentence: 'Most people who bother with the matter at all would admit that the English language is in a bad way, but it is generally assumed that we cannot by conscious action do anything about it.' In accordance with his third principle, the words 'by conscious action' should be cut, too.

Orwell created a model that has proved immensely popular, and the six precepts have been repeated time and again. His declared inheritors include the Plain English Campaign, an organization which since 1979 has been campaigning against poor expression. The Campaign offers editorial services and runs training courses. Since 1990 it has awarded something called a 'Crystal Mark' to documents and websites that its staff consider admirably clear. In case you are wondering what the criteria for achieving a Crystal Mark may be, they include 'an average sentence length of 15 to 20 words', 'the use of lists', and 'words like "we" and "you" instead of "the Society" or "the applicant" '.⁵ Obviously, too, you need to pay a fee to the Campaign. Pretty quickly it becomes clear that the Plain English Campaign is a business, not a force for universal enlightenment, and that it is bent on promoting its activities. One of the most visible of these is its Golden Bull Award, which publicly ridicules examples of gobbledygook. In many cases these are statements by building societies and local councils. A lot of them are undeniably daft. But the Campaign has mistakenly labelled some serviceable words as clichés (I feel bound to reiterate that a single word is never a cliché), and has derided some perfectly sensible utterances. For instance, it mocked Donald Rumsfeld's statement that 'Reports that say that something hasn't happened are always interesting to me, because as we know, there are known knowns; there are things we know we know. We also know there are known unknowns; that is to say we know there are some things we do not know. But there are also unknown unknowns – the ones we don't know we don't know.' Whatever you might have thought of Rumsfeld otherwise, this was an astute observation, and it could hardly have been better expressed. Gobbledygook it was not.

It is a mistake to think that plainness is always adequate. A 1986 publication entitled *The Plain English Story*, which is a manifesto for the Campaign, concludes with a quotation from Henry David Thoreau: 'Our life is frittered away by detail . . . Simplify, simplify.'⁶ The quotation is from *Walden*, Thoreau's account of his two-year retreat from society in the 1840s, and the simplicity he had in mind was of life, not language. The words immediately following 'Simplify, simplify' are 'Instead of three meals a day, if it be necessary eat but one'. It sounds austere, but the key words are 'if it be necessary'. Thoreau wants people to revise their idea of what they need. Shortly afterwards he says he could do without the post office, claiming that in all his life he has not received more than one or two letters that were worth the postage. 'And I am sure,' he continues, 'that I never read any memorable news in a newspaper.' I am sure that Thoreau, a great writer but one whose convoluted metaphysics meant that his gestures of simplicity were deeply self-conscious, is not a perfect model for modern living. Details, or what William Blake called 'minute particulars', are often the threads of amazing truths, and in a world more complicated than that experienced by Thoreau in his woodland cabin on the shore of Walden Pond we frequently need something more subtle and onion-layered than a detail-free plain English.

Newspapers and broadcasters are happy to swallow statements by the Plain English Campaign and its kindred organizations. A BBC report in March 2009 revealed that the Local Government Association had compiled a list of the two hundred worst pieces of jargon used in the public sector. A spokeswoman for the Plain English Campaign was reported as saying, 'This gobbledygook has to go. Jargon has its place within professions but it should not be allowed to leak out to the public, as it causes confusion. It could even be used to cover up something more sinister. Churchill and Einstein were both plain speakers and they did OK. Councils should follow their lead.'[7] I am certainly not going to defend items on the LGA's list such as 'predictors of beaconicity'. But if it is true that 'jargon has its place within professions', it seems unlikely that it will not 'leak out' – particularly when the 'professions' in question are local and central government or any others where people are allowed to go home at the end of the working day. The notion that Churchill and Einstein were plain speakers is open to question, and their qualities as speakers are not relevant, since the people at fault are being judged mainly on their written documents. Besides, it is hard to believe that the affairs of local government in the twenty-first century are best conducted in a language modelled on that of an aristocratic politician who has been dead for nearly fifty years or a German-born theoretical physicist whose most famous statement is an equation.

Plain English is what we demand of others, while merrily carrying on with our own not-so-plainness. In any case, the use of language that isn't plain can be a form of tact. Some people feel that to name certain things – such as death, for instance, or sickness – is to invite them. The simplest way of saying something may be too emphatic. There are departments of life better served by Latin words than by Anglo-Saxon ones. And sometimes the furriness of words, rather than their declarative simplicity, is what makes them effective.

Moreover, there are some domains where plainness of expression causes a loss of vital detail. Scientific research would be an obvious example. You cannot discuss quantum mechanics or the different regions of the brain without using complex language. When critics complain of the obscurity of this language they are often revealing an antagonism to the things of which the language is used – a fear of its significance or of its complicated nature. There is a huge difference between the properly technical and the needlessly circumlocutory: one conveys the complexity of life, the other is fatigued by it.

What frustrates people who are attentive to the subtleties of communication is the way political language has absorbed the terminology of business and management, and has channelled it onward into education, healthcare and the military. One suspects that even in his more darkly satirical moments George Orwell could not have dreamt up such locutions as 'welfare pathway', 'knowledge transfer', 'deliberative dialogue', 'negative territory', 'core competency', 'non-hostile weapons discharge', 'bespoke methodology', 'performance management solutions', 'patient outcomes', 'wrongsiding the demographic' or a 'think-feel-do' model of practice. Nor could he have imagined Ronald Reagan's Secretary of State, General Alexander Haig, with his gift for expressions such as 'the vortex of cruciality' and for statements such as 'We must push this to a lower decibel of public fixation' and 'We do have a tendency to indulge in episodic preoccupation, if you will, with one another on the strategic horizon'. A more mundane example of this kind of thing, nevertheless salient, occurs in the diaries of the Labour politician Chris Mullin. Writing about his government's obsession with setting targets, Mullin mentions a colleague telling him that there 'had even been talk of setting targets for the number of people persuaded to walk to work. A later draft of our walking document had substituted "benchmarks" for "targets". Later still, "benchmarks" had given way to "reference indicators". Orwellian.'[8]

I have picked the terms above at random; we are daily faced with others far more poisonous. Indeed, the most toxic are the ones we no longer find wholly objectionable. The language of consumption, of 'consumer choice' and branded goods, makes us tourists in our everyday lives. When I visit the local library, travel on a train, receive medical care, deal with the UK Borders Agency or communicate with my local council, I am a 'customer' – the word in each case travestying the reality of the relationship.

What may not immediately be apparent but is surely significant is the failure of this type of language to invoke the tangible realities of the world around us. If we think about Chris Mullin's example, we immediately understand what is meant in this context by a target, and we fix upon its concrete associations. The question of whether it is sensible to set a target for the number of people walking to work is not important to me at present. Rather, I am concerned with the effects of using the word *target*. Personally, when I hear this word I think of archery, and the image, if I dwell on it, is visually satisfying. Talking in terms of a target implies the need for skill – good aim, a steady hand, and so on. The word *benchmark* is more obscure. It denotes a mark made by a surveyor with a chisel, which can later be referred back to, but, when I hear this word, I don't think of surveyors and their chisels. I know what the word means and am unlikely to puzzle over why it means what it does. Yet if I do think about this, I am likely to be confused by the 'bench' part of it. The 'mark' is fine, but the concrete associations of the whole word are unclear. Now let's move on to 'reference indicators'. There is scarcely a hint of anything reassuringly physical here. The term, when I try to anchor it in my physical experience, seems to swim away from me. If I grapple it into focus, I end up with a hazy image of attempting to locate something in a library.

Physical imagery is accessible and potent. This is not to condemn abstract terminology: we need a vocabulary of the abstract. In any case, all words are abstractions. The problem is not the use of abstract words *per se*. But the abstract terms we choose to employ are ineffectual and annoying when they evoke concrete associations that simply do not fit the experience under discussion. To put it differently, we like our abstract thoughts to be grounded in bodily experience. Not all thought is grounded there – and there are strata of thought that are deeper than metaphor – but metaphor captures reality, rather than merely projecting images on to it. A metaphor is not a comparison; it asserts the essence of a thing. To underscore a point from my previous chapter: well used, it is an aid to reason. As Steven Pinker observes, '*A lawyer is a shark* says much more than *A lawyer is like a shark*.'[9]

The political and commercial infatuation with the abstract is evident in the widespread use of Microsoft's PowerPoint. To quote Edward R. Tufte, described by the *New York Times* as 'the Leonardo da Vinci of data', this software package is 'a prankish conspiracy against substance and thought', which 'allows speakers to pretend they are giving a real talk and audiences to pretend that they are listening'.[10] Note that Tufte does not say that PowerPoint forces people to act in this way; rather, the program permits it. But maladroit use is the norm, and results in presentations made up of fractured discussion points and oversimplifications, which compress the true architecture of thought. The language of the PowerPoint-ed workplace is dehydrated.

More than fifty years ago Jacques Barzun wrote about the disappearance of *the* 'as if all prose should resemble signs and captions'. He gives as an example 'Appointment of Mr Jones was announced last night.'[11] 'The appointment of Mr Jones' has a definiteness that makes us think about the appointers as well as the appointee. Doing away with the article makes the information blurrily general. The next step is 'Jones appointment announcement'. This is an example of what is sometimes ironically dubbed the Noun Overuse Phenomenon.[12] Instead of being skint or hard-up or broke, someone is in a 'money shortage situation'. 'There are more people taking part' becomes 'Participation rate spike'. Perhaps my imagination is running away with me. But on 23 July 2005 the BBC's website really did open a news item with the headline 'Cell death mark liver cancer clue', and on 6 February 2010 I spotted 'Mobility scooter river fall death'. Is it a mark of our sedentary society that we seem averse to verbs? Is this concatenation of substantives an attempt to make a slippery world seem stable? People, it seems, are replaced by processes – not in motion, but in the abstract – and verbs of action make way for nouns. More generally, the stringing together of nouns can be seen as a symptom of the complexity and dizzy pace of life. But it's not as new as we may imagine: in *Barchester Towers* (1857), a progressive bishop is gently satirized by Anthony Trollope for proposing to set up something called the Bishop's Barchester Young Men's Sabbath Evening Lecture Room.

Much of the language of modern public discourse magnifies the trivial. We live in an age of experts, and experts like to create mystique about their expertise. *Expert*, incidentally, is one of those words that has drifted away from its etymological moorings. It once denoted someone with experience; now it denotes a person who has a record of making mistakes. At the same time, much of what is debated in the political sphere is technically complicated. The issues surrounding, say, stem cell research are too elaborate to be communicated in a straightforward way. Instead of analysing and evaluating the content of what we are told, we may simply judge the people who do the telling. This accounts for the emphasis modern politicians place on their reasonableness and personal qualities. It also suggests, if we move beyond politics, why celebrity endorsements have become so important. The science behind many new products is far too complex to be explained, but an association with a trusted and revered public figure means the science does not need explaining. Or rather, that is how we are meant to feel.

28 Envoi

The word is 'very self'

I began by asking why issues of grammar, spelling and punctuation trouble us, and why we are so concerned with other people's accents and the words they use. As I tentatively suggested then, the answer is that language is at the heart of our lives. It is the instrument that has enabled us to create the world in which we live together.

We contest language because it is so important to our relationships and to our definitions and images of our selves. When I was a child I was presented with the schoolyard wisdom that 'Sticks and stones may break my bones, but words will never hurt me'. Soon enough I gathered that this was not true. Language can hurt us because we are linguistic creatures: language makes our world – we are constituted by it, or within it – and we are therefore vulnerable to it.[1] There is an irony at work here, too, for by repeating this little incantation we perform a feat of word magic: we can chant, or simply speak, our convictions into bloom.

Here is the schoolmaster John Yeomans, writing in 1759:

> Words are not, as some gross ears interpret, only a grinding or chafeing of sound of types and letters, striking the outer ear by the operation of the breath or spirit; but they are very man or mono, principle and very self, everlasting, of infinite, dread-united meaning, the express disposition of his nature in the heart, and not in the inked or graven sign. They are spirit, and they are life; they are death, and they are destruction . . . The word is very God and very Devil, good and evil, virtue and vice; and letters are as shadows.[2]

This is alarmingly expressed, but vividly also. It reminds me of the opening of John's Gospel: 'In the beginning was the Word, and the Word was with God, and the Word was God.' *In the beginning was the word* – and the word, we infer, will be present at the end.

Statements about the power of language are often couched in religious imagery. But when we talk about language, we are not always acclaiming its power: we lament its inadequacies and its obstructions, absolving ourselves of failings by blaming the organs of delivery. We speak of it as something diabolical, an affliction, a sickness; as broken, fallen or blunted. At the end of his book *The Stuff of Thought*, Steven Pinker writes, 'Language is not just a window into human nature but a fistula: an open wound through which our innards are exposed to an infectious world.'³ The sense that our linguistic constitution is fragile is one of the reasons that people invent rules about usage.

Rules are a sort of armour. Yet rule-makers miss out on the dynamism of speech. Language is democratic. Although linguistic dogma may impress many, confirming their view of the world, it is temporary. Time eats away at its pillars. In any case, the people who dole out corrections invariably include a few incorrections of their own.

We need to be more careful when we talk about the 'rules' of English. There *are* rules, which are really mental mechanisms that carry out operations to combine words into meaningful arrangements. Then there are principles: 'Express yourself clearly', 'Say no more than circumstances require', 'Keep to what is relevant'. And there are conventions: at the start of a letter to the male editor of a newspaper I write 'Dear Sir', and I sign off my letter with the words 'Yours faithfully'. The mental mechanisms are beyond our conscious control. The rest is within our power.

When we write, and also when we speak, we should pay attention to the needs and expectations of our audience, and we should never forget that we are part of that audience. In most cases, adhering to the conventions is the right decision. They are worth learning, because they enable lucid communication, and they are worth teaching. But, from an educational perspective, penalizing someone who starts every third sentence with 'And' is of less value than showing why a more varied style is preferable.

Our education never stops. We are forever learning about the effects of our use of language on the people with whom we converse. We learn the value of precision and clarity, much of the time by discovering the sore consequences of their absence. We learn, too, the usefulness of formality, as well as the occasions when formality can and even should be dropped, and we come to understand how we can be exposed by shibboleths. We master the virtues of unobtrusiveness and the versatility of standard usage. We learn that change is incessant, and that amid change there is a core of continuity.

Disputes over meaning and standards are unavoidable, and it is naïve to think that they are a special feature of our moment in history. Dig beneath the present, and instead of hitting something solid you open what appears to be a bottomless shaft into the past. If today's arguments about English seem louder and nastier than ever before, it is because they are played out through mass media, where violent imagery is normal.

Some of the language wars that are being waged today are vicious. They have grave consequences for those caught up in them. To most native speakers of English, those wars seem remote. But the future of English is not something that should be contemplated with serenity. It is worth emphasizing that, up to the present day, the most important things that have happened to English have happened in England. Worth emphasizing because in the future this will not hold true.

In the meantime there are the smaller conflicts we experience from day to day. These are in many instances eloquent about matters that otherwise find limited expression: who we think we are, where we come from, how we know what we 'know'.

Reflecting on this, I am reminded of the following deliberately improper sentence, which appeared in the *New York Times* in September 2009: 'So I say outpedant the pedants, and allow yourself to gluttonously revel in the linguistic improprieties of yore as you familiarize yourself with the nearly unique enormity of the gloriously mistaken heritage that our literature is comprised of.'[4]

The pedants are not often comprehensively outpedanted. They will usually fight back, and they are not about to go away. Their intransigence is occasionally risible. Yet, undeniably, they stimulate thought about language. That is vital, because we need to engage with language – and yes, with our language – critically. We tend to discuss it in a cantakerous or petulant way, but thinking and talking about what makes good English good and bad English bad can be, and should be, a pleasure.

Acknowledgements

In the course of writing this book I have incurred many debts of gratitude. As ever, I have drawn with pleasure on the resources of *The Oxford English Dictionary* and *The Oxford Dictionary of National Biography*. Most of my research was carried out in the British Library, and I would like to thank its staff for their assistance.

I am grateful for help of various kinds to Jag Bhalla, Jane Birkett, Jonty Claypole, Angela Cox, David Crystal, Nick de Somogyi, Bernard Dive, Robert Douglas-Fairhurst, Lesley Downer, Jonathon Green, Stephen Harrison, Jenny Hewson, Gesche Ipsen, Kwasi Kwarteng, Guy Ladenburg, Victoria Murray-Browne, Terttu Nevalainen, Jeremy Noel-Tod, Michael Quinion, Anna Saura, James Scudamore, Jesse Sheidlower, James Spackman, Ingrid Tieken-Boon van Ostade and Mary Wellesley. I must also mention two websites that have alerted me to news items I would otherwise have missed: Language Log, a blog launched in 2003 by Mark Liberman and Geoffrey Pullum, which can be found at http://languagelog.ldc.upenn.edu/nll/, and Steven Poole's Unspeak, which is at http://unspeak.net/.

Especially warm thanks are due to Richard Arundel, Robert Macfarlane and Leo Robson, as well as to Jack Lynch, who kindly shared his book *The Lexicographer's Dilemma* with me before its publication.

Finally, I reserve deep gratitude for my agent Peter Straus, my generous and sensitive editor Eleanor Birne, and my parents.

Notes

Chapter 1: 'To boldly go'

1. The short answer is that the former is dismissed because it is considered ugly, the latter because it seems pretentious. See 'The Awful Rise of "Snuck"', *The Awl*, 1 December 2009, http://www.theawl.com/2009/12/the-awful-rise-of-snuck, retrieved 17 June 2010. See also 'Some Common Solecisms' in *The Economist* Style Guide, http://www.economist.com/research/styleGuide/index.cfm?page=673903, retrieved 26 June 2010.

2. See Alan D. Sokal, 'Transgressing the Boundaries: Towards a Transformative Hermeneutics of Quantum Gravity', *Social Text* 46/47 (1996), 217–52.

3. Quoted in Kenneth Cmiel, *Democratic Eloquence: The Fight over Popular Speech in Nineteenth-Century America* (New York: William Morrow, 1990), 239.

4. D. A. Russell and M. Winterbottom (eds), *Ancient Literary Criticism: The Principal Texts in New Translations* (Oxford: Clarendon Press, 1972), 305–6.

5. William Dwight Whitney, *Language and the Study of Language* (London: Trübner, 1867), 48.

6. Ibid., 32.

7. Jacques Barzun, *Simple and Direct: A Rhetoric for Writers*, rev. edn (New York: Harper & Row, 1985), 207–9.

8. Some nice examples of invective against the usage of, among others, tailors, upholsterers and 'the architects of pastry' can be found in Richard W. Bailey, *Images of English: A Cultural History of the Language* (Cambridge: Cambridge University Press, 1991), 239–44.

9. See Deborah Cameron, *Verbal Hygiene* (London: Routledge, 1995), 218–19.

10. See Robin Tolmach Lakoff, *The Language War* (Berkeley: University of California Press, 2001), 75–6.

11. Jack Lynch, *The Lexicographer's Dilemma: The Evolution of 'Proper' English from Shakespeare to South Park* (New York: Walker, 2009), 97–8.
12. Steven Pinker, *The Language Instinct* (London: Penguin, 1995), 374.

Chapter 2: The survival machine

1. Leonard Bloomfield, *An Introduction to the Study of Language* (London: G. Bell, 1914), 17.
2. Malcolm Gladwell examines this in detail in his book *Outliers: The Story of Success* (London: Allen Lane, 2008).
3. I have been strongly influenced in my selection of cultural baggage by Anna Wierzbicka, *English: Meaning and Culture* (Oxford: Oxford University Press, 2006).
4. Noam Chomsky, *Language and Responsibility* (London: Harvester, 1979), 191.
5. See Jean-Louis Dessalles, *Why We Talk: The Evolutionary Origins of Language*, trans. James Grieve (Oxford: Oxford University Press, 2007), 282.
6. Jonathan Cott (ed.), *Dylan on Dylan: The Essential Interviews* (London: Hodder & Stoughton, 2006), 100.
7. Quoted in Ronald Carter, *Investigating English Discourse: Language, Literacy and Literature* (London: Routledge, 1997), 7.
8. My answer to this question draws on Otto Jespersen, *Mankind, Nation and Individual from a Linguistic Point of View* (Oslo: Aschehoug, 1925), 94–122.
9. Oliver Bell Bunce, *Don't: A Manual of Mistakes and Improprieties more or less prevalent in Conduct and Speech*, 3rd edn (London: Field & Tuer, 1884), 66, 45, 61.
10. Ian Michael, *The Teaching of English: From the Sixteenth Century to 1870* (Cambridge: Cambridge University Press, 1987), 380.
11. William Mather, *The Young Man's Companion*, 2nd edn (London: Thomas Howkins, 1685), 267, 279, 288.

Chapter 3: The emergence of English

1. Thorlac Turville-Petre, *England the Nation: Language, Literature, and National Identity, 1290–1340* (Oxford: Clarendon Press, 1996), 11–26.
2. Albert C. Baugh and Thomas Cable, *A History of the English Language*, 5th edn (Upper Saddle River, NJ: Prentice-Hall, 2002), 154.
3. D. G. Scragg, *A History of English Spelling* (Manchester: Manchester University Press, 1974), 7–8.

4. The subject is covered in detail by Michael Benskin in an article on 'Chancery Standard' in Christian Kay, Carole Hough and Irené Wotherspoon (eds), *New Perspectives on English Historical Linguistics: Lexis and Transmission* (Amsterdam: John Benjamins, 2004), 1–40.

5. David Crystal, *The Stories of English* (London: Allen Lane, 2004), 253.

6. Ibid., 252.

7. Ben Jonson, *The English Grammar* (London: Richard Meighen, 1640), 36. The first version of this work was destroyed by fire in 1623; Jonson put together a second version roughly a decade later.

8. Elizabeth L. Eisenstein, *The Printing Revolution in Early Modern Europe*, 2nd edn (Cambridge: Cambridge University Press, 2005), 62.

Chapter 4: From Queen Elizabeth to John Locke

1. This is convincingly explored in Richard Helgerson, *Forms of Nationhood: The Elizabethan Writing of England* (Chicago: University of Chicago Press, 1992).

2. This idea is investigated by Helen Hackett in *Shakespeare and Elizabeth: The Meeting of Two Myths* (Princeton, NJ: Princeton University Press, 2009).

3. Voltaire, visiting in 1728, noticed that Shakespeare is 'rarely called anything but "divine"'. See James Shapiro, *Contested Will: Who Wrote Shakespeare?* (New York: Simon & Schuster, 2010), 30.

4. Edward Brerewood, *Enquiries Touching the Diversity of Languages, and Religions* (London: John Bill, 1614), 42.

5. Charles Barber, *Early Modern English*, 2nd edn (Edinburgh: Edinburgh University Press, 1997), 52–3.

6. See William Nelson, 'The Teaching of English in Tudor Grammar Schools', *Studies in Philology* 49 (1952), 119–43.

7. Richard Mulcaster, *The First Part of the Elementarie* (London: Thomas Vautroullier, 1582), 81–2, 254.

8. *The Diary of Virginia Woolf*, vol. 3 (1925–30), ed. Anne Olivier Bell (Harmondsworth: Penguin, 1982), 300–1.

9. Thomas Nashe, *The Works of Thomas Nashe*, ed. Ronald B. McKerrow, 5 vols (London: A. H. Bullen, 1904), II, 183–5.

10. William Camden, *Remaines of a Greater Worke, Concerning Britaine* (London: Simon Waterson, 1605), 21.

11. Richard Verstegan, *A Restitution of Decayed Intelligence* (Antwerp: Robert Bruney, 1605), 204.

12. Jonathan Bate, *Soul of the Age: The Life, Mind and World of William Shakespeare* (London: Viking, 2009), 83–4.

13. Jonson, *The English Grammar*, 33.

14. John Wallis, *Grammatica Linguae Anglicanae* (Oxford: Leonard Lichfield, 1653), Praefatio.

15. Murray Cohen, *Sensible Words: Linguistic Practice in England 1640–1785* (Baltimore: Johns Hopkins University Press, 1977), 10–14.

16. Francis Lodwick, *A Common Writing* (privately printed, 1647), 20.

17. John Wilkins, *An Essay Towards a Real Character and Philosophical Language* (London: Gellibrand & Martyn, 1668), 386.

18. Francis Bacon, *The New Organon*, ed. Lisa Jardine and Michael Silverthorne (Cambridge: Cambridge University Press, 2000), 42.

19. Thomas Hobbes, *Leviathan*, ed. Richard Tuck (Cambridge: Cambridge University Press, 1991), 26–28.

20. John Locke, *An Essay Concerning Human Understanding*, ed. Peter H. Nidditch (Oxford: Clarendon Press, 1975), 405.

Chapter 5: Hitting le Jackpot

1. Nicola Woolcock, 'Pedants' revolt aims to stop English being lost for words', *The Times*, 7 June 2010.

2. Joseph Glanvill, *The Vanity of Dogmatizing* (London: E. Cotes, 1661), 226.

3. Joseph Glanvill, *Essays on Several Important Subjects in Philosophy and Religion* (London: J. D., 1676), 29.

4. Daniel Defoe, *An Essay upon Projects* (London: Thomas Cockerill, 1697), 233–41.

5. Jonathan Swift, *A Proposal for Correcting, Improving and Ascertaining the English Tongue* (London: Benjamin Tooke, 1712), 8, 18–19, 24–5, 30–31.

6. John Oldmixon, *Reflections on Dr Swift's Letter to the Earl of Oxford, About the English Tongue* (London: A. Baldwin, 1712), 27.

7. Jonathan Swift, *A Letter to a Young Gentleman, Lately Enter'd into Holy Orders*, 2nd edn (London: J. Roberts, 1721), 5–6, 11.

8. John Knowles, *The Principles of English Grammar*, 4th edn (London: Vernor & Hood, 1796), 1.

9. John Mullan, *Sentiment and Sociability: The Language of Feeling in the Eighteenth Century* (Oxford: Clarendon Press, 1990), 5.

10. Quoted in Robin Adamson, *The Defence of French* (Clevedon: Multilingual Matters, 2007), 27.

11. This is discussed in Ryan J. Stark, *Rhetoric, Science and Magic in Seven-*

teenth-Century England (Washington, DC: Catholic University of America Press, 2009), 177–80.

12. I owe this insight to Laura L. Runge, who explores Dryden's 'gendered' writing in her *Gender and Language in British Literary Criticism, 1660–1790* (Cambridge: Cambridge University Press, 1997), 40–79.

Chapter 6: The rough magic of English spelling

1. A. Lane, *A Key to the Art of Letters* (London: A. & J. Churchil, 1700), 6.

2. This subject is discussed in N. E. Osselton, 'Spelling-Book Rules and the Capitalization of Nouns in the Seventeenth and Eighteenth Centuries' in Mary-Jo Arn and Hanneke Wirtjes (eds), *Historical and Editorial Studies in Medieval and Early Modern English* (Groningen: Wolters-Noordhoff, 1985).

3. Lindley Murray, *English Grammar* (York: Wilson, Spence & Mawman, 1795), 174.

4. Manfred Görlach, *Eighteenth-Century English* (Heidelberg: Winter, 2001), 81.

5. Daniel Fenning, *The Universal Spelling Book* (London: Crowder & Woodgate, 1756), 96.

6. Quoted in John Carey, *William Golding: The Man Who Wrote Lord of the Flies* (London: Faber, 2009), x.

7. Walter W. Skeat, *Principles of English Etymology* (Oxford: Clarendon Press, 1892), 323–4.

8. Edward Carney, *A Survey of English Spelling* (London: Routledge, 1994), 86–94.

9. Florian Coulmas, *Writing Systems: An Introduction to their Linguistic Analysis* (Cambridge: Cambridge University Press, 2003), 182.

10. Pinker, *The Language Instinct*, 190.

11. John Hart, *An Orthographie* (London: W. Serres, 1569), 2, 5.

12. William Bullokar, *Aesop's Fables in True Orthography* (London: Edmund Bollifant, 1585), 31.

13. Mulcaster, *The First Part of the Elementarie*, 121–2.

14. Details from Anthony G. Petti, *English Literary Hands from Chaucer to Dryden* (London: Edward Arnold, 1977).

15. Examples from Lynda Mugglestone, 'English in the Nineteenth Century', in Mugglestone (ed.), *The Oxford History of English* (Oxford: Oxford University Press, 2006), 279–80.

16. H. G. Wells, *Certain Personal Matters: A Collection of Material, Mainly Autobiographical* (London: Lawrence & Bullen, 1898), 145–7.

17. David Wolman, *Righting the Mother Tongue: From Olde English to Email, the Tangled Story of English Spelling* (New York: Collins, 2008), 115.

18. Quoted in Richard L. Venezky, *The American Way of Spelling: The Structure and Origins of American English Orthography* (New York: Guilford Press, 1999), 228, n. 56.

19. Wolman, *Righting the Mother Tongue*, 121.

20. H. G. Wells, *Mankind in the Making* (London: Chapman & Hall, 1903), 217.

Chapter 7: The many advantages of a good language

1. Edward Sapir, *Language: An Introduction to the Study of Speech* (New York: Harcourt Brace, 1921), 38.

2. Sir Henry Newbolt et al., *The Teaching of English in England* (London: His Majesty's Stationery Office, 1921), 282, 289–90, 293.

3. Thomas Wilson, *The Many Advantages of a Good Language to Any Nation* (London: Knapton, Knaplock et al., 1724), 6.

4. Ian Michael, *English Grammatical Categories and the Tradition to 1800* (Cambridge: Cambridge University Press, 1970), 208, 507.

5. H. G. Wells, *An Englishman Looks at the World* (London: Cassell, 1914), 224.

6. Wells, *Mankind in the Making*, 220–21.

7. Sterling A. Leonard, *The Doctrine of Correctness in English Usage 1700–1800* (Madison: University of Wisconsin Studies in Language and Literature, 1929), 76.

8. George Snell, *The Right Teaching of Useful Knowledg* (London: W. Dugard, 1649), 49, 176–80.

9. The subject is beguilingly discussed in Nicholas Ostler, *Ad Infinitum: A Biography of Latin* (New York: Walker, 2007).

10. John Stirling, *A Short View of English Grammar*, 2nd edn (London: T. Astley, 1740).

11. Alvin Kernan, *Samuel Johnson and the Impact of Print* (Princeton, NJ: Princeton University Press, 1989), 70.

12. Lynch, *The Lexicographer's Dilemma*, 45.

13. Joan C. Beal, *English in Modern Times, 1700–1945* (London: Arnold, 2004), 9.

14. *Monthly Review* 33 (1765), 20–21.

Chapter 8: 'Bishop Lowth was a fool'

1. Samuel Johnson, *Johnson on the English Language*, ed. Gwin J. Kolb and Robert DeMaria (New Haven, CT: Yale University Press, 2005), 109.
2. Ibid., 108–9.
3. Hugh Blair, *Lectures on Rhetoric and Belles Lettres*, ed. Harold F. Harding, 2 vols (Carbondale: Southern Illinois University Press, 1965), I, 173–4.
4. *Johnson on the English Language*, 301.
5. Ibid., 102–3.
6. Ibid., 74, 84, 92, 105.
7. Ibid., 73, 100.
8. This argument is developed at length by Carol Percy in 'Periodical reviews and the rise of prescriptivism', in Ingrid Tieken-Boon van Ostade and Wim van der Wurff (eds), *Current Issues in Late Modern English* (Bern: Peter Lang, 2009), 117–50.
9. See Karlijn Navest, 'An index of names to Lowth's *Short Introduction to English Grammar* (1762), (1763), (1764)', *Historical Sociolinguistics and Sociohistorical Linguistics* 6 (2006).
10. Robert Lowth, *A Short Introduction to English Grammar* (London: Millar, Dodsley & Dodsley, 1762), 157–8.
11. Ibid., 43, 48, n., 93, n.
12. Ibid., 125, 48–9, 99, 76.
13. Mikko Laitinen, 'Singular YOU WAS/WERE variation and English normative grammars in the eighteenth century', in Arja Nurmi, Minna Nevala and Minna Palander-Collin (eds), *The Language of Daily Life in England (1400–1800)* (Amsterdam: John Benjamins, 2009), 199–217.
14. Robert Lowth, *A Short Introduction to English Grammar*, 2nd edn (London: Millar, Dodsley & Dodsley, 1763), 63.
15. Ibid., 139.
16. Cited in E. Ward Gilman (ed.), *Merriam-Webster's Dictionary of English Usage* (Springfield, MA: Merriam-Webster, 1994), 365.
17. 'Two *Negatives*, or two *Adverbs* of *Denying* do in *English* affirm' – James Greenwood, *An Essay Towards a Practical English Grammar* (London: R. Tookey, 1711), 160.
18. Robert Baker, *Reflections on the English Language* (London: J. Bell, 1770), 112–13.
19. Lowth, *A Short Introduction to English Grammar*, (1762), 1, 7.
20. Lowth, *A Short Introduction to English Grammar*, 2nd edn (1763), 63.
21. Lowth, *A Short Introduction to English Grammar* (1762), 158–9, 155.
22. Ibid., 35–6.

23. Philip Withers, *Aristarchus, or The Principles of Composition* (London: J. Moore, 1788), 23.

24. Lowth, *A Short Introduction to English Grammar* (1762), 127.

25. Ibid., 9, 15.

26. See Ingrid Tieken-Boon van Ostade, 'Robert Lowth and the strong verb system', *Language Sciences* 24 (2002), 459–69; 'Lowth's Language', in Marina Dossena and Charles Jones (eds), *Insights into Late Modern English* (Bern: Peter Lang, 2003), 241–64; and 'Eighteenth-century Prescriptivism and the Norm of Correctness', in Ans van Kemenade and Bettelou Los (eds), *The Handbook of the History of English* (Oxford: Blackwell, 2006), 539–57.

27. John Barrell, *English Literature in History 1730–80: An Equal, Wide Survey* (London: Hutchinson, 1983), 141–2.

28. William B. Hodgson, *Errors in the Use of English* (Edinburgh: David Douglas, 1881), iii.

29. Wells, *Certain Personal Matters*, 148.

30. An excellent account of changing prose styles in this period is Carey McIntosh, *The Evolution of English Prose, 1700–1800* (Cambridge: Cambridge University Press, 1998).

31. Quoted in Lynda Mugglestone, *Talking Proper: The Rise and Fall of the English Accent as a Social Symbol*, 2nd edn (Oxford: Oxford University Press, 2007), 181.

32. Joseph Priestley, *The Rudiments of English Grammar* (London: R. Griffiths, 1761), vii.

33. Ibid., vii, 56–7.

34. Ibid., x–xi.

35. See Jane Hodson, 'Joseph Priestley's two *Rudiments of English Grammar*: 1761 and 1768' in Ingrid Tieken-Boon van Ostade (ed.), *Grammars, Grammarians and Grammar-Writing in Eighteenth-Century England* (Berlin: Mouton de Gruyter, 2008), 177–89.

36. Joseph Priestley, *The Rudiments of English Grammar*, 2nd edn (London: Becket, De Hondt & Johnson, 1768), xxiii.

37. This is explored in detail in Robin Straaijer, 'Deontic and epistemic modals as indicators of prescriptive and descriptive language in the grammars by Joseph Priestley and Robert Lowth', in Tieken-Boon van Ostade and van der Wurff (eds), *Current Issues in Late Modern English*, 57–87.

38. Priestley, *The Rudiments of English Grammar*, 58.

Chapter 9: O my America, my new found land!

1. *Gentleman's Magazine* 22 (1752), 281.
2. Thomas Gustafson, *Representative Words: Politics, Literature, and the American Language, 1776–1865* (Cambridge: Cambridge University Press, 1992), 198.
3. Thomas Paine, *Rights of Man, Common Sense, and Other Political Writings*, ed. Mark Philp (Oxford: Oxford University Press, 1995), 53–4.
4. Ibid., 147.
5. Ibid., 132.
6. Quoted in David Simpson, *The Politics of American English, 1776–1850* (New York: Oxford University Press, 1986), 29.
7. Frederic G. Cassidy, 'Geographical Variation of English in the United States', in Richard W. Bailey and Manfred Görlach (eds), *English as a World Language* (Cambridge: Cambridge University Press, 1984), 186–7.
8. H. L. Mencken, *The American Language*, 4th edn (New York: Knopf, 1941), 117, 146.
9. Quoted in Allen Walker Read, *Milestones in the History of English in America*, ed. Richard W. Bailey (Durham, NC: American Dialect Society, 2002), 43.
10. Mencken, *The American Language*, 313.
11. Thomas Dilworth, *A New Guide to the English Tongue*, 13th edn (London: Henry Kent, 1751), 129–30.
12. *United States Democratic Review* 17 (1845), 5, 9.
13. Quoted in David Micklethwait, *Noah Webster and the American Dictionary* (Jefferson, NC: McFarland, 2000), 11.
14. The subject is covered at length in Makoto Ikeda, *Competing Grammars: Noah Webster's Vain Efforts to Defeat Lindley Murray* (Tokyo: Shinozaki Shorin, 1999).
15. Noah Webster, *A Grammatical Institute of the English Language*, 3 vols (Hartford: Connecticut, Hudson & Goodwin, 1783–5), I, 8, 10.
16. Noah Webster, *Dissertations on the English Language* (Boston: Isaiah Thomas, 1789), 24.
17. Ibid., viii.
18. *Dissertations on the English Language*, 394–5.
19. *A Grammatical Institute*, I, 14–15.
20. *Dissertations on the English Language*, 20.
21. Ezra Greenspan, 'Some Remarks on the Poetics of "Participle-Loving

Whitman"', in Greenspan (ed.), *The Cambridge Companion to Walt Whitman* (Cambridge: Cambridge University Press, 1995), 94.

22. Walt Whitman, *Daybooks and Notebooks*, vol. 3, ed. William White (New York: New York University Press, 1978), 717.

23. Ibid., 678.

24. These quotations all appear in F. O. Matthiessen's discussion of Whitman in *American Renaissance: Art and Expression in the Age of Emerson and Whitman* (New York: Oxford University Press, 1941), 517–625.

25. Walt Whitman, *An American Primer*, ed. Horace Traubel (London: G. P. Putnam, 1904), 2, 9, 30.

26. Ibid., 24.

27. See Shirley Wilson Logan, *Liberating Language: Sites of Rhetorical Education in Nineteenth-Century Black America* (Carbondale: Southern Illinois University Press, 2008).

28. Susan-Mary Grant, 'From Union to Nation? The Civil War and the Development of American Nationalism', in Susan-Mary Grant and Brian Holden Reid (eds), *Themes of the American Civil War*, 2nd edn (New York: Routledge, 2010), 296.

29. Maureen A. Flanagan, *America Reformed: Progressives and Progressivisms, 1890s–1920s* (New York: Oxford University Press, 2007), 13, n.

30. The subject is thoroughly dealt with in John Algeo, *British or American English? A Handbook of Word and Grammar Patterns* (Cambridge: Cambridge University Press, 2006).

31. Wells, *Mankind in the Making*, 128–9.

32. Zoltán Kövecses, *American English: An Introduction* (Peterborough, Ont.: Broadview Press, 2000), 13.

Chapter 10: The long shadow of Lindley Murray

1. Charles Monaghan, 'Lindley Murray, American', in Ingrid Tieken-Boon van Ostade (ed.), *Two Hundred Years of Lindley Murray* (Münster: Nodus, 1996), 27–43.

2. The subject is covered in detail in Jane Hodson, *Language and Revolution in Burke, Wollstonecraft, Paine and Godwin* (Aldershot: Ashgate, 2007), 21–40.

3. John Walker, *A Critical Pronouncing Dictionary and Expositor of the English Language* (London: Robinson, Robinson & Cadell, 1791), 18, 51.

4. A valuable account of the Murrays is Charles Monaghan, *The Murrays of Murray Hill* (New York: Urban History Press, 1998).

5. Peter Walkden Fogg, *Elementa Anglicana*, 2 vols (Stockport: J. Clarke, 1792–6), II, x–xi.

6. Murray, *English Grammar*, 121, 139.

7. Ibid., 105.

8. Ibid., 179–200.

9. Ibid., 55–6.

10. Ibid., 17–19.

11. Quoted in Marcus Tomalin, *Romanticism and Linguistic Theory* (Basingstoke: Palgrave Macmillan, 2009), 148–9.

12. See Emma Vorlat, 'Lindley's Murray's Prescriptive Canon', in Tieken-Boon van Ostade (ed.), *Two Hundred Years of Lindley Murray*, 163–82.

13. Murray, *English Grammar*, 188.

14. Ibid., 98.

15. Lindley Murray, *Memoirs of the Life and Writings of Lindley Murray* (York: Longman, Rees, Orme, Brown & Green, 1826), 91.

16. Alexander Gil, *Logonomia Anglica*, 2nd edn (London: John Beale, 1621), 19. My translation.

17. Francis Grose, *A Classical Dictionary of the Vulgar Tongue* (London: S. Hooper, 1785), i.

18. Jonathon Green, *Chambers Slang Dictionary* (Edinburgh: Chambers, 2008), xi.

19. Alexander Marjoribanks, *Travels in New South Wales* (London: Smith, Elder, 1847), 58.

20. Ashley Montagu, *The Anatomy of Swearing* (Philadelphia: University of Pennsylvania Press, 2001), 260.

Chapter 11: The pedigree of nations

1. John Horne Tooke, *Epea Pteroenta, or The Diversions of Purley*, ed. Richard Taylor, 2 vols (London: Thomas Tegg, 1829), I, 26.

2. Christina Bewley and David Bewley, *Gentleman Radical: A Life of John Horne Tooke* (London: Tauris Academic Studies, 1998), 6.

3. For a full account of Tooke's ideas about linguistic equality, see Susan Manly, *Language, Custom and Nation in the 1790s: Locke, Tooke, Wordsworth, Edgeworth* (Aldershot: Ashgate, 2007).

4. This is discussed by Andrew Elfenbein in *Romanticism and the Rise of English* (Stanford, CA: Stanford University Press, 2009).

5. Benedict Anderson, *Imagined Communities: Reflections on the Origin and Spread of Nationalism*, rev. edn (London: Verso, 2006), 6.

6. See Michael Billig, *Banal Nationalism* (London: Sage, 1995), 1.

7. Michel Foucault, *The Order of Things: An Archaeology of the Human Sciences*, translated by A. M. Sheridan Smith (London: Tavistock, 1970), 290.
8. Graham Robb, *The Discovery of France* (London: Picador, 2007), 50–57.
9. Robert Phillipson, *English-Only Europe? Challenging Language Policy* (London: Routledge, 2003), 146.
10. Marc Shell, 'Language Wars', *New Centennial Review* 1 (2001), 2.
11. The subject is discussed at length in Sarah G. Thomason, *Language Contact* (Edinburgh: Edinburgh University Press, 2001).
12. These ideas are explored in detail in Philip Pettit, *Made with Words: Hobbes on Language, Mind, and Politics* (Princeton, NJ: Princeton University Press, 2008).

Chapter 12: Of fish-knives and fist-fucks

1 Lawrence James, *The Middle Class: A History* (London: Little, Brown, 2006), 231.
2. These examples are from Joss Marsh, *Word Crimes: Blasphemy, Culture, and Literature in Nineteenth-Century England* (Chicago: Chicago University Press, 1998), 215–16.
3. G. M. Young, *Portrait of an Age: Victorian England*, ed. George Kitson Clark (London: Oxford University Press, 1977), 154.
4. Richard W. Bailey, *Nineteenth-Century English* (Ann Arbor: University of Michigan Press, 1996), 4.
5. Richard D. Altick, *The English Common Reader*, 2nd edn (Columbus: Ohio State University Press, 1998), 161.
6. These examples are drawn from A. N. Wilson, *The Victorians* (London: Arrow, 2003), 282–3.
7. Quoted in Theodore Zeldin, *An Intimate History of Humanity* (London: Minerva, 1995), 40.
8. Manfred Görlach, *Explorations in English Historical Linguistics* (Heidelberg: Winter, 2002), 139.
9. Quoted in Bailey, *Nineteenth-Century English*, 258.
10. Quoted in James Sambrook, *William Cobbett* (London: Routledge & Kegan Paul, 1973), 105.
11. Ingrid Tieken-Boon van Ostade, *An Introduction to Late Modern English* (Edinburgh: Edinburgh University Press, 2009), 4.
12. James Paul Cobbett, 'Pronunciation', in *A Grammar of the English Language, with an additional chapter on pronunciation by James Paul Cobbett* (London: Charles Griffin, 1866), 241.

19. John Carey, *The Intellectuals and the Masses* (London: Faber, 1992).
14. *The World*, 6 December 1753.
15. Quoted in Robin Gilmour, *The Idea of the Gentleman in the Victorian Novel* (London: Allen & Unwin, 1981), 4.
16. See Harold J. Laski, *The Danger of Being a Gentleman and Other Essays* (London: Allen & Unwin, 1939), 13–31.
17. Anon., *Woman: As She Is, and As She Should Be*, 2 vols (London: James Cochrane, 1835), I, 2, 16, 28, 74; II, 254, 257.
18. Cited in Gilman (ed.), *Merriam-Webster's Dictionary of English Usage*, 582.
19. George Vandenhoff, *The Lady's Reader* (London: Sampson Low, 1862), 1, 3, 4.
20. Peter Trudgill, *The Social Differentiation of English in Norwich* (Cambridge: Cambridge University Press, 1974), 94–5.
21. Bailey, *Nineteenth-Century English*, 84.
22. Quoted in Manfred Görlach, *English in Nineteenth-Century England: An Introduction* (Cambridge: Cambridge University Press, 1999), 174.
23. Harry Thurston Peck, *What is Good English? and Other Essays* (New York: Dodd, Mead & Co., 1899), 3.
24. Charles Mackay, *Lost Beauties of the English Language* (London: Chatto & Windus, 1874), xxii, xxiv.
25. See Virginia Tufte, *Grammar as Style* (New York: Holt, Rinehart & Winston, 1971).
26. McIntosh, *The Evolution of English Prose*, 5.
27. My figures here are from Harold Herd, *The March of Journalism: The Story of the British Press from 1622 to the Present Day* (London: Allen & Unwin, 1952), 174–5.
28. Jason Camlot, *Style and the Nineteenth-Century British Critic* (Aldershot: Ashgate, 2008), 112.
29. T. L. Kington Oliphant, *The Sources of Standard English* (London: Macmillan, 1873), 1.
30. Ibid., 323, 328, 334, 338.

Chapter 13: 'Our blood, our language, our institutions'

1. Thomas Arnold, *Introductory Lectures on Modern History, with the Inaugural Lecture*, 7th edn (London: Longmans & Green, 1885), 23–4.
2. John Mitchell Kemble, *The Saxons in England*, rev. Walter de Gray Birch (London: Bernard Quaritch, 1876), I, v.

3. J. R. Green, *A Short History of the English People* (London: Macmillan, 1874), 1.

4. Thomas R. Lounsbury, *The Standard of Usage in English* (New York: Harper, 1908), 4, 58–9.

5. I have taken these examples from William A. Craigie's *The Critique of Pure English: From Caxton to Smollett* (Oxford: Clarendon Press, 1946).

6. Claude Hagège, *On the Death and Life of Languages*, trans. Jody Gladding (New Haven, CT: Yale University Press, 2009), 104.

7. Antony Beevor, *Stalingrad* (New York: Penguin, 1999), 117.

Chapter 14: Organizing the Victorian treasure-house

1. Henry Butter, *What's the Harm of Fornication?* (London: G. Berger, 1864), 10–11.

2. Henry Alford, *A Plea for the Queen's English*, 2nd edn (London: Strahan, 1864), 6.

3. Ibid., 154.

4. George Washington Moon, *The Bad English of Lindley Murray and Other Writers on the English Language*, 3rd edn (London: Hatchard, 1869), 2.

5. George Washington Moon, *A Defence of the Queen's English* (London: Hatchard, 1863), 5.

6. This statistic comes from Peter Burke and Roy Porter (eds), *Language, Self, and Society: A Social History of Language* (Cambridge: Polity, 1991), 159.

7. *Enquire Within Upon Everything*, 27th edn (London: Houlston & Wright, 1865), 53.

8. Ibid., 54–61.

9. Ibid., 71.

10. Charles William Smith, *Mind Your H's and Take Care of Your R's* (London: Lockwood, 1866), 3, 29.

11. Alfred Leach, *The Letter H: Past, Present, and Future* (London: Griffith & Farran, 1880), 16.

12. Ibid., 11.

13. Quoted in Mugglestone, *Talking Proper*, 60.

14. Quoted in Görlach, *Explorations in English Historical Linguistics*, 191.

15. Alexander J. Ellis, *On Early English Pronunciation* (London: Trübner, 1869–89), I, 17, 19.

16. Ibid., I, 157.

17. Ibid., I, 155, n.

18. Anon., *Never Too Late to Learn: Mistakes of Daily Occurrence in Speaking, Writing, and Pronunciation, Corrected* (London: John Farquhar Shaw, 1855), 17, 54.

19. Edward S. Gould, *Good English; or, Popular Errors in Language* (New York: W. J. Widdleton, 1867), 115, 130, 135.

20. Ibid., 32–4, 89.

21. Richard Grant White, *Words and Their Uses, Past and Present* (New York: Sheldon, 1871), 183, 192, 295, 297–8.

22. Ibid., 207, 211, 216.

23. Richard Grant White, *Every-Day English* (Boston: Houghton Mifflin, 1880), 411.

24. Alfred Ayres, *The Verbalist: A Manual Devoted to Brief Discussions of the Right and Wrong Use of Words* (New York: Appleton, 1882), 128, 220.

25. Letters, *The Times*, 14 February 1872.

26. Görlach, *English in Nineteenth-Century England*, 118–25.

27. J. A. H. Murray, 'General Explanations', in W. F. Bolton and David Crystal (eds), *The English Language: Essays by Linguists and Men of Letters 1858–1964* (Cambridge: Cambridge University Press, 1969), 59.

28. This is discussed at length in Charlotte Brewer's essay '*OED* Sources', in Lynda Mugglestone (ed.), *Lexicography and the OED* (Oxford: Oxford University Press, 2000), 40–58.

Chapter 15: The warden of English

1. Quoted in Jenny McMorris, *The Warden of English: The Life of H. W. Fowler* (Oxford: Oxford University Press, 2002), 216.

2. H. W. Fowler, *A Dictionary of Modern English Usage*, ed. David Crystal (Oxford: Oxford University Press, 2009), 728.

3. Ibid., 422, 112, 444, 239, 333, 513.

4. Ibid., 558–61.

5. Ibid., 210.

6. Ibid., 204, 439, 511.

7. William Strunk and E. B. White, *The Elements of Style*, 4th edn (Needham Heights, MA: Allyn & Bacon, 2000), 71.

8. Ibid., 212.

9. Eric Partridge, *Usage and Abusage* (London: Hamish Hamilton, 1947), 103–5, 173.

10. Quoted in Jim Quinn, *American Tongue and Cheek: A Populist Guide to Our Language* (New York: Pantheon, 1980), 43–4.

11. Cody's career is examined in detail in Edwin L. Battistella, *Do You Make*

These Mistakes in English? The Story of Sherwin Cody's Famous Language School (Oxford: Oxford University Press, 2009).

Chapter 16: 'Speak that I may see thee'

1. Fowler, *A Dictionary of Modern English Usage*, 307.
2. Clive Upton, 'Modern Regional English in the British Isles', in Mugglestone (ed.), *The Oxford History of English*, 330.
3. The findings are presented in William Labov, *Sociolinguistic Patterns* (Oxford: Blackwell, 1972).
4. Anthony Burgess, *A Mouthful of Air* (London: Vintage, 1993), 235.
5. Edward Finegan, 'English in North America', in Richard Hogg and David Denison (eds), *A History of the English Language* (Cambridge: Cambridge University Press, 2006), 386–7.
6. George Bernard Shaw, *On Language*, ed. Abraham Tauber (London: Peter Owen, 1965), 47.
7. Thomas R. Lounsbury, *The Standard of Pronunciation in English* (New York: Harper, 1904), 12–20.
8. William Henry P. Phyfe, *How Should I Pronounce?* (New York: Putnam, 1885), 5.
9. George Puttenham, *The Arte of English Poesie* (London: Richard Field, 1589), 120–21.
10. Verstegan, *A Restitution of Decayed Intelligence*, 204–5.
11. A full study of London's expansion at this time can be found in A. L. Beier and Roger Finlay (eds), *London 1500–1700: The Making of the Metropolis* (London: Longman, 1986).
12. Ben Jonson, *Timber, or Discoveries*, ed. Ralph S. Walker (Westport, CT: Greenwood Press, 1953), 41–2, 45–6.
13. Greenwood, *An Essay Towards a Practical English Grammar*, 309–10.
14. Crystal, *The Stories of English*, 406.
15. Mugglestone, *Talking Proper*, 46.
16. James Buchanan, *An Essay towards Establishing a Standard for an Elegant and Uniform Pronunciation of the English Language* (London: E. & C. Dilly, 1766), xi–xii.
17. William Enfield, *The Speaker* (London: Joseph Johnson, 1774), vii–xxiv.
18. Anna Laetitia Barbauld, *The Female Speaker* (London: Joseph Johnson, 1811), v.
19. John Walker, *A Critical Pronouncing Dictionary*, xiv.

Chapter 17: Talking proper

1. John Minsheu, *Ductor in Linguas, The Guide Unto Tongues* (London: John Browne, 1617), 80.
2. John Ray, *A Collection of English Words Not Generally Used* (London: H. Bruges, 1674), 50, 74.
3. These examples are borrowed from Peter Trudgill and J. K. Chambers (eds), *Dialects of English: Studies in Grammatical Variation* (London: Longman, 1991).
4. James Milroy and Lesley Milroy, *Authority in Language: Investigating Standard English*, 3rd edn (London: Routledge, 1999), 21.
5. George Sampson, *English for the English: A Chapter on National Education* (Cambridge: Cambridge University Press, 1925), 40–41, 48.
6. Henry Sweet, *The Indispensable Foundation: A Selection from the Writings of Henry Sweet*, ed. Eugénie J. A. Henderson (London: Oxford University Press, 1971), 14.
7. Quoted in Tony Crowley, *Proper English? Readings in Language, History and Cultural Identity* (London: Routledge, 1991), 212, 214.
8. George Orwell, *Essays*, ed. John Carey (London: Everyman, 2002), 608, 611, 629, 634–6.
9. See Milroy and Milroy, *Authority in Language*, 116–130.
10. This subject is discussed at length in John Honey, *Does Accent Matter?* (London: Faber, 1989), and also in Honey's essay 'Talking Proper', in Graham Nixon and John Honey (eds), *An Historic Tongue: Studies in English Linguistics in Memory of Barbara Strang* (London: Routledge, 1988).
11. Mugglestone, *Talking Proper*, 269.
12. George Steiner, *After Babel: Aspects of Language and Translation*, 3rd edn (Oxford: Oxford University Press, 1998), 34.
13. Crystal, *The Stories of English*, 368.
14. Anne Karpf, *The Human Voice: The Story of a Remarkable Talent* (London: Bloomsbury, 2007), 2–4.

Chapter 18: The Alphabet and the Goddess

1. Kirsty Scott, 'Sounds incredible', *Guardian*, 10 July 2007.
2. Mark Wignall, 'Bad Times for a Good Relationship', *Jamaica Observer*, 4 April 2010.
3. John McWhorter, *Doing Our Own Thing: The Degradation of Language and Music and Why We Should, Like, Care* (London: William Heinemann, 2004), 3.

4. Walter J. Ong, *Orality and Literacy: The Technologizing of the Word* (London: Methuen, 1982), 125–38.

5. The key ideas here come from Ong, *Orality and Literacy*, 31–77.

6. A fuller discussion of these issues can be found in Robert Pattison, *On Literacy: The Politics of the Word from Homer to the Age of Rock* (New York: Oxford University Press, 1982).

7. Andrea A. Lunsford, *Writing Matters: Rhetoric in Public and Private Lives* (Athens, GA: University of Georgia Press, 2007), xi–xii.

8. Leonard Shlain, *The Alphabet Versus the Goddess: The Conflict Between Word and Image* (London: Allen Lane, 1998), 1, 7.

9. Quoted in Linda C. Mitchell, *Grammar Wars: Language as Cultural Battlefield in 17th and 18th Century England* (Aldershot: Ashgate, 2001), 142.

10. See Nancy Armstrong and Leonard Tennenhouse (eds), *The Ideology of Conduct* (New York: Methuen, 1987), 8–9.

11. Louann Brizendine, *The Female Brain* (New York: Morgan Road, 2006), 14, 36.

12. Mark Liberman examines Brizendine's statements in detail in his article 'Neuroscience in the Service of Sexual Stereotypes', which appears on the Language Log website: http://itre.cis.upenn.edu/~myl/languagelog/archives/003419.html, retrieved 22 March 2010.

13. Penelope Eckert and Sally McConnell-Ginet, *Language and Gender* (Cambridge: Cambridge University Press, 2003), 9.

14. See Pinker, *The Language Instinct*, 429.

15. Judith Tingley, *Genderflex: Men and Women Speaking Each Other's Language at Work* (New York: Amacom, 1994), 27.

16. Deborah Tannen, 'The Relativity of Linguistic Strategies: Rethinking Power and Solidarity in Gender and Dominance', in Deborah Cameron (ed.), *The Feminist Critique of Language: A Reader*, 2nd edn (London: Routledge, 1998), 269–70.

17. The subject is dealt with at some length in John Willinsky, *After Literacy* (New York: Peter Lang, 2001), 171–84.

18. Ann Fisher, *A New Grammar: Being the Most Easy Guide to Speaking and Writing the English Language Properly and Correctly*, 2nd edn (Newcastle-upon-Tyne: I. Thompson, 1750), 117.

19. White, *Every-Day English*, 416.

Chapter 19: Modern life is rubbish

1. John Simon, *Paradigms Lost: Reflections on Literacy and its Decline* (London: Chatto & Windus, 1981), x–xiv.

2. Edward W. Said, *Orientalism* (London: Penguin, 2003), 136.
3. H. G. Wells, *Anticipations and Other Papers* (London: T. Fisher Unwin, 1924), 204.
4. Wells, *Mankind in the Making*, 127–8.
5. Ibid., 132-3, 137.
6. W. Terrence Gordon, *C. K. Ogden: A Bio-bibliographic Study* (Metuchen, NJ: Scarecrow Press, 1990), 47.
7. Edward Finegan, 'Usage', in Richard Hogg (gen. ed.), *The Cambridge History of the English Language* (Cambridge: Cambridge University Press, 1992–2001), VI, 399.
8. Quoted in Edward Finegan, *Attitudes Toward English Usage* (New York: Teachers College Press, 1980), 121.
9. Herbert C. Morton, *The Story of Webster's Third* (Cambridge: Cambridge University Press, 1994), 173, 182.
10. Simon, *Paradigms Lost*, xv.
11. Ibid., 157.
12. Lynch, *The Lexicographer's Dilemma*, 219.
13. Geoffrey Hughes, *Political Correctness* (Chichester: Wiley-Blackwell, 2010), 3.
14. Robert Hughes, *Culture of Complaint* (London: Harvill, 1994), 4, 6, 12.
15. Ibid., 20, 21.
16. Cameron, *Verbal Hygiene*, 165.

Chapter 20: Unholy shit

1. Geoffrey Hughes, *Swearing* (London: Penguin, 1998), 243.
2. Geoffrey Hughes, *An Encyclopedia of Swearing* (London: M. E. Sharpe, 2006), 65.
3. Quoted in Andrew Murphy, *Shakespeare in Print: A History and Chronology of Shakespeare Publishing* (Cambridge: Cambridge University Press, 2003), 171.
4. Hughes, *An Encyclopedia of Swearing*, 372.
5. Steven Pinker, *The Stuff of Thought: Language as a Window into Human Nature* (London: Penguin, 2008), 331–3.
6. Jesse Sheidlower (ed.), *The F-Word*, 3rd edn (New York: Oxford University Press, 2009), xxii–xxxii.
7. Ibid., xxvii.
8. Pinker, *The Stuff of Thought*, 370.
9. Quoted in Lynda Mugglestone, *Lost for Words: The Hidden History of the Oxford English Dictionary* (New Haven, CT: Yale University Press, 2005), 84.

10. Quoted in Marc Leverette, Brian L. Ott and Cara Louise Buckley (eds), *It's Not TV: Watching HBO in the Post-Television Era* (New York: Routledge, 2008), 128.

11. Lynch, *The Lexicographer's Dilemma*, 236.

12. Simon Critchley, *On Humour* (London: Routledge, 2002), 87.

13. Maureen Dowd, 'Liberties; Niggardly City', *New York Times*, 31 January 1999.

14. Patricia O'Conner and Stewart Kellerman, *Origins of the Specious: Myths and Misconceptions of the English Language* (New York: Random House, 2009), 135.

15. Quoted in Charlotte Brewer, *Treasure-House of the Language: The Living OED* (New Haven, CT: Yale University Press, 2007), 96.

16. Quoted in Robert Burchfield, 'Dictionaries and Ethnic Sensibilities', in Leonard Michaels and Christopher Ricks (eds), *The State of the Language* (Berkeley: University of California Press, 1980), 19.

Chapter 21: 'It's English-Only here'

1. Quoted in James Crawford (ed.), *Language Loyalties: A Source Book on the Official English Controversy* (Chicago: University of Chicago Press, 1992), 85.

2. Jeremy J. Smith, 'Scots', in Glanville Price (ed.), *Languages in Britain & Ireland* (Oxford: Blackwell, 2000), 165.

3. Dick Leith, *A Social History of English*, 2nd edn (London: Routledge, 1997), 169–70.

4. Wells, *Mankind in the Making*, 209, n.

5. The rise of the 'metropolitan malcontents' is dealt with in Francis Wheen, *Strange Days Indeed: The Golden Age of Paranoia* (London: Fourth Estate, 2009), 63–95.

6. Deborah J. Schildkraut, *Press One for English: Language Policy, Public Opinion, and American Identity* (Princeton, NJ: Princeton University Press, 2005), 2.

7. MALDEF policy statement. http://maldef.org/education/public_policy/, retrieved 18 March 2010.

8. Brent Staples, 'The Last Train from Oakland', *New York Times*, 24 January 1997.

9. Marcyliena Morgan, 'More than a Mood or an Attitude: Discourse and Verbal Genres in African-American Culture', in Salikoko S. Mufwene, John R. Rickford, Guy Bailey and John Baugh (eds), *African-American English: Structure, History, and Use* (London: Routledge, 1998), 251.

10. Quoted in Hughes, *Political Correctness*, 120.

11. Ibid., 150.

12. A number of these examples come from Alice Morton Ball, *The Compounding and Hyphenation of English Words* (New York: Funk & Wagnalls, 1951).

13. Charles McGrath, 'Death-Knell. Or Death Knell', *New York Times*, 7 October 2007.

Chapter 22: The comma flaps its wings

1. Simon, *Paradigms Lost*, 8.

2. Victoria Moore, 'Apostrophe catastrophe!', *Daily Mail*, 18 November 2008.

3. Joseph Robertson, *An Essay on Punctuation* (London: J. Walter, 1785), Preface.

4. Walter Nash, *English Usage: A Guide to First Principles* (London: Routledge & Kegan Paul, 1986), 107.

5. Quoted in Nash, *English Usage*, 116.

6. Lynne Truss, *Eats, Shoots & Leaves: The Zero Tolerance Approach to Punctuation* (London: Profile, 2003), 1, 28, 30, 201.

7. Geoffrey Nunberg, *The Years of Talking Dangerously* (New York: PublicAffairs, 2009), 31.

8. Truss, *Eats, Shoots & Leaves*, 3–4, 7.

9. Louis Menand, 'Bad Comma: Lynne Truss's strange grammar', *New Yorker*, 28 June 2004.

10. David Crystal, *The Fight for English* (Oxford: Oxford University Press, 2006), 134.

11. C. C. Barfoot, 'Trouble with the Apostrophe', in Ingrid Tieken-Boon van Ostade and John Frankis (eds), *Language: Usage and Description: Studies Presented to N. E. Osselton* (Amsterdam: Rodopi, 1991), 133.

12. Elizabeth S. Sklar, 'The Possessive Apostrophe: the Development and Decline of a Crooked Mark', *College English* 38 (1976), 175.

13. M. B. Parkes, *Pause and Effect: An Introduction to the History of Punctuation in the West* (Aldershot: Scolar Press, 1992), 55–6.

14. John Ash, *Grammatical Institutes*, 4th edn (London: E. & C. Dilly, 1763), 34.

15. Quoted in Vivian Salmon, 'Orthography and punctuation', in Hogg (gen. ed.), *The Cambridge History of the English Language* (Cambridge: Cambridge University Press, 1992–2001), III, 37.

16. Parkes, *Pause and Effect*, 93.

17. A more detailed account is offered by Anthony G. Petti in *English Literary Hands from Chaucer to Dryden*, 25–8.
18. Ash, *Grammatical Institutes*, 4th edn xxiii.
19. Murray, *English Grammar*, 200.
20. Quoted in Jon Henley, 'The end of the line?', *Guardian*, 4 April 2008.
21. Richard Alleyne, 'Half of Britons struggle with the apostrophe', *Daily Telegraph*, 11 November 2008.
22. Sarah Lyall, 'Boston Journal; Minder of Misplaced Apostrophes Scolds a Town', *New York Times*, 16 June 2001.
23. Will Pavia, 'Scene is set for a pedants' revolt as city dares to banish the apostrophe from its street signs', *The Times*, 30 January 2009.
24. Philip Howard, 'A useful mark we should all get possessive about', *The Times*, 30 January 2009.

Chapter 23: Flaunting the Rules

1. Dominic Sandbrook, *White Heat: A History of Britain in the Swinging Sixties* (London: Little, Brown, 2006), 201.
2. William Zinsser, *On Writing Well* (New York: Quill, 2001), 33–4.
3. Lounsbury, *The Standard of Usage in English*, 193, 197.
4. Quoted in Mencken, *The American Language*, 4th edn, 39.
5. Ibid., 45–6.
6. Edwin Newman, *Strictly Speaking: Will America be the Death of English?* (London: W. H. Allen, 1975), xi.
7. A useful catalogue of today's salient terms is contained in Tony Bennett, Lawrence Grossberg and Meaghan Morris (eds), *New Keywords: A Revised Vocabulary of Culture and Society* (Oxford: Blackwell, 2005).
8. Raymond Williams, *The Long Revolution* (London: Chatto & Windus, 1961), 3.
9. Ernest Gowers, *ABC of Plain Words* (London: HM Stationery Office, 1951), 3.
10. Thomas de Zengotita, *Mediated: How the Media Shape the World Around You* (London: Bloomsbury, 2007), 84–6.
11. Stefanie Marsh, 'The rise of the interrogatory statement', *The Times*, 28 March 2006.
12. Ian Jack, 'Tense? Relax, it'll be clear presently', *Guardian*, 27 March 2004.
13. James Gorman, 'Like, Uptalk?', *New York Times*, 15 August 1993.
14. William Safire, 'Vogue Words', *New York Times*, 11 March 2007.
15. Partridge, *Usage and Abusage*, 349–57.

16. Frank Kermode, *Shakespeare's Language* (London: Penguin, 2001), 4–5.
17. Geoffrey Nunberg, 'What the Usage Panel Thinks', in Christopher Ricks and Leonard Michaels (eds), *The State of the Language* (London: Faber, 1990), 469–71.
18. *Légghorn* for the style of hat, *Leggórn* for poultry, and *Légghórn* for the place, apparently.
19. William Cobbett, *A Grammar of the English Language*, 3rd edn (London: Thomas Dolby, 1819), 133–5.
20. David Crystal, 'Talking about Time', in Katinka Ridderbos (ed.), *Time* (Cambridge: Cambridge University Press, 2002), 114.
21. Baker, *Reflections on the English Language*, ii–v, 48, 55.
22. My thanks to Jack Lynch for bringing this book to my attention.

Chapter 24: Technology says 'whatever'

1. Sven Birkerts, *The Gutenberg Elegies: The Fate of Reading in an Electronic Age* (New York: Faber, 2006), 237, 249.
2. Ibid., 228.
3. Tim Berners-Lee, *Weaving the Web* (London: Orion, 1999), 1–2, 224–5.
4. Sven Birkerts, 'Sense and semblance: the implications of virtuality', in Brian Cox (ed.), *Literacy Is Not Enough: Essays on the Importance of Reading* (Manchester: Manchester University Press, 1998), 20, 24.
5. Derrick de Kerckhove, *The Skin of Culture: Investigating the New Electronic Reality* (London: Kogan Page, 1997), 205, 208, 217.
6. John Seely Brown and Paul Duguid, *The Social Life of Information* (Boston, MA: Harvard Business School Press, 2002), 21.
7. Quoted in Mark Abley, *The Prodigal Tongue: Dispatches from the Future of English* (London: William Heinemann, 2008), 183.
8. Quoted in David Crystal, *txtng: the gr8 db8* (Oxford: Oxford University Press, 2008), 9.
9. Quoted in Dominic Sandbrook, *Never Had It So Good: A History of Britain from Suez to the Beatles* (London: Little, Brown, 2005), 389.
10. John Humphrys, 'We will soon be lost for words', *Daily Telegraph*, 24 October 2006.
11. De Zengotita, *Mediated*, 176.
12. Naomi Baron, *Always On: Language in an Online and Mobile World* (Oxford: Oxford University Press, 2010), 7, 171.

Chapter 25: 'Conquer English to Make China Strong'

1. See Salah Troudi, 'The Effects of English as a Medium of Instruction', in Adel Jendli, Salah Troudi and Christine Coombe (eds), *The Power of Language: Perspectives from Arabia* (Dubai: TESOL Arabia, 2007), 6.

2. H. G. Wells, *A Modern Utopia* (London: Chapman & Hall, 1905), 17, 21–2.

3. H. G. Wells, *The World Set Free* (London: Macmillan, 1914), 215, 217–18.

4. Alexander Melville Bell, *World-English: The Universal Language* (New York: N. D. C. Hodges, 1888), 7.

5. Quoted in Braj B. Kachru, 'American English and other Englishes', in Charles A. Ferguson and Shirley Brice Heath (eds), *Language in the USA* (Cambridge: Cambridge University Press, 1981), 39.

6. Edward W. Said, *Culture and Imperialism* (London: Chatto & Windus, 1993), 368–9.

7. The subject is discussed at some length in Robert Phillipson, 'Lingua franca or lingua frankensteinia? English in European integration and globalization', *World Englishes* 27 (2008), 250–84.

8. Arika Okrent, *In the Land of Invented Languages* (New York: Spiegel & Grau, 2009), 106.

9. Louis-Jean Calvet, *Language Wars and Linguistic Politics*, trans. Michael Petheram (Oxford: Oxford University Press, 1998), 197–8.

10. Mark Abley, *Spoken Here: Travels Among Threatened Languages* (London: Arrow, 2005), 90.

11. Alastair Pennycook, *Global English and Transcultural Flows* (Abingdon: Routledge, 2007), 5.

12. Robert McCrum, *Globish: How the English Language Became the World's Language* (London: Viking, 2010), 213–16.

13. Thomas L. Friedman, *The World is Flat: A Brief History of the Globalized World in the Twenty-first Century* (London: Allen Lane, 2005), 8.

14. This question is explored in Jacques Maurais and Michael A. Morris (eds), *Languages in a Globalising World* (Cambridge: Cambridge University Press, 2003).

15. Nicholas Ostler, *Empires of the Word: A Language History of the World* (London: HarperCollins, 2005), 476.

16. See Evan Osnos, 'Crazy English', *New Yorker*, 28 April 2008.

17. See, for instance, Simon Caulkin, 'English, language of lost chances', *Observer*, 24 July 2005.

18. David Graddol, *English Next* (London: The British Council, 2006), 93.

19. Quoted in William Greaves, 'Selling English by the Pound', *The Times*, 24 October 1989.

20. Phillipson, *English-Only Europe?*, 78.

Chapter 26: What do we do with the flowing face of nature?

1. Jacques Derrida, *Positions*, trans. Alan Bass (London: Athlone, 1981), 19.

2. Ferdinand de Saussure, *Course in General Linguistics*, ed. Charles Bally and Albert Sechehaye, trans. Wade Baskin, rev. edn (London: Fontana, 1974), 80.

3. These ideas are examined at length in Joseph W. Poulshock, 'Language and Morality: Evolution, Altruism and Linguistic Moral Mechanisms' (unpublished PhD thesis, University of Edinburgh, 2006).

4. George Lakoff and Mark Johnson, *Metaphors We Live By* (Chicago: University of Chicago Press, 1980), 14–21, 89–96.

5. Andrew Goatly, *Washing the Brain – Metaphor and Hidden Ideology* (Amsterdam: John Benjamins, 2007), 83–5.

6. Benjamin Lee Whorf, *Language, Thought, and Reality*, ed. John B. Carroll (New York: John Wiley, 1956), 240–1.

7. Ibid., 57–9, 61, 63.

8. Ibid., 216.

9. Bloom's work is summarized in John A. Lucy, *Language Diversity and Thought* (Cambridge: Cambridge University Press, 1992), 208–56.

10. Jack Hitt, 'Say No More', *New York Times*, 29 February 2004.

11. See Pinker, *The Language Instinct*, 57–67.

12. John McWhorter, *Our Magnificent Bastard Tongue: The Untold History of English* (New York: Gotham Books, 2008), 139.

13. A genuine example, from *The Economist* of 11 October 2003.

14. Mark Halpern, *Language and Human Nature* (New Brunswick, NJ: Transaction, 2009), 142.

15. David S. Palermo and James J. Jenkins, *Word Association Norms: Grade School Through College* (Minneapolis: University of Minnesota Press, 1964), 278–80, 406–7.

Chapter 27: Such, such are the joys

1. Steven Poole, *Unspeak* (London: Abacus, 2007), 144.

2. Orwell, *Essays*, ed. Carey, 695.

3. Locke, *An Essay Concerning Human Understanding*, ed. Nidditch, 493–6.

4. Orwell, *Essays*, ed. Carey, 966.
5. Plain English Campaign brochure, 2009.http://www.plainenglish.co.uk/services_brochure_2009.pdf, retrieved 19 March 2010.
6. Martin Cutts and Chrissie Maher, *The Plain English Story* (Stockport: Plain English Campaign, 1986), 84.
7. BBC news report – 'Councils get banned jargon list'. http://news.bbc.co.uk/1/hi/uk_politics/7948894.stm, retrieved 23 March 2010.
8. Chris Mullin, *A View from the Foothills: The Diaries of Chris Mullin*, ed. Ruth Winstone (London: Profile, 2010), 26.
9. Pinker, *The Stuff of Thought*, 262. Pinker explores metaphor closely in pp. 235–78 of this book.
10. Quoted in Don Watson, *Gobbledygook* (London: Atlantic, 2005), 105.
11. Jacques Barzun, *The House of Intellect* (London: Secker & Warburg, 1959), 233.
12. As far as I know, this name was dreamt up by Bruce D. Price for an article which appeared in the magazine *Verbatim* in February 1976.

Chapter 28: Envoi

1. See Judith Butler, *Excitable Speech: A Politics of the Performative* (New York: Routledge, 1997), 1–2.
2. John Yeomans, *The Abecedarian, or, Philosophic Comment upon the English Alphabet* (London: J. Coote, 1759), 62.
3. Pinker, *The Stuff of Thought*, 425.
4. Ammon Shea, 'Error-Proof', *New York Times*, 28 September 2009.

Bibliography of works consulted

Hans Aarsleff, *From Locke to Saussure: Essays on the Study of Language and Intellectual History* (London: Athlone, 1982)

—— *The Study of Language in England, 1780–1860* (Minneapolis: University of Minnesota Press, 1983)

Mark Abley, *Spoken Here: Travels Among Threatened Languages* (London: Arrow, 2005)

—— *The Prodigal Tongue: Dispatches from the Future of English* (London: William Heinemann, 2008)

Robin Adamson, *The Defence of French* (Clevedon: Multilingual Matters, 2007)

Jean Aitchison, *Language Change: Progress or Decay?* 3rd edn (Cambridge: Cambridge University Press, 2001)

Henry Alford, *A Plea for the Queen's English*, 2nd edn (London: Strahan, 1864)

John Algeo, *British or American English? A Handbook of Word and Grammar Patterns* (Cambridge: Cambridge University Press, 2006)

Keith Allan and Kate Burridge, *Forbidden Words: Taboo and the Censoring of Language* (Cambridge: Cambridge University Press, 2006)

Richard Alleyne, 'Half of Britons struggle with the apostrophe', *Daily Telegraph*, 11 November 2008

R. C. Alston, *A Bibliography of the English Language from the Invention of Printing to the Year 1800: A Corrected Reprint of Volumes I–X* (Ilkley: Janus Press, 1974)

Stephen G. Alter, *William Dwight Whitney and the Science of Language* (Baltimore: Johns Hopkins University Press, 2005)

Richard D. Altick, *The English Common Reader*, 2nd edn (Columbus: Ohio State University Press, 1998)

Kingsley Amis, *The King's English: A Guide to Modern Usage* (London: HarperCollins, 1997)

Benedict Anderson, *Imagined Communities: Reflections on the Origin and Spread of Nationalism*, rev. edn (London: Verso, 2006)

Anon., *Woman: As She Is, and As She Should Be*, 2 vols (London: James Cochrane, 1835)

—— *Never Too Late to Learn: Mistakes of Daily Occurrence in Speaking, Writing, and Pronunciation, Corrected* (London: John Farquhar Shaw, 1855)

—— *Enquire Within Upon Everything*, 27th edn (London: Houlston & Wright, 1865)

Jorge Arditi, *A Genealogy of Manners: Transformation of Social Relations in France and England from the Fourteenth Century to the Eighteenth Century* (Chicago: University of Chicago Press, 1998)

Nancy Armstrong and Leonard Tennenhouse (eds), *The Ideology of Conduct* (New York: Methuen, 1987)

Mary-Jo Arn and Hanneke Wirtjes (eds), *Historical and Editorial Studies in Medieval and Early Modern English* (Groningen: Wolters-Noordhoff, 1985)

Thomas Arnold, *Introductory Lectures on Modern History, with the Inaugural Lecture*, 7th edn (London: Longmans & Green, 1885)

John Ash, *Grammatical Institutes*, 4th edn (London: E. & C. Dilly, 1763)

—— *The New and Complete Dictionary of the English Language*, 2nd edn, 2 vols (London: Vernor & Hood, 1795)

Jabari Asim, *The N Word* (Boston: Houghton Mifflin, 2007)

Anita Auer, *The Subjunctive in the Age of Prescriptivism* (Basingstoke: Palgrave Macmillan, 2009)

Alfred Ayres, *The Verbalist: A Manual Devoted to Brief Discussions of the Right and Wrong Use of Words* (New York: Appleton, 1882)

—— *The Essentials of Elocution* (New York: Funk & Wagnalls, 1897)

Francis Bacon, *The New Organon*, ed. Lisa Jardine and Michael Silverthorne (Cambridge: Cambridge University Press, 2000)

Nathan Bailey, *Dictionarium Britannicum* (London: T. Cox, 1730)

Richard W. Bailey, *Images of English: A Cultural History of the Language* (Cambridge: Cambridge University Press, 1991)

—— *Nineteenth-Century English* (Ann Arbor: University of Michigan Press, 1996)

Richard W. Bailey and Manfred Görlach (eds), *English as a World Language* (Cambridge: Cambridge University Press, 1984)

Robert Baker, *Reflections on the English Language* (London: J. Bell, 1770)

Alice Morton Ball, *The Compounding and Hyphenation of English Words* (New York: Funk & Wagnalls, 1951)

Anna Laetitia Barbauld, *The Female Speaker* (London: Joseph Johnson, 1811)

Charles Barber, *Early Modern English*, 2nd edn (Edinburgh: Edinburgh University Press, 1997)

Naomi Baron, *Always On: Language in an Online and Mobile World* (Oxford: Oxford University Press, 2010)

John Barrell, *English Literature in History 1730–80: An Equal, Wide Survey* (London: Hutchinson, 1983)

Jacques Barzun, *The House of Intellect* (London: Secker & Warburg, 1959)

—— *Simple and Direct: A Rhetoric for Writers*, rev. edn (New York: Harper & Row, 1985)

Jonathan Bate, *Soul of the Age: The Life, Mind and World of William Shakespeare* (London: Viking, 2009)

Edwin L. Battistella, *Bad Language: Are Some Words Better Than Others?* (Oxford: Oxford University Press, 2005)

—— *Do You Make These Mistakes in English? The Story of Sherwin Cody's Famous Language School* (Oxford: Oxford University Press, 2009)

Laurie Bauer and Peter Trudgill (eds), *Language Myths* (London: Penguin, 1998)

Albert C. Baugh and Thomas Cable, *A History of the English Language*, 5th edn (Upper Saddle River, NJ: Prentice-Hall, 2002)

John Baugh, *Beyond Ebonics* (New York: Oxford University Press, 2000)

Joan C. Beal, *English Pronunciation in the Eighteenth Century* (Oxford: Clarendon Press, 1999)

—— *English in Modern Times, 1700–1945* (London: Arnold, 2004)

Joan C. Beal, Carmela Nocera and Massimo Sturiale (eds), *Perspectives on Prescriptivism* (Bern: Peter Lang, 2008)

Cave Beck, *The Universal Character* (London: Thomas Maxey, 1657)

Antony Beevor, *Stalingrad* (London: Viking, 1988)

A. L. Beier and Roger Finlay (eds), *London 1500–1700: The Making of the Metropolis* (London: Longman, 1986)

Henri Béjoint, *The Lexicography of English* (Oxford: Oxford University Press, 2010)

Alexander Melville Bell, *World-English: The Universal Language* (New York: N. D. C. Hodges, 1888)

Masha Bell, *Understanding English Spelling* (Cambridge: Pegasus, 2004)

Drake Bennett, 'Thinking literally: the surprising ways that metaphors shape your world', *Boston Globe*, 27 September 2009

Tony Bennett, Lawrence Grossberg and Meaghan Morris (eds), *New Keywords: A Revised Vocabulary of Culture and Society* (Oxford: Blackwell, 2005)

Tim Berners-Lee, *Weaving the Web* (London: Orion, 1999)

Christina Bewley and David Bewley, *Gentleman Radical: A Life of John Horne Tooke* (London: Tauris Academic Studies, 1998)

Ambrose Bierce, *Write It Right: A Little Blacklist of Literary Faults* (New York: Walter Neale, 1909)

Michael Billig, *Banal Nationalism* (London: Sage, 1995)

Barbara M. Birch, *The English Language Teacher in Global Civil Society* (London: Routledge, 2009)

Sven Birkerts, *The Gutenberg Elegies: The Fate of Reading in an Electronic Age* (New York: Faber, 2006)

Hugh Blair, *Lectures on Rhetoric and Belles Lettres*, ed. Harold F. Harding, 2 vols (Carbondale: Southern Illinois University Press, 1965)

W. Martin Bloomer (ed.), *The Contest of Language: Before and Beyond Nationalism* (Notre Dame, IN: University of Notre Dame Press, 2005)

Leonard Bloomfield, *An Introduction to the Study of Language* (London: G. Bell, 1914)

—— *Language* (New York: Henry Holt, 1933)

Thomas Blount, *Glossographia* (London: Thomas Newcomb, 1656)

Dwight Bolinger, *Language: The Loaded Weapon* (London: Longman, 1980)

W. F. Bolton, *The Language of 1984* (Oxford: Blackwell, 1984)

W. F. Bolton and David Crystal (eds), *The English Language: Essays by Linguists and Men of Letters 1858–1964* (Cambridge: Cambridge University Press, 1969)

Edward Brerewood, *Enquiries Touching the Diversity of Languages, and Religions* (London: John Bill, 1614)

Charlotte Brewer, *Treasure-House of the Language: The Living OED* (New Haven, CT: Yale University Press, 2007)

Louann Brizendine, *The Female Brain* (New York: Morgan Road, 2006)

G. L. Brook, *The Language of Dickens* (London: André Deutsch, 1970)

Goold Brown, *The Grammar of English Grammars* (New York: Samuel S. & William Wood, 1851)

James Buchanan, *An Essay towards Establishing a Standard for an Elegant and Uniform Pronunciation of the English Language* (London: E. & C. Dilly, 1766)

William Bullokar, *The Booke at Large, for the Amendment of Orthographie for English Speech* (London: Henry Denham, 1580)

—— *Aesop's Fables in True Orthography* (London: Edmund Bollifant, 1585)

Oliver Bell Bunce, *Don't: A Manual of Mistakes and Improprieties more or less prevalent in Conduct and Speech*, 3rd edn (London: Field & Tuer, 1884)

Anthony Burgess, *A Mouthful of Air* (London: Vintage, 1993)

Peter Burke and Roy Porter (eds), *Language, Self, and Society: A Social History of Language* (Cambridge: Polity, 1991)

David Burnley, *The History of the English Language: A source book*, 2nd edn (Harlow: Pearson Education, 2000)

Kate Burridge, *Blooming English* (Cambridge: Cambridge University Press, 2004)

—— *Weeds in the Garden of Words: Further observations on the tangled history of the English language* (Cambridge: Cambridge University Press, 2005)

Judith Butler, *Excitable Speech: A Politics of the Performative* (New York: Routledge, 1997)

Henry Butter, *What's the Harm of Fornication?* (London: G. Berger, 1864)

Jeremy Butterfield, *Damp Squid: The English Language Laid Bare* (Oxford: Oxford University Press, 2008)

Louis-Jean Calvet, *Language Wars and Linguistic Politics*, trans. Michael Petheram (Oxford: Oxford University Press, 1998)

William Camden, *Remaines of a Greater Worke, Concerning Britaine* (London: Simon Waterson, 1605)

Deborah Cameron, *Verbal Hygiene* (London: Routledge, 1995)

—— (ed.), *The Feminist Critique of Language: A Reader*, 2nd edn (London: Routledge, 1998)

Jason Camlot, *Style and the Nineteenth-Century British Critic* (Aldershot: Ashgate, 2008)

John Carey, *The Intellectuals and the Masses* (London: Faber, 1992)

—— *William Golding: The Man Who Wrote Lord of the Flies* (London: Faber, 2009)

Edward Carney, *A Survey of English Spelling* (London: Routledge, 1994)

Ronald Carter, *Investigating English Discourse: Language, Literacy and Literature* (London: Routledge, 1997)

Simon Caulkin, 'English, language of lost chances', *Observer*, 24 July 2005

Evelyn Nien-Ming Ch'ien, *Weird English* (Cambridge, MA: Harvard University Press, 2004)

Noam Chomsky, *Language and Responsibility* (London: Harvester, 1979)

Kenneth Cmiel, *Democratic Eloquence: The Fight over Popular Speech in Nineteenth-Century America* (New York: William Morrow, 1990)

Jennifer Coates, *Women, Men and Language*, 3rd edn (Harlow: Longman, 2004)

William Cobbett, *A Grammar of the English Language*, 3rd edn (London: Thomas Dolby, 1819)

—— *A Grammar of the English Language, with an additional chapter on pronunciation by James Paul Cobbett* (London: Charles Griffin, 1866)

Murray Cohen, *Sensible Words: Linguistic Practice in England 1640–1785* (Baltimore: Johns Hopkins University Press, 1977)

William A. Cohen and Ryan Johnson (eds), *Filth: Dirt, Disgust, and Modern Life* (Minneapolis: University of Minnesota Press, 2005)

Elisha Coles, *Nolens Volens* (London: Andrew Clark, 1675)

Linda Colley, *Britons: Forging the Nation 1707–1837*, 2nd edn (New Haven, CT: Yale University Press, 2005)

John Considine, *Dictionaries in Early Modern Europe: Lexicography and the Making of Heritage* (Cambridge: Cambridge University Press, 2008)

Penelope J. Corfield (ed.), *Language, History and Class* (Oxford: Blackwell, 1991)

Jonathan Cott (ed.), *Dylan on Dylan: The Essential Interviews* (London: Hodder & Stoughton, 2006)

Basil Cottle, *The Plight of English* (Newton Abbot: David & Charles, 1975)

Florian Coulmas, *Writing Systems: An Introduction to their Linguistic Analysis* (Cambridge: Cambridge University Press, 2003)

Brian Cox (ed.), *Literacy Is Not Enough: Essays on the Importance of Reading* (Manchester: Manchester University Press, 1998)

William A. Craigie, *The Critique of Pure English: From Caxton to Smollett* (Oxford: Clarendon Press, 1946)

James Crawford (ed.), *Language Loyalties: A Source Book on the Official English Controversy* (Chicago: University of Chicago Press, 1992)

Simon Critchley, *On Humour* (London: Routledge, 2002)

Tony Crowley, *Proper English? Readings in Language, History and Cultural Identity* (London: Routledge, 1991)

—— *Wars of Words: The Politics of Language in Ireland 1537–2004* (Oxford: Oxford University Press, 2005)

David Crystal, *The Cambridge Encyclopedia of Language*, 2nd edn (Cambridge: Cambridge University Press, 1997)

—— *Language Death* (Cambridge: Cambridge University Press, 2000)

—— *Who Cares about English Usage?* 2nd edn (London: Penguin, 2000)

—— *The Cambridge Encyclopedia of the English Language* (Cambridge: Cambridge University Press, 2002)

—— *English as a Global Language*, 2nd edn (Cambridge: Cambridge University Press, 2003)

—— *The Language Revolution* (Cambridge: Polity, 2004)

—— *The Stories of English* (London: Allen Lane, 2004)

—— *Language and the Internet*, 2nd edn (Cambridge: Cambridge University Press, 2006)

—— *The Fight for English* (Oxford: Oxford University Press, 2006)

—— *txtng: the gr8 db8* (Oxford: Oxford University Press, 2008)

Jonathan Culler, *Saussure*, rev. edn (London: Fontana, 1987)

Anne Curzan and Michael Adams, *How English Works: A Linguistic Introduction*, 2nd edn (New York: Pearson Longman, 2009)

Martin Cutts and Chrissie Maher, *The Plain English Story* (Stockport: Plain English Campaign, 1986)

Andrew Dalby, *Language in Danger* (London: Allen Lane, 2002)

James Dawes, *The Language of War: Literature and Culture in the U.S. from the Civil War Through World War II* (Cambridge, MA: Harvard University Press, 2002)

Hannah Dawson, *Locke, Language and Early-Modern Philosophy* (Cambridge: Cambridge University Press, 2007)

Daniel Defoe, *An Essay upon Projects* (London: Thomas Cockerill, 1697)

Jacques Derrida, *Positions*, trans. Alan Bass (London: Athlone, 1981)

Jean-Louis Dessalles, *Why We Talk: The Evolutionary Origins of Language*, trans. James Grieve (Oxford: Oxford University Press, 2007)

Guy Deutscher, *The Unfolding of Language* (London: Arrow, 2006)

Ellin Devis, *The Accidence; or First Rudiments of English Grammar*, 3rd edn (London: T. Beecroft, 1777)

Thomas Dilworth, *A New Guide to the English Tongue*, 13th edn (London: Henry Kent, 1751)

E. J. Dobson, *English Pronunciation 1500–1700*, 2 vols, 2nd edn (Oxford: Clarendon Press, 1968)

Marina Dossena and Charles Jones (eds), *Insights into Late Modern English* (Bern: Peter Lang, 2003)

Maureen Dowd, 'Liberties; Niggardly City', *New York Times*, 31 January 1999

John Dryden, *Of Dramatick Poesie, an Essay* (London: Henry Herringman, 1668)

—— *Of Dramatick Poesie, an Essay* (London: Henry Herringman, 1684)

Sarah Dunant (ed.), *The War of the Words: The Political Correctness Debate* (London: Virago, 1994)

Terry Eagleton, *After Theory* (London: Allen Lane, 2003)

Penelope Eckert and Sally McConnell-Ginet, *Language and Gender* (Cambridge: Cambridge University Press, 2003)

Elizabeth L. Eisenstein, *The Printing Revolution in Early Modern Europe*, 2nd edn (Cambridge: Cambridge University Press, 2005)

Andrew Elfenbein, *Romanticism and the Rise of English* (Stanford, CA: Stanford University Press, 2009)

Alexander J. Ellis, *On Early English Pronunciation*, 5 vols (London: Trübner, 1869–89)

William Enfield, *The Speaker* (London: Joseph Johnson, 1774)

John S. Farmer (ed.), *Americanisms – Old and New* (London: Thomas Poulter, 1889)

Barbara A. Fennell, *A History of English: A Sociolinguistic Approach* (Oxford: Blackwell, 2001)

Daniel Fenning, *The Universal Spelling Book* (London: Crowder & Woodgate, 1756)

Charles A. Ferguson and Shirley Brice Heath (eds), *Language in the USA* (Cambridge: Cambridge University Press, 1981)

Edward Finegan, *Attitudes Toward English Usage* (New York: Teachers College Press, 1980)

Edward Finegan and John R. Rickford (eds), *Language in the USA: Themes for the Twenty-first Century* (Cambridge: Cambridge University Press, 2004)

Ann Fisher, *A New Grammar: Being the Most Easy Guide to Speaking and Writing the English Language Properly and Correctly*, 2nd edn (Newcastle-upon-Tyne: I. Thompson, 1750)

John H. Fisher, *The Emergence of Standard English* (Lexington: University Press of Kentucky, 1996)

Joshua A. Fishman, *In Praise of the Beloved Language: A Comparative View of Positive Ethnolinguistic Consciousness* (Berlin: Mouton de Gruyter, 1997)

Maureen A. Flanagan, *America Reformed: Progressives and Progressivisms, 1890s–1920s* (New York: Oxford University Press, 2007)

John Florio, *A Worlde of Wordes* (London: Edward Blount, 1598)

Michel Foucault, *The Order of Things: An Archaeology of the Human Sciences*, trans. A. M. Sheridan Smith (London: Tavistock, 1970)

H. W. Fowler, *A Dictionary of Modern English Usage*, ed. David Crystal (Oxford: Oxford University Press, 2009)

H. W. Fowler and F. G. Fowler, *The King's English* (Oxford: Clarendon Press, 1906)

—— *The King's English*, 2nd edn (Oxford: Clarendon Press, 1906)

Thomas L. Friedman, *The World is Flat: A Brief History of the Globalized World in the Twenty-first Century* (London: Allen Lane, 2005)

Joseph H. Friend, *The Development of American Lexicography 1798–1864* (The Hague: Mouton, 1967)

Webb Garrison, with Cheryl Garrison, *The Encyclopedia of Civil War Usage* (Nashville, TN: Cumberland House, 2001)

Mark Garvey, *Stylized: A Slightly Obsessive History of Strunk & White's The Elements of Style* (New York: Touchstone, 2009)

Alexander Gil, *Logonomia Anglica*, 2nd edn (London: John Beale, 1621)

Stephen Gill, *Wordsworth: A Life* (Oxford: Clarendon Press, 1989)

Malcolm Gillies and David Pear, *Portrait of Percy Grainger* (Rochester, NY: University of Rochester Press, 2002)

E. Ward Gilman (ed.), *Merriam-Webster's Dictionary of English Usage* (Springfield, MA: Merriam-Webster, 1994)

Robin Gilmour, *The Idea of the Gentleman in the Victorian Novel* (London: Allen & Unwin, 1981)

Malcolm Gladwell, *Outliers: The Story of Success* (London: Allen Lane, 2008)

Joseph Glanvill, *The Vanity of Dogmatizing* (London: E. Cotes, 1661)

—— *Scepsis Scientifica: Or, Confest Ignorance, the way to Science* (London: E. Cotes, 1665)

—— *Essays on Several Important Subjects in Philosophy and Religion* (London: J. D., 1676)

Andrew Goatly, *Washing the Brain – Metaphor and Hidden Ideology* (Amsterdam: John Benjamins, 2007)

W. Terrence Gordon, *C. K. Ogden: A Bio-bibliographic Study* (Metuchen, NJ: Scarecrow Press, 1990)

Mina Gorji (ed.), *Rude Britannia* (Abingdon: Routledge, 2007)

Manfred Görlach, *Studies in the History of the English Language* (Heidelberg: Winter, 1990)

—— *Introduction to Early Modern English* (Cambridge: Cambridge University Press, 1991)

—— *New Studies in the History of English* (Heidelberg: Winter, 1995)

—— *English in Nineteenth-Century England: An Introduction* (Cambridge: Cambridge University Press, 1999)

—— *Eighteenth-Century English* (Heidelberg: Winter, 2001)

—— *Explorations in English Historical Linguistics* (Heidelberg: Winter, 2002)

James Gorman, 'Like, Uptalk?', *New York Times*, 15 August 1993

Edward S. Gould, *Good English; or, Popular Errors in Language* (New York: W. J. Widdleton, 1867)

Philip Babcock Gove (ed.), *Webster's Third New International Dictionary of the English Language: Unabridged,* 2 vols (Springfield, MA: G. &. C. Merriam, 1961)

Ernest Gowers, *ABC of Plain Words* (London: HM Stationery Office, 1951)

David Graddol, *English Next* (London: The British Council, 2006)

David Graddol, Dick Leith and Joan Swann (eds), *English: History, Diversity and Change* (London: Routledge, 1996)

Susan-Mary Grant and Brian Holden Reid (eds), *Themes of the American Civil War*, 2nd edn (New York: Routledge, 2010)

William Greaves, 'Selling English by the Pound', *The Times*, 24 October 1989

J. R. Green, *A Short History of the English People* (London: Macmillan, 1874)

Jonathon Green, *Chambers Slang Dictionary* (Edinburgh: Chambers, 2008)

Sidney Greenbaum, *Good English and the Grammarian* (London: Longman, 1988)

Ezra Greenspan (ed.), *The Cambridge Companion to Walt Whitman* (Cambridge: Cambridge University Press, 1995)

James Greenwood, *An Essay Towards a Practical English Grammar* (London: R. Tookey, 1711)

Francis Grose, *A Classical Dictionary of the Vulgar Tongue* (London: S. Hooper, 1785)

Thomas Gustafson, *Representative Words: Politics, Literature, and the American Language, 1776–1865* (Cambridge: Cambridge University Press, 1992)

Helen Hackett, *Shakespeare and Elizabeth: The Meeting of Two Myths* (Princeton, NJ: Princeton University Press, 2009)

Claude Hagège, *On the Death and Life of Languages,* trans. Jody Gladding (New Haven, CT: Yale University Press, 2009)

Mark Halpern, *Language and Human Nature* (New Brunswick, NJ: Transaction, 2009)

James Harris, *Hermes: or, a Philosophical Inquiry Concerning Language and Universal Grammar* (London: H. Woodfall, 1751)

John Hart, *An Orthographie* (London: W. Serres, 1569)

Ralph A. Hartmann, *Philosophies of Language and Linguistics* (Edinburgh: Haralex, 2007)

Einar Haugen, *The Ecology of Language* (Stanford, CA: Stanford University Press, 1972)

Terence Hawkes, *Metaphor* (London: Methuen, 1972)

William Hazlitt, *A New and Improved Grammar of the English Tongue: for the Use of Schools* (London: M. J. Godwin, 1810)

Richard Helgerson, *Forms of Nationhood: The Elizabethan Writing of England* (Chicago: University of Chicago Press, 1992)

Jon Henley, 'The end of the line?', *Guardian*, 4 April 2008

Brian Hepworth, *Robert Lowth* (Boston, MA: Twayne, 1978)

A. P. Herbert, *What a Word!*, 11th edn (London: Methuen, 1952)

Harold Herd, *The March of Journalism: The Story of the British Press from 1622 to the Present Day* (London: Allen & Unwin, 1952)

Christopher Highley, *Catholics Writing the Nation in Early Modern Britain and Ireland* (Oxford: Oxford University Press, 2008)

Jack Hitt, 'Say No More', *New York Times*, 29 February 2004

Thomas Hobbes, *Leviathan*, ed. Richard Tuck (Cambridge: Cambridge University Press, 1991)

William B. Hodgson, *Errors in the Use of English* (Edinburgh: David Douglas, 1881)

Jane Hodson, *Language and Revolution in Burke, Wollstonecraft, Paine and Godwin* (Aldershot: Ashgate, 2007)

Richard Hogg (gen. ed.), *The Cambridge History of the English Language*, 6 vols (Cambridge: Cambridge University Press, 1992–2001)

Richard Hogg and David Denison (eds), *A History of the English Language* (Cambridge: Cambridge University Press, 2006)

John Honey, *Does Accent Matter?* (London: Faber, 1989)

—— *Language is Power: The Story of Standard English and its Enemies* (London: Faber, 1997)

Philip Howard, 'A useful mark we should all get possessive about', *The Times*, 30 January 2009

A. P. R. Howatt and H. G. Widdowson, *A History of English Language Teachings*, 2nd edn (Oxford: Oxford University Press, 2004)

Geoffrey Hughes, *Swearing* (London: Penguin, 1998)

—— *An Encyclopedia of Swearing* (London: M. E. Sharpe, 2006)

—— *Political Correctness* (Chichester: Wiley-Blackwell, 2010)

Robert Hughes, *Culture of Complaint* (London: Harvill, 1994)

John Humphrys, 'We will soon be lost for words', *Daily Telegraph*, 24 October 2006

Makoto Ikeda, *Competing Grammars: Noah Webster's Vain Efforts to Defeat Lindley Murray* (Tokyo: Shinozaki Shorin, 1999)

Ian Jack, 'Tense? Relax, it'll be clear presently', *Guardian*, 27 March 2004

Ray Jackendoff, *Foundations of Language: Brain, Meaning, Grammar, Evolution* (Oxford: Oxford University Press, 2002)

Lawrence James, *The Middle Class: A History* (London: Little, Brown, 2006)

Adel Jendli, Salah Troudi and Christine Coombe (eds), *The Power of Language: Perspectives from Arabia* (Dubai: TESOL Arabia, 2007)

Otto Jespersen, *Mankind, Nation and Individual from a Linguistic Point of View* (Oslo: Aschehoug, 1925)

—— *Essentials of English Grammar* (London: Allen & Unwin, 1933)

—— *The Philosophy of Grammar*, with an introduction by James D. McCawley (Chicago: University of Chicago Press, 1992)

Charles Johnson, *The Complete Art of Writing Letters* (London: T. Lowndes, 1770)

Richard Johnson, *Grammatical Commentaries: Being an Apparatus to a New National Grammar* (London: S. Keble et al., 1706)

Samuel Johnson, *A Dictionary of the English Language*, 2 vols (London: Knapton, Longman et al., 1755)

—— *Johnson on the English Language*, ed. Gwin J. Kolb and Robert DeMaria (New Haven, CT: Yale University Press, 2005)

Richard Foster Jones, *The Triumph of the English Language* (London: Oxford University Press, 1953)

Ben Jonson, *The English Grammar* (London: Richard Meighen, 1640)

—— *Timber, or Discoveries*, ed. Ralph S. Walker (Westport, CT: Greenwood Press, 1953)

Brian D. Joseph, Johanna DeStefano, Neil G. Jacobs and Ilse Lehiste (eds), *When Languages Collide* (Columbus: Ohio State University Press, 2003)

Braj B. Kachru, *The Alchemy of English* (Oxford: Pergamon, 1986)

Anne Karpf, *The Human Voice: The Story of a Remarkable Talent* (London: Bloomsbury, 2007)

Christian Kay, Simon Horobin and Jeremy Smith (eds), *New Perspectives on English Historical Linguistics: Syntax and Morphology* (Amsterdam: John Benjamins, 2004)

Christian Kay, Carole Hough and Irené Wotherspoon (eds), *New Perspectives on English Historical Linguistics: Lexis and Transmission* (Amsterdam: John Benjamins, 2004)

Christian Kay, Jane Roberts, Michael Samuels and Irené Wotherspoon (eds), *Historical Thesaurus of the Oxford English Dictionary*, 2 vols (Oxford: Oxford University Press, 2009)

Ann Cline Kelly, *Swift and the English Language* (Philadelphia: University of Pennsylvania Press, 1988)

John Mitchell Kemble, *The Saxons in England*, rev. Walter de Gray Birch, 2 vols (London: Bernard Quaritch, 1876)

Christine Kenneally, *The First Word: The Search for the Origins of Language* (London: Penguin, 2008)

Derrick de Kerckhove, *The Skin of Culture: Investigating the New Electronic Reality* (London: Kogan Page, 1997)

Frank Kermode, *Shakespeare's Language* (London: Penguin, 2001)

Alvin Kernan, *Samuel Johnson and the Impact of Print* (Princeton, NJ: Princeton University Press, 1989)

Michael G. Ketcham, *Transparent Designs: Reading, Performance, and Form in the Spectator Papers* (Athens, GA: University of Georgia Press, 1985)

T. L. Kington Oliphant, *The Sources of Standard English* (London: Macmillan, 1873)

John Knowles, *The Principles of English Grammar*, 4th edn (London: Vernor & Hood, 1796)

Zoltán Kövecses, *American English: An Introduction* (Peterborough, Ont.: Broadview Press, 2000)

Michael P. Kramer, *Imagining Language in America: From the Revolution to the Civil War* (Princeton, NJ: Princeton University Press, 1992)

George Philip Krapp, *Modern English: Its Growth and Present Use* (New York: Scribner 1909)

William Labov, *Sociolinguistic Patterns* (Oxford: Blackwell, 1972)

George Lakoff and Mark Johnson, *Metaphors We Live By* (Chicago: University of Chicago Press, 1980)

Robin Tolmach Lakoff, *The Language War* (Berkeley: University of California Press, 2001)

Stephen K. Land, *The Philosophy of Language in Britain: Major Theories from Hobbes to Thomas Reid* (New York: AMS Press, 1986)

A. Lane, *A Key to the Art of Letters* (London: A. & J. Churchil, 1700)

Erik Larson, *The Devil in the White City* (London: Doubleday, 2003)

Harold J. Laski, *The Danger of Being a Gentleman and Other Essays* (London: Allen & Unwin, 1939)

Alfred Leach, *The Letter H: Past, Present, and Future* (London: Griffith & Farran, 1880)

Percival Leigh, *The Comic English Grammar* (London: Richard Bentley, 1840)

Dick Leith, *A Social History of English*, 2nd edn (London: Routledge, 1997)

Sterling A. Leonard, *The Doctrine of Correctness in English Usage 1700–1800* (Madison: University of Wisconsin Studies in Language and Literature, 1929)

Seth Lerer, *Inventing English: A Portable History of the Language* (New York: Columbia University Press, 2007)

Marc Leverette, Brian L. Ott and Cara Louise Buckley (eds), *It's Not TV: Watching HBO in the Post-Television Era* (New York: Routledge, 2008)

Jeff Lewis, *Language Wars: The Role of Media and Culture in Global Terror and Political Violence* (London: Pluto Press, 2005)

William Lily, *A Short Introduction of Grammar* (London: John Norton, 1608)

A. Lloyd James et al., *Broadcast English* (London: British Broadcasting Corporation, 1928)

John Locke, *An Essay Concerning Human Understanding*, ed. Peter H. Nidditch (Oxford: Clarendon Press, 1975)

Francis Lodwick, *A Common Writing* (privately printed, 1647)

Shirley Wilson Logan, *Liberating Language: Sites of Rhetorical Education in Nineteenth-Century Black America* (Carbondale: Southern Illinois University Press, 2008)

Michael Losonsky (ed.), *Humboldt on Language* (Cambridge: Cambridge University Press, 1999)

Thomas R. Lounsbury, *The Standard of Pronunciation in English* (New York: Harper, 1904)

—— *The Standard of Usage in English* (New York: Harper, 1908)

Robert Lowth, *A Short Introduction to English Grammar* (London: Millar, Dodsley & Dodsley, 1762)

—— *A Short Introduction to English Grammar*, 2nd edn (London: Millar, Dodsley & Dodsley, 1763)

John A. Lucy, *Language Diversity and Thought* (Cambridge: Cambridge University Press, 1992)

Andrea A. Lunsford, *Writing Matters: Rhetoric in Public and Private Lives* (Athens, GA: University of Georgia Press, 2007)

Sarah Lyall, 'Boston Journal; Minder of Misplaced Apostrophes Scolds a Town', *New York Times*, 16 June 2001

Jack Lynch, *The Lexicographer's Dilemma: The Evolution of 'Proper' English from Shakespeare to South Park* (New York: Walker, 2009)

Jack Lynch and Anne McDermott (eds), *Anniversary Essays on Johnson's Dictionary* (Cambridge: Cambridge University Press, 2005)

Tom McArthur, *Living Words: Language, Lexicography and the Knowledge Revolution* (Exeter: University of Exeter Press, 1998)

—— *Oxford Guide to World English* (Oxford: Oxford University Press, 2003)

—— (ed.), *The Oxford Companion to the English Language* (Oxford; Oxford University Press, 1992)

Robert McCrum, *Globish: How the English Language Became the World's Language* (London: Viking, 2010)

Robert McCrum, William Cran, and Robert MacNeil, *The Story of English*, 3rd edn (London: Faber, 2002)

Diarmait Mac Giolla Chríost, *Language, Identity and Conflict* (London: Routledge, 2003)

Charles McGrath, 'Death-Knell. Or Death Knell', *New York Times*, 7 October 2007

Carey McIntosh, *The Evolution of English Prose, 1700–1800* (Cambridge: Cambridge University Press, 1998)

Charles Mackay, *Lost Beauties of the English Language* (London: Chatto & Windus, 1874)

Erin McKean (ed.), *Verbatim* (London: Pimlico, 2003)

Jenny McMorris, *The Warden of English: The Life of H. W. Fowler* (Oxford: Oxford University Press, 2002)

John McWhorter, *The Word on the Street: Fact and Fable about American English* (New York: Plenum, 1998)

—— *Doing Our Own Thing: The Degradation of Language and Music and Why We Should, Like, Care* (London: William Heinemann, 2004)

—— *Our Magnificent Bastard Tongue: The Untold History of English* (New York: Gotham Books, 2008)

—— 'Reid's Three Little Words: The Log in Our Own Eye', *New Republic*, 9 January 2010

Peter Mandler, *The English National Character: The History of an Idea from Edmund Burke to Tony Blair* (New Haven, CT: Yale University Press, 2006)

Susan Manly, *Language, Custom and Nation in the 1790s: Locke, Tooke, Wordsworth, Edgeworth* (Aldershot: Ashgate, 2007)

John Marenbon, *English Our English: The New Orthodoxy Examined* (London: Centre for Policy Studies, 1987)

Alexander Marjoribanks, *Travels in New South Wales* (London: Smith, Elder, 1847)

Joss Marsh, *Word Crimes: Blasphemy, Culture, and Literature in Nineteenth-Century England* (Chicago: Chicago University Press, 1998)

Stefanie Marsh, 'The rise of the interrogatory statement', *The Times*, 28 March 2006

Jeremy Marshall and Fred McDonald (eds), *Questions of English* (Oxford: Oxford University Press, 1994)

William Mather, *The Young Man's Companion*, 2nd edn (London: Thomas Howkins, 1685)

F. O. Matthiessen, *American Renaissance: Art and Expression in the Age of Emerson and Whitman* (New York: Oxford University Press, 1941)

Jacques Maurais and Michael A. Morris (eds), *Languages in a Globalising World* (Cambridge: Cambridge University Press, 2003)

David Maurer, *Whiz Mob* (New Haven, CT: College & University Press, 1964)

Louis Menand, 'Bad Comma: Lynne Truss's strange grammar', *New Yorker*, 28 June 2004

H. L. Mencken, *The American Language*, 4th edn (New York: Knopf, 1941)

Ian Michael, *English Grammatical Categories and the Tradition to 1800* (Cambridge: Cambridge University Press, 1970)

—— *The Teaching of English: From the Sixteenth Century to 1870* (Cambridge: Cambridge University Press, 1987)

Leonard Michaels and Christopher Ricks (eds), *The State of the Language* (Berkeley: University of California Press, 1980)

David Micklethwait, *Noah Webster and the American Dictionary* (Jefferson, NC: McFarland, 2000)

James Milroy and Lesley Milroy, *Authority in Language: Investigating Standard English*, 3rd edn (London: Routledge, 1999)

John Minsheu, *Ductor in Linguas, The Guide Unto Tongues* (London: John Browne, 1617)

Linda C. Mitchell, *Grammar Wars: Language as Cultural Battlefield in 17th and 18th Century England* (Aldershot: Ashgate, 2001)

Nancy Mitford (ed.), *Noblesse Oblige: An Enquiry into the Identifiable Characteristics of the English Aristocrat* (London: Hamish Hamilton, 1956)

W. H. Mittins, Mary Salu, Mary Edminson and Sheila Coyne, *Attitudes to English Usage* (London: Oxford University Press, 1970)

Kusujiro Miyoshi, *Johnson's and Webster's Verbal Examples* (Tübingen: Niemeyer, 2007)

Charles Monaghan, *The Murrays of Murray Hill* (New York: Urban History Press, 1998)

Leila Monaghan and Jane E. Goodman (eds), *A Cultural Approach to Interpersonal Communication* (Oxford: Blackwell, 2007)

Ashley Montagu, *The Anatomy of Swearing* (Philadelphia: University of Pennsylvania Press, 2001)

George Washington Moon, *A Defence of the Queen's English* (London: Hatchard, 1863)

—— *The Dean's English: A Criticism of the Dean of Canterbury's Essays on the Queen's English* (London: Hatchard, 1864)

—— *The Bad English of Lindley Murray and Other Writers on the English Language*, 3rd edn (London: Hatchard, 1869)

Victoria Moore, 'Apostrophe catastrophe!', *Daily Mail*, 18 November 2008

William Morris (ed.), *The American Heritage Dictionary of the English Language* (Boston: Houghton Mifflin, 1976)

Herbert C. Morton, *The Story of Webster's Third* (Cambridge: Cambridge University Press, 1994)

Salikoko S. Mufwene, John R. Rickford, Guy Bailey and John Baugh (eds), *African-American English: Structure, History, and Use* (London: Routledge, 1998)

Lynda Mugglestone, '"Grammatical Fair Ones": Women, Men, and Attitudes to Language in the Novels of George Eliot', *Review of English Studies* 46 (1995), 11–25

—— *Lost for Words: The Hidden History of the Oxford English Dictionary* (New Haven, CT: Yale University Press, 2005)

—— *Talking Proper: The Rise and Fall of the English Accent as a Social Symbol*, 2nd edn (Oxford: Oxford University Press, 2007)

—— (ed.), *Lexicography and the OED* (Oxford: Oxford University Press, 2000)

—— (ed.), *The Oxford History of English* (Oxford: Oxford University Press, 2006)

Richard Mulcaster, *The First Part of the Elementarie* (London: Thomas Vautroullier, 1582)

John Mullan, *Sentiment and Sociability: The Language of Feeling in the Eighteenth Century* (Oxford: Clarendon Press, 1990)

Chris Mullin, *A View from the Foothills: The Diaries of Chris Mullin*, ed. Ruth Winstone (London: Profile, 2010)

Andrew Murphy, *Shakespeare in Print: A History and Chronology of Shakespeare Publishing* (Cambridge: Cambridge University Press, 2003)

K. M. Elisabeth Murray, *Caught in the Web of Words: James Murray and the Oxford English Dictionary* (New Haven, CT: Yale University Press, 1977)

Lindley Murray, *English Grammar* (York: Wilson, Spence & Mawman, 1795)

—— *Memoirs of the Life and Writings of Lindley Murray* (York: Longman, Rees, Orme, Brown & Green, 1826)

Walter Nash, *English Usage: A Guide to First Principles* (London: Routledge & Kegan Paul, 1986)

Thomas Nashe, *The Works of Thomas Nashe*, ed. Ronald B. McKerrow, 5 vols (London: A. H. Bullen, 1904)

Karlijn Navest, 'An index of names to Lowth's *Short Introduction to English Grammar* (1762), (1763), (1764)', *Historical Sociolinguistics and Sociohistorical Linguistics* 6 (2006)

William Nelson, 'The Teaching of English in Tudor Grammar Schools', *Studies in Philology* 49 (1952), 119–43

Sir Henry Newbolt et al., *The Teaching of English in England* (London: His Majesty's Stationery Office, 1921)

Edwin Newman, *Strictly Speaking: Will America be the Death of English?* (London: W. H. Allen, 1975)

David Newsome, *The Victorian World Picture* (London: John Murray, 1997)

Charles Nicholl, *A Cup of News: The Life of Thomas Nashe* (London: Routledge & Kegan Paul, 1984)

Graham Nixon and John Honey (eds), *An Historic Tongue: Studies in English Linguistics in Memory of Barbara Strang* (London: Routledge, 1988)

Geoffrey Nunberg, *The Linguistics of Punctuation* (Menlo Park, CA: CSLI, 1990)

—— *Going Nucular: Language, Politics and Culture in Confrontational Times* (New York: PublicAffairs, 2004)

—— *The Years of Talking Dangerously* (New York: PublicAffairs, 2009)

Arja Nurmi, Minna Nevala and Minna Palander-Collin (eds), *The Language of Daily Life in England (1400–1800)* (Amsterdam: John Benjamins, 2009)

Chris O'Brien, 'Confessions of a Propagandist', *Forbes*, 21 February 2008

Patricia O'Conner, *Woe is I: The Grammarphobe's Guide to Better English in Plain English*, 2nd edn (New York: Riverhead, 2004)

Patricia O'Conner and Stewart Kellerman, *Origins of the Specious: Myths and Misconceptions of the English Language* (New York: Random House, 2009)

C. K. Ogden and I. A. Richards, *The Meaning of Meaning: A Study of the Influence of Language upon Thought and of the Science of Symbolism*, ed. W. Terrence Gordon (London: Routledge/Thoemmes Press, 1994)

Arika Okrent, *In the Land of Invented Languages* (New York: Spiegel & Grau, 2009)

John Oldmixon, *Reflections on Dr Swift's Letter to the Earl of Oxford, About the English Tongue* (London: A. Baldwin, 1712)

Walter J. Ong, *Orality and Literacy: The Technologizing of the Word* (London: Methuen, 1982)

George Orwell, *Essays*, ed. John Carey (London: Everyman, 2002)

Evan Osnos, 'Crazy English', *New Yorker*, 28 April 2008

Nicholas Ostler, *Empires of the Word: A Language History of the World* (London: HarperCollins, 2005)

—— *Ad Infinitum: A Biography of Latin* (New York: Walker, 2007)

Walter R. Ott, *Locke's Philosophy of Language* (Cambridge: Cambridge University Press, 2004)

Thomas Paine, *Rights of Man, Common Sense, and Other Political Writings*, ed. Mark Philp (Oxford: Oxford University Press, 1995)

David S. Palermo and James J. Jenkins, *Word Association Norms: Grade School Through College* (Minneapolis: University of Minnesota Press, 1964)

John C. Papajohn, *The Hyphenated American: The Hidden Injuries of Culture* (Westport, CT: Greenwood Press, 1999)

M. B. Parkes, *Pause and Effect: An Introduction to the History of Punctuation in the West* (Aldershot: Scolar Press, 1992)

Eric Partridge, *Usage and Abusage* (London: Hamish Hamilton, 1947)

Robert Pattison, *On Literacy: The Politics of the Word from Homer to the Age of Rock* (New York: Oxford University Press, 1982)

Will Pavia, 'Scene is set for a pedants' revolt as city dares to banish the apostrophe from its street signs', *The Times*, 30 January 2009

Harry Thurston Peck, *What is Good English? and Other Essays* (New York: Dodd, Mead & Co., 1899)

Alastair Pennycook, *Global English and Transcultural Flows* (Abingdon: Routledge, 2007)

Anthony G. Petti, *English Literary Hands from Chaucer to Dryden* (London: Edward Arnold, 1977)

Philip Pettit, *Made with Words: Hobbes on Language, Mind, and Politics* (Princeton, NJ: Princeton University Press, 2008)

K. C. Phillipps, *Language and Class in Victorian England* (Oxford: Blackwell, 1984)

Robert Phillipson, *Linguistic Imperialism* (Oxford: Oxford University Press, 1992)

—— *English-Only Europe? Challenging Language Policy* (London: Routledge, 2003)

—— 'Lingua franca or lingua frankensteinia? English in European integration and globalization', *World Englishes* 27 (2008), 250–84

William Henry P. Phyfe, *How Should I Pronounce?* (New York: Putnam, 1885)

John Pickering, *A Vocabulary, or Collection of Words and Phrases which have been Supposed to Be Peculiar to the United States of America* (Boston: Cummings & Hilliard, 1816)

Steven Pinker, *The Language Instinct* (London: Penguin, 1995)

—— *Words and Rules: The Ingredients of Language* (London: Phoenix, 2000)

—— *The Stuff of Thought: Language as a Window into Human Nature* (London: Penguin, 2008)

Steven Poole, *Unspeak: Words are Weapons* (London: Abacus, 2007)

Robert C. Pooley, *The Teaching of English Usage* (Urbana, IL: National Council of Teachers of English, 1974)

Simeon Potter, *Our Language* (London: Penguin, 1961)

Joseph W. Poulshock, 'Language and Morality: Evolution, Altruism and Linguistic Moral Mechanisms' (unpublished PhD thesis, University of Edinburgh, 2006)

Glanville Price (ed.), *Languages in Britain & Ireland* (Oxford: Blackwell, 2000)

Joseph Priestley, *The Rudiments of English Grammar* (London: R. Griffiths, 1761)

—— *The Rudiments of English Grammar*, 2nd edn (London: Becket, De Hondt & Johnson, 1768)

George Puttenham, *The Arte of English Poesie* (London: Richard Field, 1589)

Martin Pütz, Joshua A. Fishman and JoAnne Neff-van Aertselaer (eds), *'Along the Routes to Power': Explorations of Empowerment through Language* (Berlin: Mouton de Gruyter, 2006)

Jim Quinn, *American Tongue and Cheek: A Populist Guide to Our Language* (New York: Pantheon, 1980)

Randolph Quirk and Gabriele Stein, *English in Use* (Harlow: Longman, 1990)

John Ray, *A Collection of English Words Not Generally Used* (London: H. Bruges, 1674)

Allen Walker Read, *Milestones in the History of English in America*, ed. Richard W. Bailey (Durham, NC: American Dialect Society, 2002)

Christopher Ricks and Leonard Michaels (eds), *The State of the Language* (London: Faber, 1990)

Katinka Ridderbos (ed.), *Time* (Cambridge: Cambridge University Press, 2002)

Graham Robb, *The Discovery of France* (London: Picador, 2007)

Joseph Robertson, *An Essay on Punctuation* (London: J. Walter, 1785)

David Rosewarne, 'Estuary English', *Times Education Supplement*, 19 October 1984

A. P. Rossiter, *Our Living Language* (London: Longman, 1953)

David Runciman, *Political Hypocrisy* (Princeton, NJ: Princeton University Press, 2008)

Laura L. Runge, *Gender and Language in British Literary Criticism, 1660–1790* (Cambridge: Cambridge University Press, 1997)

D. A. Russell and M. Winterbottom (eds), *Ancient Literary Criticism: The Principal Texts in New Translations* (Oxford: Clarendon Press, 1972)

William Safire, 'Vogue Words', *New York Times*, 11 March 2007

Edward W. Said, *Culture and Imperialism* (London: Chatto & Windus, 1993)

—— *Orientalism* (London: Penguin, 2003)

Vivian Salmon, *Language and Society in Early Modern England* (Amsterdam: John Benjamins, 1996)

James Sambrook, *William Cobbett* (London: Routledge & Kegan Paul, 1973)

George Sampson, *English for the English: A Chapter on National Education* (Cambridge: Cambridge University Press, 1925)

Dominic Sandbrook, *Never Had It So Good: A History of Britain from Suez to the Beatles* (London: Little, Brown, 2005)

—— *White Heat: A History of Britain in the Swinging Sixties* (London: Little, Brown, 2006)

Edward Sapir, *Language: An Introduction to the Study of Speech* (New York: Harcourt Brace, 1921)

Ferdinand de Saussure, *Course in General Linguistics*, ed. Charles Bally and Albert Sechehaye, trans. Wade Baskin, rev. edn (London: Fontana, 1974)

—— *Writings in General Linguistics*, trans. Carol Sanders and Matthew Pires (Oxford: Oxford University Press, 2006)

Deborah J. Schildkraut, *Press One for English: Language Policy, Public Opinion, and American Identity* (Princeton, NJ: Princeton University Press, 2005)

Carol L. Schmid, *The Politics of Language* (Oxford: Oxford University Press, 2001)

Kirsty Scott, 'Sounds incredible', *Guardian*, 10 July 2007

D. G. Scragg, *A History of English Spelling* (Manchester: Manchester University Press, 1974)

John Seely Brown and Paul Duguid, *The Social Life of Information* (Boston, MA: Harvard Business School Press, 2002)

James Shapiro, *Contested Will: Who Wrote Shakespeare?* (New York: Simon & Schuster, 2010)

George Bernard Shaw, *On Language*, ed. Abraham Tauber (London: Peter Owen, 1965)

Ammon Shea, 'Error-Proof', *New York Times*, 28 September 2009

—— 'Old Dictionaries', *New York Times*, 15 October 2009

Jesse Sheidlower (ed.), *The F-Word*, 3rd edn (New York: Oxford University Press, 2009)

Marc Shell, 'Language Wars', *New Centennial Review* 1 (2001), 1–17

Leonard Shlain, *The Alphabet Versus the Goddess: The Conflict Between Word and Image* (London: Allen Lane, 1998)

John Simon, *Paradigms Lost: Reflections on Literacy and its Decline* (London: Chatto & Windus, 1981)

David Simpson, *The Politics of American English, 1776–1850* (New York: Oxford University Press, 1986)

Walter W. Skeat, *Principles of English Etymology* (Oxford: Clarendon Press, 1892)

Elizabeth S. Sklar, 'The Possessive Apostrophe: the Development and Decline of a Crooked Mark', *College English* 38 (1976), 175–83

—— 'Sexist Grammar Revisited', *College English* 45 (1983), 348–58

Charles William Smith, *Mind Your H's and Take Care of Your R's* (London: Lockwood, 1866)

Olivia Smith, *The Politics of Language 1791–1819* (Oxford: Clarendon Press, 1984)

Thomas Smith, *De Recta et Emendata Linguae Anglicae Scriptione, Dialogus* (London: Robert Stephens, 1568)

Geneva Smitherman, *Talkin that Talk: Language, Culture, and Education in African America* (London: Routledge, 1999)

George Snell, *The Right Teaching of Useful Knowledg* (London: W. Dugard, 1649)

Alan D. Sokal, 'Transgressing the Boundaries: Towards a Transformative Hermeneutics of Quantum Gravity', *Social Text* 46/47 (1996), 217–52

Bernard Spolsky, *Language Management* (Cambridge: Cambridge University Press, 2009)

Julia P. Stanley, 'Sexist Grammar', *College English* 39 (1979), 800–11

Brent Staples, 'The Last Train from Oakland', *New York Times*, 24 January 1997

Ryan J. Stark, *Rhetoric, Science and Magic in Seventeenth-Century England* (Washington, DC: Catholic University of America Press, 2009)

Dieter Stein and Ingrid Tieken-Boon van Ostade (eds), *Towards a Standard English, 1600–1800* (Berlin: Mouton de Gruyter, 1994)

George Steiner, *Language and Silence* (London: Faber, 1985)

—— *After Babel: Aspects of Language and Translation*, 3rd edn (Oxford: Oxford University Press, 1998)

John Stirling, *A Short View of English Grammar*, 2nd edn (London: T. Astley, 1740)

Barbara M. H. Strang, *A History of English* (London: Routledge, 1989)

William Strunk and E. B. White, *The Elements of Style* (New York: Macmillan, 1959)

—— *The Elements of Style*, 4th edn (Needham Heights, MA: Allyn & Bacon, 2000)

Michael Stubbs, *Language and Literacy: The Sociolinguistics of Reading and Writing* (London: Routledge & Kegan Paul, 1980)

Robert D. Sutherland, *Language and Lewis Carroll* (The Hague: Mouton, 1970)

Henry Sweet, *The Indispensable Foundation: A Selection from the Writings of Henry Sweet*, ed. Eugénie J. A. Henderson (London: Oxford University Press, 1971)

Jonathan Swift, *A Proposal for Correcting, Improving and Ascertaining the English Tongue* (London: Benjamin Tooke, 1712)

—— *A Letter to a Young Gentleman, Lately Enter'd into Holy Orders*, 2nd edn (London: J. Roberts, 1721)

—— *A Complete Collection of Genteel and Ingenious Conversation, According to the Most Polite Mode and Method Now Used at Court, and in the Best Companies of England* (London: Motte & Bathurst, 1738)

Lorand B. Szalay and James Deese, *Subjective Meaning and Culture: An Assessment Through Word Associations* (Hillsdale, NJ: Lawrence Erlbaum, 1978)

András Szántó (ed.), *What Orwell Didn't Know: Propaganda and the New Face of American Politics* (New York: PublicAffairs, 2007)

Deborah Tannen, *You Just Don't Understand: Women and Men in Conversation* (London: Virago, 1991)

Sarah G. Thomason, *Language Contact* (Edinburgh: Edinburgh University Press, 2001)

Tony Thorne, *Jolly Wicked, Actually: The 100 Words That Make Us English* (London: Little, Brown, 2009)

Ingrid Tieken-Boon van Ostade, 'Double Negation and Eighteenth-century English Grammars', *Neophilologus* 66 (1982), 278–85

—— 'Female Grammarians of the Eighteenth Century', *Historical Socio-linguistics and Sociohistorial Linguistics* 1 (2000)

—— 'Robert Lowth and the strong verb system', *Language Sciences* 24 (2002), 459–69

—— 'Tom's grammar: The genesis of Lowth's *Short Introduction to English Grammar* revisited', *Paradigm* 2 (2003), 36–45

—— 'Of Social Networks and Linguistic Influence: The Language of Robert Lowth and his Correspondents', in Juan Camilo Conde-Silvestre and Juan Manuel Hernández-Campoy (eds), *Sociolinguistics and the History of English* (Murcia: Servicio de Publicaciones, Universidad de Murcia, 2005)

—— *An Introduction to Late Modern English* (Edinburgh: Edinburgh University Press, 2009)

—— (ed.), *Two Hundred Years of Lindley Murray* (Münster: Nodus, 1996)

—— (ed.), *Grammars, Grammarians and Grammar-Writing in Eighteenth-Century England* (Berlin: Mouton de Gruyter, 2008)

Ingrid Tieken-Boon van Ostade and John Frankis (eds), *Language: Usage and Description: Studies Presented to N. E. Osselton* (Amsterdam: Rodopi, 1991)

Ingrid Tieken-Boon van Ostade and Wim van der Wurff (eds), *Current Issues in Late Modern English* (Bern: Peter Lang, 2009)

Judith Tingley, *Genderflex: Men and Women Speaking Each Other's Language at Work* (New York: Amacom, 1994)

Dominic Tobin and Jonathan Leake, 'Regional accents thrive against the odds in Britain', *The Times*, 3 January 2010

Marcus Tomalin, *Romanticism and Linguistic Theory* (Basingstoke: Palgrave Macmillan, 2009)

John Horne Tooke, *Epea Pteroenta, or The Diversions of Purley*, ed. Richard Taylor, 2 vols (London: Thomas Tegg, 1829)

Elizabeth Closs Traugott, *A History of English Syntax* (New York: Holt, Rinehart & Winston, 1972)

Peter Trudgill, *The Social Differentiation of English in Norwich* (Cambridge: Cambridge University Press, 1974)

—— *Sociolinguistics*, 4th edn (London: Penguin, 2000)

Peter Trudgill and J. K. Chambers (eds), *Dialects of English: Studies in Grammatical Variation* (London: Longman, 1991)

Lynne Truss, *Eats, Shoots & Leaves: The Zero Tolerance Approach to Punctuation* (London: Profile, 2003)

—— *Talk to the Hand: The Utter Bloody Rudeness of Everyday Life* (London: Profile, 2005)

Susie I. Tucker, *Protean Shape: A Study in Eighteenth-Century Vocabulary and Usage* (London: Athlone, 1967)

Susie I. Tucker (ed.), *English Examined* (Cambridge: Cambridge University Press, 1961)

Virginia Tufte, *Grammar as Style* (New York: Holt, Rinehart & Winston, 1971)

Thorlac Turville-Petre, *England the Nation: Language, Literature, and National Identity, 1290–1340* (Oxford: Clarendon Press, 1996)

John Updike, 'Fine Points', *New Yorker*, 23 December 1996

Clive Upton and J. D. A. Widdowson, *An Atlas of English Dialects*, 2nd edn (London: Routledge, 2006)

Ans van Kemenade and Bettelou Los (eds), *The Handbook of the History of English* (Oxford: Blackwell, 2006)

George Vandenhoff, *The Lady's Reader* (London: Sampson Low, 1862)

Richard L. Venezky, *The American Way of Spelling: The Structure and Origins of American English Orthography* (New York: Guilford Press, 1999)

Richard Verstegan, *A Restitution of Decayed Intelligence* (Antwerp: Robert Bruney, 1605)

Brian Vickers and Nancy S. Struever, *Rhetoric and the Pursuit of Truth: Language Change in the Seventeenth and Eighteenth Centuries* (Los Angeles: William Andrews Clark Memorial Library, 1985)

Peter Walkden Fogg, *Elementa Anglicana*, 2 vols (Stockport: J. Clarke, 1792–6)

John Walker, *A Critical Pronouncing Dictionary and Expositor of the English Language* (London: Robinson, Robinson & Cadell, 1791)

David Foster Wallace, 'Tense Present: Democracy, English, and the Wars over Usage', *Harper's Magazine*, April 2001

John Wallis, *Grammatica Linguae Anglicanae* (Oxford: Leonard Lichfield, 1653)

Jeremy Warburg, *Verbal Values* (London: Arnold, 1966)

Ronald Wardhaugh, *How Conversation Works* (Oxford: Blackwell, 1985)

—— *Proper English: Myths and Misunderstandings about Language* (Oxford: Blackwell, 1999)

Don Watson, *Gobbledygook* (London: Atlantic, 2005)

Richard Watts and Peter Trudgill (eds), *Alternative Histories of English* (London: Routledge, 2002)

Noah Webster, *A Grammatical Institute of the English Language*, 3 vols (Hartford, CT: Hudson & Goodwin, 1783–5)

—— *Dissertations on the English Language* (Boston: Isaiah Thomas, 1789)

—— *An American Dictionary of the English Language*, 2 vols (New York: S. Converse, 1828)

H. G. Wells, *Certain Personal Matters: A Collection of Material, Mainly Auto-biographical* (London: Lawrence & Bullen, 1898)

—— *Mankind in the Making* (London: Chapman & Hall, 1903)

—— *A Modern Utopia* (London: Chapman & Hall, 1905)

—— *An Englishman Looks at the World* (London: Cassell, 1914)

—— *The World Set Free* (London: Macmillan, 1914)

—— *Anticipations and Other Papers* (London: T. Fisher Unwin, 1924)

Francis Wheen, *Strange Days Indeed: The Golden Age of Paranoia* (London: Fourth Estate, 2009)

Richard Grant White, *Words and Their Uses, Past and Present* (New York: Sheldon, 1871)

—— *Every-Day English* (Boston: Houghton Mifflin, 1880)

Walt Whitman, *An American Primer*, ed. Horace Traubel (London: G. P. Putnam, 1904)

—— *Daybooks and Notebooks*, vol. 3, ed. William White (New York: New York University Press, 1978)

William Dwight Whitney, *Language and the Study of Language* (London: Trübner, 1867)

Benjamin Lee Whorf, *Language, Thought, and Reality*, ed. John B. Carroll (New York: John Wiley, 1956)

Anna Wierzbicka, *English: Meaning and Culture* (Oxford: Oxford University Press, 2006)

Mark Wignall, 'Bad Times for a Good Relationship', *Jamaica Observer*, 4 April 2010

John Wilkins, *An Essay Towards a Real Character and Philosophical Language* (London: Gellibrand & Martyn, 1668)

Raymond Williams, *The Long Revolution* (London: Chatto & Windus, 1961)

—— *Keywords: A Vocabulary of Culture and Society* (London: Fontana, 1988)

John Willinsky, *Empire of Words: The Reign of the OED* (Princeton, NJ: Princeton University Press, 1994)

—— *After Literacy* (New York: Peter Lang, 2001)

A. N. Wilson, *The Victorians* (London: Arrow, 2003)

Edmund Wilson, *The Shores of Light: A Literary Chronicle of the Twenties and Thirties* (London: W. H. Allen, 1952)

Thomas Wilson, *The Many Advantages of a Good Language to Any Nation* (London: Knapton, Knaplock et al., 1724)

Philip Withers, *Aristarchus, or The Principles of Composition* (London: J. Moore, 1788)

Jocelyn Wogan-Browne, Nicholas Watson, Andrew Taylor and Ruth Evans (eds), *The Idea of the Vernacular: An Anthology of Middle English Literary Theory, 1280–1520* (Exeter: University of Exeter Press, 1999)

Walt Wolfram and Natalie Schilling-Estes, *American English: Dialects and Variation* (Oxford: Blackwell, 1998)

David Wolman, *Righting the Mother Tongue: From Olde English to Email, the Tangled Story of English Spelling* (New York: Collins, 2008)

Nicola Woolcock, 'Pedants' revolt aims to stop English being lost for words', *The Times*, 7 June 2010

Virginia Woolf, *The Diary of Virginia Woolf*, vol. 3 (1925–30), ed. Anne Olivier Bell (Harmondsworth: Penguin, 1982)

Laura Wright (ed.), *The Development of Standard English 1300–1800* (Cambridge: Cambridge University Press, 2000)

Sue Wright (ed.), *Language and Conflict: A Neglected Relationship* (Clevedon: Multilingual Matters, 1998)

Nuria Yáñez-Bouza, 'Prescriptivism and preposition stranding in eighteenth-century prose', *Historical Sociolinguistics and Sociohistorical Linguistics* 6 (2006)

John Yeomans, *The Abecedarian, or, Philosophic Comment upon the English Alphabet* (London: J. Coote, 1759)

G. M. Young, *Portrait of an Age: Victorian England*, ed. George Kitson Clark (London: Oxford University Press, 1977)

Theodore Zeldin, *An Intimate History of Humanity* (London: Minerva, 1995)

Thomas de Zengotita, *Mediated: How the Media Shape the World Around You* (London: Bloomsbury, 2007)

William Zinsser, *On Writing Well* (New York: Quill, 2001)

Index

Gibbon, Edward: *Decline and Fall of the Roman Empire*, 239
Gibson, Walker, 158
Gil, Alexander, 128, 197
Gladstone, Wiliam Ewart, 204
Glanvill, Joseph: *The Vanity of Dogmatizing*, 52
Globish (language), 303–4
glottal stop (voiceless glottal plosive), 213
Goatly, Andrew, 313
gobbledygook, 327–32
Godin, Seth, 322
Godkin, E. L.: 'The Growing Illiteracy of American Boys', 2
Gogate, Madhukar, 304
Golding, Sir William, 63
Good Words (magazine), 171
Google (search engine), 291–2
Gorman, James, 278
Gould, Edward: *Good English; or, Popular Errors in Language*, 175
Gove, Philip, 231–3
Gower, John, 28
Gowers, Sir Ernest: *ABC of Plain Words*, 276
Grainger, Percy, 164–5, 167, 326
grammar: imprecise, 9; universal, 16; study of, 45–7; double, 46–7; defined, 76–7; and notions of correctness, 76–7, 79–80, 86–7, 93; teaching, 77–85; Johnson on, 92; Lowth's views on, 93–100; books on, 122; Lindley Murray on, 122, 124, 126–8; as physical challenge, 220; women and, 220, 224–5; changes, 287; computer-checked, 291
Great Britain: and national identity, 142–3
Greece (ancient): education, 220
Greek language: loan words in English, 39; learning, 81

Green, Henry, 195
Green, Jonathon, 130–1
Green, J. R.: *A Short History of the English People*, 162
Greenbaum, Sidney, 13
Greenwood, James, 199; *An Essay towards a Practical English Grammar*, 96
Grimm, Jacob, 9, 65, 134, 162
Grose, Francis: *A Classical Dictionary of the Vulgar Tongue*, 128–9, 131–2
Grose, Francis, the younger, 131–2
Grundy, Mrs (imaginary figure), 237
Grzega, Joachim, 304
Guardian (modern newspaper), 215
Guardian, The (1713 newspaper), 3
Guevara, Che, 255
Gustafson, Thomas, 104

H (letter): misplacement, 172–4
Hagège, Claude: *On the Death and Life of Languages*, 167
Haig, General Alexander, 329
Halpern, Mark, 318
handwriting: and spelling, 69
Hardy, Thomas, 163–4, 167, 195; *Jude the Obscure*, 164; *The Trumpet-Major*, 164; *The Well-Beloved*, 164
Harley, Sir Robert (1st Earl of Oxford), 53
Harman, Thomas: *A Caveat or Warening for Common Cursetors*, 129
Harper Dictionary of Contemporary Usage, 188
Harris, James: *Hermes*, 98
Hart, James Morgan, 3
Hart, John, 67–8
Hartlib, Samuel, 220
Harvey, Gabriel, 42
Haugen, Einar, 285
Hayakawa, Samuel Ichiye, 255–6
Hazlitt, William, 126, 134–5, 159–60, 241

language diversity, 109–10; territorial expansion, 110; dictionaries, 113–15, 231–4; slang, 116; black language and literacy, 117–18, 257–8; Civil War (1861–5), 118–20; as name, 119–20; image, 120; urbanization, 120; different accents and dialects, 194; language societies, 230; language study, 234–5; official language question, 252, 256–7; Bilingual Education Act (1968), 255; Civil Rights Act (1964), 255; Spanish language in, 255; hyphenated citizens and immigrants, 258–9; resistance to influence on British English, 274–5
uptalk (high rising terminal), 278–9
Upton, Clive, 193, 210

Valenti, Jessica, 295
Vandenhoff, George: *The Lady's Reader*, 153–4
Vaugelas, Claude Favre de: *Remarques sur la langue française*, 18
verbs: phrasal, 59
Verstegan, Richard Rowlands, 197; *A Restitution of Decayed Intelligence*, 43–4
very (word), 276–7
Victoria, Queen: spelling, 71; reign, 143; reads *Jane Eyre* to Albert, 153; recommends *Oliver Twist* to Melbourne, 156
Victorian age, 143–5
villain (word), 149
Vives, Juan Luis: *The Instruction of a Christian Woman*, 220
Volapük (language), 305
Voltaire, François-Marie Arouet, 20, 273
vulgar (word), 149

Walker, John, *A Critical Pronouncing Dictionary*, 122–3, 173, 175, 201, 211
Wallis, John: *Grammatica Linguae Anglicanae*, 47, 92, 126, 226
Warburton, William, 99
Webster, John, 110
Webster, Noah, 110–17, 122, 126, 148, 272; *An American Dictionary of the English Language*, 113–15; *The American Spelling Book*, 112; *Dissertations on the English Language*, 111–12, 114; *A Grammatical Institute of the English Language*, 111–12, 114
Webster's Third New International Dictionary (ed. P. Gove), 231–4, 244
Weinreich, Max, 20
Wells, H. G., 73, 81–2, 100, 228, 255; 'For Freedom of Spelling', 72; *In the Days of the Comet*, 192; *Mankind in the Making*, 121, 228–9; *A Modern Utopia*, 301; *Mr Polly*, 262; *The World Set Free*, 302
Welsh language, 153
Wharton, Edith: *The Custom of the Country*, 320
whatever (word), 298
White, E. B.: *Charlotte's Web*, 185; see also Strunk, William
White, Richard Grant: *Every-Day English*, 176; *Words and Their Uses*, 176
Whitman, Walt, 116–18, 130; *An American Primer*, 117
Whitney, William Dwight, 4
whom (word), 95, 156, 188, 287–8
Whorf, Benjamin Lee, 315–17
Whythorne, Thomas, 33
Wierzbicka, Anna, 19
Wikipedia, 230